# M A S T E R I N G
## the Art of
# FLY TYING

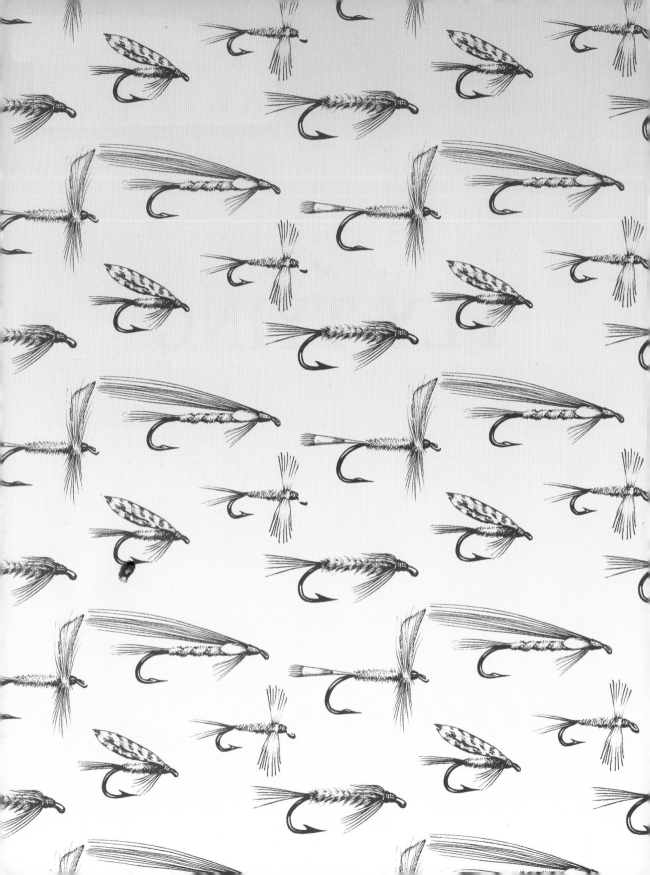

# MASTERING
## the Art of
# FLY TYING

Complete Instructions for 160 Freshwater Flies
from Simple to Complex

## G. Randolph Erskine

**Ragged Mountain Press / McGraw-Hill**

CAMDEN, MAINE ▪ NEW YORK ▪ CHICAGO ▪ SAN FRANCISCO ▪ LISBON ▪ LONDON
MADRID ▪ MEXICO CITY ▪ MILAN ▪ NEW DELHI ▪ SAN JUAN ▪ SEOUL
SINGAPORE ▪ SYDNEY ▪ TORONTO

The McGraw-Hill Companies

1 2 3 4 5 6 7 8 9 RRD Shen RRD Shen 9 8 7


Printed in China.

ISBN 13: 978-0-07144455-2

ISBN 10: 0-07-144455-6

*Library of Congress Cataloging-in-Publication Data*

Erskine, Randolph.

Mastering the art of fly tying : complete instructions for 160 freshwater flies from simple to complex / G. Randolph Erskine.

p. cm.

Includes index.

ISBN 0-07-144455-6 (pbk. : alk. paper)

1. Fly tying. 2. Flies, Artificial. I. Title.

SH451.E77 2006

688.7'9124—dc22

2005026318

Questions regarding the content of this book should be addressed to

Ragged Mountain Press

P.O. Box 220

Camden, ME 04843

Questions regarding the ordering of this book should be addressed to

The McGraw-Hill Companies

Customer Service Department

P.O. Box 547

Blacklick, OH 43004

Retail customers: 1-800-262-4729

Bookstores: 1-800-722-4726

Photographs by Jim Dugan.

Illustrations by Christopher Hoyt.

*This book is dedicated
to my beloved wife,
Madeline,
without whose help
and encouragement it
could not have been completed.*

# ACKNOWLEDGMENTS

I'D LIKE TO THANK FRED MONAHAN AND Paul Gouin for testing the detailed step-by-step instructions used in this book. Fred and Paul, who came to me as pupils in an Adult Education class, honed their tying skills while following my rough draft; their feedback, in turn, honed my writing and instructions. Their weekly tying sessions also produced many of the flies that were photographed for this book. Fred and Paul's belief in my methods and the material in this book made this project a pleasant adventure.

Thanks to my daughter, Roxanne, for typing the manuscript and for her belief in the project—and in my ability to complete it. Without her loving help and encouragement this book could not have been completed. Thanks also to my son, Peter, for his assistance and professional advice on numerous artistic features of the book.

My thanks to Jon Eaton for sensing this book's potential, to Bob Holtzman for his sensitive editing, and to Molly Mulhern and Ben McCanna for their support and assistance.

# IN MEMORIAM

GEORGE RANDOLPH ERSKINE—KNOWN to all as "Randy"—died on August 8, 2006, at the age of 93, just four days after completing his final review of this book's editing and photography.

Randy was born in Boston, Massachusetts on November 11, 1912. His father was the superintendent of the Connecticut Reformatory for Boys, and Randy's boyhood curiosity drew him to the reformatory's farm and workshops. By the time he was a teen-ager, he had learned horticulture, horsemanship, fishing, hunting, animal husbandry, slaughtering, dairying, and chicken farming. He had also developed a  lifetime love of fly fishing and fly tying.

Randy graduated from Middlebury College in 1934 and from Yale Law School in 1937. After World War II, he practiced law in Wallingford, Connecticut, for over 50 years. He believed strongly that legal representation should be available to all. Often, when a client couldn't pay his fee, Randy would accept turkey feathers, thread, and other fly tying materials instead.

He gave his full measure in all things, but nowhere was his devotion to craftsmanship and his ability to lose himself in joyful absorption in the work at hand more evident than when he was tying flies.

At age 88, after his fourth hip replacement, Randy concluded that he might not live forever. For years he had been sharing his fly tying knowledge with students and apprentices. Feeling that "the existing fly tying books really weren't worth their weight in paper," he decided to create his own.

Over the following four years, he met Monday nights with his beta-testing team of two fly-tying apprentices—whom he called "the boys"—lawyers Fred Monahan and Paul Gouin. The three men would clamp their vises side by side on the kitchen table, refining Randy's instructions line by line, fly by fly. Randy wrote the text longhand on his old legal clipboard and mailed it off a chapter at a time to his daughter, Roxanne, who keyboarded it.

The result, which you are holding in your hands, brings together Randy's artistry, his wry humor, his lawyer's logic and textual analysis, his 80 years of fly fishing and fly tying experience, and his deep knowledge of nature.

Randy was a peaceful man with an open heart. He believed that the real beauty of fly tying and fly fishing is that it hooks more humans than fish. *Mastering the Art of Fly Tying* is infused and informed by his unique combination of precision, clarity, humor, and passion.

# CONTENTS

# CONTENTS

# CONTENTS

# PREFACE

I BEGAN TO TIE BECAUSE I NEEDED SOME flies to catch fish. Seventy-five years later, I still tie some flies for occasional use, but at my age and with two artificial hips, I'm less and less comfortable standing on slippery rocks in the middle of a swift stream. Now I tie more for its own sake and for the challenge and satisfaction of making a beautiful, useful object. While my emphasis has changed from the practical to the aesthetic, the hobby has done well by me for a very long time. Also, there's the deep satisfaction of helping others acquire the skills that have meant so much to me.

In the late 1920s, my father introduced me to fly-fishing on the Housatonic and Salmon Rivers in Connecticut. After I lost a number of his flies, he introduced me to his friend and fly supplier, Len Comstock. Len offered not flies but lessons in how to tie them. I gladly agreed to take the lessons, and received an old, blacksmith-made vise; some tools; thread, beeswax, hooks, pieces of bucktail, tinsel, and other materials; and three or four lessons. My first efforts were not beautiful, but they caught fish. College, law school, and marriage thereafter reduced my fishing time, but I still tied a few flies from time to time.

During World War II, I worked at the Federal Office of Price Administration in Hartford, Connecticut, where I met Val Clementino, an active hunter, fisherman, and flytier. We came to enjoy these hobbies together, and after lunch each day we haunted the sporting section of bookstores for fly-tying literature or visited sporting goods stores for scarce hooks, feathers, and other materials.

Val was a member of a West Hartford fishing club. At its clubhouse just before meetings, eight or ten of the best amateur and professional flytiers gathered around a long, wide table, each with his light, vise, and materials, and tied flies for an hour or so. Several of these men produced the flies that Val and I had admired in the best shops in the area. These meetings provided an opportunity for the tiers to catch up on their retail quotas while explaining their techniques and materials.

Val introduced me to this group, and one night I stood too long behind one man, watching him work and asking questions. As he finished a fly he turned to me and said, "You have watched long enough! Now sit down here and tie this fly!" I was flabbergasted, but he insisted. So I sat down and, with his coaching, I finally produced a satisfactory fly that he was able to use to help meet his monthly quota.

I moved around the table and, after asking some questions about sources of materials, bought two Asiatic partial necks from another man who told me they were initially intended for ladies' hats. After two or three of these sessions and an evening of tying at Val's home, my interest in fly tying was renewed and I was well started again. Books by Ruben Cross and Herter's *Professional*

*Fly Tying Manual* provided me with new techniques and pointers, just as new supplies of hooks and materials were released at the end of the war.

I showed my creations to several stores that sold flies as a sideline and got some small orders to support my hobby. Soon, however, cheap foreign flies closed these markets to my high-priced flies, and I started tying only for my own use. Then one day while negotiating for some hooks at Cook, Newton & Smith in New Haven, the shop owners asked me to tie some high-end flies for them.

In the 1970s, Cook, Newton & Smith's successor decided to revive the old optic bucktail line of flies based on the original framed sample panel. These flies required jungle cock shoulders, which had gone up in price from $2.50 per neck when I first used them with Len Comstock to $25.00 per neck—and jungle cock was not yet on the endangered species list. During one winter I duplicated all of the patterns in the sample panel, in several sizes, and determined that I would not make a living, much less a fortune, as a professional flytier. I did, however, learn a number of useful production methods and developed considerable skill in thread control and in producing painted eyes, plus I bought a canoe with the proceeds from that one order.

For several years I taught both basic fly tying and an advanced course in tying flies that have spun/cut-and-folded hair bodies for the local adult education program. One of my early pupils went on to teach fly tying for our town's recreation department. In the mid-1970s I joined the Housatonic Fly Fisherman's Association and was soon teaching club members how to tie flies, demonstrating fly tying at the club's booth at sports shows, and writing a "Fly of the Month" column for the club newsletter.

For the past several years two of my pupils, fellow lawyers Fred Monahan and Paul Gouin, have been meeting with me weekly to improve their skills and knowledge of materials. We progressed from streamers through nymphs, small No. 28s, dry flies, fan wings, and hair body flies. Then we moved on to salmon flies, beginning with hair wing modern salmon flies, Bombers, and Green Machines, then to reduced/simplified feather wings and hair wings, Dee Strip wing and Spey flies (both present-day and traditional), and finally to whole feather wing, full-dress salmon flies. Originally, I prepared flies for my students to copy, demonstrated tying the fly, and then coached them as they tied their own copy. Over time I prepared detailed written instructions instead, which students used independently—without my usual demonstration or coaching—to produce new flies with ease. They commented that the instructions were too good to merely go into their files and should instead be made into a book and shared with other flytiers. My pupils have long said that I am a good teacher, and because many of them now tie beautiful flies and are deeply involved in the hobby, I believe them.

There is no need for you to reinvent the wheel or make mistakes for want of detailed instructions. By following the instructions in this book, you will develop a good understanding of many phases of fly tying. You can then go on tying happily or, if you are so inclined, perfect new and better methods or designs for flies.

During much of my professional life as an attorney, the results of a day's labor were not always apparent—there was little concrete evidence to show for the time and effort I invested. I might give legal advice, draw a will, and then wait for weeks or even years to find out if my proposed solution actually accomplished its purpose. Under such circumstances, a hobby that produces a useful, beautiful, physical object within a reasonable time is a boon to a person who enjoys working with his hands as much as his head. Going from the mental activity of one's work to the physical activity of tying flies can provide a change of pace that helps restore both the spirit and one's perspective on life. For me, what began as a means to meet a need for flies with which to fish developed into a much broader way of using my time and manual talents.

I have always been curious about how things work or were put together, and fly tying opened new vistas of sources for materials, other uses for materials at hand, and different ways of doing things. One thing led to another, and that to still another, while the satisfaction of taking raw materials and producing a finished product continues to bring me great joy. There is admittedly much pleasure in amazing one's family, friends, or the public by producing flies that are beautiful or tiny or, like the Hair Bumblebee, offer no explanation about their construction. Also, helping others learn and appreciate a beloved hobby is good for everyone involved. All of these aspects of fly tying have enriched my life, and I want to share my interest and knowledge with like-minded people in the hope and expectation that they too will find in this hobby the same release and enjoyment that I have experienced over these many years.

When I asked my first instructor how much I owed for his three or four lessons, vise, and materials, Len Comstock said I owed him no money. But, he said, if I would pass on my new knowledge and skills to others, he would feel well repaid. I was deeply impressed at the time and, remembering it over the years, have taken the time to help others with this hobby. I owe Len a tremendous debt for the pleasure of a lifetime of fly tying. This book is a partial payment on that very old debt, and I hope it brings you as much help and pleasure as I have had since that long-ago introduction to fly tying by my old teacher.

# HOW TO USE THIS BOOK

Most fly-tying manuals are organized according to categories of flies: dry flies, wet flies, nymphs, and so on. This book takes a different approach. It's organized to teach fly tying the way most people learn new skills most effectively: in easy stages, starting with the simplest principles and gradually advancing to the more complex. After the introductory chapters on tools, materials, and basic techniques, the flies are presented in an order that will introduce techniques and materials one by one in a logical, easy progression. Most flies are grouped in sections that use similar skills or materials or that build on a certain skill in a logical, step-by-step manner. Some of these sections naturally correspond with conventional fly categories such as dry fly, nymph, caddis, and so on. But other sections (including "Small Flies," "Spun-/Clipped-Hair Flies," and "Folded-/Bundled-Hair Body Flies") bring together flies of different types as part of the logical learning sequence. If you wish to find tying directions for a particular fly, you may refer to the Index of Flies on page 345.

If you are a beginner, however, I suggest you tie the flies *in the order they are presented* to steadily build your skills—and your confidence. Part One will guide you through basic tools, skills, and some easy flies. Start with a minimum of tools and materials until you know this hobby is right for you, but be sure those tools are adequate for the purpose and not merely the cheapest ones available. Poor, cheap tools are never a good way to save money. Nor do you need big-name, high-cost items to tie good flies. When you have worked your way through Part Two you can, if you wish, rest on your laurels. But many tiers who have progressed to that level find they have a desire to go on to the complex and complicated area that has, for the past two hundred years, been accepted as the pinnacle of fly tying: salmon flies. This is a path I have taken and have helped several others follow, and I strongly recommend it. You'll find salmon fly patterns in Part Three.

If your present level of expertise already includes salmon flies, Part Two contains a number of practical flies you may want to use. The detailed directions there will help expedite their production.

The ideal way to get started in fly tying is by joining a club or program that provides good, personalized instruction and offers access to tools and materials at little or no expense—at least until you have decided whether it is a skill you wish to learn and use on a long-term basis. Once you are sure you want to continue tying flies, the advantages of pooled resources and shared purchases that are offered by such groups are very attractive.

If you are unable to find personal instruction, however, or if you cannot or do not want to sit in front of a video screen, there is good news: you can learn how to tie flies from a book! I have done it, and you can too. Just follow these steps:

1. Read the materials and tools list for the fly you wish to tie, and have those items at hand near your vise. Materials are usually listed in their order of use.

2. Read the tying instructions carefully and thoroughly before you start tying. This should give you a clear impression of the fly and how it is put together.

3. Sit down at the vise and reread the steps, carefully following each as you tie the fly.

4. Tie two or three of each of the flies you select. You will notice improvement with each one. We all lose flies to tree branches, rocks, and sometimes to fish, so having an extra one in your fly box may make a difference in your fishing success long after it served as a confidence builder at the tying bench.

If you have good, basic fly-tying experience you can safely skip Part One and go directly to the flies you wish to tie or the techniques that interest you in Part Two.

# PART ONE

# INTRODUCTION TO FLY TYING

*Fly tying is a very old craft. Some two thousand years ago in Macedonia, Aelian wrote about a fly made of red wool and a rooster neck feather. Tied around a hook and dropped on the water, it floated like a live insect. Believing it was an insect, a fish rose to the fly and was caught.*

*Dame Julia Berners, Prioress of the Abbey at St. Albans in England about the time Columbus discovered America, wrote a book on fishing that included directions for making twelve flies, each useful in a different month of the year.*

*In the nineteenth century, a moneyed class of Victorian "gentleman fishers" supported a group of professional flytiers of great virtuosity who had access to feathers and furs from all over the world. Competition among these professionals raised fly tying from a practical application to an art form with the introduction of elaborate feather-wing salmon flies. Still generally accepted as the apex of fly tying, these flies seem designed as much to catch the attention of people as to catch fish. Apprentices of professional flytiers spent years learning techniques that are now largely forgotten, and ultimately produced extraordinarily complex designs having their own terminology and incorporating some thirty small pieces from different feathers into the wing of a single fly. Changing times have substantially reduced the use of such elaborate salmon flies in fishing, but have not eliminated the challenge these flies present to the ambitious tier or their appeal to the avid collector.*

# FLY BASICS

Flies vary widely in size, form, and materials, but they all either represent or imitate some type of food that fish eat. Some flies imitate insects that are too fragile to impale on a hook, and others mimic larger prey, such as frogs or minnows, that would be difficult or impractical to handle and store as live bait.

The insects upon which fish feed are taken either *on* the surface of the water or *under* the surface. The vast majority of flies imitate the various stages of an insect's life cycle: nymph, emerger, stillborn, dun, and spent-wing spinner. Dry flies and spiders represent the mature stages of insects that rest lightly on the water's surface, while wet flies represent the insects that drown and sink. All but the egg phase of the life cycle are represented by flies in this book.

## The Steps for Tying a Typical Fly

IT'S HELPFUL TO HAVE A GENERAL IDEA OF tying procedures before you begin tying your first fly. Most are a simple elaboration of the following outline, and I will provide such an elaboration in the Basic Skills chapter (page 43):

1. Start by placing the hook in the vise and attaching thread to the shank, opposite the hook's barb. (See page 43.)
2. Wrap the thread at least seven or eight turns toward the hook bend to form a nonslip base for the fly materials. (See page 44.)
3. Tie in the tail. (See page 44.)
4. Attach the body material to the shank at the hook bend. If there is a rib, attach that material also. Wind the thread in butting (touching) turns to ⅛ inch behind the eye and let the bobbin hang. Wrap the body toward the wing area and tie it off. Spiral the rib over the body in evenly spaced turns and tie it off at the front of the body. (See page 46.)
5. Tie in the wings. (See page 47.)
6. Attach the throat or beard. (See page 53.)
7. Form the head, whip finish, and coat it with durable nail polish. When dry, apply a coat or two of black head cement to finish the fly. (See page 54.)

Different fly-tying materials are used to imitate a particular phase of an insect's life cycle. Nymphs, for example, are sparsely tied on heavy hooks that will sink quickly and require dull-colored materials to represent or imitate their live counterparts. Emergers and stillborns are tied on lighter hooks, usually with a shuck or tail and unfolding wings. Classic dry flies sport distinctive wings,

# THE LIFE CYCLE
# OF A FLYING INSECT

THE LIFE CYCLE OF MANY FLYING insects starts when a female deposits her fertilized eggs on the surface of a stream or lake, or dives under the surface to attach them to rocks or debris. The eggs hatch into *nymphs*, which, depending on the species, spend three months to three years at or near the bottom of the stream or lake while growing. Nymphs are constantly available to fish.

As a nymph approaches adulthood, it makes several trips toward the water's surface before fully rising and floating in its splitting shell or clambering onto a rock, where its wings dry. During this phase the insect is called an *emerger*. A nymph that dies while struggling to get out of its shell is known as a *stillborn,* while one that successfully emerges flies off as a *dun* to nearby vegetation.

The adult insects usually molt, changing wing color, and then mate. The male then falls exhausted onto the water's surface, its wings half-raised (semispent) or flat (spent), thus passing into the *spent-wing spinner* phase of the life cycle. Meanwhile, the female sets about the business of laying her eggs on the water, resting lightly on top of the surface film. After laying, the exhausted female then collapses into the surface film as another spent-wing spinner, also becoming an easy meal for the resident fish. If the dying insect is not eaten while on the water surface, it drowns and sinks.

which together with their tails and stiff hackles support them on the surface. Spent-wing spinners have wide-spread wings and V-shaped tails supporting a thin body, and classic wet flies have heavier hooks and are tied with materials that will absorb water, thus successfully imitating drowned insects as they sink.

Land-based insects, also known as terrestrials, are represented in this book by several flies. Ants are represented by Hair Ants made from hollow hair bundled and humped into the proper shapes. Beetles are represented by the Horner's Deer Hair or small Tuttle's Devil Bug flies, which provide excellent fishing during hot summer days when few mayflies and caddis are hatching.

Not all flies imitate insects, of course, because fish also seek other foods. For example, Hair Mice, made from spun, hollow hair that has been cut to shape, represent mice that have fallen into the water; Hair Frogs, which are tied in a similar manner, represent live frogs that are a prime source of food for many large fish.

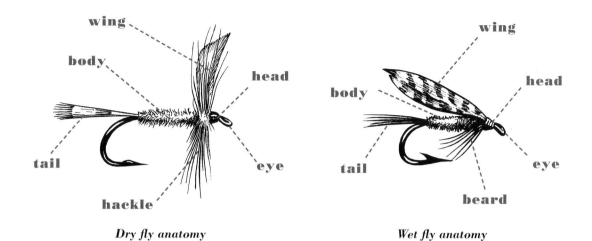

wing

body

head

tail

eye

hackle

*Dry fly anatomy*

wing

body

head

tail

eye

beard

*Wet fly anatomy*

wing

cheek or
shouldertag
of tinsel

head

tail

eye

rib of tinsel

body

throat

*Streamer/bucktail anatomy*

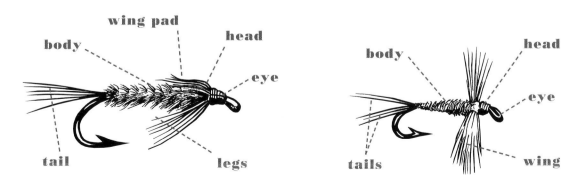

wing pad

body

head

eye

tail

legs

*Nymph anatomy*

body

head

eye

tails

wing

*Spent-wing spinner anatomy*

# FLY PROPORTIONS

CERTAIN CLASSES OF FLIES EXHIBIT RATHER fixed proportions between the sizes of their various components, while other classes exhibit more variability. Where specific instructions do not state the contrary, the following proportions are generally adhered to.

## CLASSIC DRY FLIES

**HACKLE**   *1 to 1½ times the gap of the hook*

**TAIL**   *length of body—distance from eye to bend of the hook*

**WING**   *length of body*

## WET FLIES

**TAIL**   *gap of the hook*

**WING**   *extends slightly beyond tip of the tail (if there is a tail); if no tail, then slightly beyond the bend of the hook*

**THROAT**   *just short of point of hook*

**HACKLE**   *as on Grizzly and Peacock— extends a bit beyond the bend of the hook*

## STREAMERS/BUCKTAILS

**TAIL**   *1 to 2 times the gap of the hook*

**WING**   *finger's breadth beyond the bend of the hook*

**THROAT**   *gap of the hook*

**VARIANTS**   *hackle two or three sizes larger (e.g., No. 10 fly-size hackle on a No. 14 fly)*

## SPIDER FLIES

*Hackle is a minimum of ¾ inch in diameter.*

*Hooks are 5X Short, Nos. 12–16.*

Minnows, which are also an important feature of a large fish's diet, are represented by bucktail and streamer flies that have long bodies, with red feather or hair tails and throats meant to represent blood from an injury—and hence appear to be an easy meal for large fish. Tinsel provides the flash that light produces on fish scales, and hair or feathers give the fly the appearance of life and action.

# TOOLS AND MATERIALS

## Tools

YOU NEED A RELATIVELY SHORT LIST OF TOOLS and materials to get started in fly tying. Quality tools are a good investment, but you don't need the most expensive and complicated tools to tie good flies. Buy the best tools you can afford. The latest gadgets aren't necessarily the best. Instead, look for tools that are rated for their performance and durability.

### Vise

You will need a vise to firmly hold your hooks as you tie. A pedestal-style vise has a heavy, steady base and sits flat on a desk, table, or other work surface. Clamp-style vises fasten firmly to the lip or edge of your work surface. The choice of style is yours, and it will influence at least part of your fly-tying activities.

There are, of course, both cheap and very expensive vises. I recommend something like the Thompson Pro, which was an accepted standard style sixty years ago and still does the job well, but without the bells and whistles of some of today's vises. Cabela's Master Vise is also good. Both are currently under $30. I have used a Thompson "A" vise for more than sixty years. It is simple and effective, but it does not rotate. With a rotary vise you can more easily wrap materials by rotating the hook shank rather than by wrapping the materials by hand, and you can view the placement of the materials on the opposite side of the shank without the need for a mirror.

### Hackle Pliers

Hackle pliers are used to wind feathers around the hook shank. Both Herb Howard and English styles are standard issue. You will need a regular size to tie No. 2/0 to No. 15 flies and a smaller or midge size if you tie No. 16 or smaller flies. Both cost about $3.

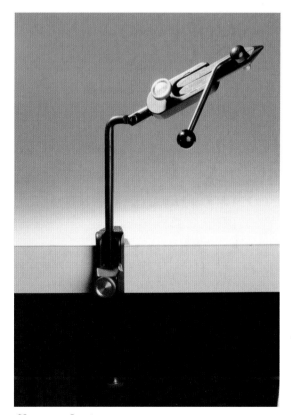

*Clamp-style vise*

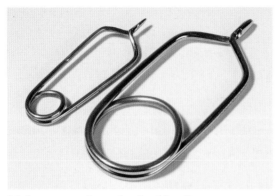

*Midge-size and regular hackle pliers*

*Dental-pick bodkin*

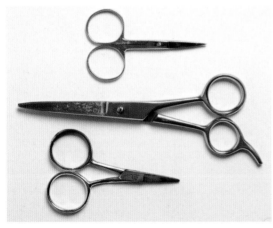

*Scissors (top to bottom): fine, heavy, and medium*

## Bodkin

A bodkin is a tool with a fine point used to manipulate thread and to separate individual hair and feather fibers. Thin-stemmed dental probes with the bent tip broken off, courtesy of your friendly dentist, make wonderful bodkins. Otherwise, you can find bodkins in a variety of finishes for a range of prices in most catalogs.

## Scissors

You will need a minimum of two pairs, although three are desirable. Flytiers generally use a light pair with fine points for feathers, threads, and similar light materials. A heavier pair is handy for tougher materials like hair and tinsel. If you do a lot of tying, a second heavy pair reserved exclusively for tinsels will prove useful, as tinsel can dull scissors quickly. Be prepared to spend some money on scissors; cheap scissors do not hold a cutting edge and are rarely worth the bargain.

## Material Clip

Material clips are used to hold loose materials out of the way and ready for use. They come in two styles. The original clip style sits on the barrel of the vise and holds the material between its lips. This is satisfactory until the day you need to put several items in the clip, out of the way, and the lips get a bit full. The second style is essentially a small diameter, helical spring fastened around the vise barrel, and the materials are simply inserted between the turns of the spring. Most suppliers carry these spring material holders; they are not expensive.

## Bobbin

A bobbin is used to control and pay out thread onto the fly. There are a number of styles, some with long tubes, others with short tubes. Bobbins with plain metal tubes are about half the cost of those with ceramic tubes or tips, and generally work well for the average tier for several years. But if you tie many flies, fine, hard threads will eventually cut and roughen the lip of the metal tube, which in turn will fray or cut the thread as it is pulled over the lip. This will inevitably occur at the least convenient time. Therefore, you may wish to purchase bobbins with ceramic tubes or tube tips. They keep their smooth surface longer and will serve the average tier for many years.

Any bobbin used for fly tying should have two arms that are pulled out to enclose the spool and hold it under slight tension as you pull the thread through the tube. The tension need not be heavy, but it must be strong enough to hold and control the thread and let the bobbin hang in order to stabilize the thread between steps. It is a busy, useful tool, so get a good one. There are times when two are desirable.

If the bobbin tube is short, threaders are unnecessary. Problems with threading a long tube are, however, easily resolved. Fold an 8- to 10-inch length of thin leader in half to make a loop. Pass 4 inches of thread through

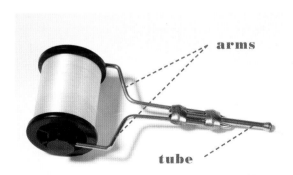

*Bobbin*

the loop and push the loop through the spool end of the tube. When you push or pull the loop through the tube, it will carry the thread with it, thus threading the bobbin.

## Hair Stacker

A hair stacker is essentially a tube in which the hair is placed, tips down. When you tap the tube on the work surface, the ends of the individual hairs will evenly align.

Before hair stackers were available, I learned to align the tips of hair for tails and wings by hand. To do this, hold the bundle of hair in one hand and, with the other, firmly grip the hairs that extend beyond most of the others. Gently pull them out and place them back in the bundle so their tips are even with the rest. Repeat the process until all the tips are even. With practice, a couple of passes generally evens the lot.

If you love gadgets and can afford it at about $10, buy a hair stacker, or else even the tips the old-fashioned way, as I continue to do. Or use a rifle shell or a lipstick tube as an improvised stacker.

## Wing Burner

This is usually a brass tong-like tool used to clamp and hold body feathers in order to form wings with stems, like fan wings. They are sold in sets of several sizes. The sets come with directions for placing the feathers inside the jaws of the tool and burning off the excess material with a candle or other flame, while the finished product is protected by the heat sink formed by the tool. Shapes for mayfly and caddis wings are available.

*Wing burner*

A drawback of wing burners is the smell of burning feathers. Instead, you can use a large nail clipper to produce the same wing shapes, but this technique requires considerable practice to duplicate wing sizes for a matched pair of feather wings.

## Whip-Finishing Tool

This is an optional tool for tying the whip finish (see page 61). Each model is slightly different, and they all come with complete instructions for their use. You need a special tool to make the whip finish at the rear of flies such as the Bomber, because the neck of most whip-finishing tools is not long enough to reach the backs of these flies. I recommend that you tie the whip finish by hand, but the choice is yours.

## Apron

A bibbed apron is a very useful garment, and I wear one regularly. A simple one that ties behind your back is fine, and pockets are optional. An apron will keep cut hair, feathers, and other by-products off your clothes and it may also catch hooks and other items that will otherwise fall to the floor.

## Lamp, Magnifier, and Mirror

Good lighting is essential for seeing small objects and following fine thread. A good, small lamp is adequate for most indoor fly tying. There are several models that combine a powerful, concentrated light with a magnifying lens. Of course, the two need not be a single unit; you can use a magnifier on a stand with an appropriate lamp. If you are on a tight budget, purchase the lamp first and secure the magnifier later.

If you don't have a rotary vise, consider adding a shaving mirror to go behind the vise you have. A mirror will allow you to see your work on the far side of the vise and is especially handy when tying in a shoulder on a feather wing. You can mount the mirror on an arm attached to the shaft of the vise and position it a few inches behind the fly. Although a mirror is not essential for tying a good fly, it can be quite helpful.

## Tools for Painting Eyes

Not all flies require eyes, painted or otherwise. For those that do, however, a home-

*Painting nails*

# ENTERING THE HOBBY ECONOMICALLY

FLY TYING IS NOT AN INEXPENSIVE hobby. Often you may be unable to buy materials cheaply in the small quantities you need for a couple of flies, so don't expect great savings if you choose to tie rather than purchase your flies. If you must purchase a whole or half neck for $25 to obtain only the three or even the dozen feathers for those three flies that retail for $2 each, you are not saving money. However, if your style of fly-fishing includes decorating every fourth overhanging branch on the stream with one of your flies, that half neck will provide enough feathers to produce all the flies you need to hang up in a season, plus you'll have a few leftover feathers for use next year. On the other hand, if you pool your order with one or two other tiers and share necks and other materials, you can reduce your expenses to a level that will compete favorably with flies sold at retail cost.

One of the most compelling reasons for tying your own flies is that you can obtain patterns and fly sizes that may not always be in stock at your local stores or available in catalogs. Even if less common flies are available, they haven't necessarily been made by careful and skillful workers. With a little experience and effort, you can learn to make better flies than most retail or mail-order flies. And most of all, you will enjoy making them.

built tool makes the job easier. Insert the head of a 1-inch No. 18 wire brad into the jaws of a hand or electric drill, allowing the point to project about ½ inch. With this makeshift drill bit, bore a ⅜-inch-deep hole in the center of the end of a ¼-inch dowel. Release the brad from the drill chuck, place its point into the hole, and tap the brad with a hammer to drive it firmly into the dowel. Cut the dowel to about a 4-inch length. You now have a tool for painting eye pupils.

For painting the whites of the eyes, make similar tools with finishing nails that have

larger heads, such as a No. 6. Several sizes of these tools are useful when tying different sizes of streamer flies.

## Building Your Own Fly-Tying Tray

While by no means essential, there are advantages in keeping your vise, tools, thread, hooks, cements, and other materials in one place. A portable fly-tying tray or station not only makes travel easier, it allows you to tie flies on virtually any suitable work surface in your home, such as your dining table. Instead of scrambling to clear the table for

# A SIMPLE FLY-TYING TRAY YOU CAN BUILD

1. Nail the back (B) and sides (C) to the base (A). These will keep things from falling onto the floor. The front edge of the tray remains open.

2. Add the corner posts (D) to the left front, left rear, and right rear corners.

3. Drill three holes of varying sizes in the tool support (E) and attach it to the top of the left-hand posts. You will clamp your vise to this support and use the holes to hold scissors, paint nails, and other tools.

4. Nail the head cement retainer (F) to the top surface of the base, parallel to the right-hand rim. Use a nail polish bottle to set the precise distance between the molding and the rim. You'll use durable nail polish such as Sally Hansen's Hard as Nails to coat the heads of your flies.

5. Stretch a taut, thin wire—not thread or string—between the tops of the two rear posts, on which you will hang your flies while their heads dry.

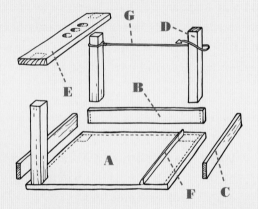

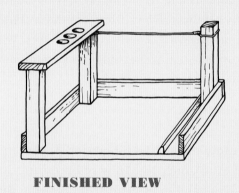

FINISHED VIEW

| KEY | COMPONENT | MATERIAL | DIMENSION | QUANTITY |
|-----|-----------|----------|-----------|----------|
| A | Base | ¾″ plywood | 12″ x 20″ | 1 |
| B | Back | ¼″ plywood | 2″ x 20″ | 1 |
| C | Sides | ¼″ plywood | 2″ x 11¾″ | 2 |
| D | Corner posts | ¾″ square lumber | 6″ long | 3 |
| E | Tool support | ¾″ plywood | 2″ x 12″ | 1 |
| F | Head cement retainer | ¾″ quarter-round molding | 11″ long (approx.) | 1 |
| G | Drying line | light wire | 28″ (approx.) | 1 |

*Not shown: Nails and/or screws, carpenter's glue, paint or varnish if desired*

the next meal or having to disassemble and put away your materials at the end of a tying session, you simply carry away the tray.

The materials you need to make your own tray are listed in the accompanying graphic. Clean, smooth scrap wood will serve to get you started. You can build or buy a furniture-grade tying station later if the spirit moves you and your budget permits.

# Materials

WHEN PURCHASING FLY-TYING MATERIALS, planning ahead saves dollars and makes good sense! In the long run, large quantities are cost-effective because you can usually find other uses for materials you buy in quantities beyond those required for your immediate needs. If you label the leftover materials and protect them against moth and silverfish infestations, they will be readily available for the next time.

Whenever possible, find a couple of people—preferably at your level of fly-tying expertise—to share the cost of materials. For example, when split three ways a Whiting 100s package (see below) allows each participant to make a mistake and still have enough material to tie several successful flies. A golden pheasant skin, from which feathers are plucked only as needed, will provide ample feathers in a variety of colors and sizes for several active tiers at a tremendous saving over buying the many individual packets of feathers you would need for different size flies. Hooks are much cheaper by the hundred, but you have to make a real investment to obtain several sizes and styles. Share, and you can each have a wide selection of hooks at a very reasonable cost. (If you are going solo, buying hooks in packets of 25 reduces the investment and keeps storage requirements to a minimum.) Another advantage of group purchases and group tying is the fun of learning new patterns and skills together.

In this book, I have endeavored to include flies that employ a minimal number of materials. You will use peacock herl, for example, for the Woodchuck Caddis (see Easy Flies for Beginners in Part One) and for four wet flies, three dry flies, and one folded-hair fly (in Part Two, Trout and Panfish Flies for Intermediate Tiers). You will use the eye to make a quill-body fly (assuming you bought the herl as an eyed feather and not in a packet of sewn herl). Similarly, natural bucktail is required for several different flies, both on its own and combined with black- or yellow-dyed white bucktail. Squirrel tail is used for trout and panfish flies and for several of the salmon flies (see Part Three), either as wings or as underwings supporting more delicate feather wings.

## Hackle

Hackle feathers are used on dry flies, wet flies, and streamers and come from the neck, the cape (the base of the neck), or the sad-

# BODY AND SPECIALIZED HACKLE

THE FEATHER TYPES LISTED BELOW, WHICH are from parts of the bird other than the neck or saddle, are usually wound around the hook shank to give a fly a lively appearance.

**SPEY HACKLE**  *Often this is "burned" goose feathers (goose shoulder feathers dipped in an acid bath to remove the secondary fibers); available in black, dun (heron gray), purple, and orange.*

**PHEASANT RUMP**  *A substitute for burned goose feathers for use as spey hackle; available in natural or dyed.*

**"CHURCH WINDOW" (FROM THE SHOULDERS AND BACK OF THE NECK OF A MALE RING-NECKED PHEASANT) AND SIMILAR ADJACENT FEATHERS**  *Employed for shoulders on streamer flies.*

**JUNGLE COCK**  *Used for shoulders on streamer and salmon flies; now often omitted because of expense.*

**MARABOU**  *Fluffy feathers from the tail end of a turkey. Available in natural and dyed colors, white, black, brown, green, orange, fluorescent yellow, and fluorescent orange. Provides good action on wet flies.*

**BLACK SPEY MARABOU**  *Thin-fibered marabou hackle utilized for spey hackle in the Black Eagle salmon fly.*

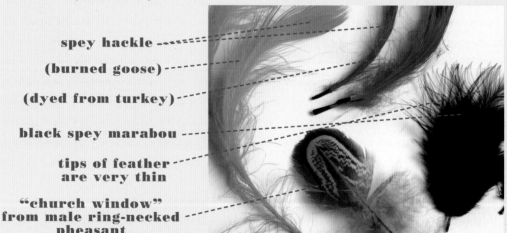

spey hackle
(burned goose)
(dyed from turkey)
black spey marabou
tips of feather are very thin
"church window" from male ring-necked pheasant

*Body hackle*

dle (the rear part of the back, just in front of the rump) of a fowl. Body feathers from some birds are also used as hackle.

Dry-fly hackle consists of stiff neck or saddle feathers, usually from a rooster, that have thin barbs and thin, flexible center shafts. The shafts of saddle hackle are generally thinner and more flexible than those of neck hackle, but the barbs are usually longer. You can buy ordinary neck or saddle hackle attached to the skin or in packets of selected neck or strung saddle feathers. Genetic hackle is higher in quality than ordinary hackle and has more usable feathers than Asiatic necks or saddles, which are smaller and contain a smaller range of feathers. We'll take a closer look at genetic hackle shortly.

Large saddle or neck hackle that has longer barbs is used for tying tails and throats, and its whole tips are used for some wings. Purchasing whole saddles and necks is efficient because they provide hackle in a variety of sizes (suitable for tying on Nos. 4–22 hooks) as well as feathers for large streamer wings.

To tie the dry flies in this book you will need dry-fly hackle in the following colors: black, white, badger, cochy (also called furnace), dark and light dun, ginger, coachman brown (also called Rhode Island Red), and grizzly. The instructions for individual flies specify the size hackle you will need to match the suggested hook size. If you look through this book you will find that some colors are used frequently; you can then determine whether there is a price advantage in purchasing half a neck as opposed to buying sev-

*Whiting 100s dry-fly hackle comes in various colors and for hooks of various sizes.*

eral packets of hackle in varying sizes to obtain the exact sizes and numbers of feathers you will need.

The greatest advance in dry-fly hackle came with Whiting Farm's breakthrough in genetic saddle hackle. Genetic hackle comes from birds that are bred specifically to produce high-quality dry-fly hackle. They have long, narrow feathers with stiff barbs, and the colors run true through the largest and smallest feathers. The individual necks are larger and much more expensive than ordinary necks, but they allow flytiers to produce a much greater number of high-quality flies—especially No. 16 or smaller—at a substantially lower cost per fly. The larger neck

# NECK HACKLE

NECK HACKLE TYPICALLY COMES FROM THE neck area of chickens and is often used to provide flotation for dry flies. It is available from various mail-order sources and retail stores.

**ASIATIC HACKLE** *Generally available as small necks with a few No. 16 or smaller dry-fly hackle feathers. Available colors include badger, cochy, ginger brown, and many dyed colors. Longer cochy feathers have a dark center that's useful for streamer wings, but this feature rarely occurs in No. 12 or smaller feathers.*

**GENETIC NECKS** *Excellent dry-fly quality in a large size; expensive hackle sold in whole or half necks. Available colors include white, badger, cochy, brown, black, dun, coachman brown, grizzly, and dyed colors.*

**CHINESE/SALTWATER NECKS** *Large necks, although not primarily of dry-fly quality. Useful for wings, tails on streamers, and wet flies. Available colors include white, black, cochy, badger, and many dyed colors.*

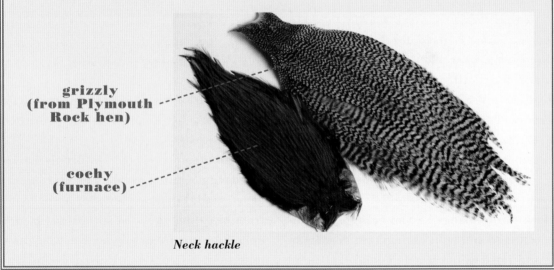

grizzly
(from Plymouth
Rock hen)

cochy
(furnace)

*Neck hackle*

feathers make good streamer wings and tails and throats for dry flies, and they work well on spiders when large spade feathers are not available.

Not all genetic breeding lines are of equal quality, but all of them show the bene-ficial effects of selective breeding to empha-size and secure high-quality dry-fly hackle. Whiting Farm, for example, produces 8- to 12-inch feathers that have a thin, flexible shaft and barbs that are nearly equal in length from one end of the feather to the

white
saddle
(genetic)

badger
saddle
(Asiatic)

*Saddles*

other. Individual feathers vary in width to match Nos. 10–22 hooks. You can purchase Whiting 100s packets of single-size feathers —which are sufficient to hackle a hundred flies—or full, half, and quarter saddles. The packets sell for a very reasonable price and are definitely a best buy.

Genetic saddle hackles solve the long-standing problem of hackling a palmered or bivisible fly, which requires at least three ordinary-length feathers to cover the allotted distance on the hook shank. Joining shorter feathers butt-to-butt creates a hump where you want a level line or silhouette. Hackling small flies with ordinary feathers, whose tips are too narrow and butts are too wide, involves much waste; often three feathers are required to adequately hackle the fly. There is no such waste using genetic saddle hackles.

Individual genetic necks are expensive, but each fly will be of better quality, cheaper, and easier to produce than the ones you make from any other source. Half necks or capes provide an adequate number of feathers for most flytiers, in a full range of sizes and for a reasonable cost. Indian and Chinese/Saltwater necks and necks from genetic hens, all of which are described in detail below, also serve a purpose, and price rather than quality becomes the determining factor in your purchase.

## INDIAN CAPES AND SADDLES

Indian neck capes and saddles are a by-product of birds produced for food rather than for fly-tying feathers. It is not easy to find dry-fly-quality small feathers with stiff fibers and the desired colors in Indian capes and saddles, so they are rarely used as a source for dry-fly feathers. Soft wet-fly and streamer grades, on the other hand, are in good supply. (Dry-fly-quality hackle is stiff and narrow and provides flotation, whereas wet-fly quality hackle is limp, webby, and produces lifelike action under water.) A wide variety of colors is usually available, and these necks and saddles are reasonably priced.

## CHINESE/SALTWATER NECKS AND SADDLES

These are improvements on the necks and saddles that are by-products of food production. They furnish large wet-fly and streamer hackle that is generally softer than the stiff barbs required for dry flies. However, some necks and saddles of medium dry-fly quality can be culled from a large lot.

Chinese/saltwater necks and saddles are the exceptions to the rule that chickens raised for food rarely produce good dry-fly hackle, and they should be welcomed if and when they are found. They come from China and some domestic sources, and given their low cost—about half the price of No. 3 domestic necks—are a good value for most uses except hackling dry flies. They come in several dyed and natural colors.

## HEN CAPES AND SADDLES

These provide soft wet-fly hackle used for tails and throats of nymphs and emergers to produce an active, lifelike effect. They are also used for wings on emergers and no-hackles, for which they can replace duck shoulder feathers with more natural—and hence more appropriate—colors. Light and dark dun, brown, partridge substitute, and grizzly are the most useful natural colors. Dyed colors of yellow, blue, orange, and black are also available.

# Other Feathers Used in Flies

The feathers we've discussed to this point all find use as hackle in various flies and all come from fowl. Now we'll look at feathers from a wider range of birds that find a wider array of uses in flies, such as wings, tails, and—when used in strips—as body materials.

## TURKEY TAIL FEATHERS

Turkey tail feathers are used in narrow strips of wings, wing pads, and throats of flies. During my lifetime the color of the majority of turkeys raised in the United States has changed from the dark bronze of wild turkeys to white, so the pinfeathers no longer show as black dots on the dressed birds. This has put a premium on the original dark shades of turkey tail and wing feathers that are called for in older patterns. When the patterns were created, dark-colored birds were plentiful and white ones were scarce freaks.

The original dark turkey tails with white tips are now almost as scarce as the specially bred cinnamon types. However, white tails and secondary flight feathers are plentiful, and they accept dyes beautifully. Red and yellow feather strips have often been used for tails and throats on streamers. Bronze/brown mottled turkey tails and wild turkey tails are also important for creating the foundations of dark salmon fly feather wings, wing pads for nymphs, and wings on wet flies like the Montreal. So-called "shorts," which grow at the base of a turkey's tail, are cheaper and have all the coloring of the larger tail feathers—and are hence a good, though often unexploited, bargain.

It is best to buy turkey feathers in matched pairs in which the feathers are asymmetrical; that is, each feather has long barbs, or fibers, on one side of the shaft and comparatively shorter barbs on other side. The two feathers should mirror each other when placed dull sides together, and will provide equal strips for well-matched wings. For every symmetrical tail feather, which has a center shaft, there are several asymmetrical tail feathers. When sold as matched pairs, asymmetrical feathers not only provide more fibers, they are significantly cheaper than their symmetrical counterparts. (The underside of turkey tails is darker than the topside, and must be used for dark wing pads, so be sure to tie the feather in with the dark side down so that it will be dark on top when folded over.)

## RING-NECKED PHEASANT TAIL FEATHERS

The underside of the ring-necked pheasant tail feather is darker than the topside. Strips from cock tail feathers are used for fly tails, wrapped onto hook shanks for bodies, and separated for nymph legs. Use the light side as an alternative to fur or dubbing to produce the segmented body on the Light Hendrickson Dry Fly (see page 189); wrap the feather onto the hook like a ribbon.

*A turkey tail feather showing characteristic asymmetry.*

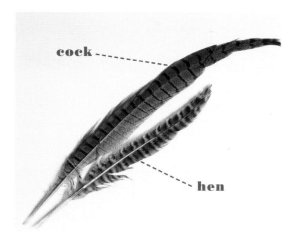

cock

hen

*Ring-necked pheasant tail feathers*

Use ring-neck pheasant tail feather strips to create wings for the March Brown salmon fly, either from a symmetrical feather or from a matched pair from which one wing

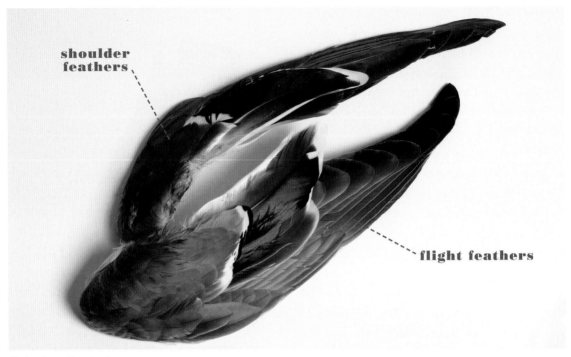

shoulder
feathers

flight feathers

*Paired mallard wings*

*Paired duck flight feathers*

feather is taken from the same side of each feather.

## DUCK FLIGHT FEATHERS

Duck wing feathers are paired by taking one feather from the same area of each wing, and are available from mail-order sources. Use paired flight feathers in strips for matched wings on wet and dry flies. You can also use individual flight feathers for wing pads on nymphs. Whole-wing pairs are also available, and provide matched, rounded shoulder feathers from the outside of the wings. From these you can make wings for no-hackles, stillborns, and emergers.

Because they contain both flight and shoulder feathers, pairs of whole wings are the best buy, but only if you need several sets of flight feathers and intend to tie no-hackles or emergers with feather wings.

## MACAW TAIL FEATHERS

When tying the Orange Parson salmon fly, use two single fibers from a tail feather for horns, one on each side. It is not possible to dye a substitute, because one side of the

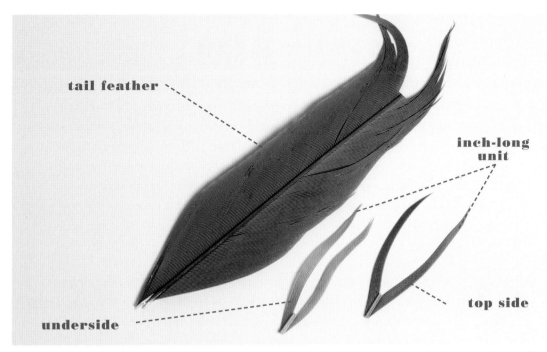

*Macaw tail feather (note the colors are not correct in the inch-long unit for the Orange Parson fly)*

macaw feather is blue and the other side is yellow; dipping a substitute in a dye bath hits both sides at the same time, making the feather all one color.

A natural, long, whole tail feather is expensive, but you can purchase inch-long units at a reasonable price, or you can omit the feather from the recipe. Pet macaws, like their wild brethren, molt every year, and I have used molted feathers effectively. Ask your bird-owning friends or the friendly zookeeper or pet shop owner to save molted

## BIRD TAILS

**CROW**  *Utilized for the Black Gnat body and wing cases on nymphs.*

**TURKEY**  *Use white to make the Garland fly body. White, cinnamon, and mottled brown (wild turkey) are employed for salmon fly wings. Red and yellow are used for streamer tails and beards, as are secondary flight feathers in the same colors.*

**RING-NECKED PHEASANT**  *Cock pheasant tail is used for nymphs. Hen tail is used for March Brown salmon fly wings.*

**BLUE/YELLOW MACAW**  *Used to make horns on salmon flies.*

# BIRD SKINS

**COCK PHEASANT CAPE** *The photo shows a few of the many colors of male ring-necked pheasant that can be used for shoulders or cheeks on streamer flies. "Church window" feathers, so-called because of their shape, are shown in place on the bird, but the other feathers can serve the same purpose effectively. To create substitutes for Indian crow and chatterer feathers, dye the white collar red and blue respectively. Rump feathers make wonderful spey-style hackle in a variety of colors.*

*Purchase a whole skin without the tail, as it is generally—but not always— the best buy. Whole skins provide a lot of feathers, and you can always purchase pheasant tail clumps separately to meet whatever need you have for those.*

**GOLDEN PHEASANT** *The crest, head, and tippet cape are sold as a unit and sometimes separately. You will also need the reddish breast feathers for the Lady Caroline salmon fly. Purchasing these feathers through mail order as part of a whole skin without the tail is the cheapest and often the only way to get them. Tails are sold separately if you need one, but a skin without a tail will probably meet your needs for most flies. All the other feathers on the skin are useful for fly tying, but they are not needed for the flies in this book.*

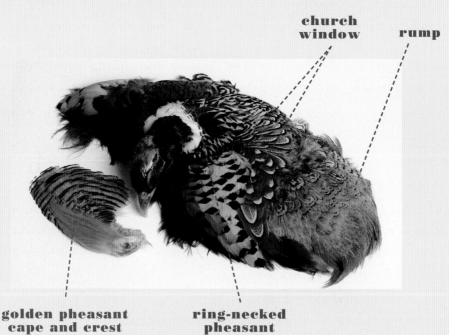

church window

rump

golden pheasant cape and crest

ring-necked pheasant

tail feathers for you. One long feather should supply the two horns for a multitude of flies. If stored properly to prevent a moth infestation, the feather should last you a lifetime.

## CROW FLIGHT FEATHERS

The tail or secondary flight feathers of the common black crow provide slips that you can wrap flat onto the hook shank like a ribbon to create a segmented body for the Black Gnat.

You can get crow feathers from friends who hunt, from molts, from birds that are hung from scarecrows, and from supply houses. I have procured feathers from each of these sources.

## PEACOCK FEATHERS

Peacock sword feathers and eyed tail feathers (called "eyes") provide herl (the barbules of the feathers), which is sold in two forms. The 8- to 12-inch tips of the feathers are cut off, and on these the herl (including the eye, if present) remains attached to the shaft and is sold as stick herl. The herl at the base of the feathers is stripped off the shaft and sewn into bundles called "pads." We use the quills from peacock-eyed sticks for quill-body flies. Turn the stick over and choose those with the lightest-color herl on the back or underside of the eye. When waxed and stripped, this herl shows the greatest contrast between the dark and light sections of the quill. The herl will be the same green or bronze as the next eye, so you get a real bonus when you select a peacock-eyed stick with a light-colored back. The eye itself is not used as herl on any fly, so picking a stick with a light color on the reverse side of the eye gives you good quill bodies and is a real bargain. Peacock herl is either green or bronze, and it is not always easy to distinguish between them.

## MARABOU FEATHERS

Soft insulating feathers from turkey rumps come in two sizes: large (5 to 8 inches long)

*Crow feather*

*Peacock sword feather*

*Eyed peacock tail feathers, one showing light side and one showing dark underside*

and "blood," which are usually bundled and sewn together and average about 4 inches in length. They are available in white and many dyed colors. For the flies in this book, you will need blood marabou in black, white, green, orange, yellow, fluorescent yellow, and brown.

The individual fibers are fluffy, but when they are wet they collapse into a very minnow-like, tapered shape and have great fish-attracting action.

Spey marabou is marabou selected to provide narrow, pointed, hairlike—rather than fluffy—ends on individual fibers. Black spey marabou, on which one side of the shaft is stripped of fibers, is used as hackle on the Black Eagle salmon fly, replacing the eagle feathers originally employed for that purpose. Spey marabou is sold separately from ordinary marabou. (See the sibebar Body and Specialized Hackle on page 14.)

# FEATHERS AND COLORS USED IN SALMON FLIES

## FEATHERS

**PEACOCK**  *Create bodies from natural herl; eyed tail feathers, called "eyes," provide stripped-quill bodies; employ sword feathers for salmon fly tails.*

**OSTRICH**  *Black herl is used for butts and joints on salmon flies.*

## COLORS

**HACKLE**  *Grizzly, badger, cochy (furnace), white, black, light dun, dark dun, brown, ginger, coachman brown.*

**DYED**  *Orange, black, yellow, lemon yellow, chartreuse, wine, blue, Indian crow substitute (red), chatterer substitute (blue), cock-o'-the-rock substitute.*

*Ostrich body feather*

# A SUMMARY OF BODY FEATHERS YOU WILL USE

**INDIAN CROW**  *A protected species of bird. For salmon flies, substitute for Indian crow feather with a white ring-necked pheasant collar feather dyed red.*

**CHATTERER**  *Another protected bird species. Substitute with a white ring-necked pheasant collar feather dyed blue.*

**COCK-O'-THE-ROCK**  *Also protected. Substitute with white chicken-body feathers that are dyed orange.*

**STARLING**  *Use neck hackle from the spring plumage of a male. Long, thin black/purple feathers are hackle for small Black Gnat flies.*

**TEAL**  *Make throats and wings for many flies from the black-barred flank feather.*

**SCAUP**  *Substitute these darker-barred flank feathers for teal. Make fan wings of the white breast feathers.*

**WIDGEON/MERGANSER**  *These are paler versions of teal flanks, and often replace them.*

**MALLARD (MALE)**  *Large bronze side feathers (called the Grand Nashua) are used to make tent-style wings on spey salmon flies.*

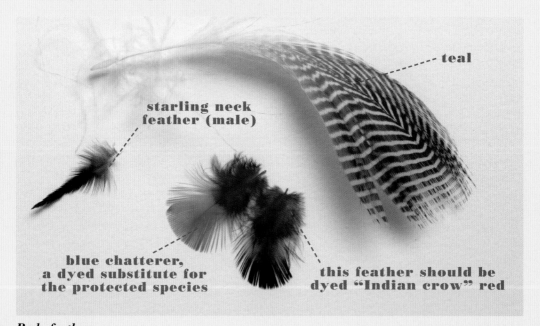

teal

starling neck
feather (male)

blue chatterer,
a dyed substitute for
the protected species

this feather should be
dyed "Indian crow" red

*Body feathers*

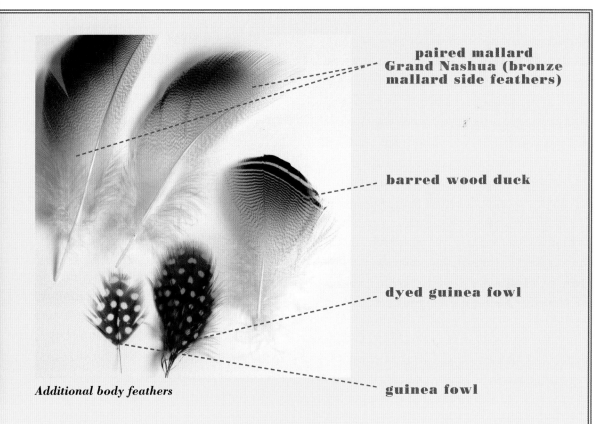

paired mallard
Grand Nashua (bronze
mallard side feathers)

barred wood duck

dyed guinea fowl

guinea fowl

*Additional body feathers*

**PEARL MALLARD**  *These are the lightest shades of the teal/widgeon series. Use flank feathers for wings and throats on several flies. They can be dyed to replace wood duck lemon flank feathers on wings, tails, and throats. Fan wings are made from white breast feathers.*

**WOOD DUCK**  *These expensive, black-barred feathers are used in thin strips to create the sides on salmon flies.*

**LEMON WOOD DUCK**  *Flank feathers for wings, tail, and throats were formerly rare and expensive. Since these ducks have returned to many areas from which they had disappeared, the feathers are now in better supply at more reasonable prices.*

**FRESHWATER COOT**  *The fibers of these feathers do not zip together as do most body feathers. The gray color and texture are suitable for Gray Nymph. I am not aware of a commercial source for these feathers, so you may have to rely on your own efforts or those of friends who hunt to secure them.*

**GUINEA FOWL**  *Spotted feathers that are available in natural colors or dyed blue, purple, or orange.*

## HERON FEATHERS

Heron are no longer hunted as vermin along trout and salmon rivers in the United Kingdom, and substitutes had to be found for these very necessary feathers, which are used as spey hackle. Commercial spey hackle is produced from goose shoulder feathers that are dipped in an acid bath to remove the zipper portions of the individual barbs, leaving the supporting quill thin and intact. They are dyed many colors, and are also sold as "burned goose." Gray is a substitute for the original heron hackle. Black, red, orange, and so on are used as hackle on spey and dee-style strip-wing salmon flies.

Other natural feather substitutes for heron are expensive blue-ear pheasant and cheap ring-necked pheasant rump feathers, neither of which are very popular.

# Body Hair

## DEER

Whitetail and mule deer provide hair for folded-/bundled-hair bodies and spun-/cut-hair bodies. The natural hair is dark gray-brown to light reddish brown depending on whether the deer live in evergreen or deciduous forests.

This hair takes dyes well, and dark colors can be achieved using the gray-brown hair that covers most of the animal. Bright colors such as yellow, green, and blue, however, are best achieved by dying white or bleached-white hair. Since there is a limited amount of white hair on each deer, dyed-over-white deer hair is more expensive.

Individual strands of natural white hair vary in length, stiffness, and coarseness (diameter). The soft hair can be made into hair wings—short for dry flies, long for streamers —and harder, stiffer white hair, either dyed or in its natural state, can be formed into spun-/cut-hair bodies.

Deer hock hair from scent glands on the animal's rear legs is tan to mahogany in color, stiff, light, hollow, and a good length for dry-fly tails. Cutting the hair patch off the leg does not result in any loss of meat, so hunters and slaughterers are usually willing

**Deer hair** in various shades

**Coastal blacktail deer body hair:** (left) light, (right) dark

*Dyed-over-white deer hair*

to give flytiers deer hock hair. Be sure to keep it in a tightly closed jar, however, because the scent gland has a disagreeable odor.

Coastal blacktail deer from the Pacific Coast have fine, often short body hair that makes good hair wings and folded hair bodies for flies such as Horner's Deer Hair. The hair is available in light and dark shades, bleached, and dyed black. Longer hair is good for spinning small flies, while shorter hair is better for hair wings.

## OTHER ANIMALS

Antelope hair makes a buoyant, high-floating fly, although when purchased from a mail-order source the tips of much hair arrive broken off and missing. For spinning, it's best to trim off both tips and butts to produce hairs of equal diameter at each end.

Antelope hair is available in natural tan, white, and several dyed colors. Caribou is another source for high-floating spinning hair. This soft, short- to medium-length hair is available in natural blue dun and white. It can also be dyed in many colors.

Other animals that are important sources for body hair include:

**MOOSE** *Black body hair is useful for creating dry-fly tails, especially those on paradrakes.*

**ELK** *This natural brown or straw-colored hair is long and, when bleached, takes light dyes very well. Natural straw, for Toth Caddis flies; and brown, dyed cinnamon, black, red, and mahogany, for ants, will cover the colors needed for the flies in this book.*

**CALF** *This body hair is taken from the animal's winter coat and is available in white, black, and often fluorescent yellow. Flytiers use calf hair for hair wings.*

**KID GOAT** *This medium to long hair is available in white and black, and is employed for hair wings. Kid goat hair can be a replacement for black bear or dyed squirrel tail. Flytiers also make the white wing on the Ingall's Butterfly salmon fly from kid goat.*

**WOODCHUCK** *Well-marked guard hairs are used for wings, and the chestnut-brown underfur makes good nymph dubbing.*

**MUSKRAT** *This provides blue dun dubbing fur of the highest quality. Cut it off in bunches from the hide and, holding the guard hairs in one hand, remove the underfur with the other. Keep the moths out, and be happy!*

**RABBIT** *This underfur is similar to the muskrat's, and it can be bleached and dyed easily on or off the hide.*

**HARE'S EAR** *This underfur comes with the guard hairs, but is not taken from the ear area anymore. At one time, the poll (head, face, and ears) of a rabbit skin was the unused by-product of felting for hats, and the face area was a very cheap source of dubbing for flies and nymphs.*

**GRAY FOX** *This is used to make Rat-series salmon fly wings. Coyote face hair is a substitute if it is well-marked black and white.*

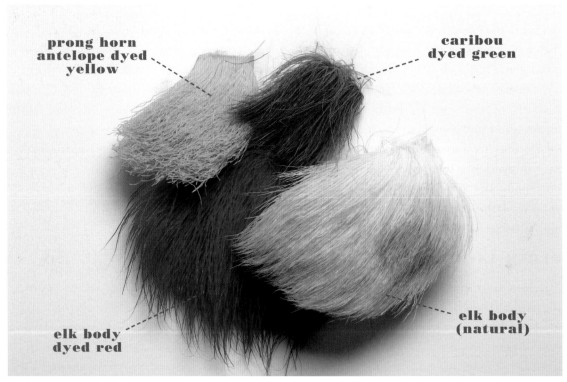

prong horn
antelope dyed
yellow

caribou
dyed green

elk body
dyed red

elk body
(natural)

*Hair from assorted other animals*

*Examples of other sources of body hair*

**FUR STRIPS (USUALLY RABBIT OR SQUIRREL)**
*The "regular" cut fur strip (i.e., the strip cut in the grain direction of the hair) is employed for the McSnake tail. Wrap cross-cut strips around the hook shank for fat fur bodies. Do not use cross-cut strips for tails, and make sure that the width you order is suitable for your needs.*

**PECCARY (WILD PIG)** *This is usually sold on the hide, and you will use only the hair (bristles)—not the thicker quills—for dry-fly tails.*

**CHINESE BOAR** *These multicolored bundles of bristles provide many shades for dry-fly tails.*

*Chinese boar fur*

# Fish Hair

Fish hair (also called Super Hair) is a synthetic fiber that you need for the tandem-

# HAIR TAILS

**DEER** *The tail color of both bucks and does is the same—the animal's body color on the top and white on the underside. Available dyed colors include black, red, yellow, and green.*

**CALF** *These tails are available with straight or crinkled hair in white, brown, and black. Straight hair is by far the best and most useful. You will need white, red, and yellow.*

**SQUIRREL** *Available natural colors include Eastern pine (formerly red), fox, and gray. Squirrel tails dyed black are purchased as a replacement for black bear, which is quite coarse.*

**MINK** *Natural shades, from black to light dun and pale cream, are used for wings on spent wings.*

*Deer tail*

hook flies in this book. It is often available in a number of colors and lengths of 6 inches or less, and individual fibers have roughly the same diameter as bucktail hair. Fish hair is sold in bundles. One end is heat sealed, and it is often used to make large saltwater flies. The most popular colors are black, white, red, and yellow. Fish hair has been in catalogs for many years, but is rarely a featured item. To make an effective tandem hook fly, purchase hair that is at least 6 inches in length.

## Hooks

Hooks, which are obviously essential for fly tying, are expensive and come in a vast number of shapes, sizes, lengths, and weights. You can spend a small fortune on them and

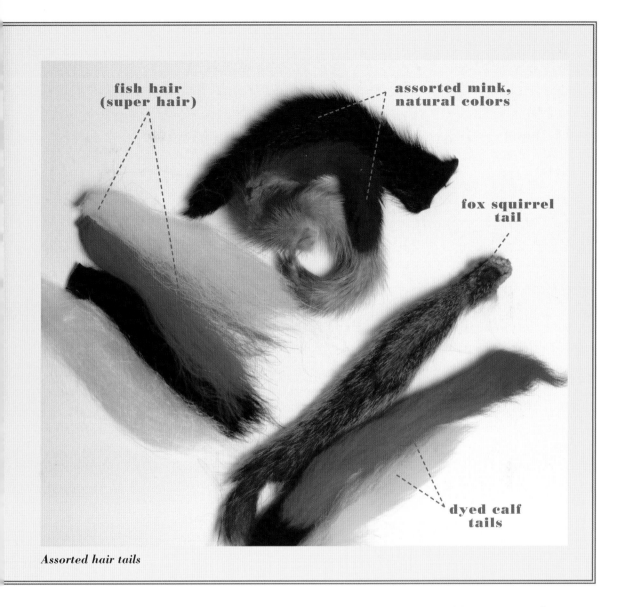

**fish hair (super hair)**

**assorted mink, natural colors**

**fox squirrel tail**

**dyed calf tails**

*Assorted hair tails*

still not have the one you need for a particular fly. Although the hooks listed in this book are made by Mustad, you can choose from a number of manufacturers; several other firms make styles that are equivalent to those made by Mustad.

Start by deciding which flies you want to tie and list the hooks and sizes needed to make them. You might also look ahead to see if there are other flies that require these hooks, and then decide whether to invest in a box of 100 at a reduced unit price or buy the smallest package (usually 25). Fortunately hooks do not deteriorate, but they can be mislaid or lost in your storage area as easily as flies are lost in trees, brush, and rocks in the water. Buy the quantity of hooks you presently need, take care of them, and keep

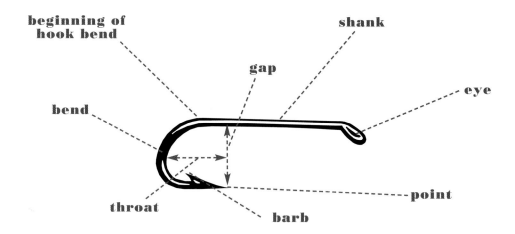

*Anatomy of a hook*

your inventory of hooks and materials within reasonable limits, and both your purse and your storage area will thank you.

Trout and panfish generally take Nos. 10–16 dry flies, unless a particular fly such as a Spent-Wing Trico or a midge pattern requires a specific size. Streamers/bucktails made for casting usually call for Nos. 6–10 hooks, up to a No. 2 for trolling flies.

Dry-fly hooks should be strong, although less weight always means a longer float for your fly. We use the following models frequently:

*Mustad #94840, Nos. 10–26*

*Mustad #94833 in regular length, 3X fine*

*Mustad #94831, twice as long as the standard length (2X), is ideal for Royal Coachman patterns, which need a long shank to accommodate a long body*

Each manufacturer selects one diameter of wire as the standard for its dry-fly hooks,

another diameter for streamer/bucktail hooks, and so on. They also make hooks for each type of fly that varies from the standard diameters. There are similar standards for the shank length of each type of fly hook. The variations from the standard hook are indicated in a code used by all hookmakers. Incidentally, 2X fine means the wire diameter of the hook is two sizes smaller than a normal hook; for example, a No. 10 2X fine is as thick as a regular No. 14 hook of the same catalog number. XL refers to length: the shank of a 2XL No. 10 hook is as long as the shank of a regular No. 6 hook of the same catalog number. Wet flies—which are intended to represent drowned insects—are tied on heavy wire hooks so they sink. Wet-fly hooks are typically medium- to short-shanked; #3906 is the Mustad standard. Nos. 6–16 are suitable for all the wet flies in this book. Nymphs—at least some of them—tend to be on the long side, and are usually tied on 1XL- to 3XL-shanked heavy hooks with turned-down eyes. You will need #9671 (2XL) and #9672 (3XL), both in Nos. 10–14, for the flies in this book. Streamers/bucktails are best tied on longer-shanked hooks such as #9575, which has a looped eye to prevent leader wear and is the Cadillac of this category.

Some hooks are forged or flattened at the hook bend after they have been formed, adding strength to the hook. Forged hooks are available for most types of flies and are well worth the extra cost. Spider hook #9523 has a 5XS (where the "S" stands for short) short shank and is made of lightweight forged wire; it can float high as a spider fly on long, stiff hackle and tail. Do not confuse spider hooks with "egg hooks," which have a similar shape but are made of very heavy wire and are used on flies representing salmon roe. An egg hook would drown a spider fly despite the best hackle and tail. Some spider-style hooks are gold- or silver-plated, which is an advantage if the hook is light.

Hooks made without barbs are somewhat rare and are more expensive than barbed hooks. Regulations for fishing in some areas, however, require barbless hooks. Luckily, with a pair of pliers, you can flatten the barbs on all hooks. When properly flattened, the barbs will cause no more injury to fish than specially made barbless hooks.

## SALMON FLY HOOKS

The salmon flies in this book require two types of hooks: *low water,* a lightweight longer-shank hook that is comparable to the usual dry-fly hooks used to catch trout, bass, and panfish; and #36890, of which Nos. 2–10 will do for spey, dee, hair, feather-wing, and

> ## QUICK TIP
>
> MAGNETS COME IN HANDY FOR PICK-ing up spilled hooks, and small hooks can be picked up from a reasonably flat surface by wetting the pad of a finger or thumb and pressing down firmly on the hook. It will stick to your finger for easy lifting. This method is quite handy if you've mislaid your tweezers.

reduced/simplified flies. The length of the #36890 hook is adequate for sunken flies and is generally available by mail order for a reasonable price.

The low-water style #90240, available in Nos. 4–10, is ideal for making floating flies, such as the Bomber and Green Machine, and various sizes of hair Bumble Bees. Use the No. 4 hook for salmon/bass-size Bivisibles with high hackles and Irresistibles, and Nos. 4–10 for Rat-Faced McDougals, which are highly effective surface lures for bass. The Nos. 4–10 hooks are lighter and stronger than many of the dry-fly hooks we would ordinarily consider using when tying these flies for trout and panfish. There is not a great difference in price, and the Japan lacquer on the salmon hook wears far better than the usual bronze finish on freshwater hooks. These low-water hooks are also used for the small-fly-on-a-large-hook style of fishing, because they have little buoyancy and sink quickly in fast water.

**94840**

VIKING, FORGED, EXTRA
FINE WIRE, STRAIGHT,
ROUND BEND, TURNED
DOWN TAPERED EYE,
BRONZED

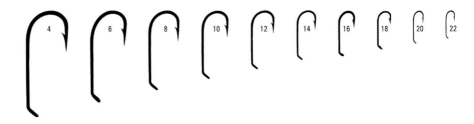

**94833**

VIKING, FORGED, 3 EXTRA
FINE WIRE, STRAIGHT,
ROUND BEND, TURNED
DOWN TAPERED EYE,
BRONZED

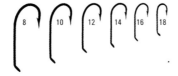

**94831**

VIKING, FORGED, 2 EXTRA
FINE WIRE, 2 EXTRA LONG
SHANK, STRAIGHT, ROUND
BEND, TURNED DOWN
TAPERED EYE, BRONZED

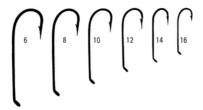

**3906**

HOLLOW POINT, SPROAT,
TURNED DOWN TAPERED
EYE, BRONZED

*Popular Mustad hook sizes and styles. Dry-fly hooks include 94840, 94833, and 94831. 3906 is the standard wet-fly hook. 9671 and 9672 are standard nymph hooks. 9575 is a standard streamer/bucktail hook, and 36890 is a salmon fly hook. Hooks are shown at actual size. (Courtesy Mustad)*

**9671**

VIKING, FORGED,
2 EXTRA LONG SHANK,
STRAIGHT, ROUND BEND,
TURNED DOWN TAPERED
EYE, BRONZED

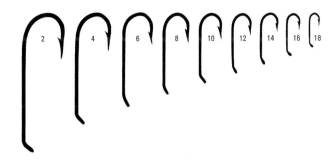

**9672**

VIKING, FORGED,
3 EXTRA LONG SHANK,
STRAIGHT, ROUND BEND,
TURNED DOWN TAPERED
EYE, BRONZED

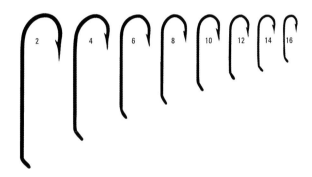

**9575**

LIMERICK, FORGED, 1/2
INCH LONGER THAN
REGULAR, TURNED DOWN
LOOPED EYE, BRONZED

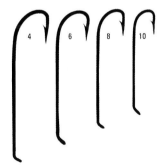

**36890**

LIMERICK, FORGED,
DUBLIN POINT, TURNED
UP LOOPED OVAL EYE,
BLACK

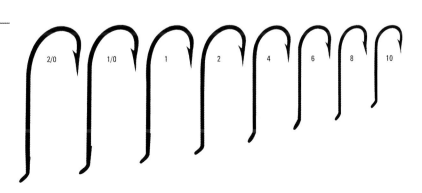

*Thread manufacturers use the* ought *system to indicate the thickness of the thread. Although the sizes haven't been standardized across all manufacturers, one thing is consistent: the bigger the number, the thinner the thread. For example, 8/0 thread is* thinner *than 6/0. The W on the leftmost spool indicates that the thread is waxed.*

## Thread and Dubbing

During my lifetime there have been remarkable changes in the size, quality, and strength of threads used for fly tying. In my youth, the preferred material was silk rather than cotton or flax. Although it was the best option available, silk was not very strong, and it rotted easily even when heavily coated with beeswax. Today synthetic fibers have replaced silk with much finer, stronger, rot-proof threads that are often waxed before or as they are spooled. The availability of fine, strong thread makes fly tying much easier, and knowing that your flies will not disintegrate because of rotting threads is a great relief.

In the 1940s, 4/0 nylon was considered very fine and strong, and was used for smaller flies. 8/0 UNI-Thread has replaced

*Dubbing is wrapped around thread, as an alternative to yarn, to make bodies. (See Dubbing on page 66 of the Basic Skills chapter.)*

it as the standard for all but the spinning of hair on flies and for some large saltwater flies. It is available in a multitude of colors and with remarkable strength for its size.

Flat waxed nylon is the popular choice for large saltwater flies. It is strong enough for the work and, because it's flat, allows for small heads. Where strength is required to hold many head materials firmly together in a short space—as is the case for larger streamers, hair bugs, and salmon flies—flat waxed nylon thread eliminates the need to tie off heavier thread and finish the head with 8/0, and produces a head of acceptable size. When used as a foundation for tinsel bodies, it will cover a hook shank effectively with fewer turns, and it has ample strength to secure heavy hair or feather wings.

When choosing threads keep these principles in mind:

1. Always use the finest thread you can manage without breaking it. Fine thread allows you to make more turns in a given space than heavier threads.
2. Use white thread, which you can see against the hook shank and materials, unless a contrasting or similar color is required, such as when making folded-hair flies. Heads tied with white thread can be easily colored with the head cement.
3. With practice you can learn to use quite fine threads for regular tying and reserve flat waxed nylon for heavier applications and for spinning hair and tying saltwater flies requiring bulky material.

For the flies in this book you will need 8/0 white UNI-Thread; 8/0 Flymaster thread in tan, beige, gray, and black; and flat waxed nylon thread.

## Tinsel

Oval tinsel is thin, narrow metal tinsel wound over a thread core and then slightly flattened. It and other tinsels come in large, medium, fine, and very fine. Gold and silver are readily available, and copper can be obtained from some dealers of salmon fly materials. To complete the salmon flies in this book you will need both gold and silver in large, medium, and small or very fine oval tinsel.

Mylar Christmas tree tinsel is available in several widths—especially just after the holidays—at a fraction of the price for its equivalent in fly-tying shops. I regularly use gold and silver in several widths. Mylar tinsel that is gold on one side and silver on the other is frequently offered by suppliers, but I recommend avoiding it; it's easy to attach this tinsel to the hook with the wrong side facing out, which is a real nuisance.

Buy flat, embossed, or oval tinsel that matches the size—small, medium, or large—of the fly you wish to tie.

## Wire

For the flies in this book you will need fine copper, gold, and silver wires, and possibly some somewhat larger gold and silver wire to make ribbing for large salmon flies. Finer wire will be adequate for salmon flies up to No. 2. For weighted nymphs, you will need lead wire or something similar. Two sizes—

Christmas
tree
tinsel

*Tinsel. Spooled tinsels are sometimes round in cross-section, sometimes flat.*

*Wire*

medium and small—should meet all your needs. Although lead shot has been banned in several areas because it causes lead poisoning in waterfowl, the use of lead wire which is then covered with other materials is still an accepted practice. Flies weighted with lead wire sink fast and deep, and are of no danger to waterfowl.

## Yarns

For fly-tying, synthetic fibers can and should replace wool to prevent flies from becoming moth bait between fishing seasons. Medium-weight yarns are the most useful, but multi-ply yarn can be separated and its strands used for various fly sizes or for flies requiring a thin body. You will need white, black, red (crimson), tan, olive, and orange yarns for the flies in this book, and not much of any of them. Before you go out and buy a large skein of yarn, consider canvassing your friends and relatives who knit for a short length instead. You will also need Antron yarn in white/cream and light (very pale) dun for spent wings and dun or slate for Hendrickson Spent Wings. Many fly shops sell yarns and chenille in short lengths that require little storage space.

*Colored yarn*

## Floss

In my youth, silk floss was the standard—if not the only—floss available for fly tying. Today synthetic fibers dominate the market, although some colors such as lilac—which you will need for the Orange Parson—are not available in the usual stock of rayon and nylon floss. In cases like this you pay a premium for the desired color in silk floss.

You will need yellow, lemon yellow, claret/wine, black, orange, red (preferably crimson to represent blood), and fluorescent green in synthetic floss, as well as a small

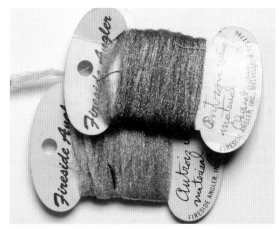

*Antron yarn, used for spent wings*

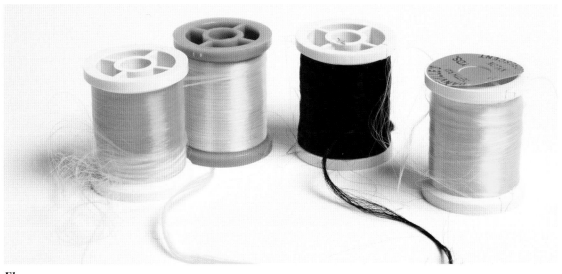

*Floss*

*Chenille comes in a variety of sizes and colors.*

## Chenille

For the flies in this book you will need both large and medium chenille in both black and yellow. Match the size of the chenille to the hook size. For the two Teasers in Easy Flies for Beginners, you can possibly get by with using either large or medium yellow chenille; the larger size may interfere with the hook gap, and hence with the fish's hold on the hook, but it will not make the fly unusable. The smaller size chenille on a No. 10 fly will assure a better setting of the hook in the fish's mouth. Wrapping larger-size black chenille near the head of the modern spey fly will not affect its hooking ability, and will aid its appearance considerably.

spool of French silk floss in each of red and lilac—for a high price.

*See Appendix 2 for sources of tools and materials.*

# BASIC SKILLS

There are some principles of construction—such as the steps for making tinsel-ribbed or yarn-and-tinsel-ribbed bodies or tying in tails and throats—that are shared by many of the flies in this book. It would be tedious and a waste of space to repeat the illustrations each time a process is described for a particular fly. Therefore we will provide a detailed, illustrated description of each process only once, here, and thereafter suggest that you return to these descriptions if you need to refresh your memory or clarify your understanding of the process.

First we will elaborate on the basic fly-tying steps previewed in the Introduction and provide some additional techniques. Next we'll take a closer look at the anatomy of a fly and explain the role of each part. Then we'll examine other skills, such as dubbing thread and spinning hair, that are used on a regular basis.

As we look at the various fly-tying processes, bear in mind that not all flies have all the parts included in the steps, nor will you need to employ every skill for every fly. Similarly, steps won't always occur in the order outlined below; for example, on some flies the throat is tied in before the wing, while on others it's tied in after the wing. Ultimately, the purpose of this chapter is simply to give you an overview of the common techniques you will encounter at the bench.

## An Elaboration of the Fly-Tying Steps

ONCE THE HOOK IS PLACED IN THE VISE AND the thread is attached to the shank (Steps 1 and 2), the process of tying in the parts of the fly will start at the rear—with the tail, which is located at or near the hook bend—and work forward, task-by-task, to the head, which is located near the eye of the hook. Occasionally a recipe will direct you to tie in a part "before its time"—say, tying in the wing before the body—but for the most part we tie flies in the order designated by the steps below.

Note that the descriptions here are generic and are intended only to give you a sense of the overall fly-tying process. The steps in the recipes themselves are written in more specific detail and provide information about how to prepare the materials you will use to make the fly.

### Step 1: Place the Hook in the Vise

Select the hook you need for the fly you are about to tie and place it in the open jaws of the vise. To hold the hook firmly in place, some tiers position it so that its point and the barb will both be covered when the jaws are closed. If the point or barb is exposed, their sharp surfaces can easily cut or fray the tying thread with annoying or disastrous results. Other tiers leave the barb just barely

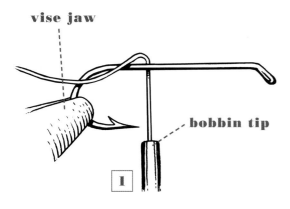

vise jaw

bobbin tip

**1**

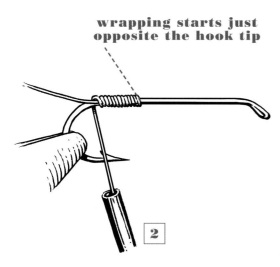

wrapping starts just
opposite the hook tip

**2**

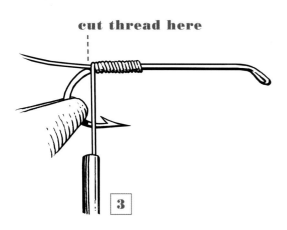

cut thread here

**3**

*Attaching thread to the hook*

exposed so as to avoid any risk of damaging it in the vise, though this is unlikely except with the smallest hooks. In the accompanying drawings and photos, the point and barb are prominently exposed for clarity.

## Step 2: Attach the Thread to the Hook

To form a foundation for the tail—or for the body materials on a fly that has no tail—begin by pulling out a couple of inches of thread from the bobbin. Holding it between your thumb and forefinger, lay the thread along the top of the hook shank so the end of the thread extends behind the hook bend and so that your turns of thread will start well down the shank from the eye, more or less directly above (across the gap from) the point of the hook. While holding this length in place, wind thread from the bobbin onto the shank so as to cover the thread end and bind it in place. Holding the thread taut, make close, firm turns, butting them smoothly, side by side, and working toward the bend of the hook. Cut off the surplus end of thread where it emerges from beneath the wraps, make a couple of turns of thread from the bobbin to cover the cut end, and let the bobbin hang.

## Step 3: Tie in the Tail

To attach a tail, place the material at the hook bend, on top of and parallel to the hook shank, so the tip of the tail extends the proper distance beyond the hook bend for the particular fly you're tying. Bind the material in place with a loose (soft) loop followed by a firm turn or two of the tying thread (see

# A BETTER MOUSETRAP (OR, MORE ABOUT ATTACHING AND WINDING THE THREAD)

IN THE CLASSIC METHOD OF TYING a trout dry fly, one begins by attaching the thread next to the hook eye and winding the thread toward the hook bend, covering about one-quarter of the hook shank. At this point, the tier ties in the wing, if the fly has one, with the butt of the wing pointing toward the rear of the fly. Next, the tier continues to wrap the thread base or foundation toward the bend, covering the area where the tail and body materials will be tied in, then wraps back over the thread base in butting turns toward the hook eye. The tier stops wrapping at the wing, where the thread will hang until the body has been wrapped up the shank. After he or she ties in the hackle, the tier will advance the thread to the eye and make the head.

Frankly, on long-shank hooks, bucktails, and streamers, this close winding of thread down, then back up, the shank is a pain in the rear! After some years of winding like this and several spools of thread, I began to start my flies at the hook bend, or at the tail if the fly had one. I attach the thread to the shank area above the barb or point of the hook and wind it in snug turns about $\frac{1}{8}$ to $\frac{3}{16}$ inch toward the hook bend (i.e., toward the left). Then I tie in the tail—if the fly has one—following which I attach the body material(s), letting them hang for the moment. From the tail or tie-in area for the body materials, I wrap the thread with butting turns back up the shank to $\frac{1}{8}$ inch behind the eye. With this modified base, you can make a fly that lasts as long as those tied in the classic manner. Also, I tie in the wing after I form the body, rather than while winding the thread toward the rear of the hook. In this method, you place the wing butt over the eye, rather than toward the rear of the wing. To form a base for the hackle, taper the wing butt toward the eye and bind it firmly with thread, which eliminates the need in that area for the double-layer thread base that's created in the classic method of tying.

This method is simply an adaptation to trout flies of the method that has proved entirely satisfactory for classic feather-wing salmon flies over the centuries. Make sure the thread base is always wrapped ahead of where you're attaching body material, until you reach the wing tie-in area. The thread is thus available to tie in items or tie them off as you build the fly.

My method saves time, temper, and a great many turns of thread, and it does not result in a sloppy fly. Try it! You should like it, unless you prefer to unnecessarily wrap thread evenly—two times—onto every hook shank.

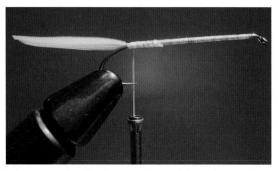

*Wrapping the Body #1. The tail has been tied on and the bobbin hangs where the body material will be attached. Note that this tier has wrapped a thread foundation from behind the eye in the standard fashion. For a recommended shortcut, see A Better Mousetrap in the accompanying sidebar.*

*Wrapping the Body #2. The body material has been tied and the thread wrapped forward in butting turns.*

*Wrapping the Body #3. The body material has been wrapped forward in butting turns to where the bobbin hangs.*

The Soft Loop Technique, page 56). Then let the bobbin hang while you check the position of the tail.

If your fly calls for a tinsel or floss body and your tail material has a thick butt, such as feather shafts or the butts of a bunch of hair, cut the butt off at a long slant toward the head end of the fly. Wrap the tapered butt with adjacent turns of thread, and then wrap back to where the tail is tied in. When you're finished, let the bobbin hang as you prepare for the next step.

# Step 4: Wrap the Body

Place the body material along the top of the hook shank so that one end will be about ³⁄₁₆ inch from the eye after you finish winding it around the shank. (This requires leaving a little extra length for the windings.) With the hanging thread, tie in the material tight against the tail, leaving no gap between the tail and where the rear of the body will be. Allow the length of the material to hang or hold it out of the way with a material clip. Wind the thread in butting turns forward to about ³⁄₁₆ inch from the eye, binding the tied end of the body material to the shank as you go. Then let the bobbin hang. Next, wrap the body material itself in butting turns up to where the thread is hanging, and tie it off. Carefully trim the excess body material; lift it above the hook shank when you trim it to avoid cutting the thread by accident!

## APPLYING A RIB

If the fly has a rib, tie in the rib material at the same time as the body material, as above

*Applying a Rib #1. When a fly has ribbing, tie it in at the same time as the body material.*

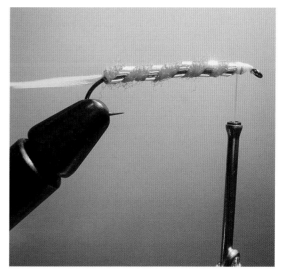

*Applying a Rib #2. The ribbing has been spiraled over the previously wrapped body.*

(i.e., you tie in the rib material *before* you bind down the end of the body material). Bind down the ends of both materials with thread, and then wrap the body onto the shank as directed. After you tie off the body, spiral the rib material over the body in evenly spaced turns. The amount of space you allow between turns will be specified in the recipe you're working on. Tie off the rib material at the front end of the body and trim the excess material.

# Step 5: Tie in the Wing

As you work through the flies in this book, you will be introduced to a number of wing styles, all of which are prepared and tied a little differently. Here is a general description of the styles of wings you will tie most frequently. (Detailed instructions for preparing and tying in the spey- and dee-style wings are provided in their respective chapters in Part Three.)

## WHOLE-FEATHER WING (DRY-FLY WING)

Select two matching feathers of the proper size. With dull sides together and tips matching, trim the soft, short fibers on each side of the shaft butts to a stubble. Place the feathers along the top of the hook shank with the trimmed shafts over the eye and the lower

*Whole feather (dry fly) wing. Two matching feathers are bound on top of the shank with their trimmed shafts over the eyes.*

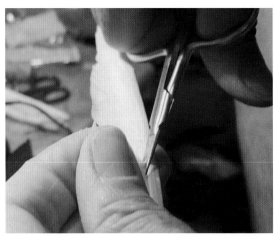

**Feather-Section Wings #1.** *Selecting a matched pair of feathers.*

**Feather-Section Wings #2.** *Cutting out matching slips.*

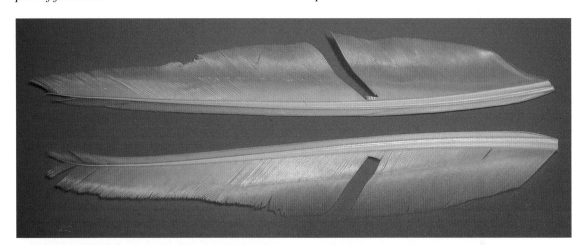

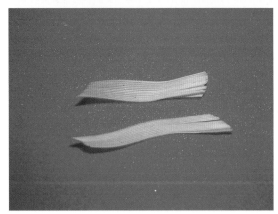

**Feather-Section Wings #3.** *The slips (above) and the feathers from which they were cut (top).*

**Feather-Section Wings #4.** *The slips bound to hook shank, butts not yet trimmed.*

edge of the feathers just touching the body. Bind them firmly in place with three or four turns of thread. Let the bobbin hang while you cut off the surplus shafts.

## FEATHER-SECTION WING (COMMONLY A DRY-FLY WING, BUT SOMETIMES A WET-FLY WING)

Remove the short, soft fibers from the wide side of a matched pair of feathers (or, if you have a symmetrical feather with a center shaft, remove the fibers from both sides of the shaft). Measure and cut off matching slips of the length and width required for the fly you're tying, from the base of the wide side of both feathers (or each side of the symmetrical feather) close to the shaft. Place the slips dull sides together and align the tips. Be sure the slips are the same size and width.

Place the unit on its edge on top of the hook shank with the tips to the rear and extending the required distance for the fly you are tying. Fasten it there using the soft loop technique and let the bobbin hang while you cut off the surplus butts.

## HAIR WING (COMMONLY A DRY-FLY WING)

Cut a small bunch of hair off the hide (see illustration page 50). Even the tips and, holding the bundle firmly by the tips, remove any fuzz or short hairs. Check its length and apply a drop of Duco Cement to the butts. Set the bundle aside to become tacky—not solid—with the wet ends hanging over the edge of a clean piece of scrap wood. (Duco Cement will ruin any painted or varnished

surface it touches, so be careful where you set that bunch of hair!) When the cement is tacky, place the wing along the top of the body so the tips extend the required distance beyond the hook bend. Use the soft loop technique to tie it in.

## Step 6: Tie in the Hackle

There are two kinds of hackle feather you can use on your flies: good-quality dry-fly neck hackle and Whiting 100s, each of which are prepared and tied in a little differently. (For more information about each kind of hackle feather, see Hackle on page 13 of the Tools and Materials chapter.)

### DRY-FLY NECK HACKLE

Select a feather that has barbs of the length required for the fly you are tying. Hold the tip of the feather firmly while you cut the soft fibers on both sides of the shaft's base to a stubble. Place the feather diagonally on the near side of the hook shank, butt downward and forward, with the first of the untrimmed

*Hair Wing. Cemented hair bound in place but not yet trimmed.*

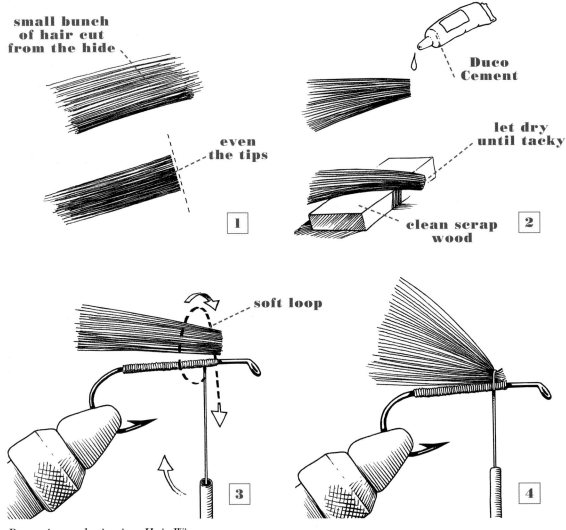

*Preparing and tying in a Hair Wing.*

part of the feather directly over the hanging thread and the feather's tip toward the rear of the hook. Fasten it there with several firm, close-butted turns of thread over the stubble area, and let the bobbin hang. Cut the surplus shaft, bind down the cut end, and let the bobbin hang.

To wind the feather, attach the hackle pliers just below the tip and at right angles to the shaft. Wind the hackle around the hook shank, either palmered (see Hackle on page 59) or as a collar.

## WHITING 100S

Select a feather (match the size to the hook) and trim the first ½ inch of both sides of the tip to a stubble. Place the stubble tip diagonally down on the near side of the hook shank with shiny side out and with the beginning of the uncut feather directly over the

soft fibers to be trimmed

**Dry-Fly Neck Hackle #1.** *An untrimmed feather.*

**Dry-Fly Neck Hackle #2.** *Soft fibers trimmed.*

**Dry-Fly Neck Hackle #3.** *The trimmed feather bound to the hook shank. Here the feather's tip points forward, but I prefer to have the tip pointing toward the rear of the hook.*

**Dry-Fly Neck Hackle #4.** *The first one or two wraps of the hackle feather have been completed.*

**Dry-Fly Neck Hackle #5.** *More hackle wraps in place.*

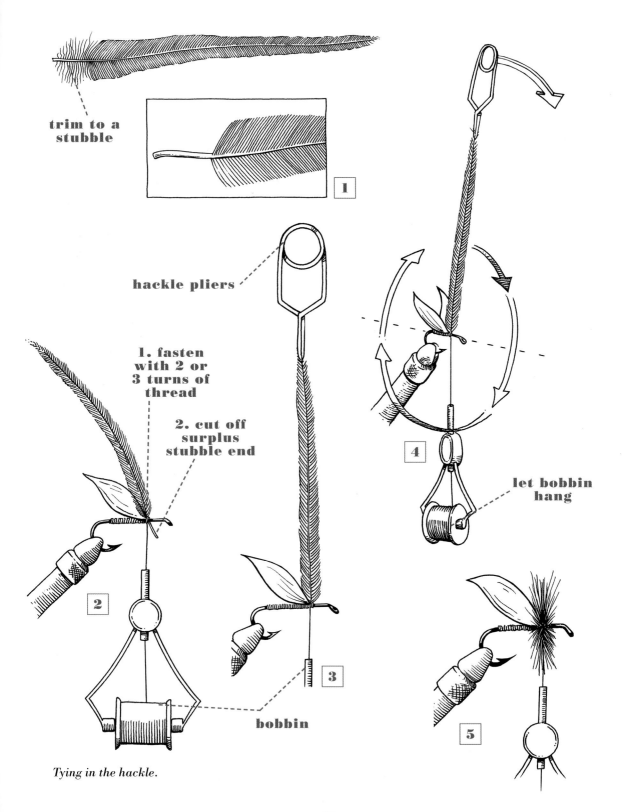

trim to a
stubble

**1**

hackle pliers

1. fasten
with 2 or
3 turns of
thread

2. cut off
surplus
stubble end

**2**

**3**

bobbin

**4**

let bobbin
hang

**5**

*Tying in the hackle.*

hanging bobbin. Fasten it there with two or three firm turns of thread, then let the bobbin hang while you cut off the surplus stubble end. Bind down the stubble end and let the bobbin hang.

To wind the feather, attach the hackle pliers about 4 inches up from the hook and at right angles to the shaft. Wind the hackle around the hook shank, either palmered or as a collar.

## UPSETTING AND DOUBLING THE FEATHER

When a feather isn't thick enough to provide the desired action in a fly, it has to be doubled before it's wound onto the hook shank (see figure on the following page). First, you'll need to *upset* the feather. Do to so, wet a clean finger and hold the tip or base of the feather between your thumb and forefinger. With your other hand, stroke the fibers against the grain (upward if holding the base of a dry-fly hackle and downward if holding the tip of a Whiting 100s). This will make the fibers stick out at right angles from the shaft. Next, you'll *double* the feather, which is done by stroking and teasing the fibers around the shaft until they appear to be all on one side. This is best done in ¾- to 1-inch sections. When you're finished upsetting and doubling the feather, wind the hackle around the hook shank, either palmered or as a collar.

# Step 7: Attach a Throat or Beard

Using the soft loop technique, tie in the throat/beard material under the hook shank just behind the eye. Trim and bind the sur-

**Whiting 100s Hackle.** *The first half-inch of a Whiting 100s feather has been trimmed to stubble, placed diagonally on the near side of a shank, and bound in place but not yet trimmed.*

plus butts to create the underside of the head. After it's tied in, you can shorten the throat to its proper size by cutting back the free, exposed end of the material. (Also see The DeFeo Method of Making a Throat, page 59.)

## CLASSIC SALMON FLY THROAT

Select a hackle feather with barbs as long as the gap of the hook and cut off the required number of barbs for the fly you're tying. Bundle them and even the tips. Place the bundle under the hook shank and take a loose turn around both the bundle and the shank. Tighten the thread and release your hold on the bundle as it spreads, with a little help from your fingers, around the lower half of the shank.

Keep the thread taut as you check for proper length and placement and identify any thin spots or gaps. To repair such problems

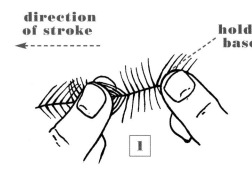

direction of stroke

hold tip or base here

**Stroking the fibers against the grain to make them stand at right angles from the shaft. This is called "upsetting the feathers."**

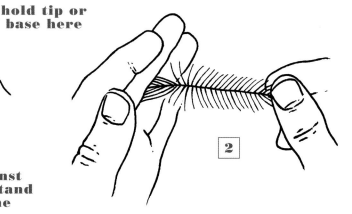

**Finishing the stroking.**

**Doubling the feather by coaxing all fibers to point upward.**

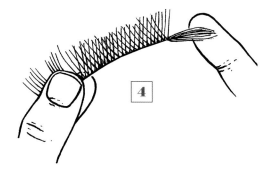

**Here the doubling is completed, and the feather is ready to be tied in by the tip at right.**

*Upsetting and doubling the feather*

prepare additional bundles of fibers sized to fill each and tie them in as you did the original bundle. When you are satisfied with the throat, secure it to the hook shank with a couple more turns of thread, and let the bobbin hang while you trim back the butts.

## Step 8: Form the Head

With thread, wrap a cone-shaped head that tapers forward toward the eye. To do this, wrap from right to left, starting near the eye, so that when pulled tight the last turns of thread provide a neat seal between body and head. Tie off the head using the whip finish (see instructions on page 61), then cut the thread close to the head.

Apply durable nail polish using the brush in the bottle (a bodkin or dental pick is more effective on small flies). Avoid getting polish on the hackle, wing, or body materials. After it dries, apply a second coat, if necessary, to achieve a smooth base for the head cement. Apply the cement with a thin bodkin or a thin dental pick with the angled tip removed.

## PAINTING EYES

Not all flies have eyes. A recipe will say whether the fly has eyes; if it doesn't say, it's safe to assume you do not have to paint on eyes or create eyes in other ways.

To paint the eyes, dip the head of a No. 6 finishing nail or a proper size painting tool

**Forming the Head.** *A cone-shaped head has been wrapped from right to left and is ready for a whip finish.*

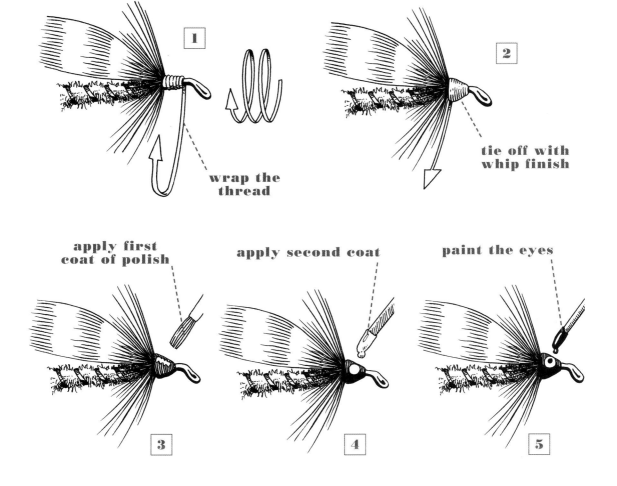

**1** wrap the thread

**2** tie off with whip finish

apply first coat of polish **3**

apply second coat **4**

paint the eyes **5**

*Forming the head*

*The Erskine Streamer*

into white head cement, just touching the surface enough to "load" the nail with paint. Lightly touch the nail to one side of the fly's head to create a round dot for the eye. Repeat on the other side of the head, and hang the fly up to dry.

When dry, use a smaller finishing nail or brad touched to black head cement to paint a pupil in the center of each eye, and allow them to dry.

# A Closer Look at Fly Anatomy

IN THIS SECTION WE'LL TELL YOU EVERY-thing you need to know about the various parts of the fly, plus provide more tips for making them, and introduce some additional techniques that will hopefully make your fly-tying experience a little easier and more efficient. (See also the illustrations on page 5.)

## Tails

Most flies have a tail located at the rear. The tails of dry flies and spinners provide flotation, and are made of stiff, hollow hair or feather barbs that are tied singly on spinners and, on most dry flies, in a bundle placed over the hook bend. Wet-fly tails, which imitate insect or nymph tails, are made with two or three hairs, feather barbs, or—in the case of an emerger's shuck—a bundle of hair or a feather.

The tails of streamers and bucktails often represent blood flowing from an injured minnow, and are hence seen by fish as an easy meal. Such tails are often made from ³⁄₁₆- to ³⁄₈-inch-wide strips of red feather or a similar-size bundle of red calftail hair. They extend ½ to ¾ inch beyond the bend of the hook. Once tied in, many tiers trim the excess on a slant toward the eye, because a real minnow is not very wide in the area just ahead of its tail. The cut ends are snugly wrapped with thread, creating a foundation for a smooth body instead of presenting an unnatural swelling in this area.

Tails for most wet and dry trout and panfish flies measure one body length: the distance between the eye of the hook and the hook bend. Because most insects are not very thick at the rear of their bodies, the excess butts on flies except those like the Bumble Bee are trimmed for a closer imitation of the natural insect. Similarly, there should be no gap or spaces between the tail and the body on any fly, because naturals have no gap or space in that area.

### THE SOFT LOOP TECHNIQUE

Although the soft loop technique is mainly used to tie in the tail, it can also be employed when tying in other parts of the fly, such as a wing or throat. The soft loop technique prevents the tail from sliding around and under the hook when tension is applied on the thread to secure the material. Obviously you don't want the tail to wind up in a mess under the hook bend—which is likely to happen if you simply wrap the thread around the tail and pull it toward you to secure the material.

You will follow the steps below many times during your fly-tying endeavors, so learn the drill now and be that much farther ahead of the game.

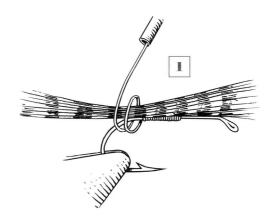

**Beginning the soft loop, with tail material laid out on shank of hook.**

1. With your left thumb and forefinger, hold the tail bundle on top of and parallel to the hook shank. With the bobbin in your right hand, carefully pass the thread between your left thumb and the shank, then up in a high, soft loop over the tail, then down behind the hook, between the shank and your forefinger, and then under the hook shank.

2. Repeat for another full turn before carefully pulling the thread downward—rather than toward you—to fix the tail firmly in place.

3. Firmly wrap several more even turns of thread around the butt of the tail barbs, securing them to the hook. Then return the thread to the tail's tie-in point, and let the bobbin hang.

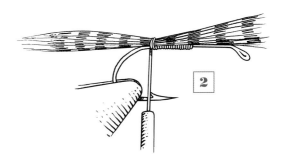

**The soft loop has been pulled tight. Finish with two more turns around the shank.**

*Soft loop technique*

## Bodies and Ribbing

Many fly bodies are made by winding flat tinsel—often with a ribbing of oval tinsel for maximum "flash and shine"—or yarn, floss, chenille, stripped quill, or a slip or strip of

feather up the hook shank. Other materials include herl, dubbing, or spun hair (the hair is cut into shape later). Smooth bodies made of tinsel and floss require the short end of the body material—that is, the end that's tied in against the tail—to extend almost to the head, and it is no mistake to treat all body materials in this way. After the material is tied down, wind the thread in adjacent turns toward the wing area.

Flytiers often employ flat and oval tinsels together to form a tinsel body, or individually as ribbing over other body materials. Use either gold or silver flat and oval tinsels together, but not both colors together. Tie in the tinsels just ahead of the main body material, before winding the thread up the hook shank.

Saddle hackle or long neck feathers are frequently spiraled up spun/clipped hair bodies or, on some salmon flies, palmered (wrapped) in spirals tight against an oval tinsel rib. (*Spiraling* is the process of winding the hackle up the body without specifying the distance between the turns. *Palmering* is when the hackle is spiraled up the body in turns ⅛ inch to ³/₁₆ inch apart.) The spey and dee flies go a step further, calling for long heron or spey hackle (burned goose) to be applied the same way over parts of the body to give the appearance of life, movement, and action in fast water.

Hair Ants and Horner's Deer Hair will obtain their characteristic humped shapes when you tie down segments of bundled hair, and are a law unto themselves, as will be seen in due course.

# Wings

The wing, which is upright on classic dry flies and tied in at a 45° angle on classic wet flies, is often made of slips from wing pointers, hackle tips, or sections of waterfowl feathers. Body feathers, fine hair, and floating synthetics are used for flotation and to imitate the wide-spread, horizontal wings of Spent-Wing Spinners lying flat against the water's surface, exhausted after their egg-laying activities. Dark-colored strips of feather can represent the growing wing pads on nymphs and are pictured in detail in the Nymphs chapter.

For dry-fly wings, hair is an adequate replacement material for feathers, as detailed in the hair wing instructions for the Royal Coachman (page 182), and makes a much more durable dry fly. For the best action, bucktail and other hair wings should not be thick and dense. To test a wing's thickness or density, lay the fly down on a printed page. You should be able to read the page through the wing. However, note that trolling streamers and trolling bucktails are usually larger flies representing large baitfish, and their wings are much thicker and should not be judged by your ability to read through them.

Although many recipes that include hair wings simply direct you to tie the hair in a loose bundle onto the hook shank, others require that the bundle be cemented first. Using cement on the wing butts and tying the wing to the hook shank while the cement is soft will lock and hold the hair together in the head area once the cement is fully dry. Now the wing cannot shed hairs, and the head becomes a solid mass under the thread wrapping, thus producing a very durable fly. Hair wings tied in without glue are faster and easier to produce, but often shed hairs singly or in large bunches, thus ruining the action of the wing in short order. The glue method also assures separation of colors in multicolored wings, which is difficult or impossible to attain when using bundles of dry hair.

Bucktail and streamer wings made of

hair, whole neck feathers, or saddle feathers provide the action of these flies. On Matukas, you can attain a minnow form by removing a shank-length area from one side of a feather wing. Then bind the feather shaft firmly to the body and hook shank in that area, while allowing an equal length of whole feather to extend beyond the bend as an active tail.

On any fly, limiting the length of the wing portion that extends beyond the hook bend to a finger's thickness will usually prevent short strikes, in which a fish seizes the end of the wing, but does not get the hook in its mouth.

## Hackle

Hackle is a neck or saddle feather tied in and wound on its edge, often in butting turns, usually in the area just behind the head. It provides flotation for dry flies and, with fewer turns, represents legs on wet flies. A hackle is palmered when there is space between the turns of the feather, and it often requires doubling first for the palmering technique to be effective. For example, particularly on wet and salmon flies, a single side of feather is not sufficiently thick to give a lifelike, vibrating appearance to the fly, so doubling the hackle is necessary. The process of doubling also creates the edge on which the hackle is wound when applied to the hook shaft.

## Throats or Beards

On bucktails and streamers we next come to the throat or beard. This is usually a feather slip, like the tail, or a thin bunch of red hair representing blood and injury. Plain or pale colors can represent legs on many wet flies, Hair Ants, and nymphs.

Feather slip throats utilize the wide side of a 1½-inch slip from a turkey tail or secondary flight feather. Tie in the thick butt and allow the feather to stick diagonally down like the rudder of a sailboat. The stiff, flat feather will give maximum exposure to the throat color.

## THE DEFEO METHOD OF MAKING A THROAT

This is an effective and accepted method of making throats/beards on salmon and other flies.

1. Select a large, webby neck feather in the desired color and having barbs along at least ½ to 1 inch of its shaft length that are 1½ times the gap distance of the hook. You can find suitable feathers on both Chinese and Saltwater necks, and both are available in many desirable colors for reasonable prices.

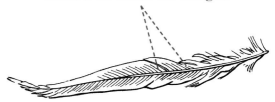

**section of shaft with fibers of desired length**

*1. Selected neck feather of proper color, having fibers of desired length along ½ inch to 1 inch of shaft length.*

2. Hold the feather between your thumb and forefinger, and, starting from the tip, find the point where the usable length of barbs begins. Upset the barbs below that point.

3. Carefully cut the shaft just above the upset barbs. Avoid cutting the barbs. Discard the surplus end.

4. Turning to the section of fibers of desired length, stroke the upper two-thirds of this section "with the grain" to return the fibers to their natural V orientation. Upset the rear one-third of the section so that the barbs are perpendicular to the shaft. Trim the butt-end fibers to leave a length of fiberless shaft as a handle.

5. Place the feather section under the

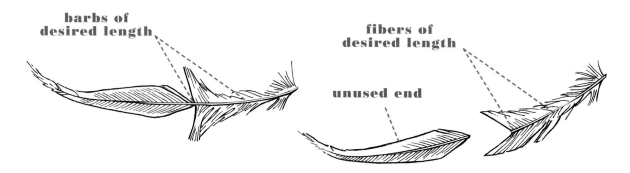

**barbs of desired length**

**fibers of desired length**

**unused end**

2. *The feather is upset at the point where the barbs are of proper length.*

3. *The surplus end of the feather is cut off. Cut only the shaft, leaving the fibers untouched.*

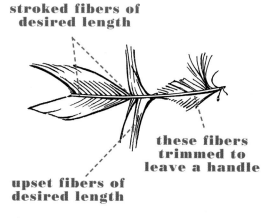

**stroked fibers of desired length**

**these fibers trimmed to leave a handle**

**upset fibers of desired length**

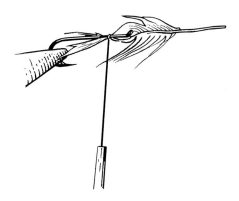

4. *At least ½ inch of fibers of desired length are stroked into their V shape. Below that, toward butt end of shaft, a shorter section of fibers of desired length is upset. And below that the fibers are trimmed away to leave a length of shaft as a handle.*

5. *Feather is secured under the hook shank with a soft loop, leaving the stroked fibers of the desired length for the throat to the rear of the tie-in point and the section of upset fibers forward of the tie-in point. Use of a soft loop allows the throat length to be adjusted (next step).*

hook shank so that the V-shaped portion faces toward the hook bend and the hanging thread is directly below the point where the upset barbs and natural barbs meet. Make a soft loop around the hook shank and the feather, and let the bobbin hang.

6. To give the throat its shape, carefully pull the feather by its shaft toward the eye. Stop pulling when the desired throat length—1½ times the gap distance—is reached.

7. Tighten the thread and make another turn or two to be sure the feather is firmly fastened. Cut off, but do not lose, the surplus feather section.

8. Repeat, using the previously upset fibers from the surplus section you just trimmed, if necessary, to fill in the throat.

# Heads

Smooth, glossy heads are one characteristic of the best professionally tied flies, and with a little effort you can attain that degree of perfection. Wrapping a smooth taper to start is also important, so make sure all excess or loose material left in the head region after tying other parts of the fly has been removed. Otherwise, your head may end up looking lumpy or too bulky.

When tying the head, always pull parallel to the hook shank. It's easy to break small forged hooks if you pull hard against their weak side. Spoiling a fly as it's being finished is not a happy experience for any flytier. Forged hooks like I-Beams are designed to resist pressure from one direction, but break

*6–8. Gently pull the "handle" ahead (i.e., to the right) in order to pull the throat through the soft loop until the remaining throat is in its proper position and of proper length. Then bind it in place with a couple of tight turns of thread, and cut off the surplus ⅛ inch behind the eye. Finally, use the section of the trimmed surplus that contains the previously upset fibers to fill in any gaps in the throat. Fasten this throat addition in the same way, with close, tight turns of thread, as the space behind the head is crowded.*

easily under pressure from another direction. Pulling the thread parallel to the hook shank not only preserves the fly, it also saves time and loss of temper.

Do not apply a heavy coat of either nail polish or the head cement to the head, as the excess may run into the hackle or body materials or blob up, closing the eye of the hook. When painting the eyes, however, using thicker head cement produces a raised, true eye shape, and is very effective.

## THE WHIP FINISH

The whip finish is used to tie off the thread as the last step of wrapping the head of a fly. In the process, the end of whatever part of the fly you tied immediately before the head —the wing, throat, perhaps the hackle—will be buried under at least three turns of thread, and the head will be both neat and secure. While learning this knot, use a large, heavy hook (perhaps even a finishing nail) and thin twine—rather than thread—weighted with a clothespin or hackle pliers, so you can easily see what you are doing. If your tying vise won't hold a big hook, you can use an ordinary workshop vise for this practice.

For the sake of clarity, the directions below have been broken down into steps, but ideally they should be executed as one continuous action. (Also note that they have been written for the right-handed flytier; left-handed tiers should make whatever adjustments are needed for comfort and ease.) Once the cord has locked the standing part in place against the nail or hook, the rest is relatively sure and simple. Understanding what you are attempting to do and keeping a controlling tension on the cord while making the turns will ensure success. After a little practice you will tie this knot with a smooth, fluid, and continuous motion, and all the steps will blend into a sure and easy whip finish.

Note that the objects referred to in the instructions are practice materials; when you perform the whip finish on a fly, thread will replace the twine or cord and the bobbin will be your weight. And, you'll be tying on a smaller hook.

1. Place a big hook (as large as 4/0 if desired) in your fly-tying vise. Secure one end of a 12- to 18-inch piece of thin cord or light twine to the hook with any convenient knot (remember, this is just practice) about 1 inch from the eye. Attach a clothespin or hackle pliers to the hanging end for weight, so that the cord imitates thread hanging on a bobbin after tying in the last piece before the head.

2. About 6 inches below the hook, rest your right hand against the dangling cord, thumb pointing down and palm away from you. Trap the cord between your thumb and forefinger, then rotate your hand so the thumb points up and the palm faces you, capturing a loop of the cord as you go. If, at the same time, you raise your right hand slightly, you will wind up with the standing part of the cord—i.e., the part between the hook and your hand—running more or less horizontally toward you to the point where it turns around your little finger. The weighted end of the cord will cross over the standing part as shown before descending. You will find this beginning loop for the whip finish much easier to execute than it is to describe!

3. Next, you want to slide the crossing point of the weighted end down the standing part until it butts up against the shank. To do this, simply raise your right hand above the hook so that the standing part slopes up from its previously horizontal position, at the same time pressing against the descending leg of the loop with your little finger in order to push it in back of the standing part, as shown. Help out with your left thumb and forefinger as necessary, until you can trap the weighted end against the shank.

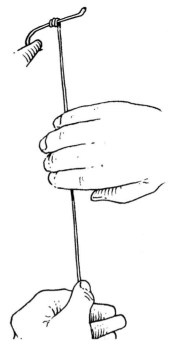

1. Cord wrapped or tied around hook shank, with its free end weighted in imitation of hanging thread.

2A. Right hand brought to bear against hanging cord, thumb down, palm away.

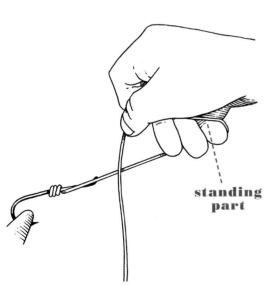

**standing part**

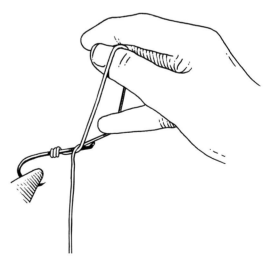

2B. Right hand raised and rotated until the standing part (the part between the hook and hand) is horizontal. This action captures a loop of the cord as shown.

3. Raise the standing part of the cord and, with your little finger, push the descending leg of the loop away from you as shown. This will cause the crossing point of the weighted end to slide down the standing part and be trapped against the shank.

4. Holding the weighted end tight against the shank with your left hand, use your right thumb and forefinger to wrap the upper part of the loop over the shank, then down and around the far side, thus binding the weighted end to the shank. At the same time, you'll drop the lower part of the loop over the eye of the hook so that only one part of the loop—not both parts—gets wrapped around the shank.

5. As this wrap progresses, you will reach the point at which your right hand is under the hook and winding toward you. At this point you need to get a new grip with your right hand in order to keep yourself from getting entangled in the loop. Fortunately, because the weighted end is now bound against the shank, your left hand is free to grasp the loop—keeping the cord taut against the underside of the hook—long enough for you to get a new grip on the cord with your right thumb and forefinger about 2 inches from the shank.

6. Now you make another complete, close, butting turn behind—i.e., to the left of—the last turn. Most fly-tying manuals advise you to make your subsequent turns to the right of the first one, but wrapping to the left on a dry

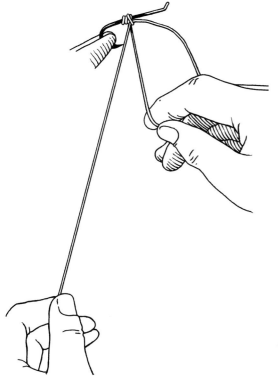

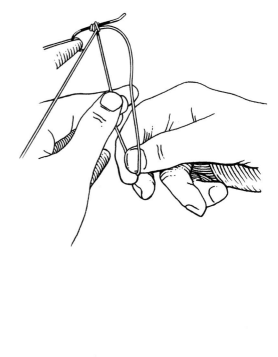

*4. Right hand passes over and down around hook shank, completely cinching the first turn.*

*5. Left hand maintains tension on cord while right hand gets a new grip for the next wrap.*

fly will have the effect of encouraging the hackle to stand up in a more natural and effective manner.

7. Make five wraps to the left in all, changing hands at each turn.

8. Holding the weighted end of the cord parallel to the shank with your left hand, pull on it to tighten the knot. As you do, hold the loop open with a finger of your right hand—or, better yet, with a bodkin—to prevent tangles from forming in the loop as you reduce it. This is especially important when you are using very fine thread.

9. Once the loop has disappeared beneath the wraps, cut off the surplus thread close to where it emerges from the wraps, and you are done.

You have just completed the whip finish. Congratulations! Tying the whip finish by hand not only allows you to tie off heads; you also can effectively tie off binding thread at the rear of a long-shanked hook, which is especially necessary when making repairs in that area. This cannot be done with the ordinary whip-finishing tool that so many use when completing the heads on their flies; the tool isn't long enough to reach the rear of the fly. This hand skill is also useful if you happen to break or mislay your whip-finishing tool!

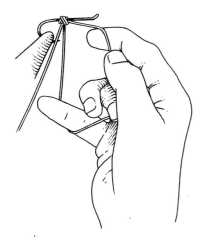

*6. Right hand makes another turn to the left of (i.e., behind) the first one.*

*7–9. With five full turns completed, use your finger or bodkin to hold the loop open as shown. You will then raise your left hand to pull the cord end to the left, along the shank. (This step is not shown here.) This will reduce the size of the loop, which you'll keep open with your right forefinger or bodkin. When the loop disappears beneath the turns, trim the cord end to finish.*

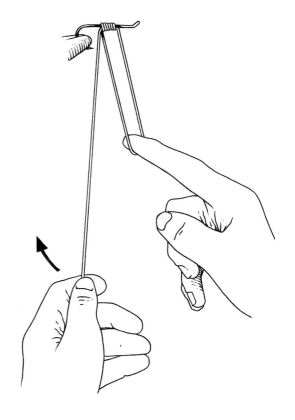

# Other Useful Skills for Tying Flies

ALONG WITH THE STANDARD STEPS FOR TYING flies, you need to learn some other basic techniques that you'll use again and again in your work. The techniques we describe below—dubbing and spinning hair—are usually employed when making the bodies and/or thoraxes of certain flies. A little practice while learning the techniques, before actually applying them to "live" flies that you're building, will go a long way toward improving your productivity later.

## Dubbing

Dubbing is natural or synthetic fur attached to a thread and wound around the hook shank to form a fly body. The production of dubbing is a useful skill at all levels of fly tying. Over the years it has been done in different ways.

During the first half of the twentieth century, fur was dubbed by twisting and compacting it between two threads, after which it was wrapped like a piece of yarn to form a body. Today the common practice is to twist fur or, more frequently, a synthetic fiber around a core of waxed tying thread. Both methods have special applications and advantages, and it is worthwhile to learn both.

## THE ORIGINAL METHOD OF DUBBING

1. The original method begins with an 8- to 10-inch length of thread, usually a dark shade or black for dark furs and light or a special color to add a subtle richness or shade for lighter colored furs. Lay the thread out straight on a smooth, flat surface.

2. Cut fur from the hide in small bunches and, if you need only the underfur, remove the guard hairs. To do this, hold the cut fur in one hand, but not too firmly, and with the other hand tightly hold the long guard hairs. Gently pull out all the guard hairs, leaving the underfur in a bunch in one hand. If the guard hairs are required for a particular fly, such as the Hare's Ear, do not remove them.

3. Separate a few wisps of the fur from the

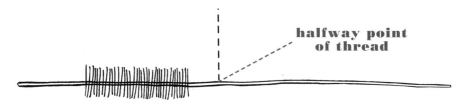

*1–3. In the original method of dubbing, place strands of fur perpendicularly over the "short half" of an 8- to 10-inch length of thread.*

bundle and place them on top of and perpendicular to the thread, beginning about 1½ inches beyond the middle of the piece of thread. Continue to thinly cover the "short" side of the thread. Cut and prepare another bunch of fur, and apply it just a little more thickly until the short side of the thread is covered to 1 to 2 inches from the end.

A couple of things to note at this point: First, far less fur is needed than most beginners expect, so start small. The purpose of spreading the second layer is to thicken the first layer if necessary. An inch and a half of dubbing will be more than enough for all but the longest hooks.

Second, placing the middle of the cut fur directly over the thread puts an equal length of fur on each side of the thread and is best for most work. However, if long legs need to be picked out later, you can place as much as three-quarters of the fur length on one side of the thread and obtain a very different final result after you have wrapped on the body.

Now back to the process.

4. About 1½ inches of thread are now covered with fur. Pick up the long side of the thread and fold it over the fur-covered side, aligning the ends. Grasp the aligned ends of thread with one hand and, with the other, grasp the folded end. Pull the thread taut between your hands. Now begin to twist the thread in one direction only, locking the fur between the turns of thread very firmly so that the fur soon becomes "chenille" with clean twisted thread at each end.

5. Put the whole unit in the palm of one

*4A. Fold the bare half of the thread over the fur-covered half, aligning the ends.*

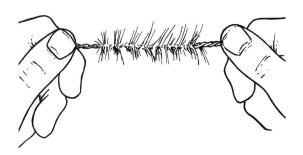

*4B. Grasp the doubled thread and twist it as shown, locking the fur between the twists.*

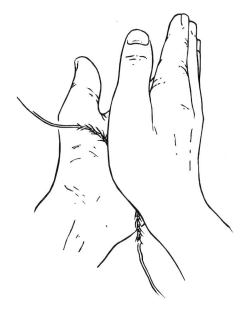

*5. Now rub the doubled and twisted length between your palms to form a noodle.*

*6. The finished dubbing is now ready to be attached to the hook shank.*

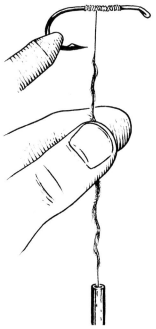

*The modern method of dubbing uses a waxed thread.*

hand and place the other palm over it. Rub your hands tightly together to make the "noodle" into a smooth yarn, noting that one end of the unit will be thinner than the other.

6. The noodle is now ready to be attached to the hook shank. To do this, tie in and then cut off the surplus twisted thread "handle" at the thinner end of the unit. Then wrap the body in the usual way, tying off the material at the front end of the body and cutting away any surplus material or thread.

## THE COMMON METHOD OF DUBBING

1. To produce dubbing the "new" way, start with the thread attached to the hook. Draw out 2 to 4 inches of thread from the bobbin and let it hang while applying a sticky, soft wax to about 2 inches of the thread nearest the hook.

2. Take small wisps of natural or synthetic fur between thumb and forefinger, apply them to the sticky section of thread, and then twist the material downward, around and onto the thread in one direction only. Add more material and continue twisting the dubbing down the thread. Continue the process until you have made about 2 inches of dubbing.

3. You can carefully push the dubbing up the thread to the hook before starting to wrap the body. This way you avoid having to wrap the bare thread several times around the hook shank just to reach the dubbing, and then having to

cover that bare thread with the thin end of the dubbing in order to start the body neatly.

Most synthetic dubbing material is made of longer strands than those of underfur, and is therefore somewhat easier to work with. To become an accomplished flytier, however, you will need to work with both types of dubbing. Very tacky dubbing wax and lots of practice will work wonders for you.

Incidentally, you will have best control of the thread, when wrapping it onto the hook shank, if the distance between the end of the bobbin tube and the hook is between 1 and 3 inches. Most of us lose considerable accuracy in butting turns of thread and other fine work when there is more than 2 inches of thread between the end of the bobbin tube and the hook.

Finally, experience will help you determine how much dubbing is needed to complete each size of body. However, these directions offer a good starting point, and you will very rarely need more than the lengths suggested here. If you have made too much, tease off the surplus fur and tie off the body with bare thread. Next time adjust the amount of material you need for that particular body. You will soon become proficient at determining the amount you need for various body sizes. Good luck!

# Spinning Hair

The hair used to spin bodies for bugs and other flies is comprised of the hollow body hair of whitetail deer, mule deer, antelope, elk, or caribou. It's available in a variety of natural colors (from black, through brown and gray, to white) and dyed (over white or bleached hair for bright yellow, green, and other strong colors; and over natural shades of hair for less brightness). The ideal hair is firm, rather coarse, and flares easily, and the individual hair shafts have a short, thin tip area and a long, even midsection. This midsection is important. By cutting off thin tips and thick hair butts we obtain hair with a consistent diameter throughout its length, and this is much easier to work with.

First attempts at spinning hair are rarely fully successful. The practice exercise below, which will not result in a fly, will help you master the art while reducing future frustration. You'll also save time, money, and materials. Starting large and simple makes learning easier and faster—so here goes.

## SPINNING HAIR ONTO THE HOOK

1. Select a good-sized hook—like a Mustad #37187 Stinger Hook #2 or a large streamer hook of that size—and put it in your vise. Load the bobbin with flat waxed nylon thread. Get out a piece of natural-color deer hide with hair that's at least 1 inch long. This is the cheapest and most easily obtained spinning hair.

2. Attach the thread to the hook near the middle of the shank and let the bobbin hang.

3. Select a bunch of deer hair that's about ¼ inch in diameter, and holding the hair together by the tips, cut it off close to the hide. While holding the

tips of the hair in one hand, clean out all short hairs and fuzz with the other. Even the tips (for the procedure, see Hair Stacker on page 9 of the Tools and Materials chapter, noting that if you held the tips tightly while cutting the hair from the hide, the tips may already be even).

4.  Trim off about ³⁄₁₆ inch from both the tips and the thick butt end of the bun-

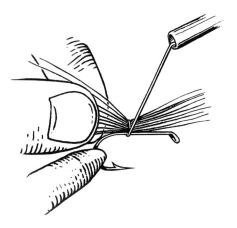

*Spinning hair, Step 5. Having selected a ¼-inch-diameter bundle of deer hair and trimmed it as described in Steps 3 and 4 of the text, attach it to the hook shank with one and a half loose turns as shown.*

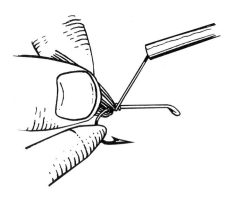

*Spinning hair, Step 6. Tighten the turns to spin the hair around the shank.*

dle. Ideally the bundle of hair should now be about ¾ inch long, and the individual trimmed hairs should have the same diameter at both ends. This shorter length makes for easier spinning, and the consistent diameter produces better texture and balance in the finished body.

5.  Place the bundle on top of the hook shank like a wing, centered directly over the hanging bobbin. Make one soft loop or loose turn completely around the hair and the hook shank, then bring a loose turn over the bundle and shank and down on the far side. You now have one and a half turns binding the bundle to the hook shank.

6.  Pull down firmly on the bobbin, tightening the turns of thread to flare and spin the hair around the shank. As the hair begins to spin, release your hold on the bundle so that it can go around the shank. Pull down until the hair stops spinning, then lift the bobbin above and over the hook shank, tightening the thread binding the spun hair. This small, extra lift/tug often moves the hair a bit farther around the hook. Be careful not to use too much pressure, which may break the thread or cause it to cut through the hair against the hook. It can also break small hooks, which is why you are using a big stout hook for this exercise.

7.  Pass the thread through the flared hair toward the eye of the hook. After pushing the flared hair toward the hook bend, take a turn or two around the

hook shank tight against the hair, and let the bobbin hang. The hair should be evenly distributed around the hook shank.

8. Place your left hand to the left of the hair as a stopper, and consolidate the flared hair. You can push the bunch back with your thumb and forefinger above and below or along both sides of the hook shank or use a special tool, such as a quarter-size fender washer, or a spool. Do what works best for you, but make a tight, compressed bundle, whatever you do!

9. Prepare another bundle of hair, and repeat the process of attaching, spinning, and compressing it on the hook shank. Do the same with two more bundles. Then tie off the thread on the shank with a couple of overhand knots or a whip finish, and cut the thread.

You now have a fuzz ball on the hook shank, and are ready to learn how to trim it into shape.

## TRIMMING THE BODY

1. Remove the hook from the vise and hold it by the bend, barb, and point. Use your strong, heavy scissors to cut along the underside of the fuzz ball about ¼ inch below and parallel to the hook shank, starting from the eye of the hook and working toward the bend. This should result in a flat cut across the bottom of the ball.

2. Make a similar cut about ¼ inch from the hook shank on both the near and

*Spinning hair, Step 7. Make a turn or two of thread on the eye side of the hair bundle.*

*Spinning hair, steps 8 and 9. After consolidating the flared hair as described in the text for Step 8, repeat steps 3 through 8 with another bundle of hair, working toward the eye. Tie on four bundles altogether. It should look as shown here.*

far sides of the fuzz ball to form the sides of the body. Then cut the top of the ball about ⅜ inch above the whole body length of the hook shank.

3. You now have a body that is ⅝ inch from top to bottom and ½ inch wide, with hair flared at each end. Trim to square off the front and rear ends of the body. Trim down the top diagonally from front to rear, with full height in front and stubble at the rear. Then nar-

*After trimming, a spun-hair body will look like this.*

row the body by making equal cuts on each side until it is about ¼ or ⅜ inch wide, rounding off the sharp edges to form an oval body.

You have now practiced spinning hair and trimming it into a reasonably shaped fly body. If the first attempt seems a bit awkward, try another one; it's sure to turn out better. Once you have gained some control of the process, you will be ready to begin working on a real fly.

You will quickly gain confidence, and your work will rapidly improve. Each of us is different, and my size suggestions are meant to meet average rather than individual needs. With practice, you will find the size bundle of hair that best suits your persona

Now that you have acquired the basic skills, you're ready to begin tying flies. The patterns in this book are arranged from the simplest to the most complex. If you're a beginner, I suggest you turn the page and begin with simple bivisible flies and move from section to section, in order, as you advance in experience and skill. In this manner, you'll be on your way to becoming quite an expert when you reach the salmon flies section. Good luck, and happy tying!

# EASY FLIES FOR BEGINNERS

The flies in this chapter are all easy to tie, use a minimum of simple materials, and put into practice several of the basic skills we covered in the last chapter. You'll experience wrapping hackle feathers and implementing the soft loop technique to tie in tails (in Bivisibles); work with chenille as a body material (Black Teaser); create wrapped tinsel bodies and feather wings (Black-and-Orange Marabou); work with peacock herl; and construct hair wings (Woodchuck Caddis). Not only are these patterns fairly simple to tie, they produce flies that catch fish. Learn them well, and you'll soon be ready to move on to more challenging patterns.

## Bivisibles

BIVISIBLES ARE HIGH-FLOATING DRY FLIES that use their many barbs and a lightweight hook for sure-footed flotation. They perform their best when they are "pocket picking" around and behind rocks in brawling freestone streams, where they can often persuade the resident fish, in a short float over a calm pocket, that something edible is available. They became popular in the 1920s and 1930s, and to this day I use them regularly and successfully.

They are also useful in water where a tree or bush has fallen, offering shelter and protection for large fish. Very often large fish live in such places and—judging from the multitude of lures that are snagged on nearby branches—few are caught there. I first read about the following fishing technique many years ago in a book by the great fishing writer Ray Bergman, and it has helped me take fish from these difficult places ever since.

Go above the downed tree and cast your high-floating bivisible directly down to it,

playing out your line and allowing the fly to float into and drown well inside the treetop. Often the resident fish will accept the drowned fly as food, as any real fly would be drowned by the turmoil and crosscurrents there. If the fly is taken on the surface, so much the better. In any event, the fish knows how to get out of his lair and into the open water; when he feels the prick of the hook he will instinctively leave that place and go outside, bringing the fly and the line with him, safely and easily past all the tangles and snags. Once he's out you must promptly and effectively prevent him from returning to his lair. After the catch, a couple of false casts will dry and fluff the fly, now ready to float high on its myriad legs over the next fish.

Bivisibles are tied with good-quality dry-fly hackle in one color for the tail and body and three or four turns of white dry-fly hackle at the face or front of the fly. The fish sees the tail and body, and the fisherman keeps track of the fly by watching its con-

*Dark Dun Bivisible*

*Cochy (furnace) Bivisible. (Head should be black lacquer, not clear as shown here.)*

*Light Blue Dun Bivisible*

*Brown-and-White Bivisible*

trasting white face—hence the name "bivisible." The tail and body can be tied with dry-fly quality neck or saddle hackle of appropriate size and color. Because neck hackle feathers are shorter, you may need several feathers to complete a body.

Feathers in badger or furnace colors each have a dark center, which appears as a distinct body, and provide the lightest possible imitation of an insect's body—a real advantage over plain-colored hackles. Black flies are useful on heavily overcast days. Fish see them readily because they contrast well against even the darkest skies.

I strongly recommend using Whiting 100s in the appropriate size and color, and

these are what I use in the instructions below. The feathers, sold in small packs of one size, are very long with barbs of almost equal width throughout their length. Their quality is excellent, and they're easy to work with. You will need black, white, and either badger or cochy (furnace) for this exercise, in sizes suitable for Nos. 12–14 hooks. See Variations at the end of the recipe if you are using some other good-quality dry-fly hackle.

Other things to note: Although the range of hook sizes listed in the materials is quite broad, Nos. 12–14 are most useful. Be aware, however, that they are made of very light wire and are easily broken. Also note that 8/0 UNI-Thread is strong thread for its size, but it requires some care and attention until you become accustomed to using the right amount of tension in wrapping and securing materials to the hook.

Bivisibles are highly useful flies, and you should tie at least three of each: one to fish, one to lose in a branch, and one to use for reference when tying replacements. The instructions below are for a Black Bivisible.

| | |
|---|---|
| **HOOK** | *Mustad #94833, Nos. 6–16* |
| **THREAD** | *White 8/0 UNI-Thread* |
| **TAIL** | *Black dry-fly hackle* |
| **BODY** | *Black Whiting 100s, size 12–14, or black dry-fly hackle* |
| **FACE** | *White Whiting 100s, size 12–14* |
| **WING** | *None* |
| **HEAD** | *Black head cement* |

*Black-and-White Bivisible (1). The tail is in place, and the body hackle is tied in by tip. The thread is being wound forward to 3/16 inch behind the eye. The feathers of the Black-and-White Bivisible appear brownish here but are in fact black. There should be no fuzz on the thread foundation.*

*Black-and-White Bivisible (2). The tail is tied in, the body hackle is wound to 3/16 inch behind the eye, and the tip of the white hackle is trimmed and tied in place.*

1. Place the hook in the vise as described in Step 1 on page 43. Be sure it is firmly held and will not be easily moved or dislodged while you are tying the fly.

2. Attach the thread to the hook and form a foundation for the tail as described in Step 2 on page 44.

3. Upset one long, good-quality hackle feather for the tail (see page 53 for upset instructions). If the barbules nearest the end of the feather are soft, strip or cut them off. Then select a bunch of 8–12 stiff barbules about ¾ inch long and cut them off close to the shaft. Even the tips and place the bundle on top of the hook shank where the bobbin hangs. The tips should extend at least ½ inch beyond the bend of the hook.

4. Tie in the tail bundle using the soft loop technique (see page 56 for instructions).

5. Upset the tip end of a long feather from the Whiting 100s packet. Trim both sides of the first ½ inch of the tip to a stubble. Continue to upset the

bivisibles

feather for about 3 inches. Place the feather's tip along the top of the hook shank, good side up. The point where the stubble ends and the barbs begin should be over the bobbin, and the bulk of the feather should be behind the hook bend. Bind the tip down using the soft loop method. The thread will catch in the stubble and hold the shaft in place. Continue winding the thread forward in close, even turns around the stubble and shank to about $\frac{3}{16}$ inch from the eye, and let the bobbin hang.

6. Grip the butt end of the feather with the hackle pliers at right angles to the shaft. To begin wrapping the body, wind the feather on its edge, good side facing toward the hook eye. Make one turn around the hook shank against the base of the tail. There should be no white thread showing between the body and the tail. Continue winding the hackle in close, even turns, pushing it back after every couple of turns so that the wraps touch each other. Wind and push the hackle back until a nice, compact body is formed up to where the bobbin hangs. Now let the pliers hang down to keep tension on the hackle. Carefully bind down the hackle with a couple of turns of thread, and let the bobbin hang.

7. Cut off the excess hackle feather, being careful not to cut the thread in the process. Bind down the cut end with close, even turns and return the thread to where the body was tied off, then let the bobbin hang.

8. Cut a half inch of the tip end of the white feather to stubble, then upset the next 1½ inches of the feather. To start the white face, tie the tip in tight against the body hackle and, with the stubble turned toward the hook eye, wind it on its edge, good side forward. Wrap three or four tight turns, the first one snug against the body, and tie it off with a couple of turns of thread. Let the bobbin hang while you cut off the excess white feather and any excess tip. Push back on the base of the face to open up about ⅟₁₆ to ⅛ inch of clearance between the face and the hook eye. Bind down all ends with even turns of thread to the eye.

9. Form a small, neat head as described in Step 8 on page 54, noting that eyes are not necessary for this fly.

## Variations

You can make other bivisibles by substituting the black hackle for the body and tail with another color. Any of the following colors will work (remember that all bivisibles have white faces): badger, cochy (furnace), grizzly, light dun, dark dun, and brown.

If you use good-quality dry-fly hackle instead of the Whiting 100s for the body, choose a feather with fibers that are 1½ times the hook gap in length. Upset the first half inch of the tip and trim both sides to a stubble. Follow the remaining instructions in Step 5 above and proceed with tying the fly. For the face, use a white dry-fly hackle that's the same size as the black one. Select a white neck hackle with barbs the length of the body hackle and trim to a stubble the first half inch of the tip. Tie in the feather good side out with the stubble end diagonally down and let the bobbin hang while you cut off the surplus tip ⅛ inch behind the eye of the hook.

Attach the hackle pliers at right angles to the stem and take three turns of the hackle toward the eye and tie off the white feather. Cut off the surplus feather, bend down the end, form the head, and finish it with a coat of nail polish followed by a coat of black cement.

This style of fly will sit on a flat surface and keep the head up while drying. Other flies, however, will dry better if hung on a wire or cord stretched between two sides of an open box. Punch a small hole in opposite sides of the box, about 1 inch down from the top, and pass the wire or cord through one side to the other. Knot it on one outside wall. Then tighten the cord and fasten it taut with a turn and knot around a nail or stick on the other outside wall. This setup will help prevent damage to or loss of flies to a gust of wind as they dry. Some commercially made fly-tying desks have such drying wires.

# Black Teaser
# (Minnow/Grasshopper Imitation)

THIS IS OUR FIRST FLY THAT REQUIRES CHEnille for the body. We will also form a throat or beard from a slip of turkey wing or tail feather and a wing of bucktail.

| | |
|---|---|
| **HOOK** | *Mustad #9575, No. 10* |
| **THREAD** | *White flat waxed nylon* |
| **TAIL** | *None* |
| **BODY** | *Yellow chenille, medium size* |
| **THROAT** | *Slip of turkey wing or tail feather, dyed red* |
| **WING** | *Black dyed bucktail* |
| **HEAD** | *Black head cement* |

*Black Teaser (1). Chenille tied on.*

1. Place the hook in the vise as described in Step 1 on page 43. Be sure it is firmly held and will not be easily moved or dislodged while you are tying the fly.

2. Attach the thread to the hook and form a foundation for the body as described in Step 2 on page 44.

3. Firmly hold an 8- to 12-inch piece of chenille about ½ inch from one end, and pull and tease the fibers off

*Black Teaser (2). Thread wrapped forward to ³⁄₁₆ inch behind eye. Chenille being wound forward.*

*Black Teaser (3). Throat in place.*

*Black Teaser (4). Wing in place.*

*Black Teaser (5). Completed fly.*

¼ inch of the extreme end. Lay the prepared end along the top of the hook shank so the long fuzzy part extends behind the hook bend. Bind down the core threads of the chenille with close, even turns of thread to about ³⁄₁₆ inch from the hook eye. Let the bobbin hang.

4.  Carefully wrap the chenille up the shank about four turns. Use your other hand, or attach hackle pliers for weight, to keep the chenille from unwinding while you push the turns back firmly. Repeat this process to form a compact body until you reach the spot where the bobbin is hanging. Then with the bobbin in hand, bind down the chenille with a couple of tight turns of thread. Let the bobbin hang while you cut off

the excess chenille, then cover the ends with a couple more turns of thread before letting the bobbin hang again.

5.  From the broad side of a turkey wing or tail feather, pull or cut the lowest inch of soft, short material (this material is not stiff enough for throats). Measure a ³⁄₁₆-inch-wide strip or slip of feather just above the stripped area, and cut it off close to the center shaft.

6.  Place the feather slip under the hook shank, with the butt end at the eye and the tip toward the point of the hook. For maximum visibility, the edge of the slip should be parallel to the hook shank so that the slip looks like a boat's rudder. When it's in place, fasten it with a soft loop (see page 56 for

instructions). Check its position and adjust it if necessary.

7. Cut and taper the butts to form the bottom of the head and let the bobbin hang.

8. Separate a bunch of bucktail about ³/₁₆ inch in diameter and at least 2 inches long, and cut it off close to the hide. Even the tips (for the procedure, refer to Hair Stacker on page 9 of the Tools and Materials chapter) and prepare the wing as described in Step 5 on page 49 (see the Hair Wing instructions).

9. When it is tacky, place the wing along the top of the hook shank, with the tips extending a finger's width beyond the bend of the hook, and secure it with the soft loop technique. Check and adjust its position as needed, and let the bobbin hang.

10. Using the angle of the hook as a guide, carefully cut and taper the excess butts to form the top of the head. Bind down

*Brown Teaser*

the tapered butts of throat and wing with tight, even, close turns of thread to the eye. Whip finish (see page 61 for instructions), wrapping at least five turns of thread before tightening the knot, and finish the head as described in Step 8 on page 54.

## Variations

To tie a Brown Teaser, use brown bucktail for the wing. All other materials and methods are the same as described above.

# Black-and-Orange Marabou

MARABOUS—CLASSIC WET FLIES THAT IMI-tate minnows—are not only easy to tie, they are also easy to cast and are effective in taking fish. (See the Classic Wet Flies chapter for other well-known wet-fly styles.) This pattern will introduce you to the use of both flat and oval tinsels and the marabou feather, for which the fly is named.

Marabous are properly tied quite full in the wing. The feather produces a fluffy wing

that slims down to a very active, thin shape when it is wet and has more action than any other wing material. Marabou is often sold strung or sewn as blood marabou, and large feathers are more likely to be sold in packages of a single size and color.

The instructions below will yield a fly that will represent the small-fry stage of a minnow's life. When tying this fly myself, I prefer a short version No. 10 3XL nymph or

black teaser | black-and-orange marabou

wet-fly hook over the longer streamer hook that's often recommended for this fly. The variations that follow the instructions will represent larger minnows and call for the streamer hook style. The larger sizes cover a lucky minnow's growth and development from fry to 3- to 4-inch adults.

All of these flies work well with either gold or silver bodies—just be sure the rib and body colors are the same—and all of the color combinations are useful imitations or suggestions of forage fish. The various color combinations can be tied on both long- and short-shanked hooks. I suggest that you tie a variety of sizes in any or all of the combinations; you will be rewarded by strikes from all of the predator species.

| | |
|---|---|
| **HOOK** | *Mustad #9672, Nos. 2–10* |
| **THREAD** | *White flat waxed nylon* |
| **TAIL** | *None* |
| **BODY** | *Gold or silver flat Mylar tinsel, medium* |
| **RIB** | *Gold or silver oval Mylar tinsel, medium* |
| **WING** | *Black and orange marabou* |
| **THROAT** | *None* |
| **HEAD** | *Black head cement* |
| **EYES** | *White or yellow with black pupils* |

1. Place the hook in the vise as described in Step 1 on page 43. Be sure it is firmly held and will not be easily moved or dislodged while you are tying the fly.

2. Attach the thread to the hook and form a foundation for the body as described in Step 2 on page 44.

3. Place the end of an 8- to 10-inch piece of flat tinsel on the side of the hook shank nearest you, about ³⁄₁₆ inch behind the hook eye. Using the bobbin, carefully tie the tinsel to the shank with three closely spaced wraps of thread, and let it and the bobbin hang. Then place the end of a 6- to 8-inch length of oval tinsel along the top of the hook shank, starting at about ³⁄₁₆ inch behind the hook eye. Tie it in place by wrapping close-butted turns of thread toward the eye until you reach the end of the tinsel. Let the bobbin hang. You now have a smooth surface on which to wrap the body.

4. Wind the flat tinsel smoothly and evenly up the hook shank to where the bobbin hangs, butting each turn so there are no gaps or overlaps. Tie down the tinsel with a couple turns of thread. Cut off the excess flat tinsel, and let the bobbin hang.

5. Next spiral the oval tinsel forward to where the bobbin hangs to create the ribbing. Between each of the turns, allow a space of about twice the width of the oval tinsel. Tie off the oval tinsel with a couple turns of thread and let the bobbin hang. Cut off the surplus tinsel, cover the ends with two or three turns of thread, and let the bobbin hang.

6. Select an orange marabou feather, strip or cut off the lowest ¼ to ½ inch of

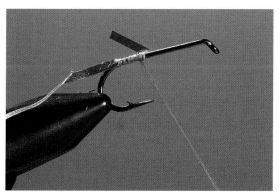

*Black-and-Orange Marabou (1). Body tinsel tied on.*

*Black-and-Orange Marabou (3). Body and ribbing wrapped forward.*

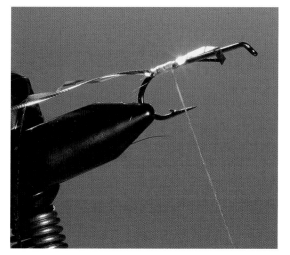

*Black-and-Orange Marabou (2). Rib tinsel tied on.*

*Black-and-Orange Marabou (4). Completed fly.*

short fibers, and then cut or strip off a section of fibers about an inch wide from one side of the shaft. Even the tips of the fibers, then place the first wing bundle along the top of the shank with the butts over the hook eye and the tips extending at least a finger's width beyond the hook bend. (Don't worry if they extend farther; they can be shortened later.) Tie in the bundle using the soft loop technique (see instructions on page 56), make a couple of extra turns of thread, and let the bobbin hang.

7. Using the same steps, make a bundle of black marabou fibers that's one-third as thick as the orange bundle. Place this wing bundle on top of the orange fibers and tie it in the same way.

8. To begin forming the head, trim off the excess butts in a taper toward the eye, using the angle of the eye as a guide.

*(side text)* **black-and-orange marabou**

Be careful not to cut the thread from the hanging bobbin. Wrap the thread forward, binding down the butts. Wrap to the eye, then back to the feathers, and then forward to the eye again. Complete with a whip finish (see instructions on page 61).

9. Finish the head and paint on eyes as described in Step 8 on page 54.

## Variations

The materials required for the variations are basically the same as those listed above, unless otherwise indicated. For all of the variations use Mustad #9575, Nos. 2–10 hooks, and tie the flies just as instructed above. Note that the dark upper portion of the bicolored wings should be about one-fourth the size of the lighter-colored lower portion.

*Black Marabou. Use silver or gold tinsel for the body and rib (flat and oval, respectively) and black marabou for the wing.*

*Black-and-Fluorescent Yellow Marabou. Use medium or large gold oval tinsel for the rib and black over fluorescent yellow marabou for the wing.*

*Black-and-White Marabou. Use medium or large gold oval tinsel for the rib and black over white marabou for the wing.*

*Brown-and-Orange Marabou. Use brown over orange marabou for the wing.*

*A marabou fly as it appears while dry.*

*Black-and-Green Marabou, shown here as it appears when wet. Use silver tinsel for the body and rib (flat and oval, respectively) and black over green marabou for the wing.*

# Woodchuck Caddis

THIS IS AN EFFECTIVE GREEN CADDIS IMITATION. Peacock herl, a hair—rather than a feather—wing, and a simple hackle make this a very durable fly. Plain brown hackle is preferred, but furnace hackle, which is also an option for bivisibles, can be substituted if you wish to keep your material purchases to a minimum at this time.

Use flat waxed nylon thread if you are a heavy-handed beginner. More advanced tiers can use 8/0 UNI-Thread, which is much lighter and will break more easily, but will allow for more turns of thread for the same size head. More turns produce a stronger head and bind the materials more tightly.

If you use flat waxed nylon thread, you may need to use two coats of durable nail polish to get a smooth head.

| | |
|---|---|
| **HOOK** | *Mustad #9671, Nos. 12–14* |
| **THREAD** | *White flat waxed nylon or 8/0 UNI-Thread* |
| **TAIL** | *None* |
| **BODY** | *Peacock herl* |
| **WING** | *Well-marked woodchuck body hair* |
| **HACKLE** | *Brown or furnace dry-fly hackle* |
| **HEAD** | *Black head cement* |

1. Place the hook in the vise as described in Step 1 on page 43. Then attach the thread to the hook and form a foundation for the body as described in Step 2 on page 44.

2. Select four or five strands of peacock herl and cut or strip them off the

*Woodchuck Caddis (1). Peacock herl bound in place.*

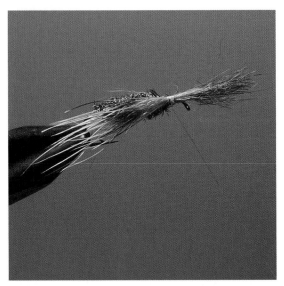

*Woodchuck Caddis (2). Herl wound forward for body. Hair wing tied on.*

feather's shaft. (If you are using a sewn unit, cut the strands free from the base.) Even the tips and place the herl along the top of the hook shank with the tips about ³⁄₁₆ inch from the eye. Tie them to the hook shank directly over the barb, then continue winding the thread forward toward the eye in close, even turns, binding down the herl to where it ends ³⁄₁₆ inch from the eye. Let the bobbin hang.

3. To form a tight, even body, pull the hanging strands of herl evenly together, and wind them forward in tight, butting turns to where the bobbin hangs. If there are gaps between the turns as you form the body, you can push them together toward the hook bend as you go. Be sure to hold the free ends of the herl firmly while you are pushing the turns together, lest the herl unravel.

4. When you have a tight, even body, attach your hackle pliers to the butts at right angles to the herl and let them hang while fastening the herl to the hook. Wrap two or three tight turns of thread, then let the bobbin hang. Cut off the excess herl, being careful not to cut the thread in the process. (If you lift the excess herl above the hook shank so that the shank is between the herl and the hanging thread when you cut the herl, there is little chance you will cut the thread.) Bind down the herl butts with close, tight turns of thread, then return the thread to where the body is tied off.

5. From a piece of woodchuck hide select a bunch of hair about ³⁄₁₆ inch in diameter. Prepare the hair wing as described in Step 5 on page 49.

6. Place the wing along the top of the hook shank, with the tips slightly

beyond the bend of the hook. Bind it in place with the soft loop technique (see instructions page 56), and cut off the surplus butts, using the angle of the eye as a guide. Bind down the cut ends, and return the thread to the front end of the body. Let the bobbin hang.

7. Select a hackle feather and upset the first half inch or so of the tip (see page 53 for instructions). Cut the fibers on each side of the shaft to a stubble.

Place the feather diagonally on the near side of the hook shank, with the stubble under the eye and the uncut portion directly over the bobbin. While holding the feather in place, bind it to the hook shank with three turns of thread, and let the bobbin hang. Carefully cut off the excess stubble tip at about ⅛ inch behind the eye. Do not cut the thread! Bind down the cut end of the stubble, and let the bobbin hang.

*Woodchuck Caddis (3). Hackle feather tied on.*

*Woodchuck Caddis (4). Hackle feather ready to wrap as soon as butt of feather is trimmed.*

*Woodchuck Caddis (5). Completed fly.*

**woodchuck caddis**

woodchuck caddis

8.  Holding the feather on edge by its shaft, carefully take three or four closely spaced turns around the hook shank forward toward the eye. You can do this either by hand or with the hackle pliers held at right angles to the feather. If necessary, push the turns back to be sure that they touch each other. Tie off the hackle with a couple of tight turns of thread, cut off the surplus hackle while holding it above the hook shank (to avoid cutting the thread), and bind down the cut end with close, even turns of thread.

9.  Form a small, neat head as described in Step 8 on page 54.

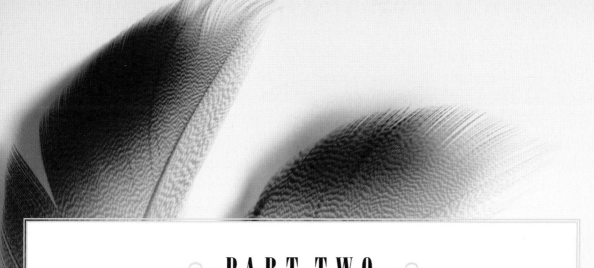

# PART TWO

# TROUT AND PANFISH FLIES FOR INTERMEDIATE TIERS

*Now that we've tied a few beginner-level flies, we are ready to explore more of the many types of flies commonly used to take trout and pan-fish. In Part Two, you will work with dubbing, folded-hair, and spun-/cut-hair bodies; tiny flies and their large, distant cousins, the tandem-hook flies; and many new materials. As you go along you will tie wet flies and dry flies, nymphs, bucktails, streamers, and more. By the time we're finished with these intermediate flies, you'll have become immersed in the craft and will be holding your own in discussions with other tiers. Maybe you'll even begin showing a thing or two to your fly-tying colleagues.*

# FOUR TO GROW ON

Here we have a group that, on the face of it, introduces flies that are rather disparate in their relationship to one another. Let's just say they will give you an opportunity to practice a few things you learned in Part One and will introduce you to a couple of others. If you've taken a break after learning the beginner flies, these will warm you up for what's to come.

Let's proceed, then, with Spiders and Woolly Buggers, both of which build on our growing skills of palmering a hackle feather. The Woolly Bugger uses a marabou feather for the tail (the material we used for the Black-and-Orange Marabou wing). Then we'll move on to the Turkey Quill Slider, which calls for a nice, productive use of a feather shaft that would otherwise be discarded as scrap. And finally we will learn to spin dubbing as we tie Spent-Wing Spinners.

## Spiders

THE SPIDER, WHICH USUALLY REQUIRES ONLY one feather, has a wide hackle. It also has a stiff tail that, on some Spiders, is made from the hackle feather itself or, on others, from a different feather. When fished, the fly will rest on its tail and the stiff, wide hackle and will dance or skate across the water to good effect on a long, light leader tippet in a little breeze.

The best hackle for this fly is from a spade feather that has long, stiff fibers at least ¾ inch long, but you can substitute a large saddle hackle if necessary. Badger and furnace hackle produce a dark center with light legs and are more effective than a plain color.

Hackle from a good Chinese or "saltwater" neck, especially the lower, larger feathers, makes excellent, stiff, high-riding Spiders, as do the larger, longer feathers from

*Brown Spider*

genetic necks, which are often too big for other dry-fly uses. Lower neck and saddle feathers are too wide for most dry flies, but they make good spiders. If using such feathers, a separate tail of stiff hackle should be tied in first.

The "sweet" spot we refer to in the steps below can be found on every feather, usually about ¼ inch from both the tip and soft butt ends. You can identify it by upsetting the feather, pulling the fibers back vertically. The barbs in the "sweet" area will be long, but will return to their original position more rapidly than the others.

*Tan Spider from neck hackle*

*Tan Spider from spade hackle*

*Badger Spider from neck hackle*

*Mahogany Spider, bivisible, from spade hackle*

| | |
|---|---|
| **HOOK** | *Mustad #9523, Nos. 12–16 5X short shank, T.U.E. ("Turned up Eye"), preferably gold-plated* |
| **THREAD** | *White 8/0 UNI-Thread* |
| **TAIL** | *Fibers from the tip of the hackle* |
| **HACKLE** | *Badger or furnace spade or large saddle hackle* |
| **HEAD** | *Black head cement* |

## If You're Using Spade Hackle

1. Attach the thread to the hook and wrap the base for the tail in the usual manner.

2. Make the tail from a section containing 6 to 12 fibers at the point of the spade hackle. With the fibers still attached to the shaft, tie the section onto the hook shank opposite the point of the hook. Then lift the shaft and, on the bare shank, wrap the thread forward in butting turns to ⅛ inch from the eye. Let the bobbin hang.

3. Wind the rest of the feather forward, on its edge, in close turns to ⅛ inch from the eye. Tie it off, cut off the excess feather, and bind down the butt.

4. Form a neat head and finish the fly.

## If You're Using Large Saddle Hackle

1. Attach the thread to the hook and wrap the base for the tail in the usual manner.

2. To make the tail, select 6 to 12 stiff, long fibers from the "sweet" section of the saddle hackle and cut them off the shaft. Even the tips and place the bundle along the top of the hook shank over the bend of the hook, keeping the fibers as long as possible. Bind the bundle in place, and trim/taper the surplus butts.

3. From the lower part of a dry-fly cape, select a wide, stiff feather that has ¾-inch or longer barbs. Cut or strip the barbs below the sweet spot from both sides of the shaft, then cut off the tip of the feather ³⁄₁₆ inch above the sweet spot. Trim both sides of the ³⁄₁₆-inch area to a stubble.

4. Place the tip of the shaft—shiny side to the right (i.e., up when held flat on the top of the hook shank)—over the tail with the stubble itself over the eye. Fasten it there with several wraps of thread, and let the bobbin hang while you cut off the stubbled tip ⅛ inch behind the eye.

5. Wrap the thread forward in tight, close turns over the stubble to ⅛ inch from the eye, and let the bobbin hang. Wind the hackle forward, on its edge, in close turns to ⅛ inch from the eye. Tie it off, cut off the excess feather, and bind down the butt.

6. Form a neat head and finish the fly.

## Variations

Spiders may also be tied bivisible style with the addition of a couple turns of smaller, white hackle at the head of the fly. This white "face" improves the visibility of a plain-colored spider. Other useful hackle and tail colors for Spiders include black, brown, cream/white, dun (both light and dark), grizzly, and badger.

spiders

# Black Turkey Quill Slider

**black turkey quill slider**

TURKEY QUILL SLIDERS OFFER A PRODUC-tive use for large flight and tail feather quills, once the fibers have been used—or even before they're used, for that matter. The broader the base section of these quills—that is, the larger its diameter—the better. The hollow quill is buoyant when sealed, and the angle of its cut end governs how deep it will run in water. Preparing several of these quills in one fly-tying session is both useful and efficient.

The placement of the quill on the hook shank (see Step 3) will allow you to pass the leader through the eye of the hook and fasten the fly to your line.

These flies are most effective when fished with slow, short jerks across the water's surface. Sudden strong jerks that pull them deep under water can break your rod tip.

| | |
|---|---|
| **HOOK** | *Mustad #9575, No. 2* |
| **THREAD** | *White flat waxed nylon* |
| **TAIL** | *None* |
| **BODY** | *Turkey wing or tail quill, base section* |
| **WING** | *Black bucktail* |
| **ALSO REQUIRED** | |
| | *Clear silicone seal, Duco Cement* |

1. Select a turkey wing or flight feather with a large diameter quill, and place a hook alongside it so the hook bend is about ¾ inch up from the end of the bare quill. Mark the quill opposite the hook eye. Then, with a sharp knife or a single-blade razor, cut off the quill's base diagonally toward its bare end. The quill base should be about a half inch longer than the hook.

2. Carefully seal both ends of the quill base with silicone seal. *Do not try to fill the hollow quill; just seal it with a plug of silicone at each end.* Let it dry.

3. When the seals are dry, put a hook in the vise, attach the thread to the hook, and wrap a nonslip base in the usual manner. Place the sealed quill along the top of the hook shank so the diagonal cut is above the hook eye and goes downward toward the hook bend. The hook eye itself should be about ⅛ inch ahead of the lower end of the diagonal cut.

4. Holding the quill in that position, wrap the thread forward in even, tight turns, butting each turn. Continue up to ³⁄₁₆ inch from the eye and let the bobbin hang. Whip finish and cut the thread. To seal and protect the thread bindings, apply one or two coats of clear, durable nail polish.

5. When the nail polish is dry, select and cut a bunch of bucktail about ³⁄₁₆ inch in diameter and 1½ inches longer than the turkey quill. Prepare the wing as direct-

ed in Step 5 on page 49 (see the Hair Wing instructions).

6. Reattach the thread ¼ inch behind the front end of the thread connecting the quill to the shank, and let the bobbin hang. Place the wing on top of the quill so the hair butts are over the eye. Bind the wing in place using the soft loop technique, and let the bobbin hang.

7. Cut the hair butts in a taper toward the hook eye to form the head. Bind down the butts, whip finish, and apply two coats of clear durable nail polish.

## Variations

This fly can also be tied with a wing of yellow or green bucktail instead of the black wing specified in the original pattern. Do not, however, use more than one color in the wing!

black turkey quill slider

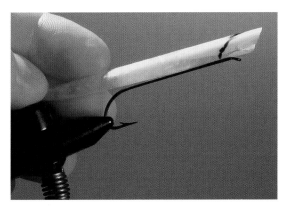

*Black Turkey Quill Slider (1). Quill marked for cutting.*

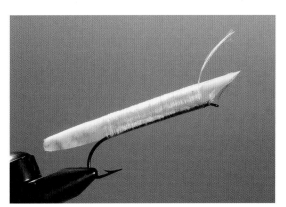

*Black Turkey Quill Slider (2). Quill cut, sealed, and wrapped in place.*

*Black Turkey Quill Slider (3). Completed fly.*

# Woolly Bugger

THE WOOLLY BUGGER IS ESSENTIALLY AN improved version of the once-popular Woolly Worm. It represents hellgrammites (the larva of the dobsonfly), which are notable live bait for trout and bass. Black is usually the best color, although brown and olive have their supporters.

The hackle length for this fly should be about twice the gap of the hook. It's somewhat loosely palmered from the rear of the fly and is wrapped more tightly to create a collar, about a half inch wide, just behind the head.

| | |
|---|---|
| **HOOK** | *Mustad #9575 (6XL) or 9672 (3XL), Nos. 2–8* |
| **THREAD** | *White flat waxed nylon* |
| **TAIL** | *Black marabou* |
| **BODY** | *Black worsted-weight yarn or black chenille* |
| **HACKLE** | *Black, soft Chinese- or saltwater-grade neck or saddle* |
| **HEAD** | *Black head cement* |

1.  After you put the hook in the vise, attach the thread, and wrap the nonslip base for the tail, select a substantial bunch of marabou fibers 1 to 1½ inches long. Cut a section of the feather ¾ inch to 1¼ inches. I suggest a section ½ to ¾ inch wide, depending on hook size.

2.  Bundle the marabou for the tail, keeping the tips even, and place it along the top of the hook bend with the tips at least ¾ inch behind the hanging thread. Fasten it there using the soft loop technique, and let the bobbin hang.

3.  Place a 6- to 8-inch length of yarn on top of the shank with one end ⅛ inch behind the hook eye, and fasten it where the bobbin hangs with three or four firm, close wraps of thread. Let the bobbin hang.

4.  Select a neck or saddle hackle feather that has barbs at least twice the size of the hook gap. Upset the barbs on ½ inch of the feather's tip and cut them to a stubble on both sides of the shaft. Place the stubble tip on top of the hook shank so the uncut section is directly behind where the bobbin hangs, and bind it in place with firm, butted turns of thread. Continue wrapping forward, binding down the stubble and the short end of the yarn, then wrapping to ⅛ inch from the eye. Let the bobbin hang.

5.  Use a material clip to hold the feather out of the way while you make the body: Wind the yarn or chenille up the shank in close, butted turns without gaps or overlaps to ⅛ inch from the eye. Fasten it there with three or four firm turns of thread, and let the bobbin hang. Cut off the surplus yarn, being careful not to cut the thread.

**Woolly Bugger (1). Tail in place.**

**Woolly Bugger (2). With yarn and hackle tied on, we are wrapping the yarn for the body.**

**Woolly Bugger (3). Body complete.**

**Woolly Bugger (4). Hackle wrapped, fly complete.**

woolly bugger

6. Attach your pliers to the feather—near the end of the shaft and at right angles to it—and with the feather on edge, spiral it up the body. Space the turns about ⅟₁₆ inch apart and continue spiraling to about ½ inch from the hook eye. At this point, begin making tightly butted turns with the feather still on its edge. Continue making the turns until you reach either the end of the feather or a point ⅛ inch from the eye, whichever comes first. (Go to the step below that is specific to where your feather ended on the hook shank.)

7. *If you have reached the end of feather and still have some distance to wrap forward to ⅛ inch from the eye,* tie the feather off with two or three firm wraps of thread, cut off the surplus shaft, bind the end down, and return the thread to the front edge of the feather wrap. If this does not apply to you, go to Step 10.

8. Prepare the second feather by making

stubble of the lowest ½ inch of the butt. Place the feather diagonally on the near side of the hook shank, butt downward and forward, with the first of the untrimmed part of the feather directly over the hanging thread and the feather's tip toward the rear of the hook. Fasten it there with several firm, close-butted turns of thread over the stubble area, and let the bobbin hang. Cut the surplus shaft ⅛ inch from the eye, bind down the cut end, and let the bobbin hang.

9.  Attach the hackle pliers below the feather's tip, at right angles to the shaft, and continue making close, butted turns—with the feather on its edge—to ⅛ inch from the eye. Tie off the feather with several firm turns of thread, and let the bobbin hang while you carefully cut off the surplus feather. (Remember not to cut the thread by accident!) Bind down the cut end of the feather. Then go to Step 11.

10. *If you have wrapped the feather to ⅛ inch from the eye and did not run out of feather*, tie the feather off, cut off the surplus shaft, and bind the end down.

11. Form a neat head and finish the fly in the usual manner.

## Variations

By substituting brown, olive, or even grizzly marabou for the tail and the same color of soft (wet-fly) hackle, you can produce Brown, Olive, or Grizzly Woolly Buggers. Brown and olive can be dyed over white or grizzly hackle, which is more frequently available.

## Dun Brown Spent-Wing Spinner

***Dun Brown Spinner** with Antron yarn wing*

SPENT-WING SPINNERS REPRESENT THE LAST stage of a flying insect's life cycle when, after mating and egg laying, the adult male and female insects fall exhausted on the surface of the water. Although there are several different spent-wing spinners, their proportions—which are very important—are all the same:

*Tail length = body length, i.e., from the hook bend to the hook eye*

*Wing length = body length*

*Wing width = 30% of body length*

*Dun Brown Spinner* with duck shoulder feather wing

*Dun Brown Spinner* with wing of pale mink tail hair

The tail and wings act as stabilizers and provide flotation, but they need to be well coated with a good flotation solution prior to casting. The tail itself is split and the two parts are separated at an angle of 45° by a small ball of body material.

We provide instructions for making three kinds of wings, and you can tie them flat (spent) or slightly raised (half-spent) to imitate various stages in the spinner fall. We will start with the whole-feather wing option, and then introduce you to the other options at the end of the recipe. Feather wings are made with matching feathers. Usually two growing side by side on a skin are similar enough in color and size to match, whereas a good match may be harder to find if you use loose feathers. The wings made from poly X (polypropylene) yarn are the simplest, although they will be in spent position when finished.

Also note that, because this fly can represent a female who has just deposited her eggs, the body you spin should be thin.

The materials listed before the instructions are for the Dun Brown Spinner. See Variations following the instructions for changes you would make to tie the Dun Cream Spinner.

| | |
|---|---|
| **HOOK** | *Mustad #94833, Nos. 12–18* |
| **THREAD** | *White 8/0 UNI-Thread* |
| **TAIL** | *Light gray dry-fly quality hackle fibers or gray hair* |
| **BODY** | *Brown fur or Poly III dubbing* |
| **WING** | *Light gray partridge or hen body feathers, Antron yarn, duck shoulder feather, or whole feather* |

**dun brown spent-wing spinner**

*Whole Feather Wing Spinner*

1. Place the hook in the vise, attach the thread, and wrap the nonslip base for the tail in the usual manner.

2. Dub a small wisp of body material onto a waxed section of the hanging thread. If in doubt about how to do this, see page 68–69 for detailed directions. After it is spun onto the thread, push it up to the top of the hook shank to form a small ball. Fasten it firmly to the hook shank with X-wraps, directly over the barb, and let the bobbin hang.

3. For the split tail, select a large dry-fly quality neck feather with barbs at least a half inch longer than the body length of the fly and cut or pull off four to six barbs. You need at least two for each side of the tail. If employing hair instead of feathers, use the same length. With the tips together, place half of the fibers on the near side of the dubbing ball, ensuring that the tail section is the proper length (i.e., 1½ times the body length should extend behind

the dubbing ball), and fasten them there with a couple of firm turns of thread. Let the bobbin hang. Repeat the process to make the other tail section and let the bobbin hang.

4. For the body, spin a thin dubbing of the same color as the ball that's separating the tail sections onto the hanging thread. Wind a dubbed body in butted turns to ³⁄₁₆ inch from the eye. Remember to keep the body thin. Tie off the body, and let the bobbin hang while you prepare the wings.

5. Select two matching feathers of the proper size for the wings. With dull sides together and tips matching, trim the lowest ³⁄₁₆ inch to ⅜ inch of soft, short fibers on each side of the shaft to a stubble. Place the feathers along the top of the hook shank with the trimmed shafts over the eye and the lower edge of the feathers just touching the body. Bind them firmly in place with three or four turns of thread. Let the bobbin hang while you cut off the surplus shafts to about ⅛ inch behind the eye.

6. Separate the wings until they are perpendicular to the hook shank and bind them with X-wraps until they lie in half-spent or spent position.

7. To build up the thorax area, spin a wisp of the body dubbing onto the thread and wind it in X-wraps, covering the white thread that binds down the base of the wings. When you are finished, tie off the dubbing with clean thread and cut off any surplus dubbing.

# MAKING AN X-BINDING

THE X-BINDING IS HANDY WHEN YOU want to separate wings or legs while securing them. It is demonstrated here with a hair wing.

**STEP 1**   *Tie the hair wing bundle in place, and follow with one or two tightly nestled turns on the eye side of the bundle to make the hair stand up. Let the bobbin hang.*

**STEP 2**   *Divide the bundle in half to form the two wings, then pass the thread back between the wings, then around the base of the far wing (not around the shank). Let the bobbin hang behind the shank.*

**STEP 3**   *Follow with a figure-eight wrap around the shank and between the wings, adding a second and third figure eight as necessary (especially with fine thread) to ensure separation of the wings.*

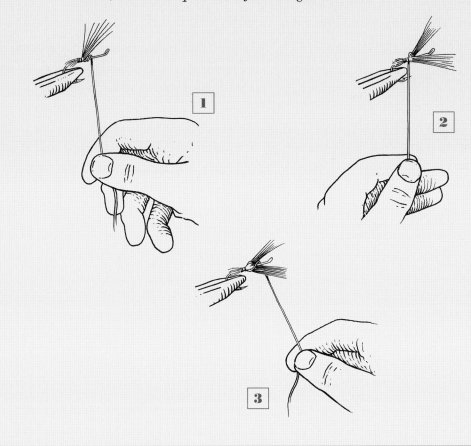

dun brown spent-wing spinner

**dun brown spent-wing spinner**

*Dun Cream Spinner with duck shoulder wing*

8. With clean thread make a small head, whip finish, and complete the fly in the usual manner.

## If You Use Bundled Materials for the Wings

For this option you would use light gray hackle tips or light gray hair such as mink tail guard hairs in a clump. (This process would replace Steps 5 and 6 above.)

1. Select a bunch of hair or feather fibers that is the desired length (wing length *plus* the area that you will attach to the hook shank) and about ⅛ to ⅜ inch thick. Even out the tips. Place the bundle along the top of the hook shank with butts over the eye and the proper length of wing behind the hanging bob-

bin. Fasten it in place with three or four firm turns of thread, and let the bobbin hang. Cut off the surplus butts to about ⅛ inch behind the eye.

2. Divide the bundle in half, and separate the wings until they are perpendicular to the hook shank. Bind them with X-wraps so they are in half-spent or spent position. Trim and bind down the wing butts.

## If You Use Poly X Yarn for the Wings

For this option you would use light gray Poly X (yarn form). (This process would replace Steps 5 and 6 above.)

1. Cut a length of light gray yarn equal to the required wing length for the fly (see the proportions above if you are in doubt). Place it on top of and perpendicular to the hook shank, with its center against the front end of the body, and firmly tie it in place with X-wraps. Let the bobbin hang.

## Variation

Follow the recipe above to tie the Dun Cream Spinner, making material substitutions as indicated below. Substitute Nos. 8–10 hooks and cream fur or Poly III dubbing for the body. The Dun Cream and Dun Brown Spinners have the same proportions.

# CLASSIC WET FLIES

et flies represent the waterlogged, sunken mayflies, caddis, and other insects that fall into the water and then sink below the surface, becoming an easy meal for the resident fish. They are important and useful flies at most times of day and in all seasons, and you will do well to use them in your fishing.

Among the classic wet flies are the marabous, which we covered in Easy Flies for Beginners (see page 79).

## Grizzly and Peacock

THIS VERY OLD WET FLY IS SIMPLE TO TIE, and it catches fish. The hackle is tied as a collar that extends to the point of the hook.

| HOOK | *Mustad #3906, Nos. 12–14; No. 6 for bass* |
|---|---|
| THREAD | *White 8/0 UNI-Thread* |
| TAIL | *None* |
| BODY | *Peacock herl* |
| WING | *None* |
| HACKLE | *Grizzly hen neck or body feather* |
| HEAD | *Black head cement* |

1. Place the hook in the vise, attach the thread, and wrap a nonslip base for the body.
2. Select three or four thick, plump peacock herls from an eye stick or sewn patch. Cut them off and place them together. Even the tips and cut off the first half inch of the tip, as it tends to be too thin and soft to tie in securely.
3. Place the bundle along the top of the hook shank so that one end is about ³⁄₁₆ inch from the eye and the other end extends beyond the hook bend. Fasten it there with the hanging thread, and continue wrapping the thread in butting turns over the end of the herl to ³⁄₁₆ inch from the eye. Let the bobbin hang.
4. While exerting even tension on the ends of the herl, wind it in butting turns up the hook shank to the hanging

*Grizzly and Peacock*

thread. Tie it off and cut off the excess herl. This forms the body of the fly.

5. Select a soft grizzly hen neck or body feather whose fibers are as long as the distance from the hook eye to the barb, and upset it. Measure the individual fibers, locate the first one of the required length, and carefully cut to a stubble all the fibers between it and the feather's tip on both sides of the shaft.

6. Place the stubble end of the prepared feather diagonally against the near side of the hook shank, good side out and with the first of the uncut fibers just to the left of the hanging thread. Fasten it there with several firm, butting turns of the thread. Let the bobbin hang while you cut off the excess stubble tip.

7. Double the hackle. Place your hackle pliers on the feather's shaft and, with two or three butting turns, wrap it tight against the body to the hanging thread. Tie it off, and let the bobbin hang while you cut off the surplus grizzly feather.

8. Bind down the cut ends of the feather. Form a neat head and finish the fly in the usual manner.

# Leadwing Coachman

THE NUMBER OF HERL FIBERS YOU USE TO tie the body of the Leadwing Coachman depends on the hook size you choose. Larger flies will obviously require more herl. The body should be thick and plump, so start with thick, plump herl fibers and use enough of them to get the desired effect. If you purchased the herl on a foot-long "stick," pull or cut the required number of fibers off either or both sides of the shaft, starting at the base.

When choosing feathers for the wing, note that the lowest ends of pointer feathers tend to be soft and curl a lot, and are unsuitable for this fly's wing; therefore, the soft part on the wide side needs to be stripped. Larger flies require wider wings as well as more and larger throat material. Note that soft hackle, not stiff dry-fly hackle, is the desired throat material.

The Leadwing Coachman and White Wing Coachman (see Variations below) are useful and productive; Nos. 4–6 are especially useful for bass and larger trout, while smaller fish prefer sizes 10–14.

| | |
|---|---|
| **HOOK** | *Mustad #3906, Nos. 4–14* |
| **THREAD** | *White 8/0 UNI-Thread* |
| **TAIL** | *None* |
| **BODY** | *Peacock herl* |
| **WING** | *Slate or shade of gray mallard wing pointer feathers* |
| **THROAT** | *Dark brown hen hackle or soft coachman brown rooster hackle such as Rhode Island Red* |
| **HEAD** | *Black head cement* |

1. Place the hook in the vise, attach the thread, and wrap a nonslip base for the tail.

2. Select three to six strands of peacock herl. Even them, then cut off about ½ inch from the tips to create a firm section to tie to the hook shank. Place the herl along the top of the hook shank so the cut tips extend about ³⁄₁₆ inch behind the eye of the hook. Bind the herl to the hook with close and continuous wraps, and continue up the shank to about ³⁄₁₆ inch from the eye. Let the bobbin hang.

3. Wrap the herl tightly up the shank to where the bobbin hangs. Pushing the herl toward the rear of the fly as you wrap will fill in any gaps and may allow a couple of extra turns of material. When finished, hold the herl in place to prevent unraveling while you bind it to the hook with a couple of tight turns of thread. Let the bobbin hang. Cut off the excess herl, and bind down the stubs to make a firm, neat foundation for the wing. Then let the bobbin hang again.

**leadwing coachman**

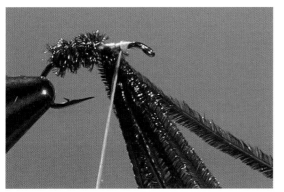

*Leadwing Coachman (1). Wrapping the herl on the shank.*

*Leadwing Coachman (2). Cut off the excess herl, and tie in the throat.*

*Leadwing Coachman (3). Tie the prepared duck wing feathers to the shaft using the soft loop technique.*

*Leadwing Coachman (4). Completed fly.*

4. Select a matching pair of duck wing pointer feathers, preferably the identical pointers from a right and left wing. Starting at about one inch from the base, strip the soft part of the wide side of both pointer feathers. Then, using the point of the scissors or a bodkin, separate a ³⁄₁₆-inch slip of feather (for a No. 14 hook) and cut it off close to the shaft. (Use wider slips on larger hooks.) Repeat the process on the second pointer to create the second slip.

5. Place the slips one on top of the other and carefully make them the same width by separating any extra fibers from the wider wing with the bodkin. With their dull sides together, place the slips on top of the body so their tips extend a little beyond the hook bend. Center them over the hook, and check all proportions before firmly tying in the slips using the soft loop technique. Let the bobbin hang. Check the position of the wings, and then cut off the surplus wing butts.

6. To make the throat, select eight to twelve fibers from a dark brown hen body feather or soft coachman brown rooster hackle. Even the tips, then bunch up the bundle and tie it in under the hook shank so the tips extend almost to the point of the hook. Use the soft loop technique to tie it in. Cut off excess feathers and tie down the butts of the throat.

7. Form a neat, small head and finish the fly in the usual manner.

## Variations

To tie the White Wing Coachman, use white pointer feathers. Also, although duck wing feathers are listed in the materials above, you may use goose or turkey feathers instead depending on the size of the fly and availability of these materials.

# Montreal

THE MONTREAL IS AN OLD STANDARD WET fly that has two less-popular body styles (see Variations below). All three flies are well worth using, however, so tie all of them.

For the tail and throat, select wet-fly hackle that has ³⁄₁₆-inch barbs. The throat hackle should be soft and webby. Choose either a large or short turkey feather for the wing—preferably one that has a center shaft and is equal in width on both sides of it—from each side of which you can cut matching wing slips (do not use the white tip of the feather for this fly). Otherwise, use a matched pair of tail feathers and cut slips from the same area of each.

A material clip attached to the barrel of your vise comes in handy for holding the lengths of tinsel and body material out of the way while you bind their ends to the shaft and do other work.

| | |
|---|---|
| **HOOK** | *Mustad #3906, Nos. 10–14 (Nos. 12–14 preferred)* |
| **THREAD** | *8/0 UNI-Thread* |
| **TAIL** | *Scarlet hackle fibers* |
| **BODY** | *Claret floss, 1-ply* |
| **RIB** | *Gold flat Mylar tinsel, fine* |
| **THROAT** | *Claret hackle fibers* |
| **WING** | *Dark-brown mottled turkey tail* |
| **HEAD** | *Black head cement* |

**Montreal**

montreal

1.  Place the hook in the vise, attach the thread, and wrap the nonslip base for the tail.

2.  Cut a bundle of about 10 to 12 fibers from the scarlet hackle for the tail. Cut close to the shaft. Even the fiber tips, then place the bundle along the top of the hook shank with the tips extending about ⅜ inch beyond the hook bend. Employ the soft loop technique to tie in the tail, and let the bobbin hang.

3.  Measure and cut off a 6- to 8-inch length of tinsel, place one end on top of the hook shank about ⅛ inch behind the eye, and tie it to the shank where the bobbin hangs.

4.  Repeat the Step 3 process for the floss, allowing its length to extend toward the rear of the hook. Then continue wrapping the tying thread in close turns to ⅛ inch from the eye, binding the tied ends of the tinsel and floss to the shank as you go. Let the bobbin hang.

5.  Wrap the floss body forward in adjacent turns, from the base of the tail to where the bobbin hangs. Tie off the floss with two or three firm turns of thread, and let the bobbin hang while you carefully cut off the surplus floss. Be careful not to accidentally cut the hanging thread.

6.  Spiral the tinsel rib up the body, allowing a space equal to twice the width of the tinsel between each turn. Tie off the tinsel and trim the excess just as you did with the floss.

7.  For the throat, cut a bunch of eight or ten barbs from one side of the claret hackle. Even the tips, then place the bunch under the body so the butts point toward the eye and the tips extend to the point of the hook. Tie the bunch to the shaft using the soft loop technique. Cut off the surplus butts.

8.  From the turkey feather(s), cut matching ³⁄₁₆-inch-wide wing slips that are at

*Montreal Silver*

*Montreal Yellow*

least ³⁄₁₆ inch longer than the hook shank. To form the wing, place the slips dull sides together with their tips aligned. Then place the unit on top of the body so its tip extends slightly beyond the hook and the butt is positioned over the eye. Tie it in using the soft loop technique. Cut off the surplus feather butts, tapering toward the eye, and bind them down.

9. Form the head and finish the fly in the usual manner.

## Variations

To tie Montreal Silver, substitute medium flat silver Mylar tinsel for the claret 1-ply floss (body), and note that this variation does not have a rib. The Montreal Yellow body calls for fine yellow yarn instead of the 1-ply floss. All other materials are the same as those listed above.

# Professor

THIS IS AN OLD, BRIGHT, WET-FLY PATTERN that can be used on its own or as the tail fly tied to the end of the leader, with a different style of wet fly tied on as a dropper about 18 inches higher on the leader. The idea is not to take two fish at once (although that may happen), but rather to offer choices and thus find out what interests the local trout at the moment. Check your local fishing regulations before you try this technique, however, as they may not permit you to cast two or more flies on your leader.

Ideally, the hackle you select for the tail and throat will be soft and webby and have ³⁄₄-inch barbs. Also, after the body and rib materials are tied in, you can hold their length out of the way with a material clip or holder while you bind their ends to the shaft or do other work.

Mallard feathers—needed for the wing—are cheaper than teal, which is in short supply at the moment. Select a medium to large natural gray flank feather that has a center shaft or a matched pair of feathers in which one feather has a wide right side and the other has a wide left side.

**Professor (1).** *Tail tied in, floss wrapped, and tinsel ready to wrap.*

| | |
|---|---|
| **HOOK** | *Mustad #3906, Nos. 12–14* |
| **THREAD** | *8/0 UNI-Thread, white* |
| **TAIL** | *Scarlet dyed wet-fly or hen hackle* |
| **BODY** | *Yellow floss, 1-ply* |
| **RIB** | *Gold flat Mylar tinsel, fine* |
| **THROAT** | *Brown wet-fly or hen hackle* |
| **WING** | *Gray mallard flank or teal* |
| **HEAD** | *Black head cement* |

1. Place the hook in the vise, attach the thread, and wrap a nonslip base for the tail.

2. From the scarlet-dyed hackle, cut off a bunch of eight or ten barbs close to the shaft. Even the tips, then place the bunch along the top of the hook shank so the tips extend about ⅜ inch beyond the hook bend. Use the soft loop technique to tie in the tail, and let the bobbin hang.

3. Measure and cut off a 6- to 8-inch length of tinsel, and place one end along the top of the hook shank about ⅛ inch behind the eye. Allow its length to extend behind the tail. Fasten the tinsel to the shank with a couple of turns of thread, and let the bobbin hang.

4. Measure and cut off about 8 inches of floss or mount the spool of floss in a second bobbin. Place the floss on top of the tinsel on the hook shank, aligning its end with the tinsel and allowing the

**Professor (2).** *Tinsel wrapped and throat tied in.*

**Professor (3).** *Wing attached.*

*professor*

*Professor (4). Completed fly.*

balance to extend to the rear of the shaftbend of the hook.

Fasten it there with two or three turns of thread. Then continue wrapping the thread in close turns to ⅛ inch from the eye, binding the tied ends of the tinsel and floss to the shank as you go. Let the bobbin hang.

5.  Starting at the base of the tail, carefully wrap the floss up the shank to form the body, butting each turn to where the bobbin hangs. Tie down the body with two or three firm turns of thread and, again, let the bobbin hang. Raise the surplus floss above the hook shank and cut it off, being careful not to cut the thread.

6.  Make a tight turn of tinsel against the tail, to cover any gap between tail and body, and spiral the rib up the body to where the bobbin hangs. Allow space twice the width of the tinsel between each turn. Tie off the rib with two or

three firm turns of thread, and let the bobbin hang while you cut off the surplus tinsel.

7.  Select a bunch of about eight to ten barbs from one side of the brown hackle and cut it off close to the shaft. Even the tips and, holding them as you did the tail, place them under the body so the butts are at the eye and the tips extend to the point of the hook. Fasten the throat there using the soft loop technique. Cut off the surplus butts, being careful not to cut the hanging thread.

8.  From the same area on each side of the mallard feather shaft, or from each of the matched pair of feathers, cut ³⁄₁₆-inch-wide slips that are ³⁄₁₆ inch longer than the hook shank. Place them dull sides together and even the tips. Place the wing on top of the body so the butts are over the eye and the tips extend just past the hook bend. Use the soft loop technique to tie it in.

9.  Taper the surplus wing butts to form the head. Bind down the butts and finish the head in the usual manner.

## Variations

For an easy and effective alternative tail, use a ⅛-inch-wide segment from the lower, soft portion of a secondary duck or turkey feather that's dyed red. Tie it on as you would the Gray Squirrel Silver tail (see page 127). The tail length is the same no matter which material you choose.

# NYMPHS

Nymphs furnish a substantial portion of trout and panfish food, so the flies that represent them are effective and popular among anglers. Nymph naturals are present year-round in our streams and lakes at various levels in the water column. Therefore, we include instructions for tying floating, weighted, and unweighted flies to meet these needs.

## Gray Nymph

HERE IS AN OLD-TIME AND EFFECTIVE NYMPH with one change from the usual pattern that improves the fly: the use of freshwater coot body feathers as legs or hackle. These unusual feathers remain separate and have excellent action in the water as well as good color. Perhaps waterfowling friends can provide you with a supply of these feathers. Soft, gray hen body feathers are perhaps the best substitute.

| | |
|---|---|
| **HOOK** | *Mustad #9672, No.12 (No. 6 for bass)* |
| **THREAD** | *White 8/0 UNI-Thread* |
| **TAIL** | *Optional* |
| **BODY** | *Muskrat underfur, dubbed* |
| **RIB** | *Gold wire (optional)* |
| **HACKLE** | *Coot body feather* |
| **HEAD** | *Black head cement* |

*Gray Nymph (1). Wire wrapped back from eye; tail tied on; body begun.*

*Gray Nymph (2). Body wraps completed.*

**gray nymph**

*Gray Nymph (3). Hackle in place.*

*Gray Nymph (4). Completed fly.*

1. Place the hook in the vise, attach the thread, and wrap a nonslip base for the body.

2. If you're using gold wire for a rib, cut off a 6- to 8-inch length and place one end on top of the hook shank about ³⁄₁₆ inch behind the eye. Fasten it in place with a couple of firm turns of thread and continue binding down the wire for at least ½ inch. Then return the thread to the tie-in point for the tail (if present) and body, and let the bobbin hang.

3. Apply soft dubbing wax to the first couple of inches of thread hanging below the hook shank. Select a small bunch of hair/fur at the edge of the muskrat hide and cut it off close to the hide. Carefully pull the long brown guard hairs out of the blue-gray underfur. Set the clean underfur aside and repeat the process with another bunch of underfur.

4. Use the fur to create dubbing for the body according to the instructions on page 66. Wind the dubbed section in close, even turns to ³⁄₁₆ inch from the

eye, pushing it back from time to time to make a compact body. Tie off the dubbing with several tight turns of bare thread and let the bobbin hang.

5. If you are creating a rib, spiral the wire over the body to the bobbin, allowing a ⅛- to ³⁄₁₆-inch space between each turn. Tie down the wire and cut off the excess.

6. Select a gray coot body feather. Separate the individual fibers and cut off six to eight that are ¾ inch or longer. Divide the bundle and place one portion on top of the other so the tips are over the butt ends, making an equally thick-ended set of legs or hackle. Place the bundle on top of and perpendicular to the hook shank immediately in front of the body and above the hanging bobbin. Each side of the bundle should extend about ⅜ to ¾ inch from the hook shank. Tightly bind the bundle down with X-wraps around the hook shank.

7. Form a small neat head and finish the fly in the usual manner.

# Hendrickson Nymph

THERE ARE A GREAT MANY NYMPHS THAT have a similar shape and coloring, so this is a useful pattern because it represents so many of them. It can also be used to specifically represent or imitate a major hatch in the East and Midwest. The rib, if you choose to wrap one, also serves as reinforcement for the body dubbing.

*Hendrickson Nymph*

| | |
|---|---|
| **HOOK** | *Mustad #9671 or #9672, Nos. 12–14* |
| **THREAD** | *White 8/0 UNI-Thread* |
| **TAIL** | *Wood duck or mallard-dyed wood duck* |
| **BODY** | *Dark brown or mahogany-dyed rabbit fur or Poly XXX dubbing* |
| **RIB** | *Copper wire, fine (optional)* |
| **WING CASE** | *Dark duck, goose, or crow flight feather or black ostrich herl* |
| **THORAX** | *Dark brown or mahogany-dyed rabbit fur or Poly XXX dubbing* |
| **LEGS** | *Wood duck or mallard-dyed wood duck* |
| **HEAD** | *Black head cement* |

1. Place the hook in the vise, attach the thread, and wrap a nonslip base for the tail.
2. Select three ¾-inch, well-marked fibers from a wood duck or dyed mallard flank feather for the tail and cut them off close to the shaft. Place the fibers on top of the hook shank with the tips extending about a shank's length beyond the bend of the hook. Tie them in with two or three firm turns of thread, and let the bobbin hang. Separate the fibers with the bodkin and hold them in place with X-wraps: one on the left, one in the middle, and one on the right. Finish with the thread hanging at the tie-in point, ready to dub the body.
3. If you plan to wrap a rib, tie in a 5- or 6-inch length of wire and let it hang.
4. Prepare the thread and dub the fur for the body as instructed on page 66, until about 1½ to 2 inches of fur is in place on the thread. If the dubbing on the thread is not close to the hook shank, carefully slide it up before starting to wrap the body. The first turn of dubbing should cover the binding that

holds the tail in place. Now wrap the dubbing forward, butting each turn to form a firm, neat body to ⅜ inch from the eye, and let the bobbin hang.

5. At the front of the body, carefully pull/tease the dubbing off the section of thread that's adjacent to the hook shank. Grasp the stripped section and carefully push the surplus dubbing down to expose an inch or so of thread. You will use this to tie in the wing case.

6. If you tied in wire for ribbing or reinforcement, spiral it up the body to just behind the eye. Allow ⅛ to 3/16 inch between turns. Tie off the rib with four or five firm turns of thread and cut off the surplus wire.

7. For the wing case, measure and cut a ⅜-inch-wide section that's at least 1¼ inches long from the broad side of the feather. Place the feather light side up on top of the hook shank so the butt is over the hook eye and the tip is over the tail. Fasten it there with several close, firm turns of thread, and let the bobbin hang while you cut off the surplus butt at ⅛ inch behind the eye. Then return the thread to where the wing case was tied in and, again, let the bobbin hang.

8. Recharge the thread with more dubbing to make a fat thorax. Push the existing dubbing a bit farther down the thread, and then wax an inch or two of bare thread directly below the hook shank. Push the surplus dubbing back to the shank and apply fresh wisps of dubbing to the thread to make a thorax twice

as thick as the body and about ⅜ to 3/16 inch long, depending on the size of the fly.

9. Wrap the dubbing in close turns, and if there is surplus dubbing, strip the thread as you did for the wing case and tie off the thorax with several butted turns of clean thread. Let the bobbin hang.

10. Lift the tip of the wing case and carefully pull it over and around the fat thorax to where the bobbin hangs. Fasten it with several firm turns of thread tight against the front of the thorax, and let the bobbin hang while you cut off the surplus tip of the wing case.

11. For the legs, select and cut off six fibers from the same wood duck or dyed mallard feather that you used for the tail. Place the bundle of fibers under the hook shank so the tips extend about a half inch behind where the thread hangs and the butts are over the hook eye. Fasten them there with two or three firm turns of thread, and let the bobbin hang while cutting off the butts at about ⅛ inch behind the eye. Then return the thread to where the legs were tied in, and let the bobbin hang.

12. With the bodkin, separate three legs for the near side of the fly and tie them in place with X-wraps. Repeat the process on the far side. The legs should all stand out at a wide angle from the hook shank. Let the bobbin hang.

13. Recharge the thread one more time with a tiny wisp of dubbing. Wind it

forward in smooth turns to ⅛ inch from the eye, neatly covering the tie-in for the legs and the front of the wing case.

14. Clean the thread and, with it, form the head. Whip finish and complete the fly in the usual manner.

# Pheasant Tail Nymph

THIS REALISTIC AND USEFUL NYMPH IS highly successful in all sizes and will please you as well as the fish.

When forming the thorax, your fingers provide better control than hackle pliers.

**HOOK**     *Mustad #9672 or #9671, Nos. 10–16*

**THREAD**  *White 8/0 UNI-Thread*

**TAIL/BODY/THORAX**

*Ring-necked pheasant tail feather (from cock)*

**RIB**       *Gold wire, fine*

**WING CASE/LEGS**

*Dark ring-necked pheasant tail feather (from cock)*

**HEAD**    *Black head cement*

*Pheasant Tail Nymph*

1. Place the hook in the vise, attach the thread, and wrap a nonslip base for the tail.

2. Cut a ³⁄₁₆-inch-wide strip of feather, preferably 1½ to 2¼ inches long depending on your hook size, from which you will make the tail, body, and thorax. Holding the feather strip with the butt over the hook eye, measure a tail length equal to the length of the hook shank, then fasten the feather to the shank at the hook bend with two turns of thread. Lift the feather strip and make two turns of thread around the shank in front of and beneath the strip to hold it up.

3. Tie in the gold wire and bind the end down to about ³⁄₁₆ inch from the eye, and let the bobbin hang. Place the free end of the wire in the material clip.

4. To make the body, wrap the feather like a ribbon—in butting turns—to where the thread hangs and bind it there with two turns of the thread. Turn the remainder of the feather until it is upright at the top of the shank, advance the thread to one turn ahead of the feather, and let the bobbin hang.

5. Cut a ³⁄₁₆- to ¼-inch strip of darker feather for the wing case. Tie it on top of

the hook shank, dark side down and just ahead of the body feather, so the butt points toward the eye (when fully tied, the dark side of the feather will show as the wing case). Bind the thorax area, trim off the excess butts (of the wing case feather only), and let the bobbin hang.

6. Wind the wire forward in spirals to form the rib, allowing ⅛ inch between each wrap, and tie it off in the thorax area.

7. Grasp the remainder of the body feather and wrap it forward, ahead of the wing case material, to form a thick thorax. Tie it off with a couple of firm turns of thread, trim any excess, bind down all ends, and let the bobbin hang forward of the thorax.

8. Pull the free end of the wing case *tightly* over the thorax. Tie it down against the thorax with two turns of thread, and let the bobbin hang. Separate out three fibers on each side of the body for legs and secure them with X-wraps.

9. Carefully cut out the remaining center section of excess fibers, bind down the ends to form a head, and whip finish. Trim the legs to about a half inch and separate the individual fibers on each side. Finish the fly by carefully applying black head cement to all the white thread in the head area.

# Floating Pheasant Tail Nymph

HERE ARE JUST A FEW THINGS TO NOTE WHEN tying this fly: Although a broader range of hook sizes is listed in the materials, Nos. 20–24 are most useful. For the tail, body, and legs, select a pheasant tail feather that has 1½ -inch or longer barbs on the wide side of the shaft. As was the case when forming the thorax for the Pheasant Tail Nymph (see page 113), your fingers will provide better feather control than hackle pliers when wrapping the body. The Poly XXX dubbing used to make the wing case provides flotation for the fly, and although the instructions call for a wing case that is ³⁄₁₆ inch in diameter, it should be larger for Nos. 14–18 flies.

**HOOK**    *Mustad #94833, Nos. 14–24*

**THREAD**  *White 8/0 UNI-Thread*

**TAIL/BODY/LEGS**
     *Ring-necked pheasant tail feather (from cock)*

**WING CASE**
     *Gray Poly XXX dubbing*

**HEAD**    *Black head cement*

1. Place the hook in the vise, attach the thread, and wrap a nonslip base for the tail.

2. Cut off a ³⁄₁₆-inch slip of pheasant tail close to the shaft. Place the slip on top of the hook shank—dark, dull side

*Floating Pheasant Tail Nymph*

down—so the tips extend slightly more than the length of the hook shank beyond the bend of the hook. Fasten it above the barb or thereabouts with a couple turns of the hanging thread.

3.  Carefully lift the front of the slip and wrap the thread in butting turns beneath it, up the hook shank to ⅛ inch from the eye. Then let the bobbin hang.

4.  To form the body, wind the raised portion of the slip in butting turns to the hanging thread. Tie it off with the thread, let the bobbin hang, and cut off the excess butts, saving three on each

side for legs. Secure the legs with X-wraps.

5.  Apply sticky dubbing wax to 1½ inches of the hanging thread next to the hook shank, and dub the Poly XXX onto the thread. Raise the bobbin and the dubbed thread above the hook and push the noodle of dubbing down the thread to form a ball about ³⁄₁₆ inch in diameter on the wing case area. Wrap the thread ahead of and behind the ball of dubbing to secure it on the wing case area.

6.  Form a neat head and finish the fly in the usual manner.

# A. P. Peacock and Pheasant Nymph

ALTHOUGH THESE INSTRUCTIONS CALL FOR the use of medium-weight lead wire, the A. P. Peacock and Pheasant Nymph is an effective fly with or without weight. The method of construction is simple and effective and can be applied to other nymphs. To tie the fly without the lead wire weight, simply skip Steps 2–3 or refer to Variations following the instructions.

The traditional method for getting flies that represent nymphs to the bottom of a stream or lake, where they are most effective, was by winding a few turns of lead wire around the shank in the thorax area or—on long, thin nymphs—binding strips of lead wire along the hook shank. Efforts to reduce lead poisoning in waterfowl and fish, however, have led to bans against the use of lead birdshot and sinkers, but no satisfactory alternatives have been found for lead wire that is wrapped onto the hook shank, then covered with fly body materials.

Of the hooks listed in the materials, No. 12 is most useful, and with that you will use a medium-weight lead wire. A coat of durable nail polish that you will apply to the lead wire and its thread covering, once they're wrapped onto the hook shank, will prevent the wire from discoloring the rest of the body.

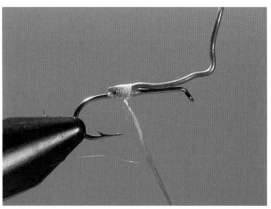

*A. P. Peacock and Pheasant Nymph (1). Binding the wire to the shank.*

*A. P. Peacock and Pheasant Nymph (2). Building the thorax.*

| | |
|---|---|
| **HOOK** | *Mustad # 9671, Nos. 10–16* |
| **THREAD** | *White 8/0 UNI-Thread* |
| **WEIGHT** | *Lead wire, medium* |
| **TAIL/WING CASE/LEGS** | |
| | *Ring-necked pheasant tail feather* |
| **RIB** | *Copper wire, fine* |
| **BODY/THORAX** | |
| | *Bronze peacock herl* |
| **HEAD** | *Black head cement* |

1. Place the hook in the vise, attach the thread, and wind it in butting turns to ³⁄₁₆ inch from the eye. Let the bobbin hang.

2. Place one end of a 5- to 8-inch piece of medium-weight lead wire along the top of the hook about halfway down the shank from the eye, allowing its length to extend toward the eye. Starting where the bobbin hangs, bind the wire to the shank—working toward the hook bend—for about ³⁄₁₆ inch, and let the bobbin hang.

3. With the free length of wire, make three to five tight, butting turns around the hook shank in the thorax area, wrapping toward the hook bend. Cut off the surplus wire, pinch the cut end against the shank, and bind it in place with the thread.

4. Cover the lead wire with turns of thread, working toward the eye and ending where the wire was tied in. Coat the thread and wire with durable nail polish and, when the polish is dry, wrap the thread back to its original tie-in point near the hook bend. Let the bobbin hang.

5. Choose a ring-necked pheasant tail feather with barbs that are about 1½ inches long to allow enough material length for the tail, wing case, and legs. Cut a segment that's about ³⁄₁₆ to ¼ inch wide. Cut close to the shaft. Place the segment dark side up along the top of the hook shank so the butts are over the eye and the tips extend about a half an inch beyond the hook bend. Bind it

*A. P. Peacock and Pheasant Nymph (3). Covering the wire with thread.*

*A. P. Peacock and Pheasant Nymph (4). Tying in the herl.*

*A. P. Peacock and Pheasant Nymph (5). Completed fly.*

a. p. peacock and pheasant nymph

**a. p. peacock and pheasant nymph**

in place, and then let the bobbin hang again while you prepare to tie in the body materials.

6. Place a 5- to 8-inch length of copper wire on the hook shank so that one end touches the rear end of the lead wire. Bind it there with a couple of turns of thread, and let the bobbin hang.

7. Even the tips of two or three strands of peacock herl and cut about a half an inch from them, as the ends are too soft and easily cut by the thread. Place the cut ends against the rear end of the lead wire and tie them in, allowing the length of the herl to extend beyond the hook bend.

8. Bind the pheasant tail feather segment to the shank with close, firm-butted turns of thread. Continue binding up the shank to the thorax area, where you will leave the segment standing up to form the wing case. Continue winding the thread forward over the thorax area, and let the bobbin hang.

9. Holding the long strands of peacock herl taut, wrap the body with even tension in butting turns to the upright pheasant tail. Wind past the pheasant tail, leaving it standing, and continue wrapping the strands in butting turns to create the thorax. Weight the herls

with hackle pliers while you tie them off. Cut off the surplus, being careful not to cut the hanging thread.

10. Wrap the copper wire up the body, in even turns about ⅛ inch apart, to form the rib. Tie it off and cut off the surplus wire.

11. Carefully pull the pheasant tail wing case firmly over the thorax, bind it down with a couple of turns of thread, and let the bobbin hang.

12. To form the legs, divide the wing case butts so that three fibers are on each side, then cut out the surplus from the center. Bind the legs down and slightly toward the rear with X-wraps.

13. Form a neat head, whip finish, and complete the fly in the usual manner.

## Variations

Here is a faster and equally satisfactory method of applying weight to this fly: Load the bobbin with white flat waxed nylon thread. Attach this thread to the hook instead of the 8/0 UNI-Thread and form the foundation with it. Also use it to cover the lead wire, then switch to the finer thread after the durable nail polish has dried. Any time you lose by changing spools in the bobbin will be returned sevenfold by using the wider thread.

# BUCKTAILS AND STREAMERS

These flies represent minnows, the small fish that comprise a large part of the larger trout and panfish diet. The difference between streamers and bucktails is simple: If the wing is made of hair, it's a bucktail; if the wing is made of a feather or feather slip, it's a streamer. The hooks on streamers and bucktails tend to be long, although short versions of these flies representing small fry are often very successful.

When in doubt, tie on a streamer or bucktail. They have taken fish even in the midst of a mayfly hatch.

## Mickey Finn

THE MICKEY FINN IS AN *ATTRACTOR* FLY, meaning it does not imitate or represent an existing creature that fish eat. Instead, attractors are usually tied with brighter materials, and their purpose is to excite fish and provoke an attack. The Mickey Finn had excellent publicity and was popular in the early 1930s, and since that time has had an excellent track record, taking many species of fresh- and salt-water fish under a wide variety of conditions. It is a relatively simple fly to tie.

The size tinsel you use for the body depends on the hook size you choose. The wide tinsel requires fewer turns to cover a given distance and is best for No. 2 hooks. Also note that the average wing diameter is about $\frac{3}{16}$ inch for a No. 10 hook and broader for larger hooks.

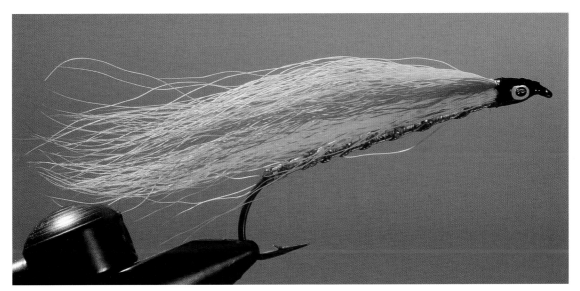

*Mickey Finn*

mickey finn

| | |
|---|---|
| **HOOK** | *Mustad #9575, Nos. 2–10* |
| **THREAD** | *White flat waxed nylon* |
| **TAIL** | *None* |
| **BODY** | *Silver flat tinsel, medium to wide* |
| **RIB** | *Silver oval tinsel, medium to large* |
| **WING** | *Top—yellow dyed bucktail; middle—red or crimson dyed bucktail; bottom—yellow dyed bucktail* |
| **HEAD** | *Black head cement* |

1. Place the hook in the vise, attach the thread, and wrap a nonslip base for the body.

2. Tie in an 8- to 12-inch length of flat tinsel on top of the hook so its end is about ³⁄₁₆ inch behind the eye. Then tie in the oval tinsel the same way, and continue wrapping the thread forward, binding down the two ends of tinsel with close, even turns. When you reach the end of the tinsel let the bobbin hang.

3. To form the body, wind the flat tinsel in tight, butting turns up the hook shank to the bobbin and tie it off with a couple of tight turns of thread. Let the bobbin hang while you cut off the surplus flat tinsel.

4. Spiral the oval tinsel up the hook shank, over the flat tinsel, to form the rib. Allow about twice the width of the oval tinsel between each turn. Tie it off with a couple of tight turns of thread, and let the bobbin hang while you cut off the surplus tinsel.

5. From the hide, cut a small bunch of yellow bucktail that's at least ¾ inch longer than the hook shank and about as thick as a kitchen match. Make it ready for the top of the wing, following the hair wing instructions in Step 5 on page 49. Then, in turn, select and make ready in the same manner a bunch of red bucktail that's about the same size as the yellow bunch for the middle of the wing and another bunch of yellow bucktail that's twice as thick and the same length as the first bunch for the bottom of the wing.

6. When all three wing sections are tacky but not yet solid, stack them so the thick yellow bunch is on the bottom, the red bunch is in the middle, and the thin yellow bunch is on top. Place the assembled wing on top of the hook so the tips extend a finger's width beyond the bend, and fasten it in place using the soft loop technique. Let the bobbin hang.

7. Trim the excess butts using the angle of the down-bent eye as a guide, and bind down the stubs to form a neat head. If you plan to add painted eyes, wrap more turns of thread to make the head larger. Finish the fly in the usual manner.

# CLASSIC BUCKTAILS

THE CLASSIC BUCKTAIL FLY FEATURES A TAIL —usually red—of hair, feather, or yarn, and a red throat. These bits of red represent blood to suggest an injured minnow, an easy meal for a hungry fish. Bucktail bodies are made of tinsel, wool yarn, peacock herl, chenille, or floss, and may have a rib of flat or oval tinsel to give the fly a little shine and sparkle. They are tied on 3X–10X long, heavy hooks.

Early in the twentieth century, when jungle cock necks were cheap, many bucktails sported jungle cock eyes and some, such as the Optic Bucktail, had large black heads with large painted eyes as well. Because of the increasing scarcity of jungle cock and its listing as an endangered species, difficulties in raising the birds domestically, and the consequent rise in price—from $2.50 per neck around 1925, to $25.00 by the 1960s, and $135.00 recently— jungle cock eyes have for some time been omitted from many of the patterns in which they formerly appeared.

Hair wings are more durable than feather wings, and bucktails should be tied with a thin, sparse, and actively moving hair wing for the best results. Such wings will have a good deal of action and provoke many strikes. Beginners tend to use too much material in the wing, which leads to bulky heads, especially when tying multicolored wings. For a bicolored wing, for example, there is often a tendency to make each color unit as large as an entire single wing, which doubles the material needed and should be avoided. (See Wings on page 58 of the Basic

Skills chapter for a tip on how to test a hair wing's thickness.)

A thick, heavy wing provides bulk at the expense of the desired movement. Trolling bucktails are generally larger than those used for casting, and they are popular for taking larger fish in many lakes and larger rivers where their extra bulk more closely represents the actual size and shape of the baitfish. Trolling flies are often used behind several revolving spinners, where the flash attracts the attention of the fish and the following fly is accepted as a meal. (Trolling is a long-accepted activity in New England and on the Great Lakes and St. Lawrence River.) Casting bucktails are generally smaller, having a thin flexible wing to both cast better and more closely replicate the size of minnows found in brooks, streams, and ponds.

Many bucktails are made from the tails of Eastern whitetail deer, either male or female, and have brown hair in various shades on the outside and white hair on the underside that is displayed like a flag when the deer is startled. This hair accepts dyes well and is sold in many colors, sizes, and lengths. It does not spin or flare like deer body hair and is much longer, softer, and more flexible.

Traditionally, black thread was used to tie bucktails because it produced a black head under clear varnish or lacquer. White thread, however, stands out far better against the hook and most body materials. Unless the color of the thread is an essential element of the fly, such as when it's used for ribbing, white thread will help you to tie a better fly

brown-and-white bucktail

simply because it's easier to see, and therefore easier to work with. So use it whenever it does not show or interfere with the pattern.

I tie almost all of my flies (except folded-hair ants) with white thread and then coat the heads with head cement in the color required for the fly. Using white thread not only reduces your thread inventory to flat waxed nylon and 8/0 UNI-Thread, it also reduces expenses.

We will first tie some flies using deer hair, starting with a simple, undyed brown and white bucktail. Then we will move on to flies whose wings are made with squirrel hair, and finish with the Black King, which calls for black bucktail.

# Brown-and-White Bucktail

ALTHOUGH A BROADER RANGE OF HOOK SIZES is listed in the materials below, the most useful hooks for the Brown-and-White Bucktail are Nos. 6–10. Also, while the recipe calls for the tail and throat to be made from a red feather slip (see materials), you can use a bunch of red calftail as an alternative in each case. (I'll say more about using hair in a minute.) Note that, if you choose to use the recommended feather for the tail, you must strip off the soft section at the base, which is too flimsy for a tail.

When starting the body, the medium-width tinsel has the advantage of an easier and often neater first turn than the large, but it requires more turns to cover the same space. If you have a problem making the first turn because of the tinsel's width, you can cut a taper or "tongue" in the first inch of the tinsel, which will start the turns off in fine shape. This technique was necessary in the early half of the twentieth century, when everyone used metal tinsel to tie flies. Metal tinsel can also—to our dismay—cut fine silk thread easily, so we strongly recommend using Mylar when a pattern calls for a flat tinsel. Remember to wrap the same color tinsel when creating both the body and rib (i.e., use silver on silver or gold on gold).

A hair throat is more durable and thicker than a feather throat. A hair throat that is prepared like a hair wing, as described in Step 5 on page 49, is especially useful on Nos. 2–6 flies, which often have matching hair tails. Hair tails can be made in the same fashion, but on small flies the extra bulk where the tail meets the body does not create a good imitation of the minnow shape that this type of fly should ideally have; for the fly to be most successful, you must employ special tapering cuts and tightly bind the butts to make the desired joint between the tail and body.

When selecting hair for the wing, bear in mind that the hair of the brown portion of the bucktail tends to be shorter than the white hair. Be sure to check the length of the brown hair to ensure that it will be long enough for the particular fly you are tying.

*Brown-and-White Bucktail*

| | |
|---|---|
| **HOOK** | *Mustad #9575, Nos. 2–10* |
| **THREAD** | *White waxed, flat nylon* |
| **TAIL** | *Red feather slip from duck or turkey wing or tail feather, or red calftail* |
| **BODY** | *Silver or gold flat Mylar tinsel, medium or large* |
| **RIB** | *Silver or gold oval tinsel, medium or large* |
| **THROAT** | *Red feather slip from duck or turkey wing or tail feather, or red calftail* |
| **WING** | *Natural brown-over-white bucktail* |
| **HEAD** | *Black head cement* |

1.  Place the hook in the vise, attach the thread, and wrap a nonslip base for the tail.

2.  To prepare the tail, strip off the soft section at the base of the wide side of the feather. With the point of your scissors or a bodkin, measure a strip about ³⁄₁₆ inch wide and cut it off close to the shaft. Place the strip on top of the hook shank so that at least ⅜ inch of the tip of the thin end extends behind the hook bend and the thicker butts point toward the eye. Use the soft loop technique to tie in the tail, and then check its length and position. Let the bobbin hang.

3.  Place one end of a 10-inch length of flat tinsel on the near side of the hook shank about ³⁄₁₆ inch from the eye and allow the remainder to hang at the rear. With the bobbin in hand, tie in the tinsel with a couple of turns of thread. Next, tie in a 6- to 12-inch length of oval tinsel so its end is about ³⁄₁₆ inch from the eye. (More than 12 inches of oval

**brown-and-white bucktail**

tinsel is hard to manage but 6 to 12 inches can rib several flies depending on their length.) To form a smooth base for the body, wind the thread—without gaps or overlaps—up the shank to the end of the oval tinsel, and let the bobbin hang.

4. Starting tight against the tail, wind the flat tinsel carefully up the hook shank in butting turns, leaving no gaps and without overlapping turns. Tie off the body with several turns of thread. Cut off the surplus tinsel while the bobbin hangs.

5. Starting at the tail, spiral the oval tinsel up the body to form the rib, leaving a space equal to two or three times the width of the oval tinsel between each turn, until you reach the end of the body. Tie off the rib with a couple of turns of thread, cut off the surplus tinsel, and bind down the ends of both tinsels. Then let the bobbin hang. (Go to the step below that is specific to the throat material you are using.)

6. If you're making a feather throat, place the thicker end of a ⅜-inch feather slip beneath and parallel to the hook shank. Use the soft loop method to tie it in where the thread is hanging. Trim off the surplus butts and bind down the cut end, then let the thread hang. Trim the throat so it extends about ½ inch for No. 10 hooks (and proportionately longer for larger flies). Then go to Step 8.

7. If you're making a red calftail throat, cut a bunch of hair that's about ³⁄₁₆ inch thick and 1 inch long from the hide. Prepare it as you would if making a hair

wing (see Step 5 on page 49). Use the soft loop method to tie in the throat where the thread is hanging. Trim the excess butts on a taper and bind down the cut end of the throat in the usual manner. Trim the throat so it extends about ½ inch for No. 10 hooks (and proportionately longer for larger flies).

8. From a clean, natural brown and white bucktail with brown hair about ¾ inch longer than the hook shank, select a bunch of brown hair that's about twice the thickness of a common kitchen match for No.10 hooks and proportionately larger for bigger hooks. Holding the tips together tightly, cut the bunch next to the hide, even the tips, and measure it for a length of one finger's width beyond the hook bend or about ³⁄₁₆ inch longer than the tail. Prepare the wing as directed in Step 5 on page 49.

9. Select and cut off a bunch of white deer tail the same size or slightly thicker than the brown bunch, and prepare it the same way.

10. When both bunches of hair are tacky, carefully place the brown on top of the white and position the unit on the top of the hook shank with butts over the eye. Tie it in using the soft loop method, then check the position and proportions of the wing, making adjustments as needed. Cut off the surplus gluey butts, tapering them toward the eye, using the angle of the hook eye as a guide.

11. Firmly bind down the butts and make a neat head with more turns of the thread. If you plan to add eyes, build

the head up with more thread. Finish the head and paint on the eyes.

## Variations

For the Black-and-White Bucktail, substitute black (dyed) bucktail for the brown bucktail in the foregoing pattern and tie the fly the same way. You can also change from silver to gold flat and oval tinsel, which make an equally useful gold-bodied Black- or Brown-and-White Bucktail. I have caught many fish with all of these fly variations!

*Black-and-White Bucktail*

## Black-and-White Shortie

THIS SMALL, SHORT VERSION OF THE BLACK-and-White Bucktail represents small fry rather than the usual bait-size minnow (see also the Brown-and-White variation below, which is a smaller version of the Brown-and-White Bucktail). Shorties are readily taken by panfish and trout, and are a useful addition to the usual minnow-size bucktails.

The bicolor wing is two-thirds white and one-third black. The white hair you select for the wing should be short and *fine*. Although the use of two bunches of hair might suggest bulk, keep the wing thin to achieve better success with the fly (see Wings on page 58 of the Basic Skills chapter for a tip on how to test a hair wing's thickness).

You can use white bucktail for the wing, but since you will use only 1 to 1½ inches of the tips, a considerable length of hair—which runs 2 to 4 inches long—will be wasted. Deer body hair carefully selected

from the rear of the body will be much finer than some bucktail and there won't be as much waste. Kid goat and calf body hair are effective substitute materials for this wing, and calftail can be used as a last resort.

| | |
|---|---|
| **HOOK** | *Mustad #9672, No. 12 3XL* |
| **THREAD** | *White flat waxed nylon* |
| **TAIL** | *Red feather slip* |
| **BODY** | *Silver flat Mylar tinsel* |
| **RIB** | *Silver oval Mylar tinsel* |
| **WING** | *Top—black (dyed) bucktail or substitute; bottom—white deer body (belly) hair or substitute* |
| **THROAT** | *Red feather slip* |
| **HEAD** | *Black head cement; large painted eyes or plastic eye shoulders* |

*Black-and-White Shortie*

*Black-and-White Shortie (another example)*

1.  Place the hook in the vise, attach the thread, and wrap a nonslip base for the body.

2.  Place the end of an 8- to 12-inch length of flat tinsel on top of the hook shank ³⁄₁₆ inch from the eye and allow the length to fall behind the hook bend. Tie it in place with a couple of turns of thread, and let the bobbin hang. Tie in an 8- to 12-inch length of oval tinsel the same way, on top of the flat tinsel, and continue wrapping the thread forward in butting turns to ³⁄₁₆ inch behind the eye. Let the bobbin hang.

3.  Wrap the flat tinsel in butting turns up the shank, binding down the tinsel to where the bobbin hangs. Fasten the body there with a couple turns of thread, and let the bobbin hang.

4.  Spiral the oval tinsel up the shank, allowing a space twice the width of the oval tinsel between each turn. Fasten the rib in place with a couple of firm turns of thread, and let the bobbin hang.

5.  From a hide, cut off a bunch of white deer body hair that's about the thickness of a kitchen match and ½ inch longer than the distance from the eye to the hook bend. Prepare the bottom portion of the hair wing as directed in Step 5 on page 49. Repeat the process for a bunch of black bucktail, except cut a bunch that's about half the thickness of the white bunch.

6.  When the wing sections are tacky but not solid, place the black bundle on top of the larger white bundle, even the tips, and place the unit on top of the hook shank with the butts over the eye. Fasten them there with a soft loop and a couple of firm turns of thread, and let the bobbin hang. Trim off the excess butts, using the slant of the hook eye as a guide.

7.  Bind down the cut ends of the butts with firm turns of thread, form a large head to accommodate the painted eyes, whip finish, and complete the fly.

## Variations

For the Brown-and-White Shortie, substitute brown bucktail for the black (dyed) bucktail in the foregoing pattern. The ratio of hair color in the wing, however, is a bit more flexible for this version of the fly: one-half to two-thirds white deer body hair to one-half to one-third brown bucktail. The fly itself is tied the same way as the Black-and-White Shortie. For either version you can substitute gold flat and oval tinsel for the silver.

*Brown-and-White Shortie*

# Gray Squirrel Silver

ALTHOUGH SILVER FLAT MYLAR TINSEL IS listed as the body material for Gray Squirrel Silver, Mylar Christmas tree icicles work just as well and may even be cheaper than your usual tinsel. If you decide to add painted eyes, white eyes with black pupils is a popular scheme.

| | |
|---|---|
| **HOOK** | *Mustad #9575, Nos. 6–10* |
| **THREAD** | *White flat waxed nylon* |
| **TAIL** | *Red (dyed) wing feather strip from turkey, duck, or goose* |
| **BODY** | *Silver flat Mylar tinsel* |
| **RIB** | *Silver oval tinsel, medium or large* |
| **THROAT** | *Red (dyed) wing feather strip from turkey, duck, or goose* |
| **WING** | *Gray squirrel tail hair* |
| **HEAD** | *Black head cement; painted eyes* |

1. Place the hook in the vise, attach the thread, and wrap a nonslip base for the tail.

2. Remove the soft lower part of the broad side of a red feather, then measure and cut off a ³⁄₁₆-inch-wide strip of firm feather close to the shaft. Place the strip on top of the hook shank where the bobbin hangs so the thin end extends ½ inch beyond the hook bend and the butts point toward they eye. Use the soft loop technique to tie in the tail, and let the bobbin hang. Cut the surplus butts in a long taper.

3. At the base of the tail, tie in an 8- to 12-inch length of flat tinsel placed so that one end is ³⁄₁₆ inch from the hook eye. Tie in a 6- to 12-inch length of oval tinsel the same way. Use a material clip to hold the lengths of tinsel out of the way while binding the ends to the shank with thread.

gray squirrel silver

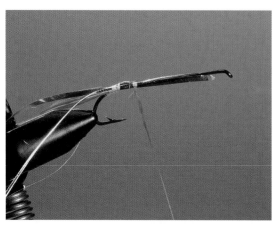

*Gray Squirrel Silver (1). Tying in the tail.*

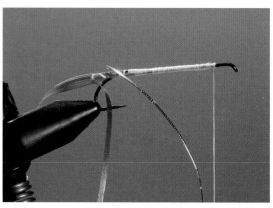

*Gray Squirrel Silver (2). Binding the ends to the shank with thread.*

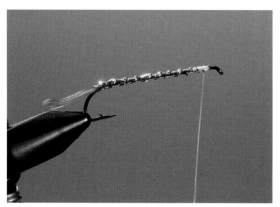

*Gray Squirrel Silver (3). Here the tinsel has been spiraled along the shank.*

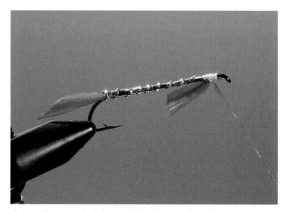

*Gray Squirrel Silver (4). Tying the throat feather in place.*

*Gray Squirrel Silver (5). Tying in the squirrel tail hair wing.*

*Gray Squirrel Silver (6). Completed fly.*

4. Starting at the base of the tail, wrap the flat tinsel in butting turns to where the bobbin hangs. Tie off the body, cut off the excess flat tinsel, and let the bobbin hang. Then spiral the oval ribbing tinsel over the body to its front end, allowing a space twice the width of the oval tinsel between every turn. Tie off the rib, cut off the excess oval tinsel, and let the bobbin hang.

5. Cut another ³⁄₁₆-inch-wide slip of red feather and place it under the hook so the thicker butts are just short of the eye. Tie the throat in place using the soft loop technique. Cut off the surplus butts, tapering toward the eye, and bind down the cut ends. Return the thread to ³⁄₁₆ inch from the eye and let the bobbin hang. Trim the throat to about ½ inch.

6. Select a ³⁄₁₆-inch-thick bunch of gray squirrel tail that's about ½ inch longer than the distance from the tip of the tail to the hook eye. Cut the hair off close to the hide. Prepare the wing as directed in Step 5 (Hair Wing) on page 49. Place the wing on top of the hook shank so the thin tips extend beyond the tail and the tacky end is positioned over the head area. Using the soft loop technique, tie in the wing. Let the bobbin hang while you trim the surplus butts on a slant, using the angle of the down eye as a guide.

7. Bind down the cut ends and form a neat head with thread. If you plan to add painted eyes, make a larger head. Finish the fly in the usual manner, referring to Step 8 on page 55 as needed for eye-painting instruction.

## Variations

The HFFA Squirrel Tail and Erskine Squirrel Tail are tied in the same manner as the Gray Squirrel Silver, with the following differences.

- The HFFA Squirrel Tail body is made with scarlet yarn and the Erskine Squirrel Tail body is made with white yarn.
- Both flies are made with medium embossed gold tinsel.
- The bodies and ribs of each are tied in the same fashion as the yarn body and tinsel ribbing of the Black King (see page 131).

## Fox Squirrel Gold

RUNNING BOTH TINSELS THE LENGTH OF THE Fox Squirrel Gold body and tapering the tail butts assures a smooth underbody not attainable otherwise. For the wing of this fly, be sure to choose fox squirrel tail hair that's well marked with dark bars.

*Fox Squirrel Gold*

| | |
|---|---|
| **HOOK** | *Mustad #9575, No. 10* |
| **THREAD** | *White flat waxed nylon* |
| **TAIL** | *Yellow turkey, goose, or duck wing or tail feather slip* |
| **BODY** | *Gold flat Mylar tinsel, medium or wide* |
| **RIB** | *Gold oval tinsel, medium or large* |
| **THROAT** | *Yellow turkey, goose, or duck wing or tail feather slip* |
| **WING** | *Fox squirrel tail hair* |
| **HEAD** | *Black head cement; painted eyes optional* |

1. Place the hook in the vise, attach the thread, and wrap a nonslip base for the tail.
2. From the bottom of the wide side of the yellow feather, strip off at least ¾ inch of short, soft material, as it is not suitable for tails. Measure a ³⁄₁₆-inch-wide section at the bottom of the wide side, and cut it off next to the shaft. Place the tail slip on top of the hook shank so the tip extends a finger's width past the hook bend, and tie it in place with a couple of firm turns of thread. Check its length and position on the shank, and let the bobbin hang. Cut the butts on a long taper and bind down the cut ends with firm close turns of thread. Then return the thread to just ahead of the original tie-in point and let the bobbin hang.
3. Place one end of an 8- to 12-inch length of flat tinsel on top of the shank, ³⁄₁₆ inch behind the hook eye. Tie it in place using the soft loop technique and let the bobbin hang. Repeat the process with an 8- to 12-inch length of oval tinsel. Then carefully wrap the thread over the ends of both tinsels in firm, close, even turns—without gaps or overlaps—to ³⁄₁₆ inch from the eye. Let the bobbin hang.

4. Wrap the flat tinsel firmly, by hand or with hackle pliers, butting every turn to where the bobbin hangs. Tie off the body with two or three turns of thread, and let the bobbin hang while you cut off the surplus flat tinsel.

5. Spiral the oval tinsel over the body to where the bobbin hangs, allowing a space twice the width of the tinsel between each turn. Tie off the oval tinsel with a couple of turns of thread and let the bobbin hang while cutting off the excess oval tinsel.

6. For the throat, cut another ³⁄₁₆-inch-wide section from the base of the wide side of the yellow feather. Hold the slip on edge under the hook shank, below the centerline of the shank and with the butts at the hook eye. Use the soft loop technique to tie it in, check that it is centered and in the proper location, and let the bobbin hang while you cut the butts in a taper at the eye. Trim the throat, from the tip of the feather, to a ½- to ¾-inch length.

7. Cut off about ½ inch of the short hairs at the base of the fox squirrel tail, as they are not long enough for a wing. From one side of the tail, select a bunch that's about as thick as a common kitchen match and cut it off close to the hide. The hair should be at least a finger's width longer than the hook shank. Prepare the wing as directed in Step 5 on page 49.

8. Place the wing on top of the hook shank so the tips extend a finger's width beyond the bend. Tie it in using the soft loop technique, and let the bobbin hang. Trim the butts using the angle of the down eye as a guide.

9. Bind down the cut ends and form a small, neat head with thread. If you plan to add painted eyes, make a larger head. Finish the fly in the usual manner, referring to Step 8 on page 55 as needed for eye-painting instruction.

## Black King

FISH CANNOT BE EXPECTED TO BITE A LURE they cannot see, but they can see the Black King and other black flies, even on a dark, moonless night. Black flies are therefore an important part of your fly-fishing gear, whether they are used on or below the water's surface. The Black King is especially useful on dull or overcast days when its dark silhouette is easily visible against even the darkest sky. Any visible light is reflected by the gold tinsel, while the red tail and throat —representing the blood of a wounded minnow—are very attractive.

When gathering your materials, select 2-ply yarn for No.10 hooks and heavier yarn for larger hook sizes (yarn is required for the body).

fox squirrel gold | black king

**black king**

***Black King (1).*** *Fasten the red calftail tail to the shank, then add black yarn and tinsel.*

***Black King (2).*** *Tying in the fly's throat.*

***Black King (3).*** *Binding the wing and throat in place.*

***Black King (4).*** *Completed fly.*

| | |
|---|---|
| **HOOK** | *Mustad #9575, Nos. 2–10* |
| **THREAD** | *White flat waxed nylon* |
| **TAIL** | *Red calftail* |
| **BODY** | *Black yarn* |
| **RIB** | *Gold embossed tinsel, medium* |
| **THROAT** | *Red calftail* |
| **WING** | *Black bucktail* |
| **HEAD** | *Black head cement; painted eyes optional* |

1. Place the hook in the vise, attach the thread, and wrap a nonslip base for the tail.

2. Select a small bunch of red calftail that's as thick as a kitchen match and cut it off close to the hide. Even the tips and then, holding the tips firmly, remove short hairs and underfur. Place the bundle of hair on top of the hook shank with the tips extending a finger's width beyond the bend of the hook. Using the soft loop technique, fasten the tail in place, and let the bobbin hang.

3. Hold an 8- to 10-inch length of yarn against the bottom or near side of the hook so that one end is about ³⁄₁₆ inch behind the hook eye and its length falls below or behind the hook. (You can also place the length in a spring clip or other material holder, out of the way, until it's needed.) Tie in the yarn with a couple of firm turns of thread, and let the bobbin hang.

4. Repeat the process with tinsel of a similar length. Then wrap the thread in even, butting turns up the hook shank, binding down the short ends of both yarn and tinsel, to about ³⁄₁₆ inch from the eye. Let the bobbin hang.

5. To form the body, wind the yarn in close, firm, even turns to where the bobbin hangs and tie it down with a couple of tight turns of the thread. Let the bobbin hang while you cut off the excess yarn.

6. Make two or three turns of tinsel around the shank to fill in the space between the tail and the body. Then spiral the tinsel up the body to form the rib, leaving about twice the width of the tinsel between each turn. Tie off the rib with a couple of turns of thread, and let the bobbin hang while you cut off the excess tinsel.

7. Select and cut off a bunch of red calf-tail that's about the same size and length as the fly's tail. Even the tips and clean out short hairs as before. Place this bunch under the hook at the front end of the body so the butts point toward the eye and the tips are at least a finger's width beyond where the bobbin hangs. Tie the throat in place using the soft loop technique, and let the bobbin hang. In preparation for the head, trim off the excess butts on a taper to the eye.

8. Select and cut a bunch of bucktail that's about ¼ inch longer than the distance from the end of the fly's tail to the hook eye and about ³⁄₁₆ inch thick. Prepare the wing as directed in Step 5 on page 49.

9. Place the wing, butts toward the eye, on top of the body so the thin tips extend about a finger's width beyond the hook bend. Use the soft loop technique to bind the wing in place. Trim the butts so they taper forward, using the angle of the eye as a guide.

10. Bind down the throat and wing butts, and form a neat head with the thread. If you plan to add eyes, build the head up with more thread. Finish the head and paint on the eyes.

**black king**

# RUBEN CROSS–STYLE BUCKTAILS

RUBEN CROSS WAS A NOTED CATSKILL FLY-tier of the 1920s and 1930s who helped lay the foundation for the genetic dry-fly hackle industry. He bred and raised his own chickens because he was unable to otherwise secure suitable feathers for tying his beautiful flies.

Cross's bucktails were designed to closely resemble the shape of minnows, and had a dark wing of bucktail above the body and a lighter-colored bucktail—usually white or yellow—tied below the body to represent the minnow's belly. In the water, the winglike back and belly pulled together, meeting at the rear of the fly to form a better shape than the conventional over-body style wing. Cross's style was accepted in his day, but did not achieve marked popularity. These flies take a bit more effort to tie, but they've worked well for me for many years on Mustad #9575 or #3665A, Nos. 6–10 hooks and No. 2 for trolling.

## Beaverkill

FOR THE BODY, USE 2-PLY YARN ON NO. 10 hooks and 4-ply yarn on larger hooks. If the ribbing tinsel gets in the way of the yarn while you're working you can either weight the end with hackle pliers or a clothespin or use a material clip on the barrel of the vise to hold it out of the way.

| | |
|---|---|
| **HOOKS** | *Mustad #9575, Nos. 2–10* |
| **THREAD** | *White flat waxed nylon* |
| **TAIL** | *None* |
| **BODY** | *White yarn, 2- or 4-ply* |
| **RIB** | *Silver flat Mylar tinsel, medium* |
| **BACK** | *Black (dyed) bucktail* |
| **BELLY** | *White bucktail* |
| **HEAD** | *Black head cement* |

1. Place the hook in the vise, attach the thread, and wrap a nonslip base for the body.

2. Place one end of an 8- to 12-inch length of yarn on top of the hook shank about 3/16 inch behind the eye, bind it in place with a couple of firm turns of thread, and let the bobbin hang. Place one end of an 8- to 12-inch length of tinsel on top of the end of the yarn and bind it down with close, tight turns of thread over both the yarn and tinsel. Continue wrapping the thread forward to 3/16 inch from the eye, then let the bobbin hang.

3. Wind the yarn in close, tight turns without gaps or overlaps up the hook shank to where the bobbin hangs. Tie off the body, let the bobbin hang, and hold the yarn above the shank as you cut off the excess to avoid cutting the thread.

4. Spiral the tinsel rib up the body to where the bobbin hangs, allowing a space twice the width of the tinsel between each turn. Tie off the rib, cut off the excess tinsel, return the thread to ³⁄₁₆ inch from the eye, and let the bobbin hang.

5. For the back, select a bunch of black bucktail at least ¾ inch longer than the hook shank and about as thick as a common kitchen match and cut it off close to the hide. Prepare it the way you would a hair wing, as directed in Step 5 on page 49. Select and prepare a similar-size bunch of white bucktail for the belly.

6. Place the black bundle on top of the body of the fly with the tips extending about a finger's width beyond the hook bend. Use the soft loop technique to tie it in and return the thread to ³⁄₁₆ inch from the eye.

7. Place the white bundle under the body so the tips align with those of the back. Tie it in place using the soft loop technique, and again let the bobbin hang.

8. Trim the excess butts in a taper, using the angle of the hook eye as a guide, and bind them down to form a neat head. Finish the fly in the usual manner.

## Variations

The materials required for the variations are basically the same as those listed above unless otherwise indicated for body, rib, back, and belly. All are tied the same way as Beaverkill.

*Beaverkill (1). Spiraling the tinsel over the yarn.*

*Beaverkill (2). Tying in the winglike back and the belly.*

*Beaverkill (3). Completed fly.*

beaverkill

- Ken Lockwood: Use scarlet yarn (2- or 4-ply) for the body and medium gold embossed metal tinsel for the rib.
- Jack Schwinn: Use orange yarn (2- or 4-ply) for the body; medium gold embossed metal tinsel for the rib; natural brown bucktail for the back; and yellow (dyed) bucktail for the belly.
- Ray Arden: Use scarlet yarn (2- or 4-ply) for the body; flat gold Mylar tinsel for the rib; and brown bucktail for the back. Make sure the brown bucktail isn't too dark; it should contrast with the few black hairs that are used as a stripe under the lower edge of the back.
- Catskill: Use red yarn (2- or 4-ply) for the body; flat gold Mylar tinsel for the rib (medium for No. 10 hooks, large for No. 2 hooks); and brown bucktail for the back.

**Ken Lockwood**

**Jack Schwinn**

**Ray Arden**

**Catskill**

# TANDEM HOOK FLIES

TANDEM HOOK FLIES REPRESENT A STYLE OF tying rather than a specific pattern, and are essentially an extension of whatever bucktail or streamer fly pattern you choose. They are large, bulky flies intended for taking large fish with heavy rods and are tied on lines that trail behind the boat or canoe. These flies have too much wind resistance to cast with lighter rods. Averaging 6 inches in length and having a front or main hook with a 2- to 2½-inch shank, there is a lot of wing that extends beyond the bend of the front hook. As a result, when the attacking fish first strikes, it will often get only a mouthful of wing from the main hook as it tugs hard on your line. However, the tandem hook located near the tip of the wing is what usually catches in the fish's mouth, along with some hair, even when the fish hits only the rear section of the long wing.

There are, of course, problems with designing and attaching the second hook on such a fly. Like the saltwater bluefish, pickerel, pike, and muskies are all notorious for their ability to shred flies and cut off leaders with their sharp teeth. If you intend to catch and land such fish, use wire connections like Sevenstrand wire—either plain or nylon-covered—instead of the 30 lb. hard nylon leader material that's usually recommended for trout and bass flies. The method of attaching the two hooks is the same in any case, so we will use the cheaper and readily available 30 lb. hard nylon leader for the following exercise.

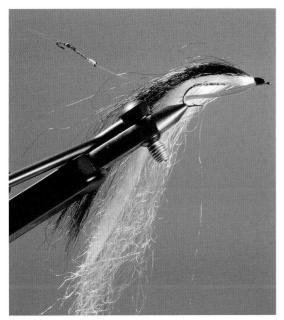 

*Two examples of tandem hook flies: **Black-and-White Bucktail** (left) and **Mickey Finn** (right).*

# Fish Hair Tandem Hook Fly

WHEN TYING THIS FLY WE START WITH THE rear (trailer) hook. The rear hook should be short shanked or standard length with a turned-down eye. It's important to have the trailer fly on its back when tying it to the main hook, and also well to the rear, so there is sure to be a hook near the end of the wing to catch and hold fish that make a short strike.

Since the tandem hook flies are essentially elongations of a particular pattern, I have not specified or detailed the steps in making the front (main) fly body. Choose a bucktail or streamer pattern that you like for the main fly, noting that for these instructions we will use 6-inch fish hair to make long wings, as there are few feathers that are long enough to be useful for this purpose. Flies with throats and tails representing blood are useful main flies, and the turned-up trailer hook can be easily concealed in the hair wing.

## TRAILER FLY

| | |
|---|---|
| **HOOK** | *Two or three sizes smaller than the front hook (see below), with a standard length shank and turned-down eye* |
| **THREAD** | *White flat waxed nylon* |
| **TAIL** | *Red feather section, wool, yarn, or calftail* |
| **LEADER** | *30 lb. hard nylon* |
| **BODY** | *Gold or silver flat Mylar tinsel* |
| **RIB** | *Gold or silver oval tinsel* |
| **WING** | *None* |
| **HEAD** | *Durable nail polish* |

1. Place the hook in the vise, attach the thread, and wrap a nonslip base for the tail.
2. Tie on a substantial tail that represents blood from an injured minnow.
3. Thread one end of a 6- to 8-inch length of leader through the hook eye from the top and push it back so it touches the hook bend underneath the shank. Bind it in place with the hanging thread.
4. Tie in the body and rib tinsels. Then wind the thread forward in butting turns, binding down the ends of the leader material and the two tinsels, to ⅛ inch from the eye. Let the bobbin hang.
5. Wind the flat tinsel in butting turns to the hanging thread. Tie off the body and cut off the surplus tinsel.
6. Spiral the oval tinsel up the body to the hanging thread, allowing a space about twice the width of the oval tinsel between each turn. Tie off the rib and cut off the surplus tinsel.
7. Whip finish the area behind the hook eye. Cut the thread and coat the whip-finish area with clear durable nail polish to complete the head of the trailer fly. Then remove the fly from the vise.

## MAIN FLY

**FRONT HOOK**

*Mustad #9575, Nos. 1/0–2*

| | |
|---|---|
| **THREAD** | *Your choice* |
| **TAIL** | *Your choice* |
| **BODY** | *Your choice* |
| **RIB** | *Your choice* |
| **THROAT** | *Your choice* |
| **WING** | *Fish hair* |
| **HEAD** | *Black head cement* |

8. Place the front hook in the vise and attach the thread in the usual manner. Then let the bobbin hang.

9. Pick up the trailer fly and place its leader on top of the main hook shank, with the trailer hook on its back and its bend about an inch ahead of where the rear end of the wing will fall. Measure this distance by holding the proposed wing up to the main hook with the trailer hook behind it. When you're satisfied with its placement, bind the trailer fly to the front hook from the bend to the eye in butting turns of thread. Cut off the surplus leader and wrap thread back to the bend of the hook to tie in the start of the main fly.

10. On the front hook, tie in your choice of tail—if desired—and body materials. Bind down the leader material, ends of body materials, and so on with butting turns of the thread to $\frac{3}{16}$ inch from the eye, and let the bobbin hang. Apply the throat in the usual manner. (For general tail, body, and throat tying instructions, see Steps 3, 4, and 7 on pages 44–45 and 53 or refer to the recipe that is specific to the fly you've chosen.)

11. Apply a dab of cement to one end of the fish hair wing and, when it is tacky, place the wing on top of the hook shank and bind it in place in the usual manner. Trim off excess butts.

12. Form a neat head and finish the fly in the usual manner.

**fish hair tandem hook fly**

# BLACK GHOST

ACCORDING TO GEORGE LEONARD HERTER in *Professional Fly Tying & Tackle Making* (1941), the original Black Ghost was invented by Carrie G. Stevens. It was a streamer fly, and she used the following materials to tie it.

**HOOK**     *Partridge, Carrie Stevens style*

**TAIL**     *Golden pheasant crest feather or 15–20 strands of dyed yellow polar bear hair*

**BODY**     *Black yarn or floss*

**RIBBING**     *Silver flat tinsel, medium*

**SHOULDER**

    *Jungle cock*

**THROAT**     *Although labeled throat, which is something under the body at the head of most flies, the dressing here calls for the golden pheasant crest or dyed yellow polar bear hair to be applied over the head of the fly and left as long as the wing. This style of treatment is a typical description of a salmon fly topping, rather than a throat.*

**WING**     *Four white webby neck or saddle hackle feathers*

The early Black Ghosts—tied at a time when tapered bodies of floss were the accepted standard for streamers, wet flies, and many dry-fly bodies—had a black floss body and a bunch of yellow hackle fibers for a tail and throat. Over the years, the popularity of floss for bodies has given way to yarn and a softer body without the sheen of floss. Yarn is easier to handle and apply, and is not split and frayed by fish teeth.

Flies have been put together in a certain order, which for most people has—over the years—assured the making of a beautiful and durable fly from the materials available at the time. A wise flytier follows accepted usage, understands its benefits and problems, and knowingly deviates only when he or she has found a better solution to a problem. Many years ago I experimented with replacing floss with yarn for streamer bodies and had great success. I also replaced the bundle of yellow hackle with a feather slip tail and throat to good effect, and have used my "improved" version of the Black Ghost for the past 60 years. I ask you to tie this fly my way now.

## Erskine Black Ghost

IN THE INSTRUCTIONS FOR THIS FLY, I HAVE included a number of wing material options and directions for tying them. When tied with a neck or saddle feather wing—the most common version of the fly—it's a streamer. You can also make a wing from a secondary or tail feather slip, create a marabou wing, or tie the fly Matuka style (see Black Ghost Matuka, page 149). In addition, you can tie a bucktail variation by employing a hair wing. All of these flies are tied with the same body, throat, and tail, except the bucktail version, whose tail and throat are also made of hair. I suggest you try each of the wing variations on individual flies because they each perform different actions in the water.

We will start with the whole-feather wing Black Ghost, and then move on to the other options. Make sure the neck or saddle hackle feathers you choose are wide and webby; they should not be dry-fly quality. Also, remember that adjacent feathers on a skin are usually the same size, which is a big advantage when making wings. Other hair and feather options often are not perfect substitutes for the original material, neither in color nor in action, but they are still both interesting and useful.

Other details to be aware of: Hook designation and sizes are the same for all the Black Ghosts. And two-ply yarn is the best body material for No. 10 hooks; otherwise the body can fill too much of the hook gap and interfere with holding the fish.

| | |
|---|---|
| **HOOK** | *Mustad #9575, Nos. 2–10* |
| **THREAD** | *White flat waxed nylon* |
| **TAIL** | *Yellow turkey, goose, or duck feather slip* |
| **BODY** | *Black yarn, 2- or 4-ply* |
| **RIB** | *Silver flat Mylar tinsel, medium* |
| **THROAT** | *Yellow turkey, goose, or duck feather slip* |
| **WING** | *White neck or saddle hackle feathers* |
| **HEAD** | *Black head cement; painted eyes optional* |

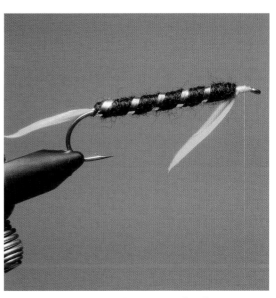

*Erskine Black Ghost (1). Winding the yarn body.*

*Erskine Black Ghost (2). Tying the throat.*

**erskine black ghost**

***Erskine Black Ghost (3). Completed fly.***

1. Place the hook in the vise, attach the thread, and wrap a nonslip base for the tail.

2. From the base of the wide side of the feather, remove about ¾ inch of the short, soft section, as it is not suitable for tails. Then measure a ³⁄₁₆-inch-wide slip at the base of that side and cut it off next to the shaft. Set the tail slip, on its edge, on top of the hook shank so the tip extends about a finger's width beyond the hook bend. Fasten it in place using the soft loop technique, and let the bobbin hang. Cut the excess butts in a long taper toward the eye.

3. Place one end of an 8- to 12-inch length of yarn on top of the hook shank ³⁄₁₆ inch behind the eye and tie it in with a couple of firm turns of thread. Repeat the process with an 8- to 12-inch length of tinsel, and continue wrapping the thread in close, even turns—binding down the

ends of the yarn and tinsel—to ³⁄₁₆ inch from the eye. Let the bobbin hang.

4. Wind the yarn body in close even turns, by hand or with hackle pliers, up the shank to where the bobbin hangs. Tie it off with a couple of firm turns of thread, and let the bobbin hang while you cut off the excess yarn. Hold the yarn above the shank while you trim it, to avoid cutting the thread.

5. Spiral the tinsel rib up the body, allowing a space of about twice the width of the tinsel between each turn. Tie it off with a couple of turns of thread, and let the bobbin hang again while you cut off the excess tinsel.

6. Cut another ³⁄₁₆-inch-wide slip from the base of the wide side of the feather for the throat. Place it on edge under the hook shank and along the centerline so the butts are at the eye. Employ the soft loop technique to tie it in, and let the bobbin hang. Cut the excess butts in a taper toward the eye, and cut off the tip of the feather so that the throat is about ½ to ¾ inch long.

7. Select four neck or saddle feathers from a package, cape, or saddle. They should be at least an inch longer than the hook shank to produce a proper wing. Put all four feathers together and match and even the tips. Then, holding the feathers firmly by the tips, cut to a stubble the fuzz and short barbs on both sides of the shaft bases until all four feathers are the same length and their tips extend a finger's width beyond the hook bend.

8. Holding the feathers together—this time near the bases—crimp the shafts by holding the feathers on edge, with the shaft tips beneath your thumbnail on a hard surface, and lifting the feathers up and forward as the crimp is created in the shafts. Crimps will raise the wing when you bind the shafts down with thread.

9. Separate the feathers and place two of them, one on top of the other, with their dull sides down. Do the same with the other pair, keeping the tips together. Place both pairs dull sides together so the bright sides form the outside of the wing and all tips align. Place the wing on edge on top of the hook shank so the tips extend a finger's width beyond the hook bend and the crimp is positioned over the hanging bobbin. Fasten it there, along the centerline of the shank, using the soft loop technique. Let the bobbin hang while you check the length and position of the wing. Then cut the excess shafts in a taper toward the eye.

10. Bind down the cut ends and form a neat head. Finish the head in the usual manner and add painted eyes if desired.

## If You Use a Feather Strip Wing

For this option the wing is made from white turkey secondary feather strips for smaller flies or tail feather strips for larger flies. Tail feathers with the shaft in the exact center are best, although they're more expensive than other tail feathers and secondary feathers. You can also use the same narrow or wide side of each feather of a matched pair of either secondary or tail feathers. To make each side of the wing, you would, for instance, cut one strip from the wide side of one feather and the other strip from the corresponding area of the matching feather. (This process would replace Steps 7–9 above. Go to the step that is specific to the type of wing material you have.)

1. If you're using *a matched pair of feathers,* strip off the short, fuzzy barbs at the base of one feather until you reach a usable section of barbs that's long enough for the wing. Repeat the process on the matching feather. Measure and cut off a ⅜- to ½-inch strip from the same side of each feather. Then go to Step 3.

2. If you're using *one feather with the shaft in the center,* cut or strip off the short, fuzzy barbs on both sides of the shaft until you have a section of usable barbs 1 inch longer than the hook shank. From each side of the shaft, measure and cut a strip that's about ⅜ to ½ inch wide.

***Erskine Black Ghost*** *with a feather strip wing*

erskine black ghost

3. Place the two feather strips on top of each other, dull sides together, so their tips align and the bright sides form the outside of the wing. Place the wing on top of the body along the centerline of the shank. The feather tips should extend a finger's width beyond the hook bend. Tie in the wing, using the soft loop technique. Trim the wing butts in a taper toward the hook eye.

## If You Use a Marabou Wing

For this option the wing is made from a large white turkey marabou feather. (This process would replace Steps 7–10 above.)

1. From one side of the base of the marabou feather, strip off the short barbs until you reach a section where they're about one inch longer than the

hook shank. Grasp and strip off a section that's about ¾ to 1 inch wide and bundle the barbs together so the ends are as even as possible.

2. Place the bundle along the top of the body so the tips extend a finger's width beyond the hook bend, and fasten it there using the soft loop technique.

3. Complete the fly in the usual manner.

## If You Use a Hair Tail, Throat, and Wing

For this version of the Erskine Black Ghost you will need yellow calftail for the tail and throat and white bucktail for the wing.

1. Place the hook in the vise, attach the thread, and wrap a nonslip base for the tail.

2. Select a bunch of yellow calftail about

*Erskine Black Ghost* with a marabou wing

³⁄₁₆ inch in diameter and ¾ to 1¼ inch in length and cut it off close to the hide. Even the tips and remove all short hairs and fuzz. Place the tail on top of the hook shank so the tips extend a finger's width beyond the hook bend, and fasten it with a couple of firm turns of thread. Let the bobbin hang while you trim the hair butts in a long taper toward the eye. Bind the butts down with firm, even turns of thread, and return the thread so the bobbin hangs over the hook barb.

3. Follow Steps 3–5 of the original Erskine Black Ghost recipe to tie the body and ribbing.

4. Select and prepare a bunch of yellow calftail hair for a throat, as directed in Step 2 of this fly option. Place the bunch under the hook so the tips extend about ½ to ¾ inch from where the bobbin hangs, and fasten it there using the soft loop technique. Trim the excess butts toward the eye and bind them down.

5. From the white part of a natural buck-tail, select and cut a bunch of hair about ³⁄₁₆ inch in diameter for No. 10 hooks and somewhat thicker for No. 2 hooks. The hair should be about 1 inch longer than the hook shank. Prepare the wing as instructed in Step 5 on page 49.

6. Place the wing along the top of the body so the tips extend a finger's width beyond the bend. Use the soft loop technique to tie it in.

7. Finish the fly in the usual manner.

*Hairwing Black Ghost (1).*

*Hairwing Black Ghost (2).*

*Hairwing Black Ghost (3). Completed fly.*

**erskine black ghost**

# MATUKAS

THE NAME *MATUKA* IDENTIFIES A STYLE OF tying rather than a pattern. Invented in New Zealand, this style of streamer solves the rather common problem in which wing tips wrap around the hook bend and cause the fly to lose its minnowlike shape and lifelike action. The solution is in how the Matuka wing—which is actually closer in appearance to a dorsal fin—and tail are tied. A general idea of the process follows, although details may vary slightly from recipe to recipe; see the individual recipes for specific measurements and tail/wing preparation instructions.

1. After the body of the fly is tied, create a tail/wing unit of four feathers. Hold the unit on its edge along the top of the hook, with the butt end of the unit at the eye.

2. Upset the fibers on the lower side of the shafts, between the hook bend and the butt end of the tail/wing unit. Remove the upset barbs of the four feathers for a distance that's equal to the length of the fly body. The barbs on the other side of the shafts will become the wing, or dorsal fin, while the full width of feather that remains at the tip of each will become the tail (the tail length should measure at least three-quarters of the body length).

3. Tightly fasten the shafts to the body, stripped sides against the body, from the base of the tail to the head of the fly. Spiral the wire, thread, yarn, or tinsel—which is tied in like ribbing

material—between sections of barbs along the top of the shaft.

The tail has considerable action and presence, and cannot get tangled in the hook bend. Together with the tail, the wing creates a very natural silhouette—which cannot be said of the classic streamer wing. A further advantage of the Matuka style is gained by using large bird body feathers and large, wide, webby hen hackle rather than narrow rooster saddle hackle for the wing/tail unit. The result is a totally different appearance and action from that of the usual streamer fly.

Body feathers from roosters, hens, or other birds produce tails that are often quite rounded but are effective because of their color. I highly recommend Whiting "Soft Hackle" with Chicaboo, which comes in several natural colors, and in dyed-over grizzly colors, which are very useful. (See Appendix 2 for sources of materials.) Sculpin imitations in barred olive or brown grizzly body feathers are popular where these baitfish are resident in local streams.

Conventional patterns can be converted to Matuka style by replacing the ribbing material with wire, fine tinsel, thread, or yarn, and using it to spirally fasten the tail/wing unit to the body. Tinsel bodies can take a rib made of the thinnest of oval or round tinsel—or wire of the same color—to fasten the tail/wing unit to the body. Obviously, a thin fastening material makes a better wing, but attachment is required throughout the entire length of the body, not just at each end (see

Steps 6 and 7 of the Black Matuka recipe).

On the other hand, if you also need the fastening material to serve as ribbing (i.e., shine or flash) for the body, you can use something a little heavier. For example, although gold or silver wire works great for fastening, it will hardly provide the shine that larger sizes of gold or silver oval tinsel can. Also, wire does not divide sections of the wing with each turn as successfully as the larger tinsel or yarn (which can be used for both the body material and as a wing fastener). However, if thin wire is all you have, you can solve this problem by making an opening—with a bodkin—just above the shaft at certain intervals for the wire turns. Or you can push the wire through the wing fibers, just above the shaft, with a minimum of disturbance to the wing.

In this section, we will first tie the Black Matuka with a black yarn body and black neck hackle wing. Next we will tie the Black Ghost Matuka, using oval tinsel to fasten down the wing. (For more information about Black Ghost flies, see page 140.) Thereafter, depending on the fly pattern you choose, you can apply hen or other large bird body feathers for wings.

## Black Matuka

HOOK NOS. 2–6 ARE MOST USEFUL FOR THE Black Matuka, and, although it's OK to use white flat waxed nylon thread for the tying thread, black is a better choice here. Note that you will also be using black flat waxed nylon thread for the "ribbing" material.

Yarn is the ideal body material for this fly. Colored thread, when applied in close

*Black Matuka*

spirals over a body of the same color, will not be very noticeable and will not ruffle the wing feathers as much as the heavier yarn that is often called for in recipes.

Be sure to choose four large, wide, webby neck hackles from the lower section of a dyed black Chinese or saltwater neck for the tail/wing unit. The length of the tail section will measure from two-thirds to a full hook shank. The wing section will be about as long as the tail. Attaching the unit to the hook at the bend and temporarily tying in the butts at the eye (Steps 6 and 7) will prevent the unit from waving in the wind while you finish binding it firmly to the body with the ribbing thread. If necessary, separate the wing fibers with a bodkin, which will allow the thread to pass through without binding down a lot of fibers. If you're careful when spiraling the ribbing thread, when finished, you will be able to smooth the separated fibers back, together, to form a solid dorsal fin (wing) rather than a series of spines. When completed, the Black Matuka's tail should be long enough to move a bit in the water.

**HOOK**     *Mustad #9575, Nos. 2–10*

**THREAD**   *Black flat waxed nylon*

**BODY**     *Black worsted yarn*

**TAIL/WING**

   *Black Chinese- or saltwater-neck hackles*

**RIB**      *Black flat waxed nylon*

**THROAT**   *None*

**HEAD**     *Black head cement*

1. Place the hook in the vise, attach the thread, and wrap a nonslip base for the body.

2. Place the end of a 6- to 8-inch length of the yarn on top of the hook shank ³⁄₁₆ inch behind the eye, allowing its length to fall beyond the hook bend, and tie it in. Then tie in a 6- to 8-inch length of ribbing thread and place its length in a material clip. Wrap the tying thread forward to ³⁄₁₆ inch from the eye, binding down the short end of the body yarn and ribbing thread as you go, and let the bobbin hang.

3. Wind the yarn body in butting turns up the hook shank to where the bobbin hangs. Fasten it there with a couple of firm wraps of tying thread, and let the bobbin hang while you cut off the excess yarn.

4. Choose four neck hackles for the tail/wing unit. Cradle one neck hackle in another so they align, and then do the same with the other two feathers. Place the two sets dull sides together so the tips align. The natural curve of the feathers should oppose each other like your hands when they are put together with the palms touching.

5. Holding the unit on top of the hook shank, so the feather tips align with the hook bend, measure about one shank length from the hook bend forward for the tail. Upset the barbs forward of that point on only one side of the feather shafts, all the way to the butt ends of the feathers. Strip off all the upset barbs of the four feathers.

6. Be sure the tips of all four feathers are still even and the wing barbs are properly aligned. Then place the unit on top of the hook shank so the tail is at or just beyond the hook bend and the stripped shafts are against the full length of the fly body. Attach the unit to the body in the following manner. With your hackle pliers securely clipped to the ribbing thread, make a complete turn of thread around the body, then let the pliers hang. With your fingers, carefully slide the next turn of thread between the barbs and down to the shaft, directly over the hanging ribbing thread. Make another turn in the same place and pull the thread tight. Let the thread hang, weighted with your hackle pliers.

7. Pull the butt ends of the feathers forward over the eye to straighten them along the body and temporarily fasten the feathers in that area by making a turn or two with the tying thread. Then let the bobbin hang.

8. Spiral the ribbing thread up the body, carefully sliding the thread down between sections of wing barbs. To properly secure the wing to the body, allow a space of ⅛ to ³⁄₁₆ inch between turns of thread. Continue to the end of the body, and let the ribbing thread hang, weighted with the hackle pliers. Bind down the ribbing thread with tying thread, then cut off the surplus feather shafts ⅛ inch behind the eye.

9. Bind down the stubs, first with the ribbing thread and then with the tying thread, with a couple of firm turns each. Cut off the surplus ribbing thread, and form a neat head.

## Black Ghost Matuka

WHEN TYING THE BLACK GHOST MATUKA, you can use either a slip of yellow dyed turkey flight or tail feather or a bunch of yellow calftail for the throat. When selecting feathers for the tail/wing unit, make sure they have good, usable sections that are at least 1¾ times the length of the hook shank (i.e., the distance from the bend to the eye of the hook). The extra length provides for the tail.

| | |
|---|---|
| **HOOK** | *Mustad #9575, Nos. 2–6* |
| **THREAD** | *White flat waxed nylon* |
| **BODY** | *Black worsted yarn* |
| **THROAT** | *Yellow dyed turkey flight or tail feather or yellow calftail* |
| **TAIL/WING** | *White rooster hackle, preferably Chinese or saltwater neck* |
| **RIB** | *Silver oval tinsel, medium* |
| **HEAD** | *Black head cement* |

*Black Ghost Matuka (1). Tying in the throat.*

1. Place the hook in the vise, attach the thread, and wrap a nonslip base for the body.

2. Tie in an 8-inch length of tinsel at the hook bend, and let the bobbin hang. Put one end of a 6- to 10-inch length of yarn on top of the hook shank about ³⁄₁₆ inch behind the eye and allow the other end to fall beyond the hook bend. Tie the yarn in place with the hanging thread, then continue wrapping the thread forward in reasonably close spirals, binding down the ends of the yarn and tinsel, to ³⁄₁₆ inch from the eye. Let the bobbin hang.

3. Wrap the yarn body in butting turns up the shank and tie it off ⅛ inch behind the eye. Let the bobbin hang while you cut off the surplus yarn. (Go to the step below that is specific to the throat material you are using.)

4. If you're making a *feather slip* throat, cut a ³⁄₁₆-inch-wide slip from the feather. Place it on edge under the hook shank and along its centerline so the butts are at the eye. Employ the soft loop technique to tie it in, and let the bobbin hang. Cut the excess butts in a taper toward the eye, and cut off the tip of the feather so that the throat is about ½ to ¾ inch long. Then go to Step 6.

5. If you're making a *calftail* throat, select a bunch of yellow calftail about ³⁄₁₆ inch in diameter and ¾ to 1¼ inch in length and cut it off close to the hide. Even the tips and remove all short hairs and fuzz. Place the bunch under

*Black Ghost Matuka (2). Completed fly.*

the hook so the tips extend about ½ to ¾ inch from where the bobbin hangs, and fasten it there using the soft loop technique. Trim the excess butts toward the eye and bind them down.

6. Select four neck hackle feathers and prepare them for the tail/wing unit as described in Steps 4 and 5 of Black Matuka (page 148). For this recipe, however, the tail length should measure three-quarters of the hook shank length.

7. Place the tail/wing unit along the top of the shank so the stripped shafts are against the length of the body and the tail extends behind the fly from the rear of the hook bend. Attach the unit to the hook with two tight turns of tinsel threaded between the fibers at the hook bend. Straighten the shafts along the body, then temporarily attach the feather butts to the shank with a turn or two of thread.

8. To fasten the unit to the shank, thread the tinsel rib between wing fibers, making tight turns not more than 3/16 inch apart to the eye. Cut off the surplus tinsel and feather butts.

9. Make a neat head and finish the fly in the usual manner.

## Ace of Spades

THE ACE OF SPADES IS A POPULAR ENGLISH lake/reservoir pattern from the 1970s. The original recipe called for a short coverage of brown mallard, but the fly is successful without this tribute to salmon-fly custom. We will omit this element and simplify the fly for your use.

For the rib, use fine tinsel on Nos. 6–10 hooks or medium for larger hooks. The size chenille you use for the body also depends on your hook size. Teasing the fibers off the end of the chenille will make tying it in easier and more secure.

This fly calls for two feathers—rather than the traditional four—for its tail/wing unit, so be sure they are as webby as possible. Otherwise the wing will not keep its dorsal fin shape under water. Also note that the prepared wing should fit exactly and tightly on the body, with no gap in the rear between the hook and the first fibers of the tail.

For the throat, you want a length of about ¾ inch for small flies and more for larger, longer flies.

*Ace of Spades (1). Chenille and tinsel bound in.*

**ace of spades**

| | |
|---|---|
| **HOOK** | *Mustad #9575, Nos. 2–10* |
| **THREAD** | *White flat waxed nylon* |
| **BODY** | *Black chenille, medium or heavy* |
| **TAIL/WING** | |
| | *Black hen feathers or large black neck hackle feathers* |
| **RIB** | *Silver oval tinsel, fine or medium* |
| **THROAT** | *Natural black-and-white Guinea fowl body feather* |
| **HEAD** | *Black head cement* |

1.  Place the hook in the vise, attach the thread, and wrap a nonslip base for the body.
2.  Tie in a 6- to 8-inch length of tinsel at the hook bend. Cut a 6- to 8-inch length of chenille and tease the fibers off about ⅜ inch of one end. Fasten that end to the shank next to the hanging tinsel, then continue winding the thread in butting turns to 3/16 inch from the eye. Bind down the ends of the tinsel and chenille as you go, and let the bobbin hang.
3.  Select a well marked, dark Guinea fowl feather having white dots and barbs that are ¾ to 1¼ inch long. Pull or cut off the soft and short fibers at the base of the feather until you reach those of the proper length. Remove a bunch of well-marked fibers that's about 3/16 inch in diameter. Even the tips and place the bundle beneath the hook shank so the butts are at the hook eye. Use the soft loop technique to tie in the throat. Trim off the surplus butts.

*Ace of Spades (2). Throat of Guinea fowl feathers has been added.*

*Ace of Spades (3). Completed fly.*

4. To form the body, wrap the length of the chenille in butting turns to the hanging thread. Tie it off, and cut off the surplus chenille.

5. Select a matched pair of feathers for the tail/wing unit. Place them dull sides together, align the tips, and, with the unit on its edge, measure a tail that's about two-thirds the length of the hook shank. Position the base of the tail at the hook bend and upset the fibers on the bottom side of the shafts only, from the base of the tail to the hook eye. (It's easiest to do this while holding the feathers against the hook.) Then carefully and firmly strip off the upset barbs.

6. Place the unit on top of the fly's body so the forward edge of the tail touches the rear of the hook bend.

7. Bind the tail/wing unit to the body with the tinsel. Measure a distance of about ³⁄₁₆ inch forward from your first turn of tinsel and open up another space between barbs for the next firm turn of tinsel. Continue the process in evenly spaced, firm turns to where the thread hangs. Tie off the tinsel rib and cut the surplus, then trim the feather butts about ⅛ inch from the eye.

8. Form a neat head and finish the fly in the usual manner.

Remember, the Matuka is a style of tying rather than a pattern. There is not enough space in this book to include more of the patterns that have been adapted to this style, so look for examples in catalogs or other books, and when you find them you will know how to tie them!

# STREAMER FLIES WITH CHEEKS

THE CLASSIC NORTHEASTERN STREAMER FLIES of the 1930s and 1940s had cheeks (also called shoulders) applied to the wing. The cheeks were made from the body feathers of various species of pheasant—then inexpensive, but now costly or altogether unobtainable—often with a jungle cock eye in the center. Flytiers used the Ripon's Silver Pheasant for the Gray Ghost, Reeves Pheasant for the Lady Ghost, and golden pheasant for the Golden Witch. As the years went by, the use of these patterns decreased in direct proportion to the increasing cost of their materials. The advantages of cheeks on a streamer, however, still remain.

Cheeks dress up a fly, keep the wing from collapsing immediately behind the eye, and give the fly the thickness needed in that area to imitate the shape of a minnow. Stabilizing the front end of a streamer wing allows the other end to move more rapidly and effectively in the current or when trolled behind a boat. For a small cost and to considerable advantage, the common ring-necked pheasant cock offers several feathers that can be used as cheeks on streamers. The "church window" feathers come to mind immediately, as do some bronze feathers with a dark spot on the center of the outer edge and blue-green feathers that can be used to imitate gill covers on the head of a small fish. If you don't have access to feathers from the previous hunting season, from either your own bounty or

a friend's, you can purchase them from a mail order supplier at a very reasonable price. If you go the mail order route, purchase a complete skin minus the tail.

Using any of the previously mentioned ring-necked pheasant body feathers as a cheek, you can make effective No. 2 trolling flies (and smaller flies for trout and bass) with the following materials: silver tinsel for the body, with an oval silver tinsel rib for extra shine; red feather or calftail for the tail and throat; and badger, cochy, or grizzly for the wing. Nos. 6–10 flies are easier to cast with a medium-weight fly rod than is the trolling fly. All should be tied on long-shank hooks such as a Mustad #9575 or #3665A. These flies have done well by me over the years in Maine, as well as in England and Scotland.

Some of the famous flytiers of the past glued the cheek onto the wing feathers before tying in the wing. This is a useful practice if you have difficulty fastening the pheasant feathers permanently in place on the fly. However, if you cut—rather than strip—the fluff from the shafts and take care to leave a stubble, the feathers will remain securely under the thread wraps for the life of your fly.

Two examples of flies with cheeks—one with a yarn body ribbed with tinsel and the other with a silver tinsel body (see Cochy [Furnace] Streamer in Variations, following the recipe)—will get you started.

# Badger Streamer

THESE CHEEKED FLIES WORK WELL FOR BASS, trout, and landlocked salmon in the Northeast and—when tied on No. 2 long-shank hooks—in Labrador. The wing calls for four equal-size, large badger neck hackles, which you can obtain from a neck, cape, or a package. They should be clean of fuzz and have good color. Tying in the wing at the crimp (see Step 8) and binding down the shaft butts raises the wing, at an angle, above the hook shank.

The cheeks will hold the wing together. You can obtain two matching "church window" feathers for the cheeks from a packet or whole ring-necked pheasant cock skin. The feathers growing next to each other assure a good match.

Be sure to make a large head on this fly to accommodate the eyes.

| | |
|---|---|
| **HOOK** | *Mustad #9575, Nos. 2–10* |
| **THREAD** | *White flat waxed nylon* |
| **TAIL** | *Red (dyed) turkey secondary, pointer wing, or tail feather* |
| **BODY** | *Scarlet yarn, 4-ply* |
| **RIB** | *Gold embossed tinsel, medium* |
| **THROAT** | *Red (dyed) turkey secondary, pointer wing, or tail feather* |
| **WING** | *Badger saltwater- or Chinese-neck hackle* |
| **CHEEKS** | *Ring-necked pheasant cock "church window" feather* |
| **HEAD** | *Black head cement; painted eyes* |

**badger streamer**

*Cochy Red-and-Gold Streamer. The loose (upper) feather can be pulled/stroked down to meet the lower part of the wing to better imitate a minnow.*

**badger streamer**

1. Place the hook in the vise, attach the thread, and wrap a nonslip base for the tail.

2. To prepare the tail, remove the lowest ¾ to 1 inch of short, soft feather from the wide side of the turkey feather. Then measure a ³⁄₁₆-inch section and cut it off next to the shaft. Place the slip on top of the hook shank so the tip extends a finger's width beyond the bend of the hook and the butts point toward the eye. Tie it down using the soft loop technique, then let the bobbin hang. Check the tail's length, make sure the slip is centered on the shank, and trim the butts in a long taper toward the eye.

3. Place the end of an 8- to 12-inch length of yarn on top of the hook shank ³⁄₁₆ inch behind the hook eye. Fasten it down with a couple of close, even, tight turns of thread. Then place one end of a 6- to 10-inch length of tinsel on top of the hook shank at least ¾ inch to the right (toward the eye) of the hanging thread. Allow its length to fall beyond the hook bend. Fasten it in place with butting turns of thread.

4. Carefully wrap the yarn in tight, butting turns up the shank to where the bobbin hangs. Tie off the body with a couple of tight turns of thread, and let the bobbin hang while cutting off the surplus yarn. Be careful not to cut the thread.

5. Spiral the tinsel rib up the body to where the bobbin hangs, allowing twice the width of the tinsel between each turn. Tie off the tinsel with a couple of turns of thread, and let the bobbin hang while you cut off the surplus tinsel.

6. Cut another ³⁄₁₆-inch slip from the feather for the throat. Place it under and parallel to the hook shank so the tip extends at least ¾ inch behind where the bobbin hangs. Tie it in place using the soft loop technique, and let the bobbin hang.

7. Cut to a stubble the soft down and fuzz found at the lower part of four neck hackle shafts. Match the feathers for size by placing the tips together. Measure their length: when placed on top of the hook shank, the tips should extend a finger's width beyond the hook bend, while the firm, bright feathers extend to where the bobbin hangs. To make one side of the wing, place one feather on top of a second one so the tips are together and the dull sides are both facing down, not together. Do the same with the other two feathers.

8. Put the two pairs of feathers dull sides together so the bright sides form the outside of the wing. Hold all four feathers near the shaft ends, place your thumbnail across all four shafts, and crimp the ends so they stand at a 30° to 45° angle to the main bodies of the feathers.

9. Place the unit on top of and along the centerline of the hook shank so the crimp is directly over where the bobbin hangs. Tie them in using the soft loop technique, and let the bobbin hang.

Check the wing for length and position, adjust if necessary, and cut off the surplus shafts at the eye.

10. Select two matching "church window" feathers for the cheeks. Put them dull sides together and, holding them by the tips, carefully cut to a stubble the down and short fluff from the base of the shafts. As you cut, make sure they remain equal in size as a matched pair. Place one of them, bright side out and with the stem over the eye, against the near side of the wing. Tie it there with the soft loop technique. Repeat the process on the other side with the second feather. Check the position and size of each, adjust if necessary, and let the bobbin hang while you cut off surplus shafts at the hook eye.

11. With the bobbin in hand, make tight, butting, close turns to bind down the stems and form a large, neat head. Finish the head in the usual manner, then apply white or yellow head cement for the eyes and add the black pupils.

## Variations

The materials required for the variations are basically the same as those listed above unless otherwise indicated. You would tie the flies just as instructed above with one exception: the Cochy Red-and-Gold Streamer head does not have painted eyes.

The neck from which you choose feathers for the wing of each variation does not

badger streamer

***Erskine Cochy Streamer Church Window.*** *The upper feather should be stroked down to cover the lower feathers, forming a neat minnow-shaped wing, which will be active in the water.*

badger streamer

*Erskine Cochy Red-and-Gold Streamer*

need to be of expensive dry-fly quality. A well-marked No. 3 neck with large, wide, soft hackle is ideal for both its action and price. Large, wide feathers from the lower end of a good dry-fly neck will also do very well, especially since there is otherwise very little use for these feathers because of their size.

   Cochy (Furnace) Streamer: Use medium or large gold or silver tinsel for the body

and rib (flat and oval, respectively); cochy (furnace) wet-fly grade or large, wide Chinese neck feathers for the wing; and dark purple/bronze ring-necked pheasant cock feather for the cheeks.

   Erskine Red-and-Gold Streamer: Use Nos. 2–6 hooks; a slip from red duck or turkey quill or tail for each of the tail and throat; cochy or furnace neck feathers for the wing; and only black head cement for the head.

# FOLDED-/BUNDLED-HAIR BODY FLIES

Hair body flies as a class are exceedingly durable, high floating, visible, and relatively easy-to-tie dry flies. There are two principal methods of construction: using either folded hair or spun hair. Folded-hair bodies include not only flies such as Hair Ants and Horner's Deer Hair, but also hair inchworms and Paradrakes, both of which use bundles of straight rather than folded hairs bound to the hook. In contrast, spun hair is tied on in bundles and spun around the hook, flaring into a fuzz ball, which is then trimmed to form mice, frogs, and light, high floating bodies on Irresistibles and Rat-Faced McDougals for trout and bass, and Bombers and Green Machines for salmon.

Flotation comes from the use of hollow hair in natural or dyed colors, of which hair taken from whitetail and mule deer are the most readily available. Some individuals are allergic to deer hair and should utilize elk hair instead. Other frequently used hair includes antelope and caribou, which can also be found in many dyed colors.

Red, green, and yellow should be dyed over white (or perhaps bleached) material in order to obtain clear, bright colors. Black can be dyed over any natural color. Rust and dark dun is often dyed over natural-colored hair to good effect. Dyed-over-white hair commands a premium price due to the scarcity of white hair on all these animals, but it is well worth paying for if you want true, bright colors, rather than dull, muddy ones.

Incidentally, caribou is a very buoyant hair. Natural white/cream colors are from the shoulder, and very good dun or gray shades cover most of the rest of the body. It is a rather soft hair, easily cut by fine thread pulled tight against a hook shank.

Coastal blacktail deer from the Pacific Coast have very fine body hair. It comes in light and dark natural shades and is also available dyed black or bleached to a ginger shade. It is especially useful for folded-hair small flies, hair wings on many regular dry-fly patterns, and Horner's Deer Hair. It can also be used for spun/clipped bodies. Be sure to specify the purpose for which it will be used, especially when ordering from a catalog. The more information you can give the suppliers, the better they can serve you. I have bought most of my materials by mail for the past 60 years with a minimum of problems. Some of the problems I have had were my fault for not making clear what I expected to use the material for.

## Peacock and Deer-Hair Bug

THE TAIL AND SHELL OF TAPP'S BUG ARE both made from one bunch of deer body hair. A portion of the head is also made from the same bunch, after a "base" head of thread is wrapped. Select a hide that has natural, gray/brown, fine-textured hair, with individual hairs about 1½ inches in length.

Also note that the tail is tied after the body has been formed, and you will whip finish both ends of the fly, not just the head. A conventional whip-finishing tool is not long enough to reach the rear of large flies, so you will have to tie this knot by hand.

**HOOK**    *Mustad #94831, Nos. 6–14*

**THREAD**  *White flat waxed nylon*

**BODY**    *Peacock herl*

**TAIL/SHELL/HEAD**

          *Natural deer body hair*

**WING**    *None*

1. Place the hook in the vise, attach the thread, and wrap a nonslip base for the body. Note that in wrapping the base, you need to leave room at the rear to tie in the tail and the shellback later.

2. Select four to six peacock herls for the body, bunch them, and even the tips, then cut off about a half inch of tip to get firm, strong herl to tie down. Place the bundle on top of the hook shank, with the trimmed end about ³⁄₁₆ inch from the hook eye and the rest beyond the hook bend. Fasten it in place with several firm turns of thread. Bind down the tied-in ends with butting turns of thread to ³⁄₁₆ inch from the eye, and let the bobbin hang.

3. Wind the bundle of herls in butting turns to the hanging thread. Tie it off

with a couple of firm turns of thread, and let the bobbin hang while you cut off the surplus herl.

4. Attach a second bobbin loaded with the same thread at the extreme rear of the body; you will now have a bobbin hanging at each end of the body.

5. From the deer hide, cut off a bunch about ³⁄₁₆ inch thick close to the hide. Holding it firmly by the tips, stroke or pull out the short hairs and any fuzz from the butt end. Even the tips and place the bunch on top of the hook shank with about ⅝ inch of the tips extending as a tail beyond the hook bend and with the butts extending over the hook eye. Fasten the tail in place using the soft loop technique, followed by several firm turns of thread, and let the bobbin hang.

6. Pull the hair together with even tension to create a shell that will smoothly and evenly cover the top of the body. Pull it over the body and down just behind the eye and fasten it there with thread from the bobbin that is hanging at that end, again using the soft loop technique. Add one or two extra turns of thread.

7. Bring the thread forward, ahead of the hair butts, and raise the butts to a vertical position. Hold them out of the way while you form a neat head, whip finish, and cut off the surplus thread. *Do not*, however, put on the head cement at this time.

8. With the bobbin that's positioned at the rear of the fly, make a tight, firm turn or two to tighten up any thread

*Peacock and Deer-Hair Bug (1). Winding the peacock herl.*

*Peacock and Deer-Hair Bug (2). Tail in place; shell being formed.*

*Peacock and Deer-Hair Bug (3). Fastening the end of the shell.*

*Peacock and Deer-Hair Bug (4). Completed fly.*

peacock and deer-hair bug

that might have loosened while the bobbin was hanging. The thread should be against the rear of the body, where you made the first tie-in turn for the tail. Complete a whip finish by hand, working toward the hook bend. Cut the surplus thread and seal both the front and rear whip-finish areas with clear or light-colored durable nail polish. Be very careful to keep the sealant off the hair.

9. Trim the excess hair butts at the eye to about ⅛ inch to form the hair tuft portion of the head.

# Horner's Deer Hair

HORNER'S DEER HAIR IS THE ANCESTOR OF the popular Humpy. It is a very durable floater and highly useful in both regular and emerger versions and in several sizes (see Variations, following the recipe, for notes on the emerger version).

Either light or dark hair makes excellent bodies. Coastal blacktail deer have very fine hair, which is good for No. 16 flies and tails. Fine whitetail deer hair works well for folded-hair flies. Spinning hair tends to be coarser and less suitable for use in folded-hair flies.

The body is made of the same type of hair as the tail, and the hair should be long enough to go from the hook eye to the hook bend and back to the eye, with an additional body length remaining for the wing. When making the body, it is essential that the folded hair is smooth and that the tips are even before beginning to form the wing.

The hackle need not be of the best quality, since the hollow deer hair body provides the flotation. Select a grizzly neck or saddle feather with barbs about 1½ times the gap of the hook.

| | |
|---|---|
| **HOOK** | *Mustad #94833 or #9672, Nos. 6–16* |
| **THREAD** | *Tan or gray monocord* |
| **TAIL** | *Fine deer body hair or coastal blacktail deer body hair* |
| **BODY/WING** | *Fine deer body hair or coastal blacktail deer body hair* |
| **HACKLE** | *Grizzly neck or saddle* |
| **HEAD** | *Black head cement* |

*Horner's Deer Hair (1). Binding in the tail hair.*

*Horner's Deer Hair (2). Bundle of hair about to be bound in for the underbody.*

1. Place the hook in the vise, attach the thread, and wrap a nonslip base for the tail.

2. Select a small bundle of deer body hair and cut it from the hide. Stroke out the short hairs and fuzz and even the tips. Place the tail on top of the hook shank so the tips extend about one body length to the rear, and tie it in with one or two loose turns of thread so the hair will bundle rather than flare. Take three or four tight turns to firmly bind the hair in place while twisting and spreading the butts with your fingers so they surround the hook shank. Spiral the thread toward the hook eye to about one-quarter body length from the eye, and let the bobbin hang. Cut off the excess hair butts and bind them down to form a base for the hackle and wing, and let the bobbin hang.

3. Select another bundle of deer body hair about ³⁄₁₆ inch in diameter and cut it from the hide. Remove the short hair and fuzz and even the tips. Make sure the hair is long enough for the body/wing (see introductory text above), and place the bundle on top of the hook so the butts are at the front of the body area and the tips are over the tail. Take a couple of loose turns of thread near the eye to bunch—not flare—the hair, and then make several tight turns to bind it in place.

4. In three or four evenly spaced turns, spiral the thread toward the rear of the fly, over the bundle of hair—thereby creating the underbody—to directly over

*Horner's Deer Hair (3). Underbody and wing are completed.*

*Horner's Deer Hair (4). Attaching the hackle.*

*Horner's Deer Hair (5). Completed fly.*

horner's deer hair

*horner's deer hair*

the hook point. Holding the bunched hair together, bind it firmly with a couple of butting turns. This action will raise the remaining length of hair. Widely spiral the thread forward, under the raised hair, to where the butts were tied down, and let the bobbin hang.

5. Collect the raised hair by the tips, taking care to separate out the tail tips, and firmly pull the bundle forward over the underbody to where the bobbin hangs. Push back on the humped hair to get a high hump and bind down the hair with tight turns of thread, which will raise the hair tips. The upright tips now form the wing. Let the bobbin hang just behind the wing.

6. Upset and cut to a stubble the lowest ½ inch of the hackle feather and place it diagonally down and toward the eye on the near side of the hook, just behind the wing. Fasten it there with couple of turns of thread, and then apply a couple more turns of thread tight ahead of the wing. Let the bobbin hang while you cut off the surplus shaft. Bind down the cut end with about five turns of thread and let the bobbin hang.

7. Attach the hackle pliers at a right angle to the shaft near the tip of the feather. Wind the hackle on edge; the first two turns should be tight against the rear of the wing, then pass the hackle under the shank and in front of the wing, where you will make at least three more turns. Allow the pliers to hang as a weight to prevent the hackle from unwinding while you tie it off. Let the

bobbin hang while you cut off the surplus hackle, and then bind down the cut ends.

8. Form a neat head and finish the fly in the usual manner.

## Variations

The emerger version of Horner's Deer Hair is tied the same way as the regular version, but has the following differences: its tail is a bit longer than the body, and it has a short wing (usually one-third to one-half the body length, instead of the full body length of its regular counterpart). Choose a hackle feather that's narrower than the regular version. The barbs should be shorter—anywhere from half the gap size to its full size—so the fly sits lower in the water. It will float lower on a total of three turns of this shorter hackle.

*Horner's Deer Hair (emerger) (1). Binding in the tail hair.*

*Horner's Deer Hair (emerger) (2).*

*Horner's Deer Hair (emerger) (3). The high hump body and wing have been formed.*

*Horner's Deer Hair (emerger) (4). Attaching the hackle feather.*

*Horner's Deer Hair (emerger) (5). Completed fly (note: the head should be black).*

# Hair Ants

HAIR ANTS ARE FLOATING, DURABLE, FOLDED-hair flies made from black, rust, red-brown, or natural deer or elk body hair. The most useful sizes are Nos. 12 to 18 (the recipe is written for No. 12 flies, so use proportion-ately thinner bundles of hair for smaller sizes). The color of the thread you use should match the color of the ant.

You may find that light 2XL hooks provide more pleasing and natural proportions. On the other hand, the fish in your area may be accustomed to dining on shorter ants, in which case the regular-length hook will fit better (e.g., Mustad #94840). Ants tied on both lengths of hook shank have taken fish for me.

The length of the deer body hair needed for this fly depends on the length of the hook shank. The hair should be at least three times as long as the distance from the hook bend to the eye, allowing three steps: fastening the hair to the shank as the underbody; folding over another length to make the body humps; and making the legs. Note that some people are allergic to deer hair, but not to elk. Either can be used for both folded- and spun-hair body flies, and both are available in the colors needed for Hair Ants.

The abdomen is about twice as long as the thorax, or a bit more than half the body length. The thorax is two-thirds of the remainder, and the ant's head is about a sixth of the body length. The head of the fly comes in front of the ant's head. When making the abdomen, thorax, and head segments, try to get these body parts plump by *humping the hair* (pushing it to the rear slightly) and tying the joints tightly without flaring the hair. Tight final turns on each of the joints will also prevent the body from turning around the hook shank.

| | |
|---|---|
| **HOOK** | *Mustad #94831 2XL, 2XF, or #94833 regular 3XF, Nos. 10–18* |
| **THREAD** | *Black, red, rust, mahogany, or brown 8/0 UNI-Thread* |
| **BODY/LEGS** | |
| | *Black, red, rust, mahogany, or brown deer or elk body hair* |
| **HEAD** | *Black head cement* |

*Hair Ant (1). Hair bound in place. Thread hanging where forward end of abdomen will be.*

*Hair Ant (2). Hair pulled forward and bound to create abdomen. Thread hanging where forward end of thorax will be.*

1. Place the hook in the vise, attach the thread, and wrap a nonslip base for the body.

2. Select deer or elk body hair of the same color as the thread and cut off a bunch about ³⁄₁₆ inch in diameter close to the hide. Remove short hairs and any fuzz. Even the tips and place the bunch on the top of the hook shank, with the tips to the rear and the butts about ⅛ inch from the hook eye. Make two close, loose turns of thread around the bundle, being careful not to flare the hair. Then make several tight turns to bind the hair in place.

3. Spiral the thread forward to ⅛ inch from the eye, bundling the hair firmly to the hook shank. Now reverse-spiral wrap back to the point that will become the forward end of the abdomen, and let the bobbin hang.

4. Now grasp the hair bundle by the tips and pull it forward evenly to form the abdomen, and bind it down with a soft (loose) turn of thread followed by two or three firm, tight turns. This will lock the bundle to the hook shank and create the waist or joint between the abdomen and the thorax. Release the hair and push it back.

5. Spiral the thread forward to bind down the thorax. Once again, pull the hair forward to form the thorax, and bind it down with a soft turn of thread followed by several firm turns. This will form the joint between the thorax and the head.

6. Spiral the thread forward again, and let the bobbin hang. Pull the hair forward to form the ant's head. Bind it down and let the bobbin hang.

7. Select three hairs on each side for legs

*Hair Ant (3). Thorax formed.*

*Hair Ant (4). Nearly completed fly. The upright hairs shown here should be stroked downward to form ant legs.*

hair ants

and cut off all the other hairs. Bind down the legs with X-wraps and bury any stubble while forming the head of the fly. Whip finish and cement the head in the usual manner.

## Variations

***Red Hair Ant.*** *Note: completed fly would have six legs pointing downward.*

***Mahogany Hair Ant.*** *Note: completed fly would have six legs pointing downward, and head would be same color as fly.*

***Black Hair Ant.*** *The upright hairs shown here should be stroked downward to form ant legs.*

# EXTENDED MAYFLY BODIES

E xtended body dry flies, the category in which mayflies fall, are designed for realistic silhouettes on short-shank hooks.

We will begin with the Darbee style, which will be used to illustrate two different ways of tying extended bodies. Having mastered these methods, you can apply them to other patterns.

After tying the extended-body flies, we will try our hand at tying stillborns.

*Example of extended body mayfly. Feather body fibers reversed and set in silicone seal.*

*Extended body mayfly.*

## Darbee-Style Blue Dun Two-Feather Extended Body

THESE FLIES WERE ORIGINALLY DESIGNED BY noted Catskill flytier Harry Darbee for use on still flats where the fish can take a really long look at your fly. It has been successful on difficult fish all over the world.

For the tail/body unit, you can use either a neck hackle or a spade feather. Using a curved spade feather produces a body curved up like a live mayfly, whereas neck hackle produces a straight, flat body better adapted

to stillborns/emergers. I suggest you begin by using the readily available neck hackle, as instructed below, and then progress to the spade hackles, since the latter are more difficult to obtain. They are not regularly listed in most fly-tying catalogs, but may be available on whole skins or from growers who process their own capes and saddles and could easily set aside spade hackle for you. Spade feathers are prepared and processed in

**Darbee-Style Blue Dun Two-Feather Extended Body.** *The trimmed feather is set in silicone.*

the same manner as neck hackle, so we will not repeat those directions here. Only note that, when tying in the body on top of the hook, the tail should curve up.

Prepare several bodies before assembling any flies. The more you make, the easier they get. Since the tail and body of this fly are one unit, it is attached to the short-shank hook over the barb.

Wings are prepared most easily by using metal wing burners, which come with detailed instructions for their use. In essence, a burner consists of two metal arms, with tips in the shape of the desired wing. One feather at a time is placed between the two arms, with the center stem of the feather a bit off-center. The arms are pinched together and a candle or alcohol lamp flame quickly burns the feather outside the metal arms, which act as a heat sink that protects the shaped part of the feather. It is an easy and effective tool to use, although the stink of the burning feather tips is unpleasant. The wing can also be cut to shape with scissors and nail clippers.

The wings are attached to the hook shank in the same manner as the Royal Coachman fan wing (see page 182).

The instructions below are for the reversed-in-silicone design, and are followed by the simplified body extension.

**HOOK**    *Mustad #94840 or 9479 4XS dry fly No. 14*

**THREAD**  *White 8/0 UNI-Thread*

**TAIL/BODY**
            *Brown or tan neck or spade hackle*

**WING**    *Blue dun hen body feathers*

**HACKLE**  *Blue dun dry-fly neck or Whiting 100s No. 14 hackle*

**ALSO REQUIRED**
            *Clear silicone seal*

**SPECIAL TOOLS**
            *Toenail clippers or No. 14 wing burners*

1. Select a soft, No. 3 grade webby wet fly rooster neck hackle with ¾-inch barbules. Find where the first barbules of that length are located, and cut off the tip above that point. Measure down ⅜ inch, cut off the shaft, and lay the shaft aside for use in Step 4. Leave the first two barbules on each side of the top end of the ⅜-inch-long section as they lay (these will become the tails), then upset the rest by stroking them toward the butt so they meet at the shaft.

2. Put a good-size dab of clear silicone seal on the upper part of the shaft and the reversed feather section. Now pull the feather several times through thumb and forefinger to coat the reversed part of the feather with the silicone seal and pull the barbules on both sides of the stem tightly together. Set the feather aside on wax paper to dry. If the barbules do not stick together, you may have to give it another coat of silicone seal.

3. When the body is dry and sticks together, make sure the tail barbs are separate from the shaft. If they aren't, free them carefully. Then apply another small dab of silicone seal to the tails and set it aside to dry.

4. Clean your hands on a dry paper towel, then take up the shaft that you set aside previously. This time the tails will be at the cut end of the feather. Measure down ⅜ inch and cut the shaft as before. Hold the cut feather by the tail and shaft, upset the feather, and repeat the silicone seal process described above. You can also start this body farther down the feather, leaving a "handle" that you treat as a "tip," and cut down to twin barbs on each side of the stem for tails.

5. Place the hook in the vise, attach the thread, and wrap a nonslip base for the tail/body unit. Set the unit on the top of the hook so it extends beyond the bend. (The body should be ⅜ inch to ⁹⁄₁₆ inch long, not counting the tails.) Tie it in over the barb with the soft loop technique and let the bobbin hang while you cut off the surplus feather. Then bind down the ends of the body.

**Extended Body,** *trimmed*

**Trimmed Body,** *reversed in silicone*

*darbee-style blue dun two-feather extended body*

**darbee-style blue dun two-feather extended body**

6. Remove the soft and short fibers from the base of the feathers you will use to make wings. Measure ½ to ¾ inch up from the butt—not the tip end—and cut off the rest of the feather tip at right angles to the shaft. Place the two feathers dull sides together and align their tips and edges.

7. If you are not using a wing burner to shape the wings, follow these nail clipper instructions. Holding the feathers firmly, use the curved toenail clippers to cut the left side quite close to the shaft (about ⅛ inch at the upper end and a bit wider at the butt end). Cut the right side of the feather so it's two to three times wider than the left side. The top of the shaped wing should be narrower than the bottom.

8. Hold the two feathers back to back with their tips curving out and away from each other. Place the unit directly ahead of and against the body so the shafts straddle the hook shank. Fasten it there with a soft loop in front of the shafts, followed by another immediately behind the shafts, then pull the thread taut. Repeat and let the bobbin hang. Cut off the shafts about 3/16 inch below the shank.

9. For the hackle, select either a neck hackle with barbs 1½ times the hook gap in length or a No. 14 Whiting 100s. Upset and trim to a stubble the first ½ inch of the tip on both sides of the feather. Place it bright side out directly behind the wing on the near side of the hook shank so the stubble tip points

diagonally down and forward and the first of the uncut upper end is just even with the top of the hook shank. Fasten it there with three or four firm turns of thread, with the last turn tight in front of the wing, and let the bobbin hang. Cut off the surplus stubble end about ⅛ inch from the hook eye, then bind down the cut end and let the bobbin hang.

10. Attach the hackle pliers at right angles to the shaft and, with the feather on edge, carefully make a turn around the hook shank close to—but not touching—the back of the wing. Make another complete turn ahead of the first turn and tight against the rear of the wing. Next, come forward up tight against the front of the wing, make two more butted turns, and let the hackle pliers hang. Make sure the turns are closely butted together and completely cover the thread binding down the wings (push the hackle back to accomplish this if necessary). Tie off the hackle with three or four firm turns of thread, and let the bobbin hang while you raise the surplus feather above the shank and carefully cut it off without cutting the hanging thread.

11. Bind down the cut ends, form a neat, small head, and complete the fly in the usual manner.

## Simplified Body Extension

This variation of the extended body does not require good dry-fly hackle. It is an innovation of Poul Jorgenson, who used it with a parachute-style hackle rather than the conventional hackle style set forth above. You might wish to try both styles. See Slate Paradrake (next recipe) for details on tying the parachute-style hackle. You will not need to use the Paradrake tail, since the body and tail are a unit, but you should wrap a dubbed thorax the color of the feather body around the wing area for additional flotation when using the parachute-style hackle.

These instructions are for creating the body extension and are intended for use with Nos. 6–10 lightweight, dry-fly hooks. The length of the body should be modified proportionately when using other size hooks. This body is attached in the same manner as the body described above. (This process would replace Steps 1–4 above.)

1. Select a brown or tan spade or neck hackle. Locate where the barbules are ¾ inch in length, and begin upsetting the feather for ½ inch to 1 inch toward the

butt, until the barbules stand at nearly right angles to the shaft. Cut the shaft at that point.

2. Holding the cut tip, cut the barbules off diagonally, starting on the left side about ⅛ inch from the shaft and finishing with a point at the base of the uncut tip. Repeat on the other side.

3. Separate the first barbules on each side of the base of the tip, spreading them away from the shaft. These will form the tails. Cut the shaft so as to leave ⅛ inch of the shaft projecting at the point between the tail barbules.

4. To reinforce the tails, apply a small dab of silicone seal to each barbule and spread it by pulling the tails between thumb and forefinger. Then add a small dab of silicone seal to the wide end of the trimmed body, spread it in the same way to reinforce it, and set it aside to dry on waxed paper.

# Slate Paradrake

THE HAIR BODY EXTENSION ON THIS FLY meets the need for natural-looking No. 10 and larger dry flies that match the largest mayflies. The hollow hair provides flotation, and the taper of the individual hairs create a naturally tapered body. Hair wings provide durability, and the scant parachute hackle serves as an outrigger and does not hide or distort the outline of the wing, which is one of the main features of the large and succulent natural flies that the fish recognize.

The hooks listed in the materials all have regular-length shanks. Hook #94840 has a downturned eye; #94842 has an upturned eye; and #94833 is 3X light for a higher float. Choose a thread color that will match the color of the body and wing hair. Expert thread handlers should feel free to use the UNI-Thread, while less experienced tiers should use the flat waxed nylon thread.

The hairs you choose for the tail should be at least 2 inches long, and the body hair at least 1 to 2 inches long. Coastal blacktail deer body hair, an option for the wing, has a much finer texture than gray or brown deer body hair. The hackle should be about two-thirds the usual 1½ times the gap of the hook—shorter than ordinary hackle so as not to disrupt the pattern of the wing, yet long enough to provide stability from the two or three turns of sparse, stiff hackle tied parachute style around the wing clump.

| | |
|---|---|
| **HOOKS** | *Mustad #94840, #94842, or #94833, No. 6* |
| **THREAD** | *Dark gray or brown flat waxed nylon or 6/0 or 8/0 UNI-Thread* |
| **TAIL** | *Any of the following—moose body or mane, peccary, porcupine body hair (not quills), boar bristles* |
| **BODY** | *Darkest gray/brown deer body hair* |
| **WING** | *Darkest gray/brown deer body hair, or darkest coastal blacktail deer body hair* |
| **HACKLE** | *Dark dun neck hackle or Whiting 100s, Nos. 12–14* |
| **HEAD** | *Black head cement* |
| **OPTIONAL TOOL** | |
| | *Hair stacker* |

1. Place the hook in the vise, attach the thread, and wrap a nonslip base for the tail.

2. Tie in two tail hairs, one on each side of the hook bend, so the tips extend two full body lengths beyond the bend. Bind them firmly in place and wind the thread forward in close butting turns, binding down the tail material to about ³⁄₁₆ inch from the eye. Let the bobbin hang, and cut off any surplus tail material.

3. Now select a bunch of deer body hair for the body, about the thickness of a kitchen match, and cut it off close to the hide. Hold it by the tips and remove all fuzz and short hairs. Even the tips by hand or with a hair stacker. *This is important!*

4. Place the bunch on top of the hook shank so the tips are about ³⁄₁₆ to ⅜ inch short of the tips of the tail and the butts are directly over the hanging bobbin. Trim the butts if they extend beyond the bobbin. Move the bundle so that the lower hairs enclose both the hook shank and the tail hairs. Holding the body in place, spiral the thread back to the hook bend, binding the bundle into a body surrounding the shank. At the bend, continue spiraling the thread around the hair bundle (but not the hook) to about ⅛ inch from the deer hair tips. Let the bobbin hang while you trim the excess tips.

5. Divide the two tails with X-wraps (see page 99) and then reverse course and spiral, with a bit more tension on the thread, back to the front end of the body, and let the bobbin hang.

6. For the wing, select a bunch of hair about half the size of the bunch used for the body. Cut off the hair close to the hide, even the tips, and remove any fuzz or short hairs. Place the wing on top of the shank so the tips extend just

*slate paradrake*

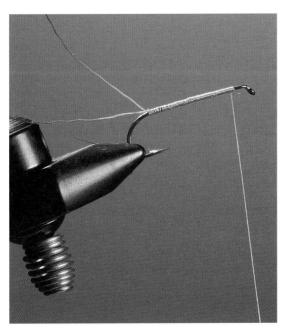

*Slate Paradrake (1). Attaching the two tail hairs.*

*Slate Paradrake (2). Spiraling the thread on the deer-hair body.*

*Slate Paradrake (3). Completed fly.*

past the hook bend and the butts are over the eye. Bind the wing in place using the soft loop technique.

7. Grasp the tips of the wing, raise it so it's vertical, and take several turns immediately behind it to set it in place. If necessary, take a turn around the base of the wing and tightly around the shank in front of the wing to hold it in place. Let the bobbin hang while you cut off surplus butts, tapering the cut toward the hook eye. Let the bobbin hang in front of and tight against the wing.

8. Upset and trim to a stubble the first ½ inch of the hackle tip on both sides of the shaft. Place the stubble tip on the near side of the base of the wing, dull side facing away from you so the feather points diagonally downward and the uncut portion is directly behind the wing. Fasten it there with several firm turns of thread, and let the bobbin

hang. Cut off the surplus stubble end.

9. Attach the hackle pliers at right angles to the shaft and, with the feather on edge, make two or three close butted turns around the wing, starting about ⅛ inch above the body and continuing down toward the body. Tie off the hackle feather between the wing and the eye. If you accidentally tie down any parachute barbs in the process, use your bodkin to release them. Hold the barbs between the wing and eye back, out of the way, while you bind down the cut end of the hackle feather.

10. Make a neat head and complete the fly in the usual manner.

## Variations

You can spin some thin, dark dubbing onto the thread before making the head, and carefully wrap a thicker thorax, covering the wing butts and the area behind the head, thereby providing more flotation.

# Slate/Tan Stillborn

THIS PATTERN COVERS MANY OF THE MOST productive mayfly hatches of early spring in the East. Stillborns represent insects that develop only partly out of the larval stage before they die of exhaustion. Since some develop a bit further than others before they expire, the flies are tied with either free (upright) or trapped wings, since both conditions occur among the natural insects.

The main instructions, below, focus on

the trapped-wing stillborn; the variations you need to make to create the freed-wing style are described at the end of the main recipe. There are three types of nymph shuck from which to choose, and they are interchangeable (i.e., you may choose any shuck for either style of this fly). The choices are whole feather, reversed-feather, and cut/shaped feather (see instructions for details). All are about one body length (excluding the tails on the last two

*Duck shoulder wing, reversed feather shuck*

options). I suggest you try a different shuck on each Slate/Tan Stillborn you tie. If you tie flies in groups of three, as I recommend, tie a different shuck on each of three trapped-wing stillborns before you start on your series of three freed-wing stillborns.

| | |
|---|---|
| **HOOK** | *Mustad #94833, Nos. 12–22* |
| **THREAD** | *White 8/0 UNI-Thread* |
| **SHUCK** | *Any of the following, in dark brown—hen hackle tip, bunch of hair, hack-le feather cut to shape, reversed hackle* |
| **WING CASE** | |
| | *Duck feather strip or poly yarn of same color pulled over the thorax* |
| **HACKLE** | *Dark sun dry-fly hackle or Whiting 100s. Use same number hackle size as your hook size.* |
| **BODY** | *Fly-Rite No. 40 or light tan fur or synthetic hair* |
| **HEAD** | *Black head cement* |

1. Place the hook in the vise and attach the thread in the usual manner. (Go to the step below that is specific to the type of shuck you are making.)

2. If you are making a *whole-feather shuck*, select a hen hackle feather about the length of the hook shank. Carefully trim to a stubble the barbs at the lowest ³⁄₁₆ inch of the shaft. Place the trimmed feather, bright side up, on top of the hook bend like a tail. Bind it in place with the thread and let the bobbin hang. Then go to Step 5.

3. If you are making a *reversed-feather shuck*, see Darbee-Style Blue Dun Two-Feather Extended Body on page 169 and follow Steps 1–4 of the main instructions. Note that you can make this shuck with or without the silicone seal. Apply the shuck to the top of the hook shank, right side up, and extending about one body length (excluding the tails) beyond the bend. Fasten it in place with the hanging thread, and let the bobbin hang. Then go to Step 5.

*Turned up duck shoulder wing; high thorax for flotation, reversed-feather shuck*

*Sidewinder wing and hair shuck*

4. If you are making a *cut/shaped-feather shuck,* see Simplified Body Extension on page 172 and follow Steps 1–4. Note that this shuck is often reinforced with silicone seal. Tie in a bunch of soft hair as long as the body, like a tail for a hair shuck.

5. Select either a slip of duck quill about ¼ inch wide or a 4-inch length of slate-colored poly yarn for the wing case. Place the chosen material on top of the hook shank (dull side up for the feather), so one end extends about ⅜ inch toward the eye and the rest extends beyond the hook bend, and fasten it in place.

6. Select a dark dun dry-fly hackle feather or Whiting 100s sized for the hook. Cut to a stubble the first ½ inch of the tip and place it, bright side up, over the hook bend on top of the short end of the wing case material; the long part of the feather should be over the eye. Fasten it there with the hanging thread. Wind the thread in butting turns to

about ³⁄₁₆ inch from the eye, binding down the hackle stubble. Return the thread to the tie-in point and let the bobbin hang.

7. Dub about 2 inches of thread for the body (refer to The Common Method of Dubbing on page 68 as needed) and wrap it in butting turns up the hook shank to about ³⁄₁₆ inch from the eye. Tie it off with a clean section of the thread, removing any surplus dubbing, and let the bobbin hang.

8. Attach the hackle pliers at right angles to the hackle feather shaft, and wind the feather forward, on edge, for three or four butting turns. Tie it off, and let the bobbin hang.

9. Cut to a stubble the upper two-thirds of the wound hackle—i.e., all of the barbules above the hook shank and a few more on each side—leaving a tuft of uncut hackle under the hook shank to float the front of the fly.

10. Pull the wing case material taut, then

*Parachute, reversed-feather tail*

*No-hackle style wing, reversed-feather shuck*

up and over the body and the clipped hackle. Tie it off in the head area, and let the bobbin hang while you cut off the surplus wing case.

11. Form a neat head and finish the fly in the usual manner.

## Freed-Wing Style Slate/Tan Stillborn

This style of Slate/Tan Stillborn has neither a wing case nor hackle, and the wings are made from dark gray duck quill slips.

1. After attaching the thread to the hook, prepare and attach the shuck of your choice according to the directions above.

2. Prepare and apply the dubbed body section (see Step 7 above). When the wound dubbing has reached about two-thirds of the body length, thicken the body so that the wings will seat properly.

3. Tie in a matched pair of duck quill slips sidewinder style (see details in

Slate/Brown No-Hackle, page 203; adapt Steps 7–9 of that recipe for the slips used here).

4. Recharge the thread with a little thin dubbing and wrap a thorax over the trimmed wing butts, filling in the area behind the head.

5. Form a neat head and finish the fly in the usual manner.

## Variations

The Gray/Yellow Stillborn and Gray/Olive Stillborn, which represents the tiny Blue-Wing Olive hatches, are tied in the same manner as either style described above. Note the following changes in materials.

- Gray/Yellow Stillborn: Use hook Nos. 16–22; dark ginger hackle for the shuck; and a mixture of half Fly-Rite No. 40 and half light tan dubbing for the body. For the trapped-wing style, use slate poly yarn for the wing case and a ginger hackle. For the freed-wing style, use duck quill slips for the wing (there is no hackle for this style).

ⅇ Gray/Olive Stillborn: Use hook Nos. 22–24; dun hen hackle tip for the shuck; and bright green or olive fur or Fly-Rite No. 24 tiny blue olive poly dubbing for the body. For the trapped-wing style, use light gray poly yarn for the wing case and a medium dun hackle. For the freed-wing style, use duck quill slips for the wing (there is no hackle for this style).

**slate/tan stillborn**

# CLASSIC DRY FLIES

The great majority of the flies in this book are ordinarily tied and used in the form described in the instructions (i.e., as a dry fly, bucktail or streamer, wet fly, and so on); however, there are equally accepted and useful, albeit less frequently tied, versions of several standard flies. For instance, the popular Royal Coachman, a pattern that does not resemble any insect or minnow, can be tied as a dry fly with hackle point or quill section wings, fan wings, a hair wing, or parachute style. It can also be tied as a wet fly with a hair or feather slip wing; in an elongated or "stretched" version of the hair wing (Bucktail Royal Coachman); and, finally, as a feather-wing fly (Royal Coachman Streamer).

When I first saw the original design for Royal Coachman dry fly in the 1920s, it had a tail of golden pheasant tippets, reddish-orange feathers with two black bars. Because this tail became waterlogged after a little use and pulled the rear of the fly into the water, it was replaced in later years with a tail made of Rhode Island Red hackle or stiff, hollow deer hock hair of the same color. The tippet tail, however, survives in the current versions of the wet fly, streamer, and bucktail because they are all used under the water's surface and the touch of color at the tail catches the eye of both fish and fishermen.

Other dry-fly patterns can also be tied in different forms to good effect. The Coachman, an accepted wet fly, can be useful as a dry fly when it's tied with stiff hackles and a supporting tail instead of the usual skimpy beard and soft tail fibers. It also makes an effective streamer or bucktail and has taken many fish in those forms.

Hair wings are more durable than feather wings, and fan wings have a unique action. That is why they are included here for your consideration and use. Hair and feather wings have long been interchangeable in fly tying, although some color combinations may be hard to match. Each material has its own set of advantages and disadvantages. You may find that you prefer hair or a particular type of hair or feather wing or tail to all the others. Only by trying each will you make this discovery. So tie the classic, standard version, in terms of both form (dry fly) and materials (hair or feather) first, and then tie the next fly with a change in materials. Try it as a fan wing, and don't forget to tie and also fish the bucktail and streamer versions of the pattern. When you do this, you will also learn to appreciate the relationship between all of the types of flies and the various materials you can use to make them, and you will broaden the scope of your fly-tying interests and activities. Tying one basic pattern as a dry fly and again as a wet fly and yet again as a bucktail or streamer, each with various wing materials, is fully explained in the Royal Coachman.

# Royal Coachman

THE ROYAL COACHMAN HAS NO COUNTERPART in nature, so it must be classed as an attractor fly rather than an imitator. It also appears as a streamer and as a wet fly, and has taken fish everywhere in all of these forms for many years. In the instructions for this fly, I have included three wing material options and directions for tying them. We will start with the classic quill section wing. Instructions for tying fan wings and hair wings—which offer the greatest durability—follow. All are tied with the same tail, body, and hackle. The tail supports the heavy rear end of the fly and should be as stiff as it is strong. The fly floats on its stiff hackle and tail—the lighter the fly, the better and longer it floats.

Deer hock hair is light, hollow, and stiff,

*Royal Coachman (1). Fastening the tail fibers to the shank.*

so it makes a wonderful tail. If you can't obtain the hair from friends who hunt or from your own bounty, you can purchase it from Feather-Craft (see Appendix 2). Alternatively, you can use stiff coachman brown dry-fly quality neck or saddle hackle, either dyed or natural.

The body is divided into three sections. The rear and front sections, each measuring one-quarter of the total body length, are made from peacock herl. The midsection, measuring half the body length, is made from a red fiber (see the materials list for options). You can use peacock herl from a sewn strip or an eyed tail feather. The tips of the herl are soft and easily cut by fine thread against a bare hook, so you must trim them before tying them in for the body. Also note that you will use hackle pliers to weight the herl, which will prevent it from unwinding between steps.

A couple of other things to note: The dry-fly hook we'll use is longer than usual, to accommodate the body style and provide space for a decent red section. It's also a very light hook, so pull the thread carefully against it as you work.

I suggest you plan to tie at least six bodies up to the wing stage before completing the first fly. Use one unit to complete the first fly. When this is done, finish another in the same fashion to be sure you have the hang of it before attempting to complete the hair wing or fan wing styles using the other

*Royal Coachman (2). Tying the herl and the tinsel in place.*

prepared bodies. By the time you complete the sixth body you should see an improvement in the bodies as well as in the time required for the work.

| | |
|---|---|
| **HOOK** | *Mustad #94833, No. 12 (2X long–2X light)* |
| **THREAD** | *White 8/0 UNI-Thread* |
| **TAIL** | *Deep mahogany deer hock hair or coachman brown neck hackle fibers* |
| **BODY** | *Rear—peacock herl; midsection—red floss or yarn or red Mylar tinsel; front—peacock herl* |
| **WING** | *White duck, goose, or turkey wing feathers* |
| **HACKLE** | *Coachman brown dry-fly quality neck hackle or Whiting 100s, No. 12* |
| **HEAD** | *Black head cement* |

**royal coachman**

*Royal Coachman (3). Finished body of the Royal Coachman.*

*Royal Coachman "standard" (4). Completed fly.*

1. Place the hook in the vise, attach the thread, and wrap a nonslip base for the tail.

2. Select a bunch of six to eight fibers for the tail that will extend about half an inch beyond the hook bend when it's tied in. Even the tips, place the bundle on top of the hook shank, fasten it there using the soft loop technique, and let the bobbin hang. If the butts of the tail extend farther up the body, cut them off about ⅛ inch beyond the tie-in point.

3. Select four peacock herls. Holding them with their tips together, cut off at least half an inch of the tips. Place the herls on top of the hook shank so the trimmed ends extend to ³⁄₁₆ inch from the hook eye, and bind them in place. Continue wrapping the thread forward, binding down the herl, for another ³⁄₁₆ inch, and let the bobbin hang.

4. Holding the four herls, even the tension so that all are equally taut. Attach the hackle pliers and wrap three close, even turns of herl around the hook shank and let the pliers hang. Tie off the herls with a couple of turns of thread—don't cut them off yet—and let the bobbin hang.

5. Place one end of a 6- to 8-inch piece of red floss, yarn, or tinsel on top of the hook directly over the hanging bobbin. Tie it in place, binding down both the short end of the red material and the layer of herl for about ⅜ inch, and let the bobbin hang.

6. To create the body's midsection, carefully wind the free end of the red material up to the hanging bobbin. Butt each turn, without gaps or overlays, to create a smooth covering. Tie off the midsection, and let the bobbin hang while you cut off the surplus red material.

7. Now carefully lift the herls with the hackle pliers and pass the thread ahead of the herl. Wind the thread in firm, close turns to ³⁄₁₆ inch from the eye, and let the bobbin hang. With the hackle pliers, wind the herl in three butted turns to the hanging bobbin, tie off the herl, and let the bobbin hang.

*You have now finished tying the body of the Royal Coachman dry fly. This is a good time to tie it off with a couple of overhand knots or a whip-finish knot and set it aside, out of the vise, while you tie the four or five more bodies that are needed to complete this exercise. When all the bodies are complete, resume building the first fly.*

8. Return one of the bodies to the vise and attach the white 8/0 UNI-Thread hard against the front end of the body, letting the bobbin hang while preparing a feather-section wing that's ³⁄₁₆ inch wide and ¾ inch long (see Step 5 on page 49 for detailed instructions). Place the sections' dull sides together on top of the hook shank, with the tips to the rear, curving down and extending about half an inch to the rear of where the thread is hanging. Fasten them there using the soft loop technique, and let the bobbin hang while you cut off the surplus butts, tapering them as a base for a small head.

9. Gently raise the wing and, holding it upright, take several turns of thread close behind the wing to hold it in place. Carefully separate the two sections with your bodkin, make an X-wrap to keep them apart, and let the bobbin hang.

10. Select a hackle with barbs 1½ times the gap of the hook. Upset and trim to a stubble the barbs on the first ½ inch of the tip. Place the stubble end diagonally downward across the near side of the hook shank so the dull side of the feather is against the shank and the first of the uncut barbs touch the base of the wing. The rest of the feather should be behind the wing. Bind it in place with three turns of thread immediately behind and against the wing, and then with at least five turns of thread in front of the wing. Let the bobbin hang.

11. Attach the hackle pliers at right angles to the feather shaft and about 2 to 3 inches from the tie-in point, and take two turns tight against the back of the wing and then two or three more tight turns in front of the wing. Tie off the hackle, and let the bobbin hang while you carefully raise the surplus stubble end and carefully trim it to ⅛ inch. Bind down the cut end and wind the thread forward in tight turns against the front of the wing.

12. Continue binding down wing butts and hackle stubble to form a small neat head, and finish in the usual manner.

## If You Use a Hair Wing

For this option, the wing can be made from white calf body hair or white calftail (kip), although calf body hair is generally better for wings than calftail hair. The hair you want for wings is fairly straight and about an inch

***Royal Coachman*** *tied with a hair wing*

long. The conventional hair wing for this fly is divided into two equal parts. For a less conventional wing, omit this division to create an undivided sail wing instead. (The process below would replace Steps 8 and 9 in the main recipe.)

1.  Starting with a Royal Coachman body in the vise, attach the thread against the front end of the body and let the bobbin hang.

2.  Select a bunch of hair about ³⁄₁₆ inch thick and cut it off close to the hide. Holding the tips firmly, remove all short or broken hairs and fuzz. Even the tips and place the bunch on top of the hook shank so the butts are over the eye and the tips extend ¾ inch behind where the bobbin is hanging. Fasten it there using the soft loop technique, and let the bobbin hang.

*Royal Coachman tied with fan wings. (Note the wings in this fly should be white, not as shown here.)*

Carefully cut the butts in a taper toward the eye, in preparation for a neat, small head.

3.  Raise the tips of the hair to a vertical position. Wrap several close turns of thread behind and against the wing to keep it upright, and let the bobbin hang. Then, with your bodkin, carefully divide the wing into two equal parts, separate them, and bind them in place with X-wraps, ending behind the wing, and let the bobbin hang.

## If You Use Fan Wings

Fan wings are beautiful, of fluctuating popularity, land lightly on the water, have a reputation for twisting leaders—and are somewhat more difficult to tie. Many dry flies have sprouted fan wings in place of their original feather or hair wings. The color and size of fan wings may differ, but they are all put together the same way. For the Royal Coachman, use a matched pair of white duck breast feathers.

The feathers you choose can be from a package or, better yet, from a white skin or patch; two feathers that grew side by side are most likely to be twins, and the feathers do need to be alike to make a good balanced fly. The feather size specified in Step 2 below works for a No. 12 hook. Other size hooks will require proportionately larger or smaller feathers.

There are several methods for mounting fan wings, and all do the job. One method is included in the instructions, and another is offered in Wet Fly below. In the method described in the instructions, you will put the wings on the fly at the same time, with the shafts straddling the hook shank. This helps align the wings as they are tied in.

Experiment and find the method that suits your style. In any case, you do not want more than about ⅛ inch of base shaft above the hook shank or the wing will be too tall for the fly. (The process below would replace Steps 8 and 9 in the main recipe.)

1. Starting with a Royal Coachman body in the vise, attach the thread against the front end of the body and let the bobbin hang.

2. Hold the feathers, one on top of the other, by their rounded tips and reduce to a stubble the short barbs and fuzz at the base of both feathers equally. The firm section of the feather should now be about ⅜ inch wide and ½ to ¾ inch long.

3. Put the feathers back to back so their tips curve out and away from each other. Place the unit directly ahead of and against the body so the shafts straddle the hook shank with the wings upright. Fasten them there with a soft loop in front of the shafts, followed by another immediately behind the shafts, followed by another immediately behind the shafts. Then pull the thread taut, repeat the soft loop wraps, and let the bobbin hang. Cut off the shafts about ³⁄₁₆ inch below the shank.

4. Bend the feathers up toward the hook eye and bind them firmly in place. Cut off any excess butts ⅛ inch from the

eye. Separate the feathers and fasten them in place with X-wraps, finishing behind the wing, and let the bobbin hang.

## Wet Fly

Another method of applying fan wings is to tie them in separately, starting on either the near side or the far side of the hook shank.

For the Royal Coachman Wet Fly, use

*Royal Coachman Wet Fly (1).*

*Royal Coachman Wet Fly (2).*

royal coachman

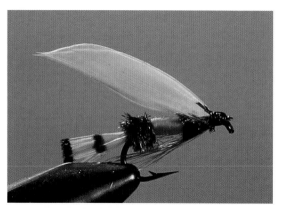

*Royal Coachman Wet Fly (3). Completed fly.*

Mustad #3906, No. 12 wet-fly hooks, and coachman brown hen hackle for the throat.

The Royal Coachman Streamer is essentially an elongated version of the classic Royal Coachman wet fly and shows how a wet-fly pattern can be converted to streamer form by using a longer hook and stretching out the body and wing. In this case, use Mustad #9575, Nos. 2–10 (I suggest No. 6) streamer hooks and coachman brown hen hackle (Rhode Island Red) for the throat.

*Royal Coachman Streamer*

*Royal Coachman Bucktail*

# Light Hendrickson Dry Fly

THE HENDRICKSON IS A MAJOR EASTERN AND Midwestern mayfly hatch and is important to early-season trout fishermen. The female mayfly is represented by the Light Hendrickson—the original pattern—and the male is represented by the Dark Hendrickson, which came later. There is considerable variety among individual mayflies of the same sex in any one stream, as well as between the sexes.

There are two styles of feather wing from which to choose when tying this fly—the classic quill section wing and the rolled/bundled wing made from the fibers of one slip—and instructions for both are provided below. When selecting feather material from which to cut slips, remember that a feather with a center shaft will provide equal-length barbs on both sides of the shaft and allow you to cut sections of equal length and width from the same area on each side. If such a feather is not available, choose two equal-size feathers—one with the wide part on the right side of the shaft and the other with the wide part on the left. In either case, feather sections of equal length are critical for making a balanced wing.

The challenge with creating the rolled/bundled wing is that it's often difficult to prevent flank feather wing sections from splitting apart, and quite a few tiers won't even try this method. (Mallard dyed wood duck is a popular substitute for wood duck flank.) Either method of wing production seems to please the fish, however, as long as the size of the fly matches the hatch.

Other things to note: Make sure the tail material you use is stiff enough to create a high-floating fly. And, for those of you who don't know, pink fox—the body material you need for the Light Hendrickson—is urine-stained fox belly hair.

After the main recipe, we provide instructions for tying an optional feather strip body style. Notes for tying the Dark Hendrickson and Slate Wing Mahogany Dun versions of this fly appear in Other Variations. Also see Hendrickson Nymph (page 111 of the Nymphs chapter) if you want to tie nymph and spinner phases of this insect.

*Light Hendrickson*

**light hendrickson dry fly**

| | |
|---|---|
| **HOOK** | *Mustad #94833, Nos. 12–14* |
| **THREAD** | *White 8/0 UNI-Thread* |
| **TAIL** | *Dark blue dun neck or saddle hackle barbs* |
| **BODY** | *Pink fox or Hendrickson Pink Poly XXX* |
| **WING** | *Wood duck flank or mallard dyed wood duck* |
| **HACKLE** | *Dark blue dun dry-fly hackle neck or Whiting 100s, No. 12* |
| **HEAD** | *Black head cement* |

1. Put the hook in the vise, attach the thread, and wrap a nonslip base for the tail.

2. Select a stiff dry-fly quality neck or saddle feather with barbs at least ¾ inch long, and cut three or four stiff barbs from each side of the shaft for the tail. Place the barbs on top of the hook shank so the tips extend about half an inch beyond the hook bend, fasten them in place with three or four firm turns of thread, and let the bobbin hang.

3. Produce 1½ to 2 inches of dubbing for the body, following the instructions provided in The Common Method of Dubbing (see page 68 in the Basic Skills chapter).

4. Push the noodle of dubbing up close to the hook shank and, starting hard against the base of the tail, wrap the dubbing in butted turns to ³⁄₁₆ inch from the eye. Let the bobbin hang while you clean the excess dubbing off the thread. Tie off the body with two or three tight turns of the clean thread, and let the bobbin hang. (Go to the step below that is specific to the type of wing you are preparing.)

5. If you are making the *classic quill section wing,* select a feather (or feathers, if you can't obtain one with a center shaft) with barbs at least ¼ inch longer than the hook shank. Prepare the feather(s) and cut ³⁄₁₆-inch-wide slips according to the instructions in Step 5 on page 49. Place the sections' dull sides together and with the tips aligned to form the wing. Then go to Step 7.

6. If you are making a *rolled/bundled wing,* cut a ³⁄₈-inch-wide section from one side of the feather shaft. Roll it into a bundle, making sure the tips are even.

7. Place the wing along the top of the hook shank so the butts are over the eye and the tips are a shank length behind the hanging thread. Fasten it there using the soft loop technique, cut off the surplus butts, bind down the cut ends, and return the thread to the rear of the wing.

8. Lift the wing by the tips to a vertical position. Holding the wing in place, make several turns of thread tight against the rear of it, and then let the bobbin hang. With your bodkin, carefully separate right and left equal-size sections of the wing, keeping the fibers in each section together as units, and fasten them with X-wraps ending behind the wing. Then let the bobbin hang.

9. Prepare and attach either a dry-fly hackle or a Whiting 100s according to the instructions in Step 6 on page 49, noting these additional directions: If you use dry-fly hackle, select a feather that has barbs 1 to 1½ times the gap of the hook; choose a Whiting 100s that matches the size of your hook. Tie in either one so the dull side faces the shank.

10. Attach the hackle pliers at right angles to the feather shaft, near the tip of the neck hackle or 3 inches from the shank if you're using a Whiting 100s feather. With the feather on edge, carefully make a turn between the body and the wing and then another turn tight against the rear of the wing. Then make two turns against the front of the wing. Let the hackle pliers hang to keep the hackle from unwinding while you tie it off with two or three firm, close butted turns of thread, and let the bobbin hang while you cut off the excess feather.

11. Bind down the cut ends of the hackle, form a small, neat head, whip finish, and complete the fly in the usual manner.

## The Feather Strip Body Style

This body style is lighter and "buggier" than the original dubbed style, and often a closer match to many of the insects in the hatch on a particular stream. It makes a useful fly when the fish are slow to take the dubbed style. The body material we use here is light-colored ring-necked pheasant tail (from a cock), which can be purchased as one or paired feathers, a tail clump, or a whole pheasant skin. (This process would replace Steps 3 and 4 above.)

1. Select a feather with barbs of 1½ to 2½ inches on the wide side, and separate and cut off a ³⁄₁₆-inch-wide strip, close to the center shaft.

2. Place the thin tip of the feather strip on top of the hook shank at the base of the tail where you usually tie in the body material with the light side of the strip on top, and bind it in place with three or four firm, close turns of thread. Continue winding the thread up the hook shank, butting each turn, to ³⁄₁₆ inch from the eye, and let the bobbin hang.

3. Carefully attach the hackle pliers at right angles to and at the end of the feather strip. Carefully wind the strip up the hook shank, butting every turn without gaps or overlaps, to where the bobbin hangs. Tie off the feather with three or four firm, close turns of thread, and let the bobbin hang while you trim off the surplus feather butts. Bind down the cut butts, return the thread to the front end of the body, and let the bobbin hang. You have completed the body.

## Dark Hendrickson

The Dark Hendrickson is tied in the same manner as the Light Hendrickson except that the body is made of dark blue-gray underfur, without guard hairs, from cottontail

light hendrickson dry fly

*Dark Hendrickson*

rabbit or muskrat. If you can't obtain the fur, use dark dun Poly XXX instead. This variation represents a change in color rather than technique, so follow the directions for the dubbed Light Hendrickson body, using the appropriate color instead of Hendrickson Pink, and you should have no problems.

The Slate-Wing Mahogany Dun is smaller but similar to the Dark Hendrickson, and is tied just like it, except for these changes: the hook size is No. 16–18; the body is made of mahogany-colored fur or synthetic dubbing; and the Whiting 100s hackle size is 18. To more accurately match this mayfly hatch, you could also use light gray dry-fly quality hackle fibers or gray hair for the tail and one of the following materials for the wing: light gray hackle tips, light gray Poly X (yarn form), light gray partridge or hen body feathers, or light gray hair (mink tail guard hairs in a clump).

## Housatonic Quill

THIS PATTERN IS VERY USEFUL DURING THE white fly hatch, and a No. 16 was my father's favorite small, light-colored dry fly. I still have some in that size, tied by Ray Bergman, that I inherited from my father.

The body segments on the natural fly are narrower in the rear, and this is also true for this quill body. There are two ways in which you can prepare the wing: Either tie the wing as two separate feather sections or in the rolled/bundled style. In each case the wing length on this fly is equal to the body

*Housatonic Quill tied with a classic quill section wing*

*Housatonic Quill with a rolled/bundled wing*

length (i.e., it's as high as the body of the fly is long). The hackle should be stiff and No. 1 quality, but it's graded lower because of the lack of a dark center. The proper shade is sometimes found in No. 2 or No. 3 quality necks.

| HOOK | Mustad #94833, Nos. 12–18 |
|---|---|
| THREAD | White 8/0 UNI-Thread |
| TAIL | Wood duck or mallard dyed wood duck |
| BODY | Well-marked, stripped peacock eye quill |
| WING | Wood duck or mallard dyed wood duck speckled flank feather |
| HACKLE | Gray badger (lighter center strip) |
| HEAD | Black head cement |

1. Place the hook in vise, attach the thread, and wrap a nonslip base for the tail.

2. Select a small, stiff-fibered wood duck or dyed mallard flank feather and cut off six to nine fibers to form a tail about the length of the hook from the bend to the eye. Even the tips, and use the soft loop technique to tie in the bunch just ahead of the hook bend, with the tail extending the length of the hook shank beyond the bend.

3. With a bodkin, separate out one segment of peacock eye quill from the waxed eye. (See below for details on preparing this item.) Remove it and strip off the waxed herl by running it between your fingernails until the quill is clean.

4. Tie in the quill, by its tip or thin end, against the first turn of thread at the

base of the tail. There should be no gap between tail and body. Wrap the thread in butting turns to the wing area—i.e., about two-thirds of the distance to the eye—and let the bobbin hang.

5. Attach hackle pliers to the free end of the quill, at right angles to it, and wind it carefully in butting turns up the shank to form the body. Tie it off and let the bobbin hang while you cut off the excess quill shaft. (Go to the step below that is specific to the type of wing you are preparing.)

5. If you're making a *classic quill section wing*, select a well-marked wood duck or dyed mallard feather that has a center shaft. Cut two sections about ³⁄₁₆ inch wide, one from each side of the shaft. Place the tips of the two sections dull sides together and align the edges to form the wing. Then go to Step 7.

6. If you're making a *rolled/bundled wing*, select a well-marked wood duck or dyed mallard feather. Cut and fold a ³⁄₈-inch-wide segment from one side of the shaft to make a ³⁄₁₆-inch-wide wing, or roll the segment into a bundle. Make sure the tips are even.

7. Place the wing on top of the hook shank so the tips are over the hook bend and the butts are over the eye. Use the soft loop technique to tie it in, and let the bobbin hang. Do not separate the wing into two parts at this time, and cut off the surplus butts.

8. Raise the wing by the tips to a vertical position. Make several close turns of thread behind the wing to hold it up, and let the bobbin hang. Using your bodkin, carefully divide the wing into equal halves and bind them in place with X-wraps, ending behind and against the rear of the wing, and let the bobbin hang.

9. Select a small gray badger neck hackle feather with barbs one to two times the size of the gap of the hook. Trim the soft fibers on the bottom ¼ inch of the shaft to a stubble, and place the feather just behind the wing, with the shiny side out and the butt slanting diagonally forward toward the eye. Tie it in with two turns of thread behind the wing, then bring the thread ahead of the wing for a turn or two, and let the bobbin hang. Cut off the excess shaft ⅛ inch from the eye and bind it down.

10. Attach the hackle pliers to the tip of the feather, at right angles to the shaft. Make one or two tight turns behind the wing, directly against it, and then make two or three more turns tightly ahead of and against the wing. Let the hackle pliers hang. While holding tension on the hackle tip, catch it with the thread loop, complete the turn, and pull the thread tight. Make two more turns of thread to fasten it firmly, and let the bobbin hang while you cut off the surplus hackle, being careful not to cut your thread. Bind down the cut end of the hackle.

11. Form the head and finish the fly in the usual manner.

## Preserving Peacock Eye Quill for Fly Bodies

Below we describe a method of preserving peacock eye for future use when making quill bodies. When the wax coating has hardened, the eye will keep for years, free of moth damage and without becoming brittle. The wax into which you dip the eye can be reused many times. Individual sections or quills of the peacock eye can be separated with a needle or bodkin, then stripped of herl and wax in preparation for use.

1. Select a peacock-eyed tail feather by looking at the backside. The lighter it is, the better the color contrast will be in the finished quill body. (You can use the herl below the eye for bodies on Coachman, Woodchuck Caddis, and other flies. Save the "eye" for quill bodies.) Hopefully there will be a handle on the "eye"—i.e., the stem from which the other herls were taken.

2. Secure a tin can or a small pot, 2 or 3 inches in diameter, and several bars of paraffin such as is used to seal jelly or jam jars. You will need about 2 inches of hot wax in the container for this process. Since it is flammable, it is best to melt the paraffin by standing the container in a pot of boiling water rather than placing it directly over an open flame or electric heating unit. Stirring the paraffin well will speed up the melting process. The paraffin must be liquid, but should not be bubbling.

3. Holding the eye by the handle or with tongs or pliers, immerse the whole eye in the melted wax, then remove, drain, and allow it to cool on newspaper.

## Light Cahill

THE LIGHT CAHILL IS A GOOD STANDARD FLY that's useful throughout much of the trout season in the East and Midwest. This is my version of the lightest, toughest Light Cahill, and it has done well for me and many of my friends and pupils for the past 50 years. I usually want my dry flies to float high off the water, supported by a tail and stiff hackles for a long float. Here, the combination of light hook, feather strip body, light, stiff tail, and stiff hackle makes for a high-floating fly.

The wood duck wings and tail of the traditional Light Cahill are fragile, and the feather tail rarely supports the fly well. To remedy this, I have replaced the feather tail with a stiff hair tail. Deer hock hair is very stiff, strong, and light and, at least at the time of this writing, can be obtained from Feather-Craft (see Appendix 2 for contact information). Choose hairs that are as long as the body.

There are two styles of wing from which to choose when tying this fly—a feather wing and a hair wing—and instructions for both are provided below. I strongly recommend a

housatonic quill  light cahill

light cahill

hair wing, for which deer mask hair or light coastal blacktail deer body hair make light and very durable wing materials.

This fly is tied in the same manner as the pheasant tail body version of the Light Hendrickson (page 191). Note the following proportions.

*Body = eye to bend of the hook*

*Tail = body length*

*Wing length = body length*

*Wing width = 30 percent of body length*

*Hackle = 1½ times gap of the hook*

If you have tied the flies in the order in which they appear in this book, you should have no problem completing this fly.

| | |
|---|---|
| **HOOK** | *Partridge 2X long, 4X light, or Mustad #94833 (3X light), Nos. 12–16* |
| **THREAD** | *White 8/0 UNI-Thread* |
| **TAIL** | *Tan/ginger deer hock hair* |
| **BODY** | *White turkey tail or secondary feather* |
| **WING** | *Wood duck flank or mallard dyed wood duck (feather wing); tan/ginger deer mask hair or light coastal blacktail deer body hair (hair wing)* |
| **HACKLE** | *Ginger neck or Whiting 100s, No. 12–16 hackle* |
| **HEAD** | *Black head cement* |

**Light Cahill** *with a feather wing*

*Light Cahill with a hair wing*

1. Starting with the thread about ³⁄₁₆ inch ahead of the hook bend, attach the thread to the shank.

2. At the bend of the hook, tie in six to eight deer hock hairs for the tail, then bundle and bind down the excess length to the wing area and cut it off there. Return the thread to the tail in smooth, even turns.

3. For the body, cut a ³⁄₁₆-inch-wide strip of white turkey tail or secondary feather that's 1½ to 2½ inches long. Tie in the strip so that the tip is about ³⁄₁₆ inch behind the eye on top of the hook shank and the butts are beyond the bend of the hook. (If the tip is very thin, you can shorten it so the thread won't cut through the soft feather.)

Wind thread forward to the wing area, and let the bobbin hang.

4. Wind the body feather slip as a flat ribbon, with the turns butted tightly together, and tie it off. Cut off the excess, bind down the ends, and let the bobbin hang. (Go to the step below that is specific to the type of wing you are choosing.)

5. If you're making a *feather wing*, decide whether you will cut and prepare a two-section wing or a rolled/bundled wing. Select the required number of medium-size wood duck or mallard dyed wood duck flank feathers for your wing style, with fibers a bit longer than the length of the fly's body, and prepare the slip(s). Then go to Step 7.

6. If you're making a *hair wing,* select a bunch of hair the thickness of a kitchen match and cut it off close to the hide. Holding it firmly by the tips, remove any fuzz or short hairs. Even the tips by hand or with a hair stacker.

7. Place the wing on top of the hook shank so the butts are over the eye and the tips extend just beyond the hook bend. Fasten the wing in place using the soft loop technique, and let the bobbin hang while you cut off the surplus butts.

8. Raise the wing to a vertical position and make several close turns of thread behind and tight against the back of the wing to hold it in place. Divide the wing into two equal parts and secure them with X-wraps. Bind down the cut butts and return the thread to hang behind the wing.

9. Pick up either a neck hackle with barbs 1½ times the gap of the hook or a long Whiting 100s sized for the hook you are using. In either case, upset the first ⅜ inch of the tip and cut to a stubble

the upset barbs on both sides of the shaft. Place the stubble end against the near side of the hook shank so the shiny side of the feather is facing you. The feather should be pointing diagonally forward and downward and the first of the uncut barbs should be just behind the wing. Fasten it there with three or four firm turns of thread, ending in front of the wing, and let the bobbin hang. Cut off the surplus stubble end about ⅛ inch from the hook eye.

10. Attach the hackle pliers at right angles to the shaft and wind two turns around the hook shank, the first behind and the second close against the rear of the wing. Bring a third turn under and then in front of the wing, and continue for two or three more close-butted turns. Let the pliers hang so the hackle doesn't unwind while you tie it in. Carefully cut off the excess hackle and bind down the cut end.

11. Make a small, neat head, whip finish, and complete the fly in the usual manner.

## Henryville Caddis

HENRYVILLE CADDIS IS AN OLD, EFFECTIVE, high-floating dry caddis pattern. It's originally from Pennsylvania, and when it's tied correctly it's accepted as one of the best caddis patterns from coast to coast.

Note that this fly floats on the palmered ribbing, not on the hackle. The barbs of the rib palmer should be a little longer than the hook gap, while those of the hackle should be 1½ times the hook gap. Before tying the underwing, which will extend just past the hook bend, trim off the top of the ribbing. Experience will show you how much needs to be removed, but one-third of the barb length above the hook shank is a good start.

The wing itself is tied like a tent over the body and extends to just beyond the tip of the underwing. Although the instructions suggest tying in the wings together, you can also tie them in one at a time, but be sure they sit the same on each side. In nature, in-sect wings are in matched pairs and equally spaced; they should be the same on your fly.

| | |
|---|---|
| **HOOK** | *Mustad #94840 or #94831, Nos. 14–18* |
| **THREAD** | *White 8/0 UNI-Thread* |
| **TAIL** | *None* |
| **BODY** | *Olive yarn or dubbing* |
| **RIBBING** | *Grizzly neck hackle or Whiting 100s equivalent* |
| **UNDERWING** | *Lemon wood duck or mallard dyed wood duck flank feather* |
| **WING** | *Dark gray duck quill sections* |
| **HACKLE** | *Brown neck or Whiting 100s equivalent* |
| **HEAD** | *Black head cement* |

1. Place the hook in the vise, attach the thread, and wrap a nonslip base for the body.
2. For the ribbing, select either two neck hackles or Whiting 100s equivalent. Upset and trim to a stubble the first ⅜ to ½ inch of the feather tip(s) and tie the tip(s) in at the hook bend. Let the feather(s) and the bobbin hang.
3. Dub the thread (see The Common

*Henryville Caddis*

Method of Dubbing, page 68) and wind it forward, forming a thin body, to ³⁄₁₆ inch from the hook eye, and let the bobbin hang.

4. Attach the hackle pliers at right angles to the rib hackle shaft(s), and palmer the ribbing in close turns to the hanging thread. Tie it off and cut off the excess feather. Bind down the stub, then cut off the surplus ribbing.

5. With your scissors cut off about ⅓ of the height of the ribbing above the hook shank to provide space for the underwing.

6. For the underwing, cut a ³⁄₁₆-inch-wide section of feather that extends from the hook eye to the hook bend. Place it on top of the cut section of the ribbing with the tip of the underwing extending to the bend of the hook and tie it in using the soft loop technique. Cut off the butts, and let the bobbin hang.

7. Prepare a feather-section wing (refer to Step 5 on page 49 as needed) and place it on top of the underwing, covering it like a tent. Fasten the wing in place using the soft loop technique. Trim the wing butts and bind them down, return the thread to where you first tied in the wing, and let the bobbin hang.

8. Select a feather for the hackle, then upset and trim to a stubble the barbs on the first ⅜ inch of the tip. Place the stubble tip diagonally forward on the near side of the hook shank so the first barbs that are 1½ times the hook gap in length are at the base of the wing. Fasten it there with several turns of thread. Cut off the excess stubble tip ⅛ inch from the eye.

9. Wind the hackle forward for two or three butting turns tight against the rear and then tight against the front of the wing, and tie it off. Cut off the surplus feather and bind down the stub.

10. Form a neat head and finish the fly in the usual manner.

## Toth Elk-Hair Caddis

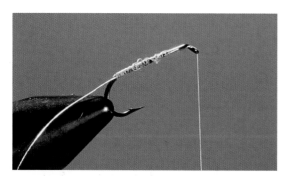

*Toth Elk-Hair Caddis (1). Fastening the wire to the hook shank.*

THE TOTH ELK-HAIR CADDIS IS A DURABLE and effective dry caddis fly that can be tied in several other colors with equally good results. It represents a style of tying, and is a very useful fly in a wide range of sizes. A couple of things to note: You will wrap the rib after you wrap the hackle. Also, when making the head, use the head cement on thread only, not on the tuft of hair that remains after you trim the wing butts.

This tuft is the characteristic trademark of this fly.

| | |
|---|---|
| **HOOK** | *Mustad #94840, Nos. 10–18 (No. 12 is used most often)* |
| **THREAD** | *White 8/0 UNI-Thread* |
| **TAIL** | *None* |
| **RIB** | *Gold wire, fine* |
| **BODY** | *Hare's ear dubbing or synthetic dubbing in that color* |
| **HACKLE** | *Furnace (cochy) neck hackle or Whiting 100s sized for the hook* |
| **WING** | *Tannish-cream elk hair* |
| **HEAD** | *Black head cement* |

1. Place the hook in the vise, attach the thread, and wrap a nonslip base for the body.

2. Place a 5- to 8-inch length of wire on top of the hook shank so that one end is about ⅛ inch from the eye and the rest falls behind the bend. Fasten it there with several turns of thread. Continue winding the thread to the end of the wire and then back to the tie-in spot, and let the bobbin hang.

3. Dub the thread for the body as directed in The Common Method of Dubbing on page 68. When you have 1½ to 2 inches of dubbing prepared, wrap it in even, butted turns to about ³⁄₁₆ inch from the eye, tie it off, and let the bobbin hang.

4. Choose a neck hackle that has barbs

*Toth Elk-Hair Caddis (2). Wrapping the dubbing.*

*Toth Elk-Hair Caddis (3). Tying on the neck hackle.*

*Toth Elk-Hair Caddis (4). Palmering hackle through body.*

*Toth Elk-Hair Caddis (5). Completed fly.*

toth elk-hair caddis

1½ times the hook gap in length and trim to a stubble the ½ inch nearest the butt on both sides of the shaft. If you select a Whiting 100s, upset the first ½ inch of the tip and then trim the barbs to a stubble on both sides.

5. Place the stubble portion of the feather on the near side of the hook shank at the front end of the body, good side out, so the shaft is diagonally downward and forward and the uncut portion of the feather is touching the body. Tie it in with three to five firm turns of thread, and let the bobbin hang while you cut off the surplus shaft about ⅛ inch from the eye.

6. Attach the hackle pliers to the feather, a couple inches from the tie-in point and at right angles to the shaft. With the feather on edge, spiral it in even turns to the hook bend, where the gold wire hangs. Let the pliers hang to keep the hackle in place.

7. Tie off the hackle with two or three turns of wire, then attach the hackle pliers to the wire as a weight while you cut off the surplus hackle.

8. Spiral the wire rib to the hook eye, bind-ing down the feather shaft, *but not the hackle fibers.* Make two close turns of wire around the hook shank and let the hackle pliers hang. Tie off the wire with thread, and cut off the surplus wire.

9. For the wing, select a bunch of hair about twice the thickness of a kitchen match. Cut it off close to the hide, even the tips, and pull out any fuzz and short hairs. Place it on top of the hook shank so the tips extend slightly beyond the hook bend and the butts are over the eye. Fasten it there with several firm turns of thread. Take hold of the wing tips and pull the wing upright. Now take several tight turns of thread behind the wing to keep it firmly in place as a single unit. The wing butts should still extend over the eye.

10. Raise the wing butts and form a neat head just behind the eye. Whip finish and complete the head in the usual manner.

11. Trim the wing butts to free the eye and create a small tuft for the head. Apply durable nail polish and head cement to the thread, but not the tuft, and the fly is finished.

# NO-HACKLE FLIES

## Slate/Brown No-Hackle

GOOD DRY-FLY HACKLE HAS ALWAYS BEEN IN short supply, and other means of flotation had been the norm until the latter part of the nineteenth century. Genetic hackle as a commercial product is only about 25 years old. Some few tiers raised their own birds to supply a small quantity of good feathers for their own use, and from these bloodlines, hackle like Metz, Herbert, and Whiting developed. These hackles far surpassed the best Asiatic hackle, which was for many years the standard of the commercial fly-tying trade. During most of my life, however, good hackle was hard to find and expensive to purchase. No wonder there was great interest in alternative means of flotation.

Slate/Brown No-Hackle, introduced by Doug Swisher and Carl Richards in the 1970s, is a revival of the fifteenth-century Dame Berners style of tying. The style is ancient, but it has always taken fish, so it must have some merit. It floats much like the natural insect, and the wings—various as they are and of many materials—are well accepted by fish everywhere. Whole books have been written about these no-hackle flies; however, space in this book only allows us to touch on the essentials of the style and introduce you to a representative pattern and optional wing styles.

Swisher and Richards claim that a few basic color combinations, in different sizes, can cover almost all the mayflies of North America, so prototype patterns are highly useful in many sizes. We will use the Slate/Brown for this tying exercise. This particular color combination is useful in Nos. 10–24, and we will use No. 14 for this recipe, as it is large enough to tie easily and matches many different mayflies in size. The proportions listed here apply to all flies of the no-hackle style.

*Body length = bend of the hook to the eye*

*Wing length = same as the body*

*Wing width = one-third of the body length*

*Tail = body length*

*Wing is set two-thirds of the body length from the hook bend*

The wide, V-shaped tails of no-hackle flies are usually made from long, stiff fibers from a large, good dry-fly quality neck hackle or stiff hairs of the same color, and serve as outriggers to balance the fly on the water, in addition to providing a certain amount of buoyancy for the fly. They can be attached a bit forward of the hook bend and then separated to form a V, or can even have a third, more realistic tail tied in between the arms of the V. On dry flies, a small, compact ball of dubbing is often used to separate the arms of the V. Employ firm X-wraps on all parts of the tail.

The dubbing used for the tail and body

provides flotation for this fly. The instructions call for dark brown body material, and medium brown is a good alternative and useful in its own right. All bodies are constructed the same way, but the wings differ in materials, from individual feathers to slips of wing pointers to clumps of feather barbs. Each requires different methods of preparation, attachment, and trimming into shape. We will begin with the whole-feather wing, and then provide instructions for the other wing options after the main recipe.

| | |
|---|---|
| **HOOK** | *Mustad #94833, Nos. 10–24* |
| **THREAD** | *White 8/0 UNI-Thread* |
| **TAIL** | *Dark blue dun dry-fly fibers; body dubbing* |
| **BODY** | *Dark brown natural or synthetic dubbing* |
| **WING** | *Dark gray or slate duck wing feathers* |
| **HEAD** | *Black head cement* |

1. Place the hook in the vise, attach the thread, and wrap a nonslip base for the tail.

2. Spin a very thin ¼ inch noodle of dubbing on the thread, push it up to form a ⅛-inch ball of dubbing (see The Common Method of Dubbing on page 68 for detailed instructions) on the hanging thread, secure it to the hook shank where the bobbin hangs, and let the bobbin hang.

3. Select four stiff fibers at least 1 inch long for the tail. Place two fibers, with their tips evened, on the far side of the dubbing ball so they extend about ¾ inch behind the hook bend. Tie them in place with a couple of turns of thread, and let the bobbin hang.

4. Repeat the process on the near side of the dubbing ball, making sure the fiber tips are even with those of the other tail. Return the thread to the near side of the dubbing ball and let the bobbin hang. The tails should be spread in a wide V.

**Slate/Brown No-Hackle (1).** *Tail feathers and first dubbing ball attached.*

**Slate/Brown No-Hackle (2).** *Body dubbing complete.*

*Slate/Brown No-Hackle (3). Wings attached.*

5. Spin about 2 inches of dubbing for the body. Wrap the dubbing in butting turns, starting hard against the ball at the tail and continuing to about ³⁄₁₆ inch from the eye. Release any excess dubbing from the thread and cut off the excess dubbing, tie off the body with the bare thread, and let the bobbin hang.

6. From the dark topside of one of a matching pair of duck wings, select a ½- to ¾-inch-long, dark gray or slate round-tipped feather. Pull it off the wing and measure it against the hook. If it is the correct length (see proportions above), find a similar feather from the same part of the opposite wing and remove it.

7. Hold the two feathers dull sides together and tips even, and trim to a stubble the fuzz and short, soft feath-ers from both sides of the shafts. Trim an equal amount from both feathers. Place the shafts on top of the hook shank, against the front of the body, bind them there with several firm turns of thread, and let the bobbin hang.

8. Raise the wing upright and support it there with several turns of thread against the rear of the feather shafts. Let the bobbin hang while you cut off the surplus shafts about ⅛ inch from the eye. Separate the feathers, fasten them apart with X-wraps, and let the bobbin hang.

9. Prepare about 1½ inches of dubbing and wrap the thorax or wing area, including the space just behind the head area. Tie off the dubbing.

10. Make a neat head and complete the fly in the usual manner.

slate/brown no-hackle

*Slate/Brown No-Hackle with the wing sidewinded*

*Slate/Brown No-Hackle with a high wing*

## If You Use a Feather-Section Wing

For this wing, you would use matching slate-colored duck pointer wing segments. (This process would replace Steps 6 and 7 above.)

1. Trim the short, soft fibers from the butts of two matching flight feathers, and measure and cut off ¼- to ⅜-inch-wide segments from the same area of the wide side of each. The segments should be ¾ inch long.

2. Holding the segments dull sides together and with the tips aligned and curving up, place the wing on top of and slightly surrounding the hook shank, directly over the hanging bobbin. The butts should be over the eye and the tips should extend to just behind the bend. Fasten the wing there using the soft loop technique, and let the bobbin hang.

## If You Use a Hackle Fiber Bunch Wing

For this wing option you can use hen or rooster body hackle or turkey flats that are dyed slate. Hen neck or saddle feathers dyed dark dun or slate can be used in place of the duck shoulder feathers and are tied in the same way. You can trim all these feather varieties to better imitate mayfly wings. (This process would replace Steps 6 and 7 above.)

1. Select a bunch or bundle of hackle fibers about ⅛ to 3⁄16 inch in diameter and 1 inch in length, and cut it off the feather shaft.

2. Even the tips and place the bunch on top of the hook shank so the butts are over the eye and the tips are over the hook bend. Fasten it there using the soft loop technique, and let the bobbin hang.

3. Pull the bundle forward and upright by the tips, and then wrap several firm turns of thread tight against the rear of the wing to keep it there. Cut and bind down the excess butts at about ⅛ inch from the eye. Return the thread to just behind the wing and let the bobbin hang.

# Yellow Dun

THE YELLOW DUN NO-HACKLE COVERS A SUB-
stantial number of common mayflies in the
same sizes as given for the preceding fly. The
only change is that the body is tied using natural or synthetic yellow dubbing and the wings
can be as varied as those of the preceding fly.

*Yellow Dun*

*Yellow Dun (overhead view)*

*Yellow Dun tied with a feather clump wing*

*Yellow Dun Slate/Yellow No-Hackle tied with a
duck shoulder wing*

# SMALL FLIES

**M**idges—small flies—are an important and at times an essential means of taking fish. When fish are feeding on small flies they usually refuse all other sizes. Natural midges are present and available as food, especially early and late in the season when they are often the only flying insects on the water.

Present-day 8/0 threads, starling neck hackle, and Whiting genetic hackle facilitate tying these small flies, and, with such thin materials and small hooks, you must be careful to handle them gently and stay within their limitations. For example, pull the whip finish parallel to the thin hook shank, rather than at an angle.

## Mouse Turd

THIS SIMPLE, TINY FLY, WHICH REPRESENTS minute insects and larva floating in or under the surface film of the water, is very successful on the Housatonic River in Connecticut when the fish are "smutting." The body is small and rather thin, so be sure to prepare thin dubbing for it.

| | |
|---|---|
| **HOOK** | *Mustad #94842, Nos. 20–22* |
| **THREAD** | *White 8/0 UNI-Thread* |
| **BODY** | *Blue-gray muskrat underfur or synthetic dubbing of that color* |
| **HEAD** | *Black head cement* |

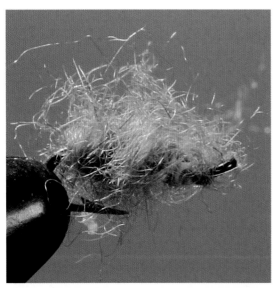

***Mouse Turd.** Dubbing should be tight, not loose as pictured.*

1. Place the hook in the vise, attach the thread, and wrap a nonslip base for the body.
2. Select a small bunch of muskrat fur, cut it off the hide, and, holding the long guard hairs firmly, pull out the underfur.
3. Apply some soft, sticky wax to about 1½ inches of the hanging thread and dub a tiny wisp of the fur or synthetic. Wrap the dubbing in butting turns up the hook shank, in an effort to create the shape of a grain of rice, to about ⅛ inch from the hook eye. Clean off any surplus dubbing, then tie off the body with the clean thread.
4. Form a small, neat head and finish the fly in the usual manner.

# Black Gnat

THIS IS AN OLD ENGLISH PATTERN THAT I have used with great success for at least 60 years. All sizes are useful, but Nos. 16–24 probably get the most use, as smaller sizes are too hard to attach to the leader! Start with a No. 16, and later, as you build confidence, test your skills on smaller hooks—say No. 24s—if you are feeling cocky.

Frankly, tying Nos. 24–28s is an act of faith rather than skill. Even after all these years, if I am not in the mood after a fly or two, I know it is time to put the tiny hooks away and start a 6XL No. 2 bucktail or streamer tied with heavy flat waxed nylon thread. However, when all goes well, the little No. 26s or 28s come surely and without strain, and amaze me as well as others who view them.

Properly tied, this small, dark fly floats *in* the water—not on the surface—accurately representing the behavior of the natural insect. Trout feed heavily on them while they are smutting, excluding all larger forms. The materials required to tie them are all soft, and the hooks are small and delicate. When tying in materials, be sure not to pull too hard before taking a second turn or two, or the thread will cut through the materials like a knife. Also, it is for such times that I told you early on to pull the whip finish carefully, with the thread parallel to the hook shank. If you forget or are heavy-handed, you will be promptly rewarded with disaster—in the form of a broken hook— just as you're preparing to finish the fly.

Some things to note: Use the up-eye hook (#94842) for Nos. 24–28 flies. The long, thin, deep purple neck feathers of the male starling provide proper-sized hackle for tiny flies, rivaling even genetic hackle. The strip of crow tail or secondary feather makes an unusually fine, almost weightless, segmented body.

| | |
|---|---|
| HOOK | *Mustad #94833 or #94842, Nos. 16–26* |
| THREAD | *White 8/0 UNI-Thread* |
| TAIL | *None* |
| BODY | *Crow tail or secondary feather* |
| HACKLE | *Purple/black adult male starling neck feather* |
| HEAD | *Black head cement* |

***Black Gnat***

black gnat

1. Place the hook in the vise, attach the thread, and wrap a nonslip base for the body.

2. Select a feather for the body. Then cut off a strip, close to the shaft, that's three to five barbs wide and 1½ inches long. Long strips are easier to handle.

3. Place the strip on top of the hook shank so the tip is ⅛ inch from the hook eye, and tie it in where the bobbin hangs. Carefully wind the thread forward, binding down the tip of the strip, to ⅛ inch behind the eye and let the bobbin hang.

4. Attach the hackle pliers at right angles to the feather near its butt. To form the segmented body, carefully wind the feather like a ribbon in butting turns up the shank to the bobbin, tie it off with a couple of firm turns of thread, and let the bobbin hang while you cut off the surplus feather.

5. For the hackle, select a long, narrow starling feather that has barbs slightly longer than the hook gap. Cut off about ⅛ inch from the extreme tip of the feather. (It, too, is too soft to use.) Hold the feather diagonally against the near side of the shank at the front (eye) end of the body. With the shaft to the rear, fasten it there with a soft turn of thread, followed by three or four firmer turns to fix it in place. Tying it in this way will help prevent the feather from pulling out when you wind the hackle.

6. Attach small hackle pliers at right angles to the feather shaft and carefully make a turn around the hook shank, close against the body of the fly. If there is enough feather, continue wrapping it around the shank to complete one-and-a-half to three turns maximum; quit while you're ahead! Tie off the hackle and let the bobbin hang again. Cut off the surplus feather and bind down the stub.

7. Form the head and finish the fly in the usual manner.

## Black Caddis

THESE FLIES ARE DESIGNED TO FLOAT ON the water's surface, and they work well there. They are also extremely effective when pulled under the surface, where they represent rising egg-laying females after they've deposited their eggs on the bottom of the stream. Two or three flies can be fished on short tippets on the same leader, either on the surface or under it, with good effect.

The naturals are small, typically caddis-shaped flies that are most vulnerable below the surface on their many egg-laying trips to the bottom of the stream. Black caddis appear from early July to the middle of September on the Housatonic River in western Connecticut.

Tying with white thread against a black body and wing allows you to follow thread

*Black Caddis*

placement easily, and the use of black head cement as a final step assures a truly black fly. Also, No. 20 hooks are small and light, so be sure not to pull hard, especially at a right angle to the hook shank, since it is quite easy to break off the point of the hook.

Because the wing will be so short, it's important to even the tips of the hair you will use to make it. If the wing is too thin, you can improve it by adding more tips or some medium-size hair that's left over from another wing you made. Long, fine tips may well be too thin by themselves to make a proper wing. The finished wing should not be coarse, but it needs some bulk on the sides of the fly for flotation, as well as to outline the wing, and extremely long, fine tips of hair do not meet these requirements.

| | |
|---|---|
| **HOOK** | *Mustad #94840 or #94842, Nos. 18–22* |
| **THREAD** | *White 8/0 UNI-Thread* |
| **TAIL** | *None* |
| **BODY** | *Black XXX dubbing* |
| **WING** | *Black (dyed) deer body hair* |
| **HEAD** | *Black head cement* |

1. With the hook set in the vise, start the thread base at the middle of the hook shank, wrap back to the hook bend, and let the bobbin hang.

2. Prepare a thin dubbing of fine black material (refer to The Common Method of Dubbing, page 68, as needed for

direction). Wrap the body to about ⅛ inch from the eye, tie it off, and let the bobbin hang.

3.  Select a bunch of deer body hair about the thickness of a kitchen match and cut it off close to the hide. Even the tips by hand or by tool, whichever you prefer. If the tips are too long and fine, trim about ⅛ to 3/16 inch off the ends, and then use the somewhat thick tips to form the wing. Holding the bunch about an inch from the tips, measure the wing against the hook. The tips should not extend more than ⅛ to 3/16 inch beyond the hook bend when the butts are over the eye. Look at the thickness of the wing as well as its length.

4.  Bind the wing in place with a soft loop turn. Allow the wing to come down on both sides of the hook shank to about level with the lower side of it. This placement provides both flotation and stability for the fly.

5.  When you are satisfied with the length and position of the wing, make a couple of firm turns of thread to bind it in place. Cut off the excess hair at the eye, leaving a Toth-type tuft (see page 200).

6.  Finish the head between the tuft and the wing, whip finish, and apply black head cement to the head bindings as follows: use a bodkin or needle, and apply the head cement with the shaft, rather than attempting to control a drop of cement at the tip of the tool in the narrow space between the wing and the tuft.

# Spent-Wing Trico

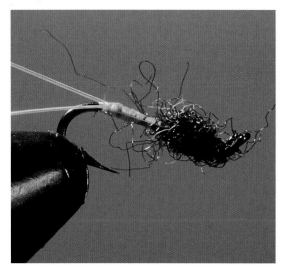

*Spent-Wing Trico*

THE SPINNER IS THE MOST EFFECTIVE FORM for these insects, which have a long season with little competition. This fly represents the male gender of the insect. The natural wing for both males and females is transparent to white depending on how the light hits it. To represent them, poly wings are easier to tie (see Variations), but small hen hackle taken from the head area is a bit more effective with fish.

The stubble you will create at the base of the wing feathers will help secure them to the hook shank and makes a stronger wing. Therefore, do not strip the soft material, as doing so will leave a smooth, slippery surface. Such a surface will allow the thread to slide, and the connection between the feathers and the shank will not be secure.

**HOOK**   *Mustad #94840, Nos. 24–26*

**THREAD**   *White 8/0 UNI-Thread*

**TAILS**   *Natural or dyed black cock hackle fibers*

**BODY**   *Black or brownish-black fur or synthetic*

**WING**   *Light dun hen hackle*

**HEAD**   *Black head cement*

1. Put the hook in the vise, attach the thread, and wrap a nonslip base for the tails.
2. Select a cock hackle feather with barbs ¾ inch long. Cut off or strip the soft, short fibers at the base of the feather until you hit good, firm tail material. Cut off three barbs for the tail.
3. Place one fiber on top of the hook shank so the tip extends three shank lengths beyond the hook bend. Fasten it in place with firm turns of the thread and let the bobbin hang.
4. Place another tail fiber on top of the hook shank so it forms a V with the first fiber and its tip extends the same distance. Fasten it there with a couple of firm turns of thread and let the bobbin hang.
5. Apply the third tail fiber to the far side of the hook in the same manner. Make

a couple of X-wraps between the three tails to spread them apart, and let the bobbin hang.

6. Spin a thin wisp of the black dubbing (see page 68 as needed for instructions) to make a thin body, and wrap it to ⅛ inch from the eye. Tie the body off and let the bobbin hang.
7. Select two matching feathers and prepare a whole-feather wing that is equal to the length of hook shank (refer to Step 5 on page 49 as needed while preparing the feathers). Place the feathers shiny sides together on top of the hook shank so the stubble is toward the eye and the beginning of the barbs is against the forward edge of the body. Bind them there with several turns of thread and let the bobbin hang.
8. Separate the two feathers so they lie flat and are at right angles to the hook shank. Bind them there with the thread

***Spent-Wing Trico*** *tied with a Poly wing*

spent-wing trico

and take X-wraps between them, and let the bobbin hang while you cut off the surplus feather butts.

9. Apply a thin wisp of dubbing to the thread and, to create a thorax, make X-wraps of the dubbing over the base of the wing. Then fill in the area between the wing and the head area. Note that very little of this thin dubbing is needed to do this.

10. Tie off the dubbing, and complete the head in the usual manner.

## Variations

For the Poly wing, use a section of light cream or light gray yarn that is twice the length of the hook shank. Center the wing at right angles to the shank, tight against the forward end of the body, and bind it in place with X-wraps.

# Caenis Spinner (Modified Pattern)

A SMALL BALL OF DUBBING HOLDS THE TAIL fibers apart, forming a V-shaped tail. The deer body hair you use for the abdomen should be thick to create segments and provide flotation.

| | |
|---|---|
| **HOOK** | *Mustad #94842, Nos. 22–28* |
| **THREAD** | *White 8/0 UNI-Thread* |
| **TAIL** | *Light blue dun hackle; white Poly XXX dubbing* |
| **ABDOMEN** | |
| | *White deer body hair, hard and thick* |
| **THORAX** | *Black Poly XXX dubbing* |
| **WING** | *Light gray or cream Antron yarn* |
| **HEAD** | *Black head cement* |

1. Place the hook in the vise, attach the thread, and wrap a nonslip base for the tail.

2. Select four 6-inch-long hackle fibers from a large neck or saddle feather. Cut them off the shaft and put them aside for the tail.

3. Spin a small amount of white dubbing on a short, waxed area of the hanging thread. Push it up to the shank, form a small ball on the top of the shank, and fix it there at the end of the bend with X bindings.

4. Attach half of the tail fibers to the far side of the hook shank so the tips extend half an inch beyond the hook bend on a No. 22 hook. Place and tie in the other half of the tail the same way on the near side of the shank, so the ball of dubbing is between the two halves. Let the bobbin hang while you cut off the excess tail butts close to the tail.

5. Select one deer body hair at least 1 inch long and cut it off the hide. Tie it in by the tip so the thick end points

*Caenis Spinner (1). Attaching the tail, dubbing, and wings.*

*Caenis Spinner (2). Separate wings with X-wraps.*

toward the rear of the fly. Continue binding the hair down to about ³⁄₁₆ inch from the eye, and let the bobbin hang.

6. Attach the hackle pliers to the thick end of the hair and wind it onto the shank to where the bobbin hangs. Let the hackle pliers hang to keep the deer hair in place while you tie it down with two turns of thread. Then let the bobbin hang while you cut off the surplus deer hair. Bind down the cut ends of hair and let the bobbin hang.

7. Apply dubbing wax to 1½ inches of the thread close to the hook, then spin a thin film of black Poly XXX dubbing onto the thread for the thorax. Push the dubbing up to the hook shank and wind a plump, short thorax. Tie off the thorax with two turns of thread and let the bobbin hang again.

8. Measure slightly more than two hook-shank lengths of Antron yarn and cut it off. Place the yarn on top of and perpendicular to the hook shank, between the thorax and the hook eye,

*Caenis Spinner (3). Completed fly.*

so it extends an equal distance from each side of the shank. Fasten it there with X-wraps, ending in front of the wings, and let the bobbin hang.

9. While holding onto the body and thorax, push the wing back firmly against the thorax to make room for a neat head. Form the head and finish the fly in the usual manner.

# Badger Midge

WHEN YOU ARE FINISHED MAKING THE BODY of this fly, you may find that the remainder of the peacock eye quill is long enough for another body, so set it aside for future use. Choose your hackle from a genetic dry-fly quality badger neck or Whiting 100s.

| | |
|---|---|
| **HOOK** | *Mustad #94842, Nos. 20–24* |
| **THREAD** | *White 8/0 UNI-Thread* |
| **TAIL** | *None* |
| **BODY** | *Peacock quill, stripped* |
| **WING** | *None* |
| **HACKLE** | *Badger genetic neck or Whiting 100s, Nos. 18–20* |
| **HEAD** | *Black head cement* |

1. Place the hook in the vise, attach the thread, and wrap a nonslip base for the body.

2. With a bodkin, separate out one segment of peacock eye quill from a waxed eye. Remove it and strip off the waxed herl by running it between your fingernails until the quill is clean. Tie in the thin end of the quill at the bend of the hook, then wind the thread in close, even turns up the shank to ⅛ inch behind the eye and let the bobbin hang.

3. Attach the hackle pliers to the quill and wind the body, carefully butting each turn, to ⅛ inch from the eye. Tie off the body and cut off the surplus quill.

*Badger Midge*

4. For the hackle, select a small neck feather with barbs 1½ times the hook gap in length. Trim the lowest ¼ inch of the feather to a stubble on both sides of the shaft. If using the Whiting 100s hackle, upset ½ inch of the tip and cut both sides of that area to a stubble.

5. With two or three turns of thread, tie in the stubble end of the feather directly over the hanging bobbin so the shaft slants horizontally against the near side of the hook shank. Let the bobbin hang while you cut off the surplus stubble close behind the eye.

6. Attach small or midge-size hackle pliers to the free end of the hackle. With the feather on edge, take two or three turns toward the eye, then let the pliers hang while you tie off the hackle and cut off the excess feather. Bind down the end of the hackle shaft.

7. Form a small, neat head and finish the fly in the usual manner.

# Dun Midge

When tying Dun Midge, use the same color feather material for the tail and the hackle. The length of the fibers should be 1½ times the body length for the tail and 1½ times the hook gap for the hackle.

| | |
|---|---|
| **HOOK** | *Mustad #94842, Nos. 20–28* |
| **THREAD** | *White 8/0 UNI-Thread* |
| **TAIL** | *Dark blue dun hackle fibers* |
| **BODY** | *Blue-gray muskrat underfur or dubbing* |
| **HACKLE** | *Dark blue dun* |
| **WING** | *None* |
| **HEAD** | *Black head cement* |

The Dun Midge is tied like the Dark Hendrickson. See page 191 for details.

## Variations

The Brown/Cochy Midge is tied the same way as the Dun Midge, with the following materials substitutions: use brown or cochy

*Dun Midge*

*Brown/Cochy Midge*

*Brown/Cochy Midge (overhead view)*

(furnace) hackle fibers for the tail; one strand of pheasant tail feather (from a cock) for the body; and brown or cochy hackle.

The required length of hackle fibers for the tail is the same as that for the Dun Midge. The body material is tied in by its tip, or thin end, and wound in butting turns up the hook shank. Select hackle that is 1½ times the hook gap in length, and apply only two or three turns of it to the shank.

## Bumble Bee

THIS IS AN EFFECTIVE, HIGH-FLOATING FLY for trout and panfish. Review Spinning Hair in the Basic Skills chapter (page 69) for the details on spinning and trimming this type of fly.

When you are finished tying the first Bumble Bee, tie another one. It will come easier the second time and you can then afford to lose the first one to a rock, tree, or fish.

| HOOK | *Partridge 01 or Mustad #94840, Nos. 8–10* |
|---|---|
| THREAD | *White flat waxed nylon; 8/0 UNI-Thread* |
| TAIL | *None* |
| BODY | *Black and yellow deer, elk, or antelope body hair* |
| WING | *None* |
| HEAD | *Black head cement* |

1. Place the hook in the vise and attach the flat waxed nylon thread. *Do not wrap a nonslip base.*
2. Select a bunch of black hair about ¼ inch thick and at least 1 inch long, and cut it off close to the hide. Trim both ends of the bundle to shorten it to about ¾ inch of even-diameter hair, and spin it onto the hook shank. Spin on another bunch, then let the bobbin hang.
3. Prepare and spin on a yellow bunch to form the middle of the body, making it at least ³⁄₁₆ inch wide. Let the bobbin hang while you prepare and spin at least two more bunches of black hair to bring the compacted fuzzy ball to about ⅛ inch from the eye.
4. Tie off the thread and trim the fuzz ball to attain the shape of a bumble bee (see Trimming the Body on page 71 for detailed instructions).
5. Attach the bobbin charged with 8/0 UNI-Thread or flat waxed nylon thread, make a neat head, and finish the fly in the usual manner.

*Bumble Bee*

# Hair Popper/Pusher

THIS FLY IS A NOISY ATTRACTOR THAT MUST be used carefully. By pulling too hard or fast on the retrieve, the fly will go deeply under the water, and the broad, hardened face may create enough resistance to break your rod tip. If used properly, however—in short jerks with pauses, rather than long pulls—it will chug merrily along the surface, making lots of noise and bubbles and exciting all the fish within hearing range.

Although there are several hook size options, we will tie a No. 6 fly, and you can tie other sizes in proportion. Color is not a critical feature, so cheap, natural gray/brown deer body hair works very well for the spun body (see Variations for a night version of the fly). Elk and antelope hair can be substituted for deer body hair.

This fly has a widely divided tail. For No. 6 hooks the tail should be about 1½ to 2 inches long. For No. 2 hooks, they may be up to 2½ inches long. Saddle trimmings may offer a cheaper option for tail material and work about as well as saddle hackle, but they do not look as nice. The stubble you will create on the shafts of the tail hackles will hold the thread well and keep the tail in place better than when using a stripped, smooth hackle shaft. It is well worth the extra effort to trim the tail hackles.

Larger size hooks require proportionately larger tails and bodies, but do not get such a large "face" (see Step 12) that it digs into the water when you fish. And remember,

even with a proper-size face, don't pull too hard or fast or you may break a rod tip.

| | |
|---|---|
| **HOOK** | *Mustad Stinger #37187, Nos. 2–6* |
| **THREAD** | *White flat waxed nylon* |
| **TAILS** | *Brown, black, badger, or furnace saddle hackles or saddle trimmings* |
| **BODY** | *Natural deer body hair* |
| **HEAD** | *Black head cement* |
| **ALSO REQUIRED** | *Clear silicone seal* |

1. Place the hook in the vise, attach the thread, and wrap a nonslip base for the tail.
2. Select four short, matching feathers for the tails. Pair them up, tips together, so each pair has a good side and a dull side. Place the pairs dull sides together and trim to a stubble the fuzz and short, soft fibers.
3. Place one pair on the far side of the hook so the stubble is over the hanging thread and the first barbs are behind the hook bend. Bind it in place so the curve of the feathers (if any) goes out and away from the hook shank.
4. Tie in the other pair on the near side of the shank in the same manner. Make several X-wraps to spread and secure the tails. Cut off the excess feather shafts and bind down the butts. Make

*Hair Popper/Pusher, before trimming*

*Hair Popper/Pusher, completed fly*

a last turn of thread against the first pair of tail fibers, fastening the turns so there will be no bare space at the base of the tails when you start spinning on the body. Let the bobbin hang.

5. Select a ¼-inch-thick bundle of hair for the body, about 1½ inches long for No. 6 hooks and longer, if available, for No. 2 hooks. Cut it off close to the hide and, holding it firmly by the tips, remove all fuzz and short hairs. Reduce it to a length of ¾ inch by cutting equal lengths from both ends of the bundle.

6. Spin the hair onto the hook as directed in Spinning Hair onto the Hook on page 69 of the Basic Skills chapter, and let the bobbin hang. Repeat the process with another bunch of hair, spinning it on tight against the first bunch. Push the hair back while holding it from the rear to form a tight, dense body, and let the bobbin hang.

7. Continue preparing and spinning more bunches of hair, but cut less and less from the tips and butts until the last two bundles, at least, are full-length, untrimmed hair and the pushed-back bundles are about ³⁄₁₆ inch from the hook eye.

8. After the last bunch is in place, make two turns of thread around the hook shank, tie off the thread with a couple of half hitches, and cut it off, leaving an end about 1 inch beyond the knot.

9. Take the fly from the vise and trim the body, using the steps described in Trimming the Body, on page 71 of the Basic Skills chapter, as a guide. To define the flat belly of the fly, begin cutting at about ½ inch below the hook eye (for No. 6 hooks) and continue diagonally back to slightly below the tail. To define one side of the body, begin cutting at about ½ to ¾ inch to the left of the hook shank and continue

diagonally back to the tails (*do not* cut the tails). Repeat the cut on the opposite side of the body. Trim the top last, again starting at about ½ to ¾ inch above the eye, to define the tip of the body.

10. The body should now be 1 inch square at the eye end, tapering to the tail. Cut off the corners of the square to make a rounded, cone-shaped body about 1 inch in diameter at the eye for a No. 6 fly and as much as 1½ inches for a No. 2 fly.

11. Replace the hook in the vise and attach the thread between the eye and the front of the hair. Bind down the end of the original spinning thread before making a neat head and finishing it in the usual manner.

12. Trim the face of the fly flat behind the eye and apply a coat of clear silicone seal. This will hold the hair together and allow the face to push water, pop, and gurgle.

## Variations

There may be some advantage in using a black popper at dusk or for night fishing, as the dark silhouette against the lighter sky makes it easier for the fish to pinpoint the noisy fly. The black version of Hair Popper/Pusher is tied as described above, using black feathers for the tails and black dyed deer body hair for the body.

# G. H. Caddis

THE SPUN HAIR BODY OF G. H. CADDIS provides high flotation and a wing silhouette in typical caddis form. The length of hair required for the body will spin easily and, hopefully, will not foul on the lower part of the hook in the process. Once perfected, the extra little lift created when you cinch the hair after it stops turning on the shank (see Step 3) will vastly improve the durability of your spun hair flies. Be sure to consult the photos for shaping the body, as the body outline is of great importance to this fly.

Note that the hackle on the bottom of the fly remains untrimmed to look like legs. Leaving the bottom hackle full length also helps float the fly.

| HOOK | Mustad #94831 (2XL or 2X fine), Nos. 12–14 |
|---|---|
| THREAD | White flat waxed nylon; 8/0 UNI-Thread |
| TAIL | None |
| BODY/WING | Natural deer body hair |
| HACKLE/ANTENNAE | Brown dry-fly neck hackles |
| HEAD | Black head cement |

1. Place the hook in the vise and attach the thread. Do *not* wrap a nonslip base.

2. Select a bunch of hair about 1 to 1¼

G. H. Caddis (1). Body hair spun on.

G. H. Caddis (3). Tying the feathers in place.

G. H. Caddis (2). Body trimmed.

G. H. Caddis (4). Preparing the hackle.

g. h. caddis

inches long and as thick as a pencil for the body, and cut it off close to the hide. Holding it firmly by the tips, remove any short hairs and fuzz. Cut off about ³⁄₁₆ inch from the tips and a bit less from the butts to create a bundle that is about ¾ inch long and having hair of the same diameter throughout its length.

3. To create the body, spin two such bundles according to the directions provided in Spinning Hair onto the Hook (page 69 of the Basic Skills chapter). When finished, the front of the body should be about ³⁄₁₆ inch from the hook eye. Tie the thread off with two overhand knots before cutting it about an inch ahead of the knots.

4. Remove the fly from the vise and trim the body as follows, referring to Trimming the Body on page 71 of the Basic Skills chapter as needed for detailed instructions. Make a cut about ³⁄₁₆ inch below and parallel to the hook

**G. H. Caddis (5). Completed fly.**

shank, from the eye to the hook bend, to expose the hook point and barb and form the bottom of the fly. Square off the near side of the body, making the cut about ³⁄₁₆ inch from the shank. Then make a similar cut the same distance from the shank on the other side of the fly. At this point, examine the body and carefully trim it to about ³⁄₁₆ inch in width, with the hook shank as the centerline. Carefully trim out the hook gap. You can also trim more off the bottom of the fly to good effect. When finished, you should have a body that's flat on the bottom, ³⁄₁₆ inch wide, and has flat sides and an untrimmed top or crest.

5. To shape the wing, start at the extreme rear of the untrimmed top and cut forward in a diagonal, from the full length of the hair to the eye. Square off the extreme rear of the body and, with judicious clipping, flatten the first one-third of the top of the body behind the eye, starting at the eye rather than from the rear.

6. When satisfied with the shape of the body and the height of the wing, carefully trim and thin the top edge, from both sides, to about one-half its thickness. To obtain a more natural, typical caddis shape, round over the rear corner of the wing and the areas where the bottom and side cuts meet.

7. Return the fly to the vise and attach white 8/0 UNI-Thread to finish the rest of the fly. Be sure to first cut off the excess flat nylon thread and bury the

cut end under the new thread, tight against the hair body.

8. Select two equal-size hackle feathers that have barbs 1½ times the hook gap in length, and strip the fuzz and barbs from the lowest ¾ inch of each. Place the feathers together, dull sides down, on top of the hook shank so the shafts extend over the eye and the first usable barbs are tight against the body. Tie the feathers firmly in place with about six turns of thread, and let the bobbin hang.

9. Align the tips of the feathers, then attach hackle pliers at right angles to the shafts. Wrap the feathers, on edge, tight against the clipped body. Continue forward, making three close, tight turns, then let the hackle pliers hang so the feathers will not unwind. Tie off the hackle with a couple turns of thread, and let the bobbin hang while you cut off the surplus *tips* of the feathers; *do not* cut off the feather shafts. Bind down the cut ends of the feathers.

10. To make antennae, raise the feather shafts that extend over the hook eye. Wrap a couple of turns of thread to hold them up well above the eye, then separate them and hold them apart with X-wraps.

11. Remove the fly from the vise and trim the hackle above and a bit down on each side of the hook shank to stubble. Do not trim the hackle on the bottom.

12. Return the fly to the vise, make a small, neat head, and finish the fly in the usual manner.

# Tuttle Devil Bug (Shellback)

TUTTLE DEVIL BUG IS A HIGH-FLOATING, durable shellback bug pattern. Relatively easy to make, it replaces the cork of the old Tuttle Devil Bug with softer spun/clipped hair. It will take lots of use and abuse and still interest many species of fish. Bass and pickerel attack the large sizes, and trout, bluegills, and other panfish accept the No. 12 as a beetle. It's a good *search fly*—a fly that resembles nothing in particular but everything in general. The construction is similar to Peacock and Deer-Hair Bug (page 159), but this fly has a spun/clipped hair body and is tied onto larger size hooks. The spun/clipped hair body is much more durable than peacock herl (which we used for the Peacock and Deer-Hair Bug body) and offers white, yellow, black, and natural gray and brown for body colors with a natural or black shellback for contrast.

The shellback should cover the back of the fly completely and extend down to the top of the hook shank on each side. Tying the shellback bundle firmly in place will flare the tips and spread the shellback. Spiraling the thread forward *under* the raised shellback will completely conceal the passage of the tying thread from the rear to the front end of the fly, where it will be used to tie down the other end of the shellback.

If you tie this fly for trout, use a Mustad #94831, Nos. 6–12 2XL dry-fly hook.

| | |
|---|---|
| **HOOK** | *Mustad Stinger #37187, Nos. 2–6 or #90240* |
| **THREAD** | *White flat waxed nylon* |
| **BODY** | *Natural, white, or yellow deer, elk, antelope, or caribou body hair* |
| **TAIL/SHELLBACK** | |
| | *Dark natural, black (dyed), or brown deer, elk, or antelope body hair* |
| **WING** | *None* |
| **HEAD** | *Black head cement* |

1. Place the hook in the vise and attach the thread. Do *not* wrap a nonslip base.
2. Select a ⅜-inch-diameter bundle of hair for the body and cut it off the hide.

Prepare and spin the hair into a fuzz ball body. (See Spinning Hair onto the Hook on page 69.) Repeat until the body is within ³⁄₁₆ inch of the hook eye, tie off the thread, and cut it about 1 inch above the half hitches.

3. Trim the body of the fly to a width and top-to-bottom dimension of ¾ inch for No. 2 hooks and about ¼ inch for No. 12 hooks (see Trimming the Body on page 71 as needed for detailed instructions). Round off and taper both ends of the body and leave no sharp points where the sides meet the top and bottom.
4. Select a bundle of shellback hair that will provide good color contrast with the body. It should be 1½ inches long or more, or long enough to extend from about ¾ inch beyond the rear of the body (the tips will form the tail), over the top of the body, and at least ⅜ inch beyond the hook eye. Cut a bundle about ⅜ inch thick for No. 2 hooks or about ³⁄₁₆ inch thick for No. 6 hooks.

*Tuttle Devil Bug (1). Hair spun into fuzz ball body.*

*Tuttle Devil Bug (2). Body has been trimmed.*

**Tuttle Devil Bug (3).** *Attaching the bundle of shellback hair.*

**Tuttle Devil Bug (4).** *Shellback formed.*

**Tuttle Devil Bug (5).** *Completed fly (tied on a Mustad #90240).*

5.  Attach the thread to the hook shank, hard against the rear of the body, and let the bobbin hang. Even the tips of the shellback bundle and place it on top of the body so the tips extend about ¾ inch beyond the hanging bobbin and the butts are over the eye. Bind it in place with several firm turns of thread. Then carry the thread forward—in taut spirals under the raised shellback and buried in the clipped body hair—to the eye area, and let the bobbin hang.

6.  Gather the butt ends of the flared shellback and, with even tension, spread it over the back and top of the fly, without any gaps. While holding the butts in one hand, carefully bind down the shellback just behind the eye with the other, with several turns of thread. Then bring the thread ahead of the shellback and trim the shellback butts to ½ to ³⁄₁₆ inch.

7.  Form a neat head, whip finish, and complete the fly in the usual manner.

# White Hair Frog

FOR SPINNING THE HAIR FROG BODY, CARI-bou hair is softer than deer hair, spins well, floats the fly even higher, and can be dyed—but it's not as readily available. Whichever you use, there must be enough hair to go completely around the hook, but not so much that you can't spin it easily. With a little experience you will discover how large a bunch you can handle. The width of the body is controlled by the length of the hair bundles, so keep the body depth very short at the legs to maintain good hooking ability.

The "tails" of Hair Frogs actually represent legs—so we will refer to them as legs henceforth—and they serve many purposes. The feather legs and spun/cut hair body share the job of floating and/or stabilizing the fly on the water's surface. The legs "kick" well due to the curve of the feathers, giving a very lifelike action to this fly. The method of tying on the legs is the same as that for the V-shape tail of a No-Hackle (page 203), except without the ball of dubbing. Also, here the two feathers curve outward for maximum action when the frog is jerked through the water.

The arms should extend at least 1 inch on each side of the body. They should be cut a bit long and then trimmed to size when the fly is finished, especially if you did not get an equal length on each side on the first try. When in the water, they should bend back each time the fly is pulled; they must not be too thick and stiff, but should make some commotion in the water as the fly moves forward.

Other things to note: Use No. 4 or No. 6 hooks if you're fishing for bluegills or using a lighter fly rod. White flat waxed nylon is recommended for all steps, but you can use "A" nylon for spinning hair if you often break the flat waxed nylon.

**White Hair Frog (1).** *Tying the "tail"—the frog's legs, in place.*

**White Hair Frog (2).** *Body spun on.*

| HOOK | *Mustad #90240, No. 4 salmon dry fly hook, or Stinger #37187, Nos. 2–6* |
|---|---|
| THREAD | *White flat waxed nylon* |
| LEGS | *Badger saddle hackles or trimmings from saddles* |
| BODY | *White deer body hair* |
| ARMS | *Crimped fine nylon* |
| HEAD | *Black head cement* |

**White Hair Frog (3).** *Body trimmed to an angle.*

white hair frog

1. Place the hook in the vise and attach the thread about ⅛ inch ahead of the hook bend. Wrap the thread ⅛ inch toward the rear to provide a nonslip surface for the legs.

2. From the upper edge of the saddle, choose four similar-size, short hackles that are proportionate to the size of the fly and the hook. Pair these and trim the soft, lower part of the feathers to a stubble. Place a pair on one side of the hook shank, so the feathers curve out, and bind them in place. Repeat with the second pair on the opposite side of the hook, placing it so the legs are separated. Cut off the excess hackle shafts and bind them down smoothly so the hair bundles will easily spin over them. Then let the bobbin hang.

3. Select a piece of hide containing coarse, white deer hair from the lower chest area, and cut off a bunch that's a little thinner than a pencil. Trim from both ends until you have a length of about ¾ inch. Spin a hair body as directed in Spinning Hair onto the Hook (page 69 of the Basic Skills chapter). If hairs are caught on the hook point, free them with your bodkin so they spin evenly and completely around the hook shank. Use longer bunches of hair when you are past the hook point, and continue spinning until the closely packed body is about ¼ inch from the hook eye. Tie off the thread with at least two half hitches, then cut it, leaving about 2 inches of it hanging.

4. Trim the body to the proper size and shape, being careful not to cut off the hanging thread (see Trimming the Body on page 71 as needed for detailed instructions). Trim the bottom at an angle, from the front edge to the legs, leaving at least ½ inch of body depth on the underside of the fly. Be sure not to cut the legs. Next cut both sides, leaving the maximum width at the front and tapering toward the legs. Then cut the top as you did the bottom. Carefully

**white hair frog**

*White Hair Frog (4). Completed fly.*

trim the rear of the body, where it over-hangs the legs. To do this, slide the thick, dull side of one scissors blade along the feathers, and then close the scissors to trim away the unwanted hairs. Finish trimming as needed, rounding the edges between the sides and top and bottom cuts.

5. Return the fly to the vise and attach the thread at the same spot where you tied it off before you trimmed the fuzz ball. Bind down the cut end of the original thread and cut off any excess.

6. Cut a bundle of crimped nylon as thick as a kitchen match and 3 to 4 inches long for the arms. Place it on top of and perpendicular to the hook shank,

against the body, and bind it firmly in place with X-wraps.

7. Form a head, whip finish, and finish the fly in the usual manner. Trim the arms to size, if needed.

If you have difficulty tying in the arms close to the body, a hackle guard will solve your problem. This is easily made from a sheet of metal or stiff plastic such as a pocket calen-dar card. In the card, drill a hole large enough to put the hook eye through, then make a slit from the hole to one edge of the card. Put the eye of the hook through the hole after attaching the thread, then push the guard firmly back against the hair. Work the thread forward through the slit. Because the thread is already tight against the body, it is also in place to bind down the arms tightly against the hair. When you finish the head, remove the guard by spreading/twisting the split side to release it from the fly.

If you experience problems fastening the feather legs firmly to the hook shank, and they move around the shank when you spin the first bunch of hair, here is a simple and effective cure. It does, however, add 10 or 15 minutes of drying time to the process.

After you bind the legs in place in the usual manner, apply a couple of half hitches or the whip finish and cut the thread. Apply a generous coating of durable nail polish. Any color will do, as it will be buried and forever out of sight. This will bind the thread and feather legs firmly to the hook shank, and should be thick enough—perhaps with a second coat—to provide a smooth surface upon which to spin the first bunches of hair.

## Variations

All of the following flies are tied in the same manner as the White Hair Frog by substituting the appropriate colored materials.

- Black Hair Frog: Excellent for overcast days and night use. For the legs, use short black saddle hackle, or spade hackle for smaller sizes.
- Natural Hair Frog: Use light tan to dark gray body hair, with short brown or furnace saddle hackles for the legs.
- Yellow Hair Frog: Use short badger saddle hackle for the legs.
- Green Hair Frog: Use short grizzly saddle or spade feathers for the legs.

## Hair Mouse

THE HAIR MOUSE IS AN OLD, FAVORITE, top-of-the-water fly for bass and large trout. The basic construction follows that of the Hair Frog, which I suggest you read before tackling the mouse. The rubber or leather tail is used in place of the feather legs. The fuzz ball body is made the same way, but with increasingly shorter bundles of hair at the front so it is easier to trim the nose. Leather or rubber arms and legs can be tied in front and rear, but frankly they are a nuisance to tie in, and if well done, they will catch more fishermen than fish! Keep it simple. You cannot duplicate the frantic foot action of a swimming mouse with any artificial or natural material. However, you can achieve the body shape, including the tail, and that is usually more than enough to produce hard strikes. Another distinct advantage: The recipe calls for natural, undyed deer body hair, which will produce a buoyant, natural-looking mouse.

Stinger hooks give good clearance, and Nos. 2, 4, and 6 are useful. Anything larger will produce a fly that is hard to cast with the average trout fly rod. When spinning the body, be sure to start the first bundle so there is no gap showing white thread between the tail and the body. No self-respecting mouse has such a white area, and your Hair Mouse doesn't need one either!

Trimming the body and head area of the Hair Mouse can be tricky business. When shaping the ears especially (see Step 6), slow and easy does it! You cannot put hair back, no matter how much you want to do it! A dab of clear silicone seal smoothed onto each ear will greatly improve and stabilize most ears.

If you find this fly a challenge to tie, remember this: Your second mouse will be easier, and should look better too.

| | |
|---|---|
| **HOOK** | *Mustad Stinger #37187, Nos. 2–6* |
| **THREAD** | *White flat waxed nylon* |
| **TAIL** | *Rubber band or leather strip* |
| **BODY** | *Natural gray-brown whitetail or mule deer body hair* |
| **EYES** | *Black head cement* |
| **HEAD (NOSE)** | |
| | *Black head cement* |

1. Place the hook in the vise, attach the thread, and wrap a nonslip base for the tail.

2. Select a 2½-inch section of leather or rubber band (gray or black preferred) about ⅛ to 3/16 inch wide and, if desired, taper one end to match the taper of a mouse's tail. Place the untapered end on top of the hook shank about ½ inch ahead of the hook bend and bind it firmly in place. Then return the thread to the rear of the binding and let the bobbin hang.

3. Select a bundle of hair 1¼ to 2 inches long and about as thick as a pencil for the body, and cut it off close to the hide. If there is fuzz, clean it out. Trim both ends of the bundle until it's 1 inch long for No. 2 hooks and a bit shorter for No. 6 hooks. Spin the first bundle and the rest of the body according to the directions on page 69 (see Spinning Hair onto the Hook), keeping the following instructions in mind: As you cut and trim subsequent bundles of

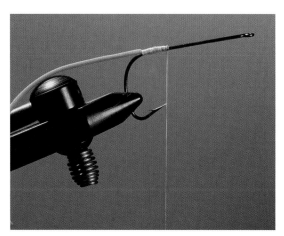

*Hair Mouse (1). Tying in the tail.*

*Hair Mouse (2). Body hair spun on.*

hair, shorten their length to form the taper of the nose, but make none under ½ inch in length, as it is then too hard to control. When pushed back, the last bundle should be about ³⁄₁₆ inch from the eye. Tie off the thread with a couple of half hitches, cut it, and remove the fly from the vise.

4. Trim the body, referring to the instructions on page 71 of the Basic Skills chapter as needed. Cut flat across the bottom of the fly, parallel to the hook shank and about ³⁄₁₆ inch below it, to the tail. Make a straight cut about ½ inch from the hook shank on both sides to create a body width of 1 inch. Make a flat cut on top, about ½ inch above the hook shank and starting 1 inch behind the hook eye (the 1-inch space is for the head and face). When you are finished, the depth of the body should be about ¹¹⁄₁₆ inch.

5. Leave a ³⁄₁₆-inch-wide collar of uncut hair between the last cut you made for the body and the one you're about to make for the head. You will shape the collar into ears later. To start the head, make a cut at right angles to the hook shank, and about a half an inch above it, across the top of the fuzz ball. Starting in the hook eye area, make a cut about ⅛ inch above the hook shank and slanting up to meet the previous cut. This forms the top of the face. Make similar cuts on both sides of the hook shank to shape the sides of the mouse head/face, and another at the bottom to shape the pointed chin in that area.

6. To shape the ears, go back to the uncut collar and, starting directly over the hook shank, cut out about a ³⁄₁₆-inch slot of hair to separate them. (Ears are quite large on a real mouse.) Measure off about ¼ inch for the left ear and define it by cutting away the excess hair. Do this in small cuts and stop while you still have a bit more to trim off! You can trim it later if need be. Repeat the process to define the right ear.

*Hair Mouse (3). Completed fly.*

*Hair Mouse tied with alternative body hair.*

7. Take a good, long look at what you have done, and slowly and carefully clean up whatever is necessary. For example, round off square edges to create a more realistic shape, and, if necessary, cut a little closer to the hook shank on the bottom toward the rear. Round or thin the ears as needed.

8. Use a matchstick—or, better yet, a finishing nail with a medium-size head—to make the eyes. Dip the tool in black head cement and touch the wet end onto each side of the head, fairly well behind the nose area. You may need to apply two coats of head cement to bind the hair together in a little ball of paint.

9. Reattach the thread behind the hook eye, form a small, neat head—in this case, the mouse's nose—whip finish, and complete the fly in the usual manner.

# Rat-Faced McDougal

THE RAT-FACED MCDOUGAL, AND THE IRRE-sistibles in the next recipe, are hair-body search flies that function well in a variety of situations in which matching the ongoing hatch is not essential. They are all very useful and durable flies that should be in your tackle box, especially Nos. 6 and 8 for large trout and bass.

The Rat-Faced McDougal that follows is a Harry Darbee pattern. When preparing the body, remember that shorter hair is easier to spin, and the consistent diameter of the hairs makes a better body.

Variations on this pattern follow the main recipe. These flies can also be tied on lightweight hooks, but the hair body provides ample flotation for the heavier hooks, so the choice is yours. Use a No. 12 hook for trout and a No. 6 hook for bass and salmon.

*Rat-Faced McDougal (1). Tying in the tail.*

*Rat-Faced McDougal (2). Attaching body hair.*

*Rat-Faced McDougal (3). Body trimmed, wing hackle on and neck hackle being attached.*

*Rat-Faced McDougal (4). Completed fly.*

| HOOK | *Mustad #94833 or #94840, Nos. 4–14* |
|---|---|
| THREAD | *White flat waxed nylon* |
| TAIL | *Light tan elk hair or deer hock hair* |
| BODY | *Light tannish-gray deer body hair* |
| WING | *Light grizzly hackle tips* |
| HACKLE | *Light ginger neck hackle or Whiting 100s* |
| HEAD | *Black head cement* |

1. Place the hook in the vise, attach the thread, and wrap a nonslip base for the tail.

2. Select a bunch of hair about as thick as a common kitchen match and at least 1 inch long for the tail, and cut it off the hide. Even the tips and remove any fuzz or short hairs. Place the bunch on top of the hook shank so the tips extend about ¾ inch beyond the hook bend. Fasten it there using the soft loop technique, and let the bobbin hang. Cut off the surplus butts in a taper toward the eye. Bind down the cut ends, return the thread to the soft loop, then let the bobbin hang.

3. Select a ¼- to ³⁄₁₆-inch-thick bunch of hair for the body and cut it off close to the hide. Remove any fuzz, and then cut equal amounts from the tips and butts to yield a ¾-inch-long bundle of hairs that are nearly equal in diameter.

4. Place the bundle on top of the hook shank and spin the hair body (refer to Spinning Hair onto the Hook on page 69 of the Basic Skills chapter as needed). If the ends of the flared hair are caught in the hook gap, use the bodkin to free them before passing the thread through the hair and around the hook shank. When the body reaches ³⁄₁₆ inch from the hook eye, tie two half hitches around the hook shank to hold

everything in place and cut off the thread 1 inch beyond the knots.

5. Remove the fly from the vise to trim the body into shape. Make a cut from the eye to inside the hook bend, about ³⁄₁₆ inch below the shank, to clear the point and gap of the hook. Starting at the eye, cut each side of the body about ³⁄₁₆ inch from the hook shank and tapering to the base of the tail. Then cut the top, starting ³⁄₁₆ inch above the shank at the eye and tapering to the base of the tail. Last, redo the first cut, starting at about the middle of the body and tapering to the tail. To form an oval or round insect-like body, round over the sharp edges where the several cuts meet,

6. Select two light grizzly neck hackle feathers about 1 to 1½ inches long, preferably they are growing side by side on the skin. Place them dull sides together and, holding them firmly by their evened tips, measure down a hook-shank length from the tips. Separate the tips from the rest of the feather with the bodkin. Reduce part of the feathers below the tips to a stubble. Place the wing, dull sides together, on top of the hook shank so the butts are over the eye and the rear end of the untrimmed feather tips is directly over where the bobbin hangs. Fasten the wing in place, using the soft loop technique, and let the bobbin hang while you carefully cut the hackle shafts off about ⅛ inch from the eye.

7. Lift up the wing by the tips and wrap several turns of thread tight behind it to keep it in a vertical position. Separate the feathers and fix them there with X-wraps, ending behind the wing, and let the bobbin hang.

8. Prepare and tie in either a neck hackle or a Whiting 100s of a size to match your hook size (refer to Step 6 on page 49 as needed) with three or four firm turns of thread behind the wing and then two or three turns of thread in front of the wing. Trim the excess stubble end.

9. Attach the hackle pliers at right angles to the shaft (about 4 inches up from the hook if using the Whiting 100s) and turn the feather on edge. Start the first turn close to the rear of the wing, then make a second turn very tight against the rear of the wing. Bring the feather forward tight against the front of the wing for one turn, and continue for two more closely butted turns. Let the hackle pliers hang while you tie off the hackle with three or four tight firm turns of thread. Let the bobbin hang while you carefully cut off the surplus hackle, raising it above the hook shank to avoid cutting the thread. Bind down the cut ends of the hackle.

10. Form a neat head, whip finish, and complete the fly in the usual manner.

## Variations

To make a more durable fly, you can substitute hair for feather wings. For a hair-wing fly use light tan deer hair or bleached coastal blacktail deer hair, which has a finer texture. Employ a dark ginger wing if you're tying the Orvis style. Review Step 5 on page 47 of the Basic Skills chapter as needed to prepare and tie in a hair wing.

# Irresistibles

THIS IS A FAMILY OF HIGH-FLOATING, LONG-lasting flies. Nos. 10–12 are successful with trout and panfish and Nos. 4–8 will attract and catch bass and salmon. Tying smaller sizes is difficult because of the spun/clipped hair body. The light hooks do not withstand the strain of heavy thread and a strong hand. The fine hair needed for small flies, combined with the pressure needed for spinning it, accentuate the usual problems—thread-cut hair and broken hooks—and close trimming can result in the accidental cutting of the tying thread. However, in the proper sizes they are remarkably useful search flies. They do not match the hatch, but they offer a real mouthful to a hungry fish and produce a lot of action from both pocket-water and lake fishing.

Here's a word of caution about applying the tail hair to the shank: If the hair flares when you use the soft loop technique, stop! Undo it and start again (see Step 3). The tail should be *bundled*, not flared. Body hair spins best on a bare hook shank and often catches and turns the tail around the shank when you exert the pressure needed to properly spin the hair body. Care in preparing a tight, smooth tail binding—without flaring the hair—will pay great dividends and prompt rewards.

The tying instructions below are for the Regular Irresistible (several other Irre-sistibles follow the end of the recipe). If you need a heavier hook than what's listed in the materials, use #7957B, especially for salmon or large bass. For No. 12 hooks, a bunch of about fifteen hairs is ample for the tail, but use more for Nos. 4–8 hooks.

| | |
|---|---|
| **HOOK** | *Mustad #94831 2XL, Nos. 4–12* |
| **THREAD** | *White flat waxed nylon* |
| **TAIL** | *Coastal blacktail deer body hair or equivalent* |
| **BODY** | *Gray (dyed) deer body hair or caribou body hair* |
| **WING** | *Coastal blacktail deer body hair or similar fine deer body hair* |
| **HACKLE** | *Dark dun or rusty dark dun neck hackle or Whiting 100s* |
| **HEAD** | *Black head cement* |

1. Place the hook in the vise, attach the thread, and wrap a nonslip base for the tail.
2. Select a small bunch of hair for the tail and cut it off close to the hide. Place the bundle on top of the hook shank so about one hook-shank's length of hair extends beyond the hook bend, and fas-

*Regular Irresistible, 1.*

*Regular Irresistible, 2.*

ten it there using the soft loop technique. Then let the bobbin hang.

3.  If the tail hair spins when you tie it in,
    start again, taking your first turn of
    thread at least ⅛ to ³⁄₁₆ inch ahead of
    where the thread hangs. This first turn
    should be a bundling, gathering turn
    rather than one that binds the hair
    firmly to the hook shank. The next turn

or two should be tighter, and the fourth
turn should bind the hair firmly to the
hook shank. Now reverse the direction of
the thread for several turns, firmly binding the hair to the hook so it will not
turn or spin when you spin the first few
bunches of body hair. The thread should
now be where the bobbin was hanging
before you started tying in the tail.

4. Cut a bunch of hair about ³⁄₁₆ to ¼ inch thick for the body. Prepare the bundle and spin the body to within ³⁄₁₆ inch of the eye, tie off the thread with a couple half hitches, and cut the thread about an inch from the hook shank. (Refer to Spinning Hair onto the Hook on page 69 of the Basic Skills chapter as needed.)

5. Remove the fly from the vise to trim the body. Make the first cut flat across the fuzz ball, from the eye to the hook bend and about ³⁄₁₆ inch below and parallel to the hook shank. Cut one side about ³⁄₁₆ inch from the hook shank, starting at the eye and tapering to the tail. Repeat for the other side. Cut the top, ³⁄₁₆ inch above the hook shank, starting at the eye and tapering to the tail. You now have a rather squared-off body ⅜ inch wide at the eye and tapering to the tail. Turn the fly bottom-up and cut the underside, first to free up the hook gap and then to cut back the belly at the front—to about ⅛ inch on small flies and somewhat more on Nos. 4–8. Then round over the square edges of the body.

6. Return the fly to the vise and attach the thread tight against the body. For the wing, select a ⅜-inch bundle of hair that's at least ³⁄₁₆ inch longer than the hook shank, and cut it off close to the hide. Prepare the hair wing as directed in Step 5 on page 49. Place it on top of the hook shank against the front end of the body so the tacky end is toward or over the eye, and fasten it there using the soft loop technique. Trim off the surplus butts at about ⅛ inch behind the eye.

7. Divide the wing into two equal parts with your bodkin. Fasten them in that position with X-wraps, then return the thread to the rear of the wing.

8. Choose a neck hackle that has barbs that are 1½ times the hook gap in length or a Whiting 100s that's the same size as the hook. Remove any fuzz or soft parts at the butt end of the feather, then upset about a ⅜-inch section of the barbs at that end and trim them to stubble.

9. Place the stubble end against the near side of the hook shank, immediately behind the wing, so the butt points diagonally forward and down and the bulk of the feather is behind the wing. Fasten it there with a couple firm turns of thread behind the wing, and let the bobbin hang while you cut off the surplus butt. Wrap the thread forward in butting turns to ⅛ inch from the eye and let the bobbin hang.

10. Attach the hackle pliers at right angles to the feather shaft and carefully take a turn or two around the hook shank between the body and the wing. Then take three or four turns tight against the front of the wing. Fasten the hackle there with a couple of firm turns of thread and let the bobbin hang. Cut off the surplus hackle feather, being careful not to cut the hanging thread, and bind down the cut end.

11. Form a neat head, whip finish, and complete the fly in the usual manner.

*irresistibles*

*Black Irresistible*

*White Irresistible*

*Adams Irresistible*

## Other Irresistibles

The Black, White, and Adams Irresistibles are tied in the same manner as the Regular, substituting materials for the tail, body, wing, and hackle as listed below. Consider replacing the well-known White Wulff with the White Irresistible. It floats better, is more durable and, with a hair wing, is almost indestructible. I highly recommend the fly and have used it for many years.

- Black Irresistible: Use dyed black deer or elk body hair for the tail; black deer or caribou body hair for the body; badger hackle tips or gray squirrel tail for the wing; and black dry-fly neck or Whiting 100s for the hackle.
- White Irresistible: Use stiff white deer body hair for the tail and a regular white deer body hair (spinning grade) for the body as it is easier to handle. Use badger hackle tips for the wing or, alternatively, white calf body hair for Nos. 10–14 or white soft deer belly hair or straight (not excessively curly) calf-tail. Substitute badger for the hackle.
- Adams Irresistible: Use medium brown deer hock hair for the tail; caribou or gray (dyed) deer or elk body hair for the body; and grizzly hackle or gray squirrel tail for the wing. For the hackle, use grizzly and brown tied and wound on together.

irresistibles

# McSnake

THIS TEXAS BASS PATTERN BY DAVID McMIL-lan introduces several new elements: a fur strip tail, glass eyes, nylon leader weed guard, and more advanced trimming of cut/ spun deer hair in color segments (see The Multicolor Head Style, below). It catches fish, too!

Since this is the most complicated of the spun/clipped patterns in this book, we will begin with a simple approach for your first attempt and recommend you tie the first fly on a large hook; it will be much easier. For the simple version, the head is a solid color and the tail is a fur strip that's the same color as the head. Once you have the hang of the process you can try your hand at ty-ing the multicolored head, for which details are offered after the main recipe.

You can choose from two methods of ty-ing in the weed guard. One is presented in the main instructions and the other is de-scribed in Variations, below.

The head and body together are about ¾ inch long, ½ inch wide at the rear, and ³⁄₁₆ inch wide at the hook eye. All sizes and meas-urements provided in the instructions are based on these overall dimensions. When spinning the layers for the head/body, be sure you make the second, third, and fourth bands with shorter hair so that you do not later mistake those bands for the long first band, or vice versa (see Step 8). Shortening the last couple of bundles will save much trimming of the "nose." You want the first,

or rear, band to present bulk and push water, so trim it under the hook shank only, to pro-vide clearance for the hook.

When you begin trimming the head/ body, remember that you cannot put hair back on after you've cut it off. "Measure twice and cut once" is good advice here.

With its weed guard, this fly will be right at home in very thick cover, and can be worked through heavy lily pads and popped along the edges of weed beds to lure bass and pickerel out of places where other flies cannot go. Make sure you tie several of these flies; your friends will want to bor-row some.

| | |
|---|---|
| **HOOK** | *Mustad Stinger #37187, Nos. 1–6* |
| **THREAD** | *White flat waxed nylon* |
| **WEED GUARD** | |
| | *20–30 lb. hard nylon monofilament* |
| **TAIL** | *Natural rabbit fur strip* |
| **OVERWING** | |
| | *Black Krystal Flash* |
| **HEAD/BODY** | |
| | *Deer or elk body hair, natural gray brown* |
| **EYES** | *Glass doll eyes, medium (⅛ inch)* |
| **HEAD** | *Black head cement* |
| **ALSO REQUIRED** | |
| | *Clear silicone seal* |

mcsnake

1. Place the hook in the vise and attach the thread about ¾ inch behind the eye of the hook.

2. Place one end of the 6-inch-long section of monofilament on top of the hook shank directly over the hanging thread so the long end extends beyond the hook bend. Bind the monofilament to the hook shank with butting turns of thread, wrapping toward the hook bend. Continue winding around the bend, but not as far as the barb, and end with a whip finish. Cut off the thread, and let the long end of the monofilament hang.

Apply a coat of clear head cement or durable nail polish to the entire binding to protect it and secure it to the hook shank.

*If you are making several of these flies, hang the hook up to dry while you prepare other hooks up to this point. Simply reattach the thread to one of the hooks when you're ready to proceed with tying the fly.*

3. Cut off a 4- to 6-inch section of rabbit fur strip depending on the hook size you're using. Hold the strip so the "grain"—the direction in which the

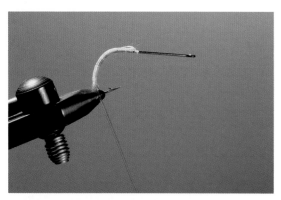

*McSnake (1). Binding on the monofilament.*

*McSnake (2). Tying on the charcoal tail.*

*McSnake (3). Spinning on the body hair.*

*McSnake (4). Body not yet trimmed.*

**McSnake (5).** *Completed fly with optional olive tail.*

hairs grow—goes to the left, and trim to a stubble ½ to ¾ inch of the fur at the right end of the strip. Place the stubble end on top of the hook shank, fur side up, so the strip's length extends beyond the hook bend and the beginning of the uncut fur is over the hanging thread. Bind the strip in place with forward-butting turns of thread, until the stubble is completely covered, then wind the thread back to the uncut fur and let the bobbin hang.

4. Cut a 2½-inch-long section of Krystal Flash that's a bit thicker than a common kitchen match or about ⅛- to ³⁄₁₆-inch thick depending on the size of the fly. Even the ends and place the bundle on top of the hook shank so one end is over the tied-in end of the tail and its length extends over and beyond the hook bend. Fasten it there with a cou-

ple of turns of thread, and let the bobbin hang. Taper the surplus tied-in end of Krystal Flash toward the eye. Apply a drop of durable nail polish or Duco Cement to the butts and, before the cement dries, bind them down with firm, butting turns of thread. Then return the thread to the near or front end of the fur tail and let the bobbin hang.

5. We will now spin the four-layer, one-color head/body (refer to Spinning Hair onto the Hook on page 69 of the Basic Skills chapter as needed). For the first layer at the rear of the body, select a ³⁄₁₆- to ⅜-inch-diameter bunch of deer or elk body hair that's 1½ inches or longer, and cut it off the hide. Even the tips, but do not cut them off. Place the bundle on top of the hook shank so at least an inch, including the tips, extends to

the rear of the hanging thread. Spin and spread the bundle completely around the hook shank. Push the spun hair firmly back to form a ⅛-inch-wide collar or skirt.

6. Select a bunch of hair that's shorter than the first bunch and of a similar diameter, and cut it off the hide. Even the ends and cut off the tips and butts so the bundle is at least ¾ inch long and the hairs have a consistent diameter. Spin this in the usual manner, then continue with similar-size bunches to produce a tight, ¼-inch band of ¾-inch-long hair when it is firmly pushed back.

7. Prepare and spin a ⅛-inch-wide skirt or band of hair that's ½ inch long, then let the bobbin hang. Then prepare and spin a ¼-inch-wide band of hair that's ½–⅜ inches long for the McSnake's "nose," and let the bobbin hang. After the hair is spun on and pushed firmly back to make a firm, tight body, tie off the thread and cut it off.

8. Review Trimming the Body on page 71 of the Basic Skills chapter as needed before starting this step. Remove the fly from the vise, and with your heavy scissors, rough out the "body." Begin about ³⁄₁₆ inch below the hook shank and cut parallel to the shank, from the head toward the tail. Cut the top so it slants forward and downward from about ½ or ⅜ inch behind the head area to a point at the rear of the hook eye. Rough out the "head" and then carefully trim it to size. Place a rubber band around the long-haired rear segment of the "body" to hold it together and hold the hair and flare it back toward the rear. Trim the bottom of the first collar section last.

9. Locate the proper position for each eye close to the rear collar. Do this by holding a glass doll eye at the proposed location to see if it looks right. Trim flat, depressed areas for the eyes, making sure they are in similar areas of the "head" before cutting a lot of the hair away to make "sockets." Do not set the eyes too deep into the finished head. Apply a dab of silicone seal to the hair and each eye and set the eyes in place.

10. Put the fly back in the vise. Attach the thread between the hook eye and the spun-hair nose and let the bobbin hang. Hold the long end of the monofilament weed guard under the hook shank at the hanging thread. Tighten the weed guard to allow about ⅛ inch of slack below the point of the hook. Take a couple of turns of thread around the weed guard and the hook shank, and let the bobbin hang.

11. Thread the long surplus end of the weed guard up through the eye of the hook, bend it down tight against the upper side of the hook shank, and fasten it with several turns of thread. Cut off the surplus monofilament about ⅛ inch behind the hook eye and bind down the end.

12. Form a neat head, and finish the fly in the usual manner.

# The Multicolor Head Style

The multicolor head style is put together the same way as the one-color style, except you alternate colors when spinning the layers for the head/body. For this version you will use natural brown/gray deer body hair and black (dyed) deer body hair.

Here's a breakdown of the layers, including their colors and layer thicknesses. The length of hair for each layer is the same as described in the main recipe.

**FIRST (REAR) LAYER**  *⅛ to 3/16-inch-wide layer of long natural brown/gray hair spun with its tips to the rear*

**SECOND LAYER**  *¼-inch-wide layer of spun black hair*

*McSnake variations*

mcsnake

**THIRD LAYER** *⅛-inch-wide layer of natural brown/gray hair*

**FOURTH LAYER** *¼-inch-wide layer of black deer body hair*

# Variations

Here's a good alternative method for tying in the weed guard. Attach the thread just above the beginning of the "flat" section between the bend and the barb of the hook, and let the bobbin hang while you place one end of the monofilament on the top of the hook shank about ¾ inch from the eye. Bend the long end around the hook bend and down to the hanging thread. Bind it there with a couple turns of thread, and let the bobbin hang while you see if the short end still reaches to within ¾ inch of the eye. Now bind down the short end of the monofilament with butting turns of thread, up the bend and along the shank to the end of the monofilament. Then let the bobbin hang at ¾ inch from the eye. Apply Duco Cement or clear durable nail polish to the entire binding.

As stated in the recipe, if you are making several of these flies, you can prepare several hooks in advance: whip finish after you bind in the end of the monofilament, cut the thread, apply the clear head cement, and hang the hook up to dry while you prepare other hooks up to this point. Simply reattach the thread to one of the hooks when you're ready to proceed with tying the fly.

# PART THREE

# SALMON FLIES FOR ADVANCED TIERS

An immense number and variety of Atlantic salmon flies have been developed over the last couple of centuries. With the diminishing number of salmon returning to rivers from the ocean, those who tie salmon flies today are clearly split into two groups. One group ties these flies to catch fish, and at least as many tie them—especially the older, classic feather-wing flies—for the challenge they present. Most of us would like to fish for salmon, but few of us have the chance, and so the rest of us tie these intricate and beautiful flies simply for the pleasure of doing so. Their beauty and the mystique surrounding the materials for and the methods of tying them make salmon flies the pinnacle of fly tying, and a growing number of people tie them each year.

In Part Three you will use some now-familiar techniques, and learn about some new materials and techniques particular to the class. The salmon flies included in this section were chosen to ease you gently from the trout/panfish, spun/cut hair patterns to their salmon fly cousins made from the same materials. Therefore, by easy stages, you will progress through a variety of different styles, both old and new, and ulti-mately tie one classic, whole-feather-wing fly, the Orange Parson.

It is rather generally accepted that the feather-wing salmon flies catch the attention of more people than fish (perhaps because there are so few salmon left to catch). Even in Britain, where the feather wings were developed, they are rarely fished except in their reduced/simplified versions, or where spey or dee styles hold local priority. In any event, as works of art, feather-wing salmon flies do attract people. Their intricate and complex structure has evolved over two centuries but, as a class, they are largely without action and do not catch fish as well as the hair-wing flies in common use nowadays. The hair-wing salmon flies have more action, are more durable and less complicated, and employ cheaper and more readily available materials than the feather-wing flies. So while feather-wing flies tend to be accepted as works of art and signs of virtuosity in fly tying, hair-wing flies are what a majority of the present salmon fishers use. A well-rounded flytier is able to tie both types.

Among the things that separate classic salmon flies from those for trout and panfish are the peculiar size and shape of the heads and the unique methods of tying in materials and dealing with surplus material. In the preceding chapters, for instance, we always tied in materials at the point of first use, and then usually cut off any surplus promptly, wherever it was tied off. When tying salmon flies, however, we will attach most materials under the hook shank so the short end is just behind the hook eye. Also, we will not cut off the surplus material—not even the butt of the tail material—but will instead carry it ahead, on top of the hook shank, to a point just behind the eye. Carrying so many items up the shank may seem to congest the head area with both the tied-in ends of the material and the tied-off surplus, but they are combined there to make the short, fat, typical salmon fly head. (Not to mention the carrying process provides an even, smooth base upon which to construct a complicated body.) The salmon fly head is, of course, larger than those of similar size trout and panfish flies, and this is both expected and accepted. The only time such a large head would be accepted on a trout fly is when an optic style eye is painted on a head specifically enlarged for that purpose.

An additional unique characteristic: When golden pheasant crest tails and toppings are used together on a salmon fly, they are intended to enclose the rear of the fly, and the tips of the tail and topping should meet, or very nearly meet, to do this. Also, unlike saltwater flies, the tails, wings, and topping of salmon flies do not extend very far beyond the hook bend, so the salmon, upon striking the fly, will get the iron well into its mouth, and thus be securely hooked.

Special features and details of classic salmon flies include tags of tinsel or wire, often with a tip of floss, to give shine and color to the rear of the body; butts of ostrich or peacock herl; joints dividing a body into segments; and veilings of small, bright feather or floss. Palmered sections—usually made with five turns of long, soft wet-fly hackle—are spaced much farther apart to give the appearance of life and activity under water, rather than closely wrapped to provide flotation, as in the bivisibles.

Finally, you need to know the names of several new and distinctive fly parts, and here we refer you to the diagram of a typical salmon fly for that information.

# THE PARTS OF SALMON FLIES AND SOME BASIC TECHNIQUES

## TAG

The tag is the first part dressed on the hook and consists of flat, embossed, round, or oval tinsel or wire in gold, silver, or copper. A typical tag is two or three turns of fine oval tinsel applied directly over the barb of the hook, with a floss segment—often called a tip—wrapped tight against the tinsel and extending to a point directly over the point of the hook.

## TAIL

On old patterns the tail is invariably made of golden pheasant crest feather, usually 1½ hook gaps (see below) in length, either by itself or in combination with other feather strands about half its length.

## BUTT

Located just ahead of the tag, the butt is wound after the tail is tied in. When used to separate other parts of a body it is often called a joint. Butts and joints are often made with ostrich or peacock herl, wool, or dubbing in black, red, or green.

## VEILING

The veiling consists of Indian crow (red) or toucan (orange) breast feathers that are incorporated into bodies that are broken up into several segments. Floss is used in a similar way in the Rusty Rat hair-wing fly. The veiling is tied flat, above and often also below, body parts.

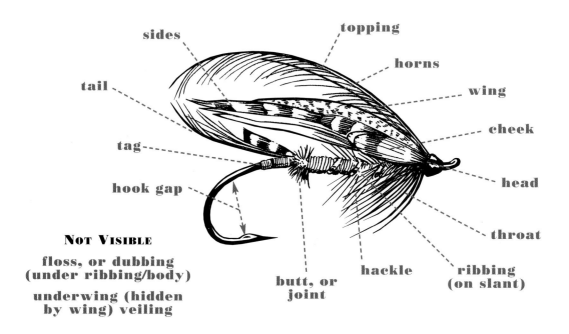

*Parts of a salmon fly*

## UNDERWING

Hair or other material that is used to support the main wing is called the underwing. Pine squirrel, fox, and gray squirrel tail hair, white-tipped turkey, golden pheasant tippets, and many other materials are used for this purpose.

## WING

The wing may be made from a broad strip of tail, wing, or body feather or assembled from several thin strips of natural or dyed feathers. The wing materials are assembled in the order given in the material lists, starting with the lower edge of the wing. The width should be about half the hook gap and the length should extend to just inside the tail, unless otherwise indicated. See also Wings of Flank Feathers, below.

## SIDE

The side consists of a jungle cock feather or a broad strip of teal, black barred wood duck, or plain hackles placed outside the main or outer wing. Jungle cock is usually one-third to one-half the wing length, and the other feathers are usually longer or the length specified in the pattern.

## CHEEK

Indian crow or blue chatterer is employed for the cheek, and is set on the outside of the sides. They are one-half to one full hook gap in length.

## TOPPING

The topping is made from a golden pheasant crest feather—or feathers—that is tied in over the finished wing. It follows the upper perimeter of the wing, and its tip extends to join exactly with the tip of the tail.

## HORNS

Two single strands of macaw tail, either red, orange/red, or blue and yellow are tied in at or above the middle of the cheek. They extend slightly upward to the end of the wing, where the tips meet a little above the wing. However, because of the scarcity of the materials, for which no substitutes have been found, horns are often left out.

## HOOK GAP

If you have skipped the earlier parts of the book, take note of this definition, which is critical for tying salmon flies. The hook gap is the distance between the point of the hook and the hook shank immediately opposite it. See the description of salmon fly hooks on page 35.

# Wings of Flank Feathers

The soft, fine-fibered feathers from teal, mallard, scaup, pintail, and widgeon typically do not have enough bulk and stiffness to produce adequate wings under normal conditions. One solution is to use several times the usual amount of material, but this tends to exacerbate the problem of too much material in the head area. Another solution is to apply the required segments or slips of the desired wing material over a base or underwing of light or dark squirrel tail hair, which adds an additional step to the process but can prove very helpful. The third method is to use the center tips of two flank feathers that have some barbs or fibers long enough for the particular wing, although not necessarily in sufficient quantity to produce a proper wing by themselves. The feather shaft does not have to be in the center, although this can be a distinct advantage. The two feathers must be the same size and shape. If there are barbs or fibers longer than you need within ½ inch on either side of the shaft, when measured from the tip edge of the feather, you can remove them to reduce the width of the finished wing to the desired size for your hook size.

There are several advantages of this third method: (1) The width and volume of the wing are sufficient for the hook and fly size, without the need for an underwing; (2) the barbs at the feather tip are stiffer; and, most significantly, (3) the tips of the feather wing assume a good shape when wet. The disadvantage of this method? It wastes a large part of feather, but we will suggest a cure for that later, so wait for the details.

Here's how you can prepare such a wing:

1. Choose two similar-sized flank or bronze mallard feathers and place them dull sides together. Upset the barbs on one side of the shafts, starting at the butt end of the feather, to find where the fibers are as long as the proposed finished wing length. Check the length of the proposed wing against the wide side of the feather to see if it will supply a large enough piece.
2. Be careful. The finished wing is wide, and both sides of the wing need to be of equal size. Adjust the width by including or removing the necessary barbs. Then mark the same place on the opposite side of the shaft and upset the same area of the feather on that side. Both sides should look alike now.

*As you will be tying in a throat or beard of the same material as the wing on many flies, this is a good time to see if some or most of the barbs in the "upset" area of the feather can be salvaged for the bundle method of throat construction (rather than either the collar or the DeFeo method [see page 53]). If the barbs are long enough, the two feathers will usually provide enough bulk to make a good throat, and you will have made efficient use of the two feathers.*

3. Cut off the upset barbs, and do not cut off the bare shafts. They will provide a good handle with which to adjust or position the wing.
4. Place the two feathers, dull sides together, on top of the body and secure them with the soft loop technique. The tip of the wing should extend to a point just within the curve of the tail—if it's curved. If it isn't curved, the wing should not extend beyond the tail. Cut off the surplus feather and trim the shafts to about ⅛ inch from the eye.
5. Finish the fly in the usual manner.

One of the three methods of using flank feathers for wings should suit your style of tying. All of them are effective and useful, so take your choice, do it well, and enjoy.

# Salmon Bivisibles

SALMON BIVISIBLES ARE ESSENTIALLY VERY large versions of the Bivisibles described in Part One, tied on low-water salmon fly hooks. Just as the others float over trout, these float over salmon. They have been used successfully for years, when salmon are responding to surface lures, and I have also caught many smallmouth bass on them over the years.

| | |
|---|---|
| **HOOK** | *Mustad #90240, Nos. 10–14* |
| **THREAD** | *White 8/0 UNI-Thread* |
| **TAIL** | *Black dry-fly neck barbules (from a cock)* |
| **BODY** | *Black dry-fly hackle* |
| **FACE** | *White dry-fly neck or saddle hackle* |
| **WING** | *None* |
| **HEAD** | *Black head cement* |

Here we will tie a black Salmon Bivisible. Turn back to the Bivisibles recipe on page 73 of the Easy Flies for Beginners chapter for detailed instructions for tying this fly.

Select 12–24 stiff barbules at least ¾ inch long for the tail.

The dry-fly hackle you select for the body should measure 1 to 1½ times the hook gap in length. Use the large feathers on the lower part of a black neck or the largest saddle hackle, but not Whiting 100s, as even the largest barbs will be far too short for this fly. Saltwater or Chinese necks will serve you well here.

You will probably need to tie in the rearmost feather by the tip and wind it in place. Tie it off and push it back, holding the rear, to compact it into a tight body. Now strip the soft, short barbs from the butt of the next feather until you reach barbs of the required length. Then tie the feather in by the butt end and wind it forward in butting turns, incorporating only full-length barbs into the fly body. Tie it off, push it firmly to the rear, and prepare another feather. Repeat until the hook shank is filled to within ³⁄₁₆ inch of the eye.

Apply the white face, and finish the fly as directed in Steps 8 and 9 of the Bivisibles recipe. The hackle you use for the face can be

***Badger Bivisible***

*salmon bivisibles*

the same size as the body hackle, or somewhat smaller if desired.

## Variations

Badger, Cochy, Grizzly, and Light and Dark Dun Salmon Bivisibles are tied in the same manner, substituting feathers of the appropriate colors. All of them are effective, useful flies, and they are a good use for those long hackles that are otherwise destined to serve as wings on streamer flies, as they are too long for most dry flies.

# SPUN-/CLIPPED-HAIR SALMON FLIES

H istorically almost all salmon flies were fished under the surface. However, for the past century floating salmon flies have become an accepted method of taking these great fish. The Spun-/Clipped-Hair body floats very high and can also be finished with a riffle hitch around the eye to produce a V-shaped wake that, at times, interests large salmon.

## Green Machine

THE GREEN MACHINE IS A SALMON DRY FLY that we will tie on a low-water hook. The size tinsel you use for the tag will depend on your hook size. We recommend medium for a No. 6 hook and fine for No. 10. The shank space that is covered by the tag and the tip is divided into the following propor-

tions: one-quarter is tinsel, and the remaining three-quarters is divided into two equal-size bands of red and green fluorescent floss. The length of the hook shank, which depends on the hook size you use, will govern the actual length of each band.

Although the materials list doesn't

*Green Machine*

specifically call for it, you can use white flat waxed nylon thread to spin the hair body if the 8/0 UNI-Thread breaks while spinning. When trimming the body, go slow and keep control, or risk having to spin and then shape a new body. (If you have not created a spun/clipped hair body recently I strongly suggest you reread Spinning Hair [on page 69 of the Basic Skills chapter] before you start this hair body.)

You can choose from two ways to attach the hackle; one is presented in the main instructions and the other is described in Variations, below. You may want to review each and choose your method ahead of time. After it's attached, you will spiral the hackle over the body.

| | |
|---|---|
| **HOOK** | *Mustad #90240, Nos. 6–10* |
| **THREAD** | *White 8/0 UNI-Thread* |
| **TAG** | *Silver flat nylon tinsel, fine or medium* |
| **TIP** | *Fluorescent green floss; fluorescent red floss* |
| **BODY** | *Green deer, elk, or antelope body hair* |
| **HACKLE** | *Brown or furnace neck or saddle hackle* |
| **HEAD** | *Black head cement* |

1.  Place the hook in the vise, attach the thread, and wrap a nonslip base for ³⁄₁₆ inch.
2.  Place the end of a 6- to 8-inch length of tinsel on the underside of the hook shank such that one end is equal to three-quarters of the length of the hook shank. (This will be shorter than the other end.) Tie it in place and let the bobbin hang.
3.  Advance the thread in butting turns for one-quarter of the distance between the hanging thread and the tip of the short end of the tinsel and let the bobbin hang while you wind the tinsel in butting turns to the hanging thread. Tie off the tinsel but do not cut it off as it will be carried forward.
4.  Cut off a 6- to 8-inch length of red fluorescent floss and place one end under the hook shank on top of the short end of the tinsel and bind it in place with the hanging thread. Continue winding the thread to the right for twice the width of the band of silver tinsel. This will bind down the surplus tinsel on the top of the hook shank and the short end of the floss under the hook shank.
5.  Pick up the red floss and wind it in butting turns to the hanging thread. Tie it off but do not cut off the surplus floss.
6.  Cut off a 6- to 8-inch length of green fluorescent floss and place one end on the red floss under the hook shank. Tie it in place and wind the thread in butting turns to a point over the forward edge of the short end of the tinsel to bind down the tinsel and surplus red floss. Let the bobbin hang.
7.  Pick up the green floss and wind it in butting turns to the hanging thread.

Tie it off and let the bobbin hang while you cut off the surplus tinsel and red and green floss.

8. If you are using flat waxed nylon thread to spin the body, recharge the bobbin with it at this point, attach it to the forward edge of the red floss, and let the bobbin hang.

9. Select a bunch of hair that's at least as thick as a pencil and 1 inch in length, and cut it off close to the hide. Trim both the tips and butts so the bunch is about ¾ inch in length. Spin the hair body, referring to Spinning Hair onto the Hook (page 69) as needed. Tie off the thread with a couple of half hitches and cut it off, leaving about 1 inch of thread beyond the knot.

10. Take the fly out of the vise and trim the body with small cuts—you can always cut off more later if you wish. The desired body shape is a collar about ⅜ to ½ inch in diameter. The length of the collar will vary depending on the length of the hook you're using.

11. Return the fly to the vise. Choose a feather for the hackle that has barbs at least as long as the hook gap. Upset the first ½ inch of the tip, and then cut that area to a stubble. Fasten the stubble end to the hook shank at the rear of the body, and bury ⅛ to ³⁄₁₆ inch of the excess stubble tip by working it into the hair body. Spiral the thread forward to the eye, carefully pulling it deep into the hair and out of sight.

12. Spiral the hackle for two to four turns to the eye, applying firm pressure to embed one side of the feather in the hair body. Tie it off and cut any surplus.

13. Form a neat head, and complete the fly in the usual manner.

## Variations

If you choose to do so, you can tie in the hackle *before* you spin the hair body. To do this, upset and trim to a stubble the first half an inch of the feather tip. Then fasten the stubble end to the hook shank, just before you begin to spin the hair, and let the feather hang. With this method you must be careful not to accidentally cut off the feather while trimming the body.

# Bomber

THIS IS A HIGH-FLOATING, VISIBLE, DURABLE dry salmon fly that can also be used to take bass on the water's surface. Its action is somewhere between that of a Turkey Quill Slider and a Hair Frog, which moves both arms and legs in an active, breaststroke-like swimming action.

The Bomber may be tied in a variety of colors and combinations of body colors and palmered "caterpillar" hackle. Originally the

green machine bomber

bomber

tail and body were made of natural gray/brown deer body hair, and the "wing" at the head was made of the same material and color. Although a good floater, it was not easy to see on the water. Over time the tail and "wing" became white or some more visible fluorescent color. The body also became more colorful, with contrasting color in the palmered hackle. Judging from fly catalogs, all the variations catch both salmon and fly fishers, but perhaps not in equal numbers.

You can use heavier hooks than what's listed in the materials, as there is sufficient flotation in the clipped deer hair, but the extra length and light weight of the low-water hook is a distinct advantage. The hair you choose for the tail should be short and soft. The tail needs to be securely fastened, then bound to the shank (see Step 2), or it will turn around the shank when you spin the body hair.

There are two methods of attaching the feather hackle. If you are new to spinning hair and the problems of trimming such bodies to the proper size and shape, it will be less frustrating to use the method detailed in the recipe rather than the option provided in Variations, below. When tying in the hackle, be sure to secure the stubble end of the feather firmly. Otherwise it will pull out when you spiral the feather up and into the clipped hair body, and you will have to do it all over again. Turns of hackle that are spaced about ³⁄₁₆ inch apart usually look good, but they can be spiraled closer or farther apart depending on your preference.

The wing should be large enough so you can easily follow the travels of the fly on the water. When choosing hair for the wing, I strongly suggest you use the same color as the tail. That's how the original pattern was tied, and despite many variations, it remains the accepted practice many years later.

| | |
|---|---|
| **HOOKS** | *Mustad #90240, Nos. 4–10* |
| **THREAD** | *White flat waxed nylon* |
| **TAIL** | *White deer body hair or calftail, or calf body hair* |
| **BODY** | *Natural gray/brown deer body hair* |
| **HACKLE** | *Black or brown saddle hackle or Whiting 100s, No. 12 or larger* |
| **WING** | *White calftail or white calf body hair* |
| **HEAD** | *Black head cement* |

1. Place the hook in the vise, attach the thread, and wrap a nonslip base for the tail.

2. Select a ³⁄₁₆-inch-diameter bundle of white deer body hair (preferably not of the spinning type) and cut it off close to the hide. Even the tips, remove any fuzz, and place it on top of the hook shank so the tips extend about ½ inch (or a finger width) beyond the hook bend. Fasten it there with several firm turns of thread, then bind down a section about ³⁄₁₆ inch long and cut off the surplus butts. Bring the thread back to where you made the first tie-in turn and let the bobbin hang.

3. Select a bunch of hair for the body

*Bomber (1). Tail and first part of body tied on.*

*Bomber (2). Body spinning complete.*

*Bomber (3). Body has been trimmed.*

*Bomber (4). Tying in the hackle feather.*

that's ³⁄₁₆ to ⅜ inch in diameter and 1 to 1½ inch long and cut it off close to the hide. Trim the tips and butts so the bundle is about ¾ inch long and the fibers are about equal in diameter at both ends of the bundle. Spin the body to ³⁄₁₆ inch from the hook eye. Tie off the thread with a couple of half hitches, then cut the thread an inch or so from the knot.

4. Take the fly out of the vise and trim the fuzz ball into proper shape. Make the first cut on the underside of the fly, starting from the eye, to make a flat bottom about ³⁄₁₆ inch below the hook shank. Cut the right side about the

same distance from the hook shank. Do the same on the left side and the top, creating a ⅜-inch-square shape with the hook passing through the middle. Round off the corners and taper the rear end to a cigar shape to yield a large body. To yield a smaller body, trim the whole fly to about ¼ inch in diameter. (The maximum diameter should be between ¼ and ⅜ inch.) Then return the fly to the vise.

5. For the hackle, select a saddle feather or Whiting 100s having a usable length of at least 5 inches (longer if you are tying No. 4 flies; shorter if you are tying smaller flies). Upset the first

bomber

*Bomber (5). Completed fly. Note: This fly was tied with a yellow body rather than natural body.*

⅜ inch of the tip and cut both sides of that area to a stubble.

6. Reattach the thread at the back end of the body, over the tail. Cut off any surplus end, and let the bobbin hang. Place the hackle feather diagonally against the hook shank so the stubble end points forward and the beginning of the usable barbs are over the base of the tail. Fasten it in place with several firm turns of thread.

7. With your bodkin push, shove, and work the hackle tip surplus into the clipped hair of the body and out of sight. Then either whip finish the feather binding or wind the thread tightly, in wide spirals, through the hair to the front of the body. Keep the thread taut to bury it in the hair.

8. Attach your hackle pliers at right angles to the feather shaft near its butt end, or hold the feather in your hand, and carefully spiral it up the body with enough tension to sink the stem into the body surface. If possible take an extra turn or two close together at the front of the body before you tie off the feather and cut off the surplus.

9. For the wing, select a bunch of straight calftail hair that's about 1 inch long and ³⁄₁₆ to ¼ inch in diameter, and cut it off close to the hide. Prepare the wing as described in Step 5 on page 49. Set the wing, butts forward, on top of the hook shank and fasten it in place with three to four firm turns of thread. Then raise the tip vertically and take several close turns behind the wing to keep it

upright for the best visibility. Trim the surplus butts and bind them down.

10. Form a neat head, whip finish, and complete the fly in the usual manner.

## Variations

Alternative colors for the tail hair include dyed fluorescent yellow or orange. For the body you can substitute white, yellow, green, or black (dyed) deer body hair, each with a contrasting feather hackle palmered over the spun/clipped body. If you are using the hackle tie-in method that's described in the recipe, employ a thread whose color is as close as possible to the body color.

Useful color combinations, all tied along with a white tail and wing, include

- Black body and white hackle
- White body and black hackle
- Yellow body and brown hackle
- Yellow body and black hackle
- Green body and brown hackle or grizzly hackle

Or choose your own combination—it may become a winner! In any event, all of these flies are tied in the same manner, whatever colors are used.

As an alternative method of tying in the hackle, place the stubble end on top of the hook shank—before you spin the body—so the tip is forward and the beginning of the uncut feather is directly over the tie-in point of the tail. Fasten it there with several firm turns of thread. Return the thread to the tie-in point, and let it and the feather hang. If you use this method to tie in the hackle, be very careful not to accidentally cut the feather when you trim the body. Spiral the hackle after you trim the body.

*Bomber tied with a black body and white hackle*

*Bomber tied with a yellow body and brown hackle*

# HAIR-WING SALMON FLIES

Hair-wing salmon flies display more action in the water than their feathered counterparts. Hair is also more durable than feathers. Feathers, on the other hand, have different density and action and take dyes differently. Each type has its uses and they are not always interchangeable.

## Ingall's Butterfly

INGALL'S BUTTERFLY CAN BE FISHED AS A dry fly and then allowed to sink. After it has sunk, give it slight action with the rod tip to make it pulsate or "breathe." It is often used with a ruffling hitch to form a V wake on the water's surface. It is an action fly that's intended to get the salmon's attention, and thus to cause a strike, when the usual flies or methods of presentation fail to get a response from the fish.

The wing is very sparse for lots of action, and the hackle is applied as a sparse collar.

| | |
|---|---|
| **HOOK** | *Mustad #90240, Nos. 6–10* |
| **THREAD** | *White 8/0 UNI-Thread* |
| **TAIL** | *Bright red calftail or hackle fibers* |
| **BODY** | *Peacock herl* |
| **WING** | *White kid-goat hair* |
| **HACKLE** | *Dark brown (Rhode Island Red) neck or saddle hackle* |
| **HEAD** | *Black head cement* |

1. Place the hook in the vise, attach the thread, and wrap a nonslip base for the tail.

2. Select and cut a bunch of calftail hair or hackle a little longer than the hook shank length and about the diameter of a common kitchen match for the tail. Clean out any short hairs and fuzz, and place the bunch on top of the hook shank so the tips are about a body-length beyond the hook bend. Fasten it there using the soft loop technique.

3. Select four to six good, plump herls from an eyed tail feather stick or a sewn patch of peacock herl, and cut them off. Put them together, tips evened, and cut off about ½ inch from the tips. Place the bunch on top of the hook shank so the cut tips are about ³⁄₁₆ inch behind the hook eye. Fasten them there with firm turns of thread, then carry the thread forward, over the herl, in butting turns to ³⁄₁₆ inch from the eye. Let the bobbin hang.

4. To form the body, apply even tension to the strands of herl and wind them, in butting turns, to the hanging thread. Tie them off and cut off the surplus.

5. Select a bundle of kid-goat hair about the thickness of a common kitchen

*Ingall's Butterfly (1). Fastening the tail.*

*Ingall's Butterfly (2). Tying in the herl for the body.*

*Ingall's Butterfly (3). Fastening the wings.*

*Ingall's Butterfly (4). Completed fly.*

match, with fibers a little longer than the hook length, and cut it off close to the hide. Remove any short hairs or fuzz, even the tips, and put the bundle aside. Then make a similar bundle for the other wing. Measure each again for length.

6. Place one bundle on top of the hook shank so the butts are over the hanging thread and the tips point toward the rear, raised to a 45° angle, and tie it in. Repeat the process for the second wing on the opposite side, and separate the wings with X-wraps to form a V-shaped wing. Trim the butts of each bundle

and bind them down, returning the thread to where the wing was first tied in, and let the bobbin hang.

7. Select a hackle feather with barbs one-half the length of the body. Upset the tip of the feather to where the barbs are of the proper length, and cut to a stubble the upset portion on both sides of the shaft. Place the stubble end diagonally down and forward on the near side of the hook shank, bright side out, with the first usable barbules immediately to the left of the hanging thread, and fasten it there. Continue wrapping the thread in butting turns to ⅛ inch

from the eye, then let the bobbin hang.

8. Holding the feather at right angles to the hook shank with your hackle pliers, make two turns tight against the front

edge of the wing and tie off the hackle. Trim off the surplus feather.

9. Make a neat salmon fly head, and finish the fly in the usual manner.

# Black Bear Green Butt

THIS FLY WAS ORIGINALLY TIED WITH BLACK bear hair, but now uses softer hair for better action in the water. If the golden pheasant crest feather you choose for the tail is thin, use two of them. If you use fitch tail for the wing, select one with good black hair at its tip. Note the tail and throat alternatives described in Variations, below.

| HOOK | Mustad #36890, Nos. 2–10 |
|---|---|
| THREAD | White 8/0 UNI-Thread |
| TAG/RIB | Silver flat Mylar tinsel, fine |
| TIP | Bright green fluorescent floss |
| TAIL | Golden pheasant crest |
| BODY | Black floss |
| THROAT | Black hackle |
| WING | Black fitch tail, or black (dyed) squirrel or kid-goat hair |
| HEAD | Black head cement |

1. Place the hook in the vise, attach the thread, and wrap a nonslip base for the tag.

2. Place one end of a 6- to 8-inch length of tinsel under the hook shank about ⅛ inch from the eye and fasten it in place

with firm turns of thread. Continue wrapping the thread forward in butting turns for ³⁄₁₆ inch, and let the bobbin hang. To form the tag, wind the tinsel in butting turns to the hanging thread, and tie it off.

3. Place the end of a 6- to 8-inch length of bright green fluorescent floss under the hook shank, on top of the tied-in tinsel end. Wind the thread to the right, binding down the long end of the tinsel, for a distance of ³⁄₁₆ inch and let the bobbin hang. To form the tip, wind the green floss in butting turns to the hanging thread. Tie it off and let the bobbin, floss, and tinsel hang.

4. Select a small to medium golden pheasant crest feather from a skin or packet. The feather should have a good gold color throughout a section as long as the hook gap. Trim to a stubble the fibers that are not needed for the tail.

5. With the tip curved up, place the tail on top of the hook shank so the beginning of the usable fibers is just behind the hanging thread. Fasten it in place with firm turns of thread, and let the bobbin hang. Place the tinsel you used to tie the tag in a material clip, out of

*Black Bear Green Butt*

the way, until you need it for the rib.

6. Place one end of a 6- to 8-inch length of black floss under the hook shank, on top of the tied-in end of green floss, and fasten it in place. Continue wrapping the thread in butting turns—binding down the tail butts, the long end of the green floss, and the short ends of the tinsel and black floss—to ⅛ inch from the eye, and let the bobbin hang.

7. Wind the black floss body in butting turns to the hanging thread, then back to the hanging tinsel, and again to the hanging thread. Tie it off, and let the bobbin hang while you cut off the surplus black and green floss.

8. To form the rib, spiral the tinsel up the body to the hanging thread, allowing twice the width of the tinsel between each turn. Tie it off, and let the bobbin hang while you cut off the surplus tinsel.

9. Select a hackle feather with barbs as long as the hook gap and cut off 18 to 24 barbs of the proper length. Bundle them and even the tips. Place the bundle under the hook shank as a throat and make a loose turn of thread to tie it in. Tighten the thread and release your hold on the bundle as it spreads around the lower half of the shank with a little help from your fingers.

10. Keep the thread taut as you check the throat for proper length and placement, and identify any thin spots or gaps, which you will now repair with bundles of black feather sized to match the trouble spots. Repair bundles are prepared and applied the same way as the original bundle. When you are satisfied with the throat, make two more turns of thread to secure it, and let the bobbin hang while you trim back the butts.

**black bear green butt**

11. For the wing, select a ³⁄₁₆-inch bunch of black hair long enough to extend from the hook eye to the tip of the tail and cut it off the hide or tail. Place the bundle on top of the body so the tips are over the tips of the tail and the butts are over the hook eye. Secure it there using the soft loop technique, then let the bobbin hang while you cut off the wing butts. Put a drop of Duco Cement or durable nail polish on the butts of both the wing and the throat.

12. Form a neat salmon fly head. While the cement is still wet, whip finish, and complete the fly in the usual manner.

## Variations

An alternative tail of recent date is made from short black hair or hackle instead of the golden pheasant crest, and is similar to the change that's taken place, over time, in the tail of the Royal Coachman Dry Fly, from golden pheasant tippet strands to dark brown hackle fibers or mahogany deer hock hair.

To make the alternative tail for this fly, select a ³⁄₁₆-inch bundle of the same black material you will use to make the wing and cut it off the hide or tail. It should be 1 to 2 inches long. Even the tips and place the bundle on top of the hook shank so the tips are about ³⁄₈ inch beyond the hook bend. Fasten it there using the soft loop technique, and let the bobbin hang.

For a hair throat, measure a length of black (dyed) kid-goat hair that's as long as the hook gap, cut off a ³⁄₁₆-inch bundle, even the tips, and attach it as described in Steps

9 and 10 above. You can also make repairs as described in Step 10, if needed.

If you followed the recipe above, you have tied a fly in the classic salmon fly manner by carrying all of the materials forward to be cut off at the head, contributing to a very smooth body. The body materials for Black Bear Green Butt do not actually require this type of construction, but many other salmon flies do. Learning with these easy-to-handle materials builds your confidence and is a good initiation into one of the long-accepted "mysteries" that separate classic salmon flies from flies intended for other fish.

While you are congratulating yourself for completing this fly, sit down and tie at least two more. This will reinforce your new skills, and each fly will prove easier than the one before it.

Take a good look at the shape of the typical head on a classic salmon fly. Notice that it's shorter and plumper than the heads on other flies. It's shorter because, by the time you are ready to form the head, there is very little space between the body and the hook eye; and it's plumper because there are so many ends to bind down and secure before the fly is ready for the whip finish and head cement.

The body is like many other yarn and tinsel bucktail and streamer bodies, and so are the throat and wing. The hook is heavier and shorter, and the head area is far more crowded, which dictates a different head shape. So, you see, the path here among the salmon flies is the same one you followed when tying bucktails and streamers. You are simply farther along that path and, although some things have changed, most of the steps and skills you learned while tying bucktails will continue to assist you and build your confidence, like old friends. You are learning to tie salmon flies!

# Black Fitch Tail

THERE ARE JUST A FEW QUICK THINGS TO note before you tie the Black Fitch Tail. When selecting tinsel for the tag/rib, use fine for Nos. 8–10 hooks and medium for Nos. 2–6. You can use two golden pheasant crest feathers for the tail if they are thin, and you can use black (dyed) squirrel tail or kid-goat hair as an alternative material for the wing.

| | |
|---|---|
| **HOOK** | *Mustad #36890, Nos. 2–10* |
| **THREAD** | *White 8/0 UNI-Thread* |
| **TAG/RIB** | *Silver flat Mylar tinsel, fine or medium* |
| **TIP** | *Fluorescent orange-yellow floss* |
| **TAIL** | *Golden pheasant crest* |
| **BODY** | *Black floss* |
| **THROAT** | *Black neck or saddle hackle fibers* |
| **WING** | *Black fitch tail* |
| **HEAD** | *Black head cement* |

1. Place the hook in the vise, attach the thread, and wrap a nonslip base for the tag.
2. Place one end of a 6- to 8-inch length of tinsel under the hook shank, about ⅛ inch from the eye. Fasten it in place, then advance the thread in butting turns toward the eye for ³⁄₁₆ inch, and let the bobbin hang. To form the tag, wrap three to four butting turns of tinsel, tie it off, and let the bobbin hang.
3. Place one end of a 6- to 8-inch length of fluorescent orange-yellow floss under the shank of the hook, on top of the tied-in end of tinsel, and fasten it there. Advance the thread in butting turns, for ³⁄₁₆ inch, binding down the long end of the tinsel, and let the bobbin hang. Wrap the floss in butting turns to the hanging thread to form the tip. Tie it off and let the bobbin hang.
4. Choose a medium sized golden pheasant crest feather. The amount of good-colored feather you need for the tail is at least the length of the hook gap. Trim to a stubble the fibers you don't need for the tail.
5. With the tip curved up, place the feather on top of the hook shank so the good-color portion of the feather is showing. Fasten the tail in place with firm turns of thread, then let the bobbin hang.
6. Place one end of a 6- to 8-inch length of black floss under the hook shank, on top of the tied-in end of the fluorescent floss, bind it in place, and let the bob-

*Black Fitch Tail*

bin hang. (At this point, place the
length of tinsel in the material clip, out
of the way until you're ready to rib the
body.) Wind the thread in butting
turns—over the tail butts, two layers of
floss, and the tied-in end of the black
floss—to ⅛ inch from the eye, then let
the bobbin hang.

7. Wind the black floss body in butting
turns to the hanging thread, then back
to the hanging tinsel, and forward
again to the hanging thread. Tie it off
and cut off the surplus floss.

8. Spiral the tinsel rib up the body, allowing twice the width of the tinsel
between each turn. Tie it off, and let
the bobbin hang while you cut off the
surplus tinsel.

9. Select a large neck or saddle hackle,
from a Chinese or saltwater rooster,
that has fibers at least as long as the
hook gap. Cut off 18 to 24 usable
fibers, even the tips, and place the bun-

dle under the hook shank for a throat.
Tie in and repair the throat as
described in Step 7 on page 53. When
satisfied with the throat, make two
more turns of thread to secure it, and
let the bobbin hang.

10. Select a fitch tail that has a tip of black
hair long enough to extend from the
hook eye to the tip of the tail, and cut
off a bundle that's about ³⁄₁₆ inch in
diameter from the black portion of the
tail. Place the bundle on top of the
body so the tips are over the tips of the
tail and the butts are over the eye. Use
the soft loop technique to fasten the
wing firmly in place, and let the bobbin
hang while you trim the surplus wing
butts and other materials. Put a drop of
clear head cement or durable nail polish on the trimmed butts.

12. Form a neat head while the cement is
still wet, whip finish, and finish the fly
in the usual manner.

black fitch tail

# Hot Orange

SOME THINGS TO NOTE AS YOU TIE HOT Orange: If the golden pheasant crest feather you choose for the tail is thin, use two of them. If the body seems too fat after you tie the first of these flies, next time only wrap the floss to the hanging thread and do not wind it back and forth again (see Step 9). When making the throat, use saltwater or Chinese hackle for larger fly sizes; however, note that large saddle hackle will do nicely for all sizes. And, lastly, you can use black (dyed) squirrel tail or kid-goat hair as an alternative material for the wing.

| | |
|---|---|
| **HOOK** | *Mustad #36890, Nos. 2–10* |
| **THREAD** | *White 8/0 UNI-Thread* |
| **TAG/RIB** | *Gold flat Mylar tinsel, fine* |
| **TIP** | *Fluorescent yellow floss* |
| **TAIL** | *Golden pheasant crest* |
| **BODY** | *Black floss* |
| **THROAT** | *Bright orange neck or saddle hackle* |
| **WING** | *Black fitch tail* |
| **HEAD** | *Black head cement* |

1. Place the hook in the vise, attach the thread, and wrap a nonslip base for the tag.
2. Place one end of a 6- to 8-inch length of tinsel under the hook shank about ⅛ inch from the eye, allowing its length to extend over the hook bend, and bind it in place. Advance the thread ³⁄₁₆ inch in butting turns, and let the bobbin hang. Wind the tinsel tag in butting turns to the hanging thread. Tie it off with a couple of firm turns of thread, and let the bobbin hang.
3. Place one end of a 6- to 8-inch length of fluorescent yellow floss under the hook shank, on top of the tied-in end of tinsel, and fasten it in place. Advance the thread in butting turns for ³⁄₁₆ inch, binding down the tinsel. Wind the floss tip in butting turns to the hanging thread. Fasten it in place, then let the bobbin hang.
4. Select a small to medium golden pheasant crest feather that has good color in a section that's at least as long as the hook gap. Trim the surplus/unwanted fibers to a stubble. With its tip curved up, place the tail on top of the hook

*Hot Orange*

shank so the beginning of the usable barbs are at the hanging thread. Bind it in place, then let the bobbin hang. At this point, place the length of tinsel in the material clip or holder, out of the way until you're ready to rib the body.

5.  Place one end of a 6- to 8-inch length of black floss under the hook shank, on top of the tied-in end of the yellow floss, and fasten it in place. Advance the thread in butting turns—binding down the tail butts, yellow floss, and so on—to ⅛ inch from the hook eye, and let the bobbin hang.

9.  Wind the black floss body in butting turns to the hanging thread, then back to the ribbing tinsel, then once again to the hanging thread. Tie it off with firm turns of the thread, and let the bobbin hang while you cut off the surplus ends of the black and yellow floss.

10. Spiral the tinsel rib up the body, allowing space equal to twice the width of the tinsel between each turn, and tie it off. Let the bobbin hang while you cut off the surplus tinsel.

11. Select a hackle for the throat. The barbs should be at least as long as the hook gap or, even better, as long as the distance between the hook eye and the point of the hook. Upset the feather and measure to be sure the barbs are long enough. Cut off 18 to 24 barbs, even the tips, and place the bundle under the hook shank. Tie in and repair the throat as described in Step 7 on page 53. When you are satisfied with the throat, make two more turns of thread to secure it, and let the bobbin hang while you cut off the surplus butts.

12. For the wing, select a bundle of hair long enough to extend from the eye to just beyond the hook bend and about ³⁄₁₆ inch in diameter, and cut it off the hide. Even the tips and place the bundle on top of the body so the tips are over the bend and the butts are at the eye. Fasten the bundle in place using the soft loop method, and let the bobbin hang. Trim the surplus butts and apply a drop of head cement or durable nail polish to the cut ends.

13. Form a neat head while the cement is still wet, whip finish, and finish the fly in the usual manner.

# Blue Charm
# (Hair Wing, Reduced and Simplified)

THIS IS A GOOD, POPULAR, STANDARD HAIR-wing pattern.

Take note of these matters before you tie Blue Charm: For the tag/rib, use fine tinsel for Nos. 8–10 hooks and medium tinsel for larger ones. After you wind the tag, you will bring the long section of tinsel forward, under the floss tip, so it's available when you're

**Blue Charm**

ready to spiral the rib. Hen hackle is preferred for the throat, or you can use Chinese or saltwater neck hackle. To test the length of hackle fibers, upset the feather so the individual fibers are at right angles to the shaft. And, lastly, use fox squirrel to make the wing of large flies and pine squirrel hair for the wing of smaller flies.

| | |
|---|---|
| **HOOK** | *Mustad #36890, Nos. 1/0–10* |
| **THREAD** | *White 8/0 UNI-Thread* |
| **TAG/RIB** | *Silver flat Mylar tinsel, fine or medium* |
| **TIP** | *Fluorescent yellow floss* |
| **TAIL** | *Golden pheasant crest* |
| **BODY** | *Black floss* |
| **THROAT** | *Bright blue hackle fibers* |
| **WING** | *Fox squirrel or pine (red) squirrel* |
| **HEAD** | *Black head cement* |

1. Place the hook in the vise, and attach the thread.

2. Place one end of a 6- to 8-inch length of tinsel under the hook shank, about ⅛ inch from the hook eye, and fasten it in place. Continue winding the thread forward in butting turns, covering the tied-in end of the tinsel for ³⁄₁₆ inch, and let the bobbin hang. Wind the tinsel tag in butting turns to the hanging thread, tie it off with a couple of tight turns of thread, and let the bobbin hang.

3. Place one end of a 6- to 8-inch length of yellow fluorescent floss under the hook shank, on top of the tinsel behind the eye. Bind it in place, then carry the thread forward in butting turns for ³⁄₁₆ inch and let the bobbin hang. Wind the yellow floss tip in butting turns up the shank, covering the short end of the floss and two layers of the tinsel (short end and length) for ⅛ inch, and tie it off with a couple of firm turns of thread.

blue charm

4. For the tail, select a short, full golden pheasant crest feather from a crest, whole skin, or packet. A portion of the feather equal to the hook gap in length should show good color. Trim off the fuzz and short fibers from the base of the feather. Then, with the tip curving up, place the feather on top of the hook shank, tie it in place, and let the bobbin hang.

5. Place one end of a 6- to 8-inch length of black floss—flat, rather than multiply—under the hook shank, on top of the floss. Fasten it in place, then wind the thread in butting turns to ³⁄₁₆ inch from the eye, binding down the surplus yellow floss, tail butts, and tied-in ends of the yellow floss, tinsel, and black floss. At this point, place the long section of tinsel in the material clip.

6. Wind the black floss body in butting turns to the hanging thread, then back to the hanging tinsel, then forward again to ³⁄₁₆ inch from the eye. Tie it off, and let the bobbin hang while you cut off the surplus floss.

7. Spiral the tinsel rib up the body, allowing a space equal to twice the width of the tinsel between each turn. Tie it off, and let the bobbin hang while you cut off the surplus tinsel.

8. Select a hackle feather that has fibers at least as long as the hook gap for the throat. Remove the fuzz and short fibers, then select 16 to 24 fibers for a No. 10 hook (select proportionally more for larger hook sizes) and cut or strip them off as a bunch or bundle. Even

the tips and place the bundle under the hook shank. Tie in and repair the throat as described in Step 7 on page 53. When the throat is satisfactorily completed, tie it off with several firm turns of thread, and let the bobbin hang while you trim off the surplus butts.

9. Select a bunch of squirrel tail hair a little thicker than a kitchen match for the wing. The hair should extend from the fly head area to just short of the tip of the tail. Even the tips and place the bundle on top of the shank so the wing tips are just within the tips of the tail. Bind it firmly in place, and let the bobbin hang while you cut off the surplus hair butts. Apply a drop of clear head cement or clear durable nail polish to the cut butts.

10. Form a neat salmon fly style head while the cement is still wet, and finish the fly in the usual manner.

## Variations

To tie the Orange Charm Hair Wing (reduced and simplified), substitute bright orange hackle for the blue hackle.

*Orange Charm Hair Wing*

# Hairy Mary

THIS BASIC HAIR-WING FLY IS USED IN MANY sizes and places for Atlantic salmon. If the golden pheasant crest feather you choose for the tail is thin, use two of them. Employ fine or medium tinsel for the rib depending on the hook size you're using. When you prepare the throat, note that larger fiber butts will provide a good handle for putting the throat in place; the butts are trimmed off later as the head is formed.

| | |
|---|---|
| **HOOK** | *Mustad #36890, Nos. 1/0–10* |
| **THREAD** | *White 8/0 UNI-Thread* |
| **TAG** | *Gold oval tinsel, fine* |
| **TAIL** | *Golden pheasant crest* |
| **BODY** | *Black floss* |
| **RIB** | *Gold oval tinsel, fine* |
| **THROAT** | *Bright blue (dyed) hackle* |
| **WING** | *Reddish-brown fitch tail, or pine or fox squirrel tail* |
| **HEAD** | *Black head cement* |

1. Place the hook in the vise, and attach the thread.

2. Place one end of a 6- to 8-inch length of fine tinsel under the hook shank, about ⅛ inch from the eye, and bind it in place. Advance the thread in butting turns to a point directly over the hook point and let the bobbin hang. Wind the tinsel tag in butting turns to the hanging thread, tie it off, and let the bobbin hang.

3. Select a small to medium golden pheasant crest feather that has good color and is long enough to extend about the length of the hook gap. With the tip end curved up, place the tail on top of the shank so the good color extends one hook-gap length from the tie-in point. Fasten it there firmly, bind down the surplus long end of the fine tinsel, and let the bobbin hang.

4. Place one end of a 6- to 8-inch length of black floss under the hook shank, on top of the tied-in end of fine tinsel. Fasten it in place, then let the bobbin hang.

5. For the rib, place one end of a 6- to 8-inch length of oval tinsel under the hook shank, on top of the tied-in end of the black floss. Bind it in place, then wind the thread forward in butting turns—binding down the fine tinsel, tail butts, and tied-in ends of floss and oval tinsel, forming the underbody— and let the bobbin hang.

6. Wrap the black floss body in butting turns to the hanging thread. If the body looks too thin, wind the floss in butting turns back to the hanging tinsel, then forward to the hanging thread. Tie off the floss and let the bobbin hang.

7. Spiral the oval tinsel rib over the body

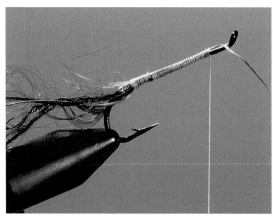

*Hairy Mary (1). Black floss is tied into place.*

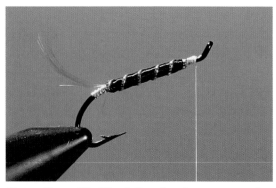

*Hairy Mary (2). Black floss has been wrapped for the body, and the tinsel has been spiraled to form the rib.*

*Hairy Mary (3). The throat has been tied in.*

*Hairy Mary (4). Tying off the bundle of hair for the wing.*

*Hairy Mary (5). Completed fly.*

to the hanging thread, allowing a space of twice the tinsel width between each turn. Tie it off and let the bobbin hang.

8. Select a hackle feather that has fibers at least as long as the hook gap and upset it. Remove the short fibers at the base of the shaft, then cut or pull off 12 to 24 fibers long enough for the throat. Place the bundle, preferably with the dull side of each fiber inside, under the hook shank. Tie in and repair the throat as described in Step 7 on page 53. When satisfied, take a couple of turns of thread to secure the throat, and let the bobbin hang.

9. For the wing, select a bundle of hair that's ⅛ to 3/16 inch thick and long enough to extend from the head area of the fly to ⅛ inch beyond the tip of the tail. Cut it off close to the hide, even the tips, and place the bundle on top of the hook shank. Check its length and position, bind it firmly in place, and let the bobbin hang.

10. Carefully trim off all surplus material to form a good salmon fly style head. To help make the head a solid unit, apply a drop or two of clear head cement or durable nail polish to the trimmed butts. Bind down the damp head materials with thread, and finish the fly in the usual manner.

# Rat

THE RATS ARE A SERIES OF FAMOUS AND USE-ful American hair-wing salmon flies that were originated by Roy Angus Thompson around 1910 for use in Canadian rivers. They take their name from his initials. Originally they all had red heads; nowadays their heads are often black, following the trend of the great majority of flies. All have grizzly hackle collars, and salmon take the flies in a variety of sizes.

When tying the tag, use fine tinsel for Nos. 8–10 hooks and medium tinsel for larger hooks. If the golden pheasant crest feather you choose for the tail is thin, you can use two. Also note that by applying a drop of durable nail polish to the wing butts just before you tie in the collar, you can complete the head while the glue is still pliable.

After you tie the Rat, Silver Rat, and Rusty Rat, you will have a dark, light, and mixed-body fly, which should cover most fishing conditions, and you will have become acquainted with several new materials.

| | |
|---|---|
| **HOOK** | *Mustad #36890, Nos. 2–10* |
| **THREAD** | *White 8/0 UNI-Thread* |
| **TAG/RIB** | *Silver oval tinsel, fine and medium* |
| **TAIL** | *Golden pheasant crest* |
| **BODY** | *Peacock herl* |
| **WING** | *Gray fox guard hairs (small bunch)* |
| **COLLAR** | *Grizzly hen or soft hackle* |
| **HEAD** | *Red head cement* |

**rat**

1. Place the hook in the vise, and attach the thread.

2. Place one end of a 6- to 8-inch length of tinsel under the hook shank, about ⅛ inch from the hook eye, and fasten it in place with firm turns of thread. Advance the thread in butting turns to a point directly over the hook point, and let the bobbin hang. Wind the tinsel tag in butting turns to the hanging thread. Tie it off, then let the bobbin and the tinsel hang.

3. From a skin, head, or packet, select a small, short golden pheasant crest feather that has good color extending the distance from the hanging thread to ½ inch beyond the hook bend. Trim the unneeded fibers to stubble on both sides of the shaft. With the tip curving up, place the feather on top of the hook shank so the first golden fibers are immediately to the left of the hanging thread. Fasten it there with firm turns of the thread, and let the bobbin hang.

4. Cut off three to five strands of peacock herl from a tail feather stick or a sewn bundle. Even the tips, then cut off ½ inch from the tips and place the herls under the hook shank, on top of the tied-in end of the tinsel. Fasten them in place with several turns of thread. Continue winding the thread forward in butting turns to ⅛ inch from the eye, binding down the tail butts and short ends of herl and tinsel as you go. Then let the bobbin hang.

5. With equal tension on the strands, wind the bundle of peacock herl in butting turns to the hanging thread. Tie it off, and let the bobbin hang while you cut off the surplus herl.

6. Spiral the tinsel rib up the body, allowing a space twice the width of the tinsel between every turn. Tie off the rib, and let the bobbin hang while you cut off the surplus tinsel.

7. Select a well-marked bundle of hair for a wing about the thickness of a common kitchen match and at least long enough to extend from the eye to the tip of the tail. Cut it from the hide, remove any fuzz and short hairs, even the tips, and place the bundle on top of the body so the tips are over the end of the tail and the butts are over the hook eye. Fasten it in place using the soft loop technique, and let the bobbin hang while you trim the butts.

8. Select a hackle feather with fibers long enough to extend from the eye to the midpoint of the body. Upset the feather and trim the fibers at the butt end, up to the first of the proper-length fibers, to a stubble. Before you tie in the feather, put a drop of clear durable nail polish on the trimmed wing butts. Then place the hackle, with its dull side toward the body of the fly, diagonally on the near side of the hook shank. The stubbled butt should be under the eye area and the long tip should extend above the fly body. The first uncut fibers should be immediately to the left of the hanging thread. Fasten the feather there with several firm turns of the thread, and let the bobbin hang.

*Rat (1).* Tinsel, golden pheasant crest feather, and herl all bound in place.

*Rat (2).* Herl has been wrapped, and tinsel has been spiraled around the herl.

*Rat (3).* Wing tied in place.

*Rat (4).* Hackle feather tied in.

*Rat (5).* Completed fly.

rat

**Silver Rat**

9. Double the feather, attach your hackle pliers to the shaft, and wind the hackle in three or four butting turns to form the collar. Allow the pliers to weight the feather while you tie it off and trim off any surplus feather and shaft. Make five or six turns of thread hard to the left, against the base of the collar to merge it with the wing.

10. Form a neat salmon fly head and finish the fly in the usual manner.

## Variations

The materials required for the Silver Rat are basically the same as those listed for Rat, with these substitutions: use oval gold Mylar tinsel (sized to fit the hook) for the tag and ribbing, and medium or large flat, silver Mylar tinsel for the body.

Everything is tied the same way as described in the recipe above except the body. (The following process would replace Steps 4 and 5 above.)

1. Tie in one end of the flat tinsel under the hook shank, $3/16$ inch behind the eye. Bind down the tied-in end of the tinsel and the tail-feather shaft with butting turns of thread, making a firm, smooth underbody.

2. Wind the tinsel up the shank in butting turns to the bobbin, then tie off the body. Let the bobbin hang while you cut off the surplus tinsel $1/8$ inch from the eye.

# Rusty Rat

HERE ARE JUST A FEW THINGS TO NOTE WHEN you tie the Rusty Rat. For the tag/rib, use fine tinsel for Nos. 8–10 hooks and medium for Nos. 2–6. The fluorescent yellow floss you will use for the rear half of the body will also form the veiling, from the middle of the body to the end of the wing. (In the original recipe the veiling was made from yellow or yellow-orange floss, as fluorescent floss had not yet been invented.) Therefore, you will not have to carry the floss under the front half of the body to the head of the fly.

| | |
|---|---|
| **HOOK** | *Mustad #36890, Nos. 2–10* |
| **THREAD** | *White 8/0 UNI-Thread* |
| **TAG/RIB** | *Gold oval tinsel, fine or medium* |
| **TAIL** | *Peacock sword fibers* |
| **BODY** | *Rear half—yellow (or orange) fluorescent floss; front half— peacock herl (fat and full)* |
| **WING** | *Gray fox guard hairs* |
| **COLLAR** | *Grizzly feather* |
| **HEAD** | *Red head cement* |

*Rusty Rat (1). Peacock sword feather tied on, and orange floss tied in (recipe indicates yellow but either is fine).*

*Rusty Rat (2). Herls tied in for the front half of the body.*

*Rusty Rat (3). Completing the herl bundle that creates the front half of the body.*

*Rusty Rat (4). Hair attached for the wing. Note: This version has been tied with the yellow floss.*

1. Place the hook in the vise, and attach the thread.

2. Place one end of a 6- to 8-inch length of tinsel under the hook shank, about ⅛ inch from the hook eye, and fasten it in place with firm turns of thread. Advance the thread in butting turns to a point just over the hook, then let the bobbin hang. Wind the tinsel tag in butting turns to the hanging thread, tie it off, and let the bobbin and the tinsel hang.

3. From a peacock sword feather, select three to six fibers about 1 inch long for the tail and cut them off close to the shaft. Even the tips and place them, bright side up, on top of the hook shank so the tips extend about ½ inch beyond the hanging thread. Fasten them there with firm turns of thread.

4. Place one end of a 6- to 8-inch length of yellow fluorescent floss under the shank, on top of the tied-in end of the tinsel. Tie it in place, then advance the thread in butting turns to the middle of the hook shank and let the bobbin hang.

5. Wind the rear, floss half of the body in butting turns to the hanging thread, binding down the tail butts and the tied-in ends of the tinsel and floss, and tie off the floss.

6. To create the veiling, extend the remaining length of floss back to the beginning of the hook bend, then cut it off at that point.

7. From a sewn patch of herls or an eyed tail feather, select four to six long, plump herls for the front half of the body and cut them off. Even the tips and cut off about ½ inch of them, as that area is very soft and may break off as you make the first turn of herl. Place the tip of the herl bundle under the shank, on top of the tied-in end of floss, and bind it in place. Advance the thread in butting turns to ⅛ inch from the hook eye, binding down the herl tips and tied-in ends of tinsel and floss, and let the bobbin hang.

8. With even tension on the strands, attach the hackle pliers to the herl bundle. Wind the bundle in butting turns to make a plump, full body. Tie it off at the hanging thread, and let the bobbin hang while you cut off the surplus herl.

9. Spiral the tinsel rib up the body, allowing a space twice the width of the tinsel between each turn, and tie it off. Then let the bobbin hang.

10. For the wing, select a well-marked bundle of hair about the thickness of a common kitchen match and at least long enough to extend from the eye to the tip of the tail. Cut it from the hide, remove any fuzz and short hairs, even the tips, and place the bundle on top of the body so the tips are over the end of the tail and the butts are over the hook eye. Fasten it in place using the soft loop technique, and let the bobbin hang while you trim the butts.

11. Select a grizzly feather that has fibers as long as the hook gap. Upset the feather and trim to a stubble both sides of the tip to where the first usable fibers begin. Apply a drop of clear durable

*Rusty Rat (5). Completed fly.*

nail polish on the wing butts, and while they are still pliable, place the feather under the hook shank so the stubble tip is under the eye and its length is under the body. The first usable fibers should be immediately to the left of the hanging thread. Fasten the feather there with several firm turns of thread, then let the bobbin hang while you double the feather and cut off the surplus ⅛ inch behind the eye.

12. With your hackle pliers at right angles to the shaft, wind the feather in three to four butting turns to form a collar. Allow the pliers to weight the feather while you tie off the surplus. Then make five or six turns of thread, hard against the base of the collar, to merge the collar with the wing.

13. Form a neat salmon fly head and finish the fly in the usual manner, noting that the head is red.

## Cosseboom Hair Wing

THIS IS AN OLD (1923), DEPENDABLE, STANdard hair-wing fly widely used for salmon in the Canadian Maritime Provinces. The usual recipe, provided by Joseph D. Bates, Jr., in *Atlantic Salmon Flies and Fishing*, 1st edition, calls for a red head. However, on page 236 of that book, the colored reproduction of the fly that was actually tied by its originator shows a black head, which I have also used.

Once again, the tinsel width you use for the tag/rib should be sized to the fly: fine for No. 10, medium for No. 6, and wide for Nos. 1/0–2.

*Cosseboom Hair Wing*

**HOOK**      *Mustad #36890, Nos. 2–10*

**THREAD**    *White 8/0 UNI-Thread*

**TAG/RIB**   *Silver embossed tinsel*

**TAIL/BODY**

             *Olive green floss*

**WING**      *Gray squirrel tail*

**THROAT**    *Bright lemon yellow hen hackle*

**HEAD**      *Black head cement*

1. Place the hook in the vise, and attach the thread.
2. Place one end of a 6- to 10-inch length of tinsel under the hook shank, about ³⁄₁₆ inch from the hook eye, fasten it in place with several firm turns of thread, and let the bobbin hang. To create the tag, wrap three to five butting turns of tinsel toward the hook eye, tie it off, and let the bobbin hang. Put the tinsel in the material clip on your vise for later use.

4. Place a 6- to 10-inch length of olive green floss on top of the hook shank, not under it, so the tip of one end—the tail—extends ³⁄₈ to ½ inch beyond the hook bend and the rest extends toward the eye. Fasten it with several firm turns of thread. Lift up the long end of the floss and place it in the material clip, out of the way, while you wind the thread in butting turns to ³⁄₁₆ inch from the eye, and let the bobbin hang.
5. Carefully wrap the floss body in even, butting turns to the hanging thread, tie

it off, and let the bobbin hang while you cut off the surplus floss.

6. Starting at the rear of the body, spiral the tinsel rib up the hook shank, allowing twice the width of the tinsel between every turn, and tie it off at the hanging thread. Let the bobbin hang while you cut off the surplus tinsel.

7. Select a well-marked bunch of hair for the wing, about as thick as a common kitchen match and at least as long as the distance from the end of the tail to the hook eye. Prepare the wing as described in Step 5 on page 49.

8. Place the wing on top of the body so the tips are just over the end of the tail, and fasten it in place with the soft loop technique. Let the bobbin hang while you trim the wing butts to ⅛ inch from the eye before the glue sets firmly.

9. For the throat, select a feather that has barbs 1½ times the hook gap in length. Upset the feather and trim to a stubble the unusable fibers on both sides of the shaft, until you reach the point where the proper-length fibers begin. Place the feather diagonally on the near side of the shank, bright side toward the hook eye, leaving ⅛ inch of stubbled stem above the hook shank. Fasten the feather there with several turns of thread, then let the bobbin hang.

10. Double the feather, then cut off the surplus stem ⅛ inch from the eye. Attach the hackle pliers at right angles to the shaft and carefully wind the collar for three to four complete turns forward, tight around the body and wing, and tie it off. Trim off the surplus feather, then make a few tight turns of thread against the body/wing to sweep and merge the hackle with the wing. Let the bobbin hang while you trim and bind down the butts of material.

11. Form a neat salmon fly style head. Whip finish and complete the fly in the usual manner.

cosseboom hair wing

# REDUCED/SIMPLIFIED
# FEATHER WINGS

A reduced/simplified (R/S) salmon fly results when you take a complicated feather-wing pattern and omit one or more materials or parts. For example, the Lady Caroline salmon fly is a spey-style fly with a long hackle. The reduced/simplified version of the same fly omits the hackle. This omission reduces both tying steps and materials, but it retains effectively the somber tones and colors that characterize the Lady Caroline.

The R/S designation also indicates that the omission or subtraction of parts or materials was intentional and not merely a mistake by the flytier. The R/S designation can be applied to both feather-wing and hair-wing salmon flies.

## Crossfield

CROSSFIELD IS A SALMON FLY THAT REQUIRES many of the skills you learned while tying trout flies. Here are some things to note as you tie the fly: The size feather you choose for the tail will vary depending on the hook size you use. The feather wing will be more durable and easier to tie satisfactorily if you first tie in a small to medium bunch of squir-

rel tail hair to support it. Pine squirrel tail hair is a good length for Nos. 8–10 hooks; for larger hook sizes, use gray squirrel tail hair with teal, widgeon, and other gray/black feathers, and fox squirrel with brown mallard or brown turkey feathers.

When choosing a mallard side or flank feather (sometimes called pearl or gray mal-

*Crossfield*

lard) for the wing, select a medium feather for No. 10 hooks and a large one for other sizes. If the shaft is not at or near the center of the feather, you will need to match a pair of feathers for overall size as well as the width of their opposite sides.

| | |
|---|---|
| **HOOK** | *Mustad #36890, Nos. 2–10* |
| **THREAD** | *White 8/0 UNI-Thread* |
| **TAG/RIB** | *Silver oval tinsel, fine* |
| **TAIL** | *Golden pheasant crest (topping)* |
| **BODY** | *Silver flat Mylar tinsel, medium* |
| **THROAT** | *Blue dun hackle fibers* |
| **UNDERWING** | |
| | *Gray squirrel tail* |
| **WING** | *Barred mallard flank* |
| **HEAD** | *Black head cement* |

1. Place the hook in the vise, and attach the thread.

2. Place one end of a 6- to 10-inch length of oval tinsel under the hook shank, ⅛ inch from the hook eye. Bind it there with butting turns of thread to the front end of the nonslip base, and let the bobbin hang. Wind the tinsel tag forward in tight, butting turns to where the bobbin hangs, bind it down with a couple of firm turns of thread, and let the bobbin and tinsel hang.

3. From a golden pheasant crest or a package of crest feathers, select a small to medium feather that will extend from the forward end of the tag to a point above the hook bend, at least ⅛

inch behind the barb. To double-check the tail length, hold a straightedge at right angles to the rear of the hook bend. The tail should extend about ⅛ inch beyond this line.

4. With the tip curving up, place the feather on top of the hook shank, bind it there with a couple of firm turns of thread, and let the bobbin hang. Do not cut off the shaft.

5. Place one end of a 6- to 10-inch length of flat tinsel under the hook shank, ⅛ inch behind the eye, and fasten it there with a couple of firm, butting turns of thread. Advance the thread to the eye area in close, butting turns, binding down the tail butt and tinsel ends.

6. Wind the flat tinsel body in butting turns to the hanging thread. Tie it off with a couple of turns of thread, cut off surplus flat tinsel ⅛ inch from the eye, and let the bobbin hang.

7. Wind the oval tinsel rib in tight turns to the hanging bobbin, allowing about twice the width of the tinsel between each turn. Tie off the rib, cut off the surplus, and let the bobbin hang.

8. Select a feather that has barbs about ¾ inch long for the throat. Strip off the soft, short barbs at the base of the feather and select a ½- to ¾-inch-wide band of barbs that are ½ to ⅝ inch long (perhaps a bit shorter for No. 10 hooks). Cut or strip the barbs from the shaft and place the bundle underneath the hook shank. It should extend to at least the rear half of the hook shank. Fasten it in place, then add more fibers

*crossfield*

to either side of the hook shank as needed to yield an ample throat. Fasten the finished throat firmly in place and cut away any surplus fibers until it's even with the body materials.

9. For the underwing, select a bunch of hair about ³⁄₁₆ inch in diameter and cut it off close to the hide. Pull out any fuzz or short hairs, even the tips, and place the bundle on top of the hook shank so the tips are at the start of the hook bend and the butts are over or beyond the eye. Fasten the bundle in place, and let the bobbin hang while you cut off the surplus butts. Place a small drop of glue or clear head cement on the trimmed butts to make a very secure wing.

10. Select a feather or pair of feathers and remove the short, soft fibers from both sides of the shaft at the base of each.

For the wing, prepare two matching feather sections that are ³⁄₈ inch wide and long enough to extend from the hook eye to the bend. Pair the slips, dull sides together, and place them one at a time, tentlike, so they cover the underwing. Tie them in with a couple of firm turns of thread and let the bobbin hang. Check the wing for length and placement, make any needed adjustments, and trim the surplus butts.

11. Make a typical short, fat salmon fly head. Bind down the surplus butts while forming the head, and finish the fly in the usual manner.

## Variations

You can also use the DeFeo method to make the throat. See page 59 of the Basic Skills chapter for instructions.

## Silver-Gray Reduced Feather Wing

*Silver-Gray Reduced Feather Wing*

KEEP THE FOLLOWING SUGGESTIONS IN MIND when tying this fly: Because the mallard flank sections you will use for the wing do not have a distinct curve, crest feathers with a slight curve are more useful as a topping than those with a greater curve at their tip. Allowing the crest feather to divide with fibers on each side of the wing will assure good topping placement. Also note that having a little extra length of pure gold color in the topping feather is a distinct advantage when adjusting its final position.

**HOOK**  *Mustad #36890, Nos. 2–10*

**THREAD**  *White 8/0 UNI-Thread*

**TAG/BODY**
*Silver flat Mylar tinsel, medium or fine*

**TIP**  *Fluorescent yellow floss*

**TAIL**  *Golden pheasant crest*

**BUTT**  *Black ostrich herl*

**RIBBING**  *Silver oval tinsel, fine*

**UNDERWING**
*Gray squirrel tail*

**WING**  *Barred mallard flank feather*

**THROAT**  *Barred mallard flank feather*

**TOPPING**  *Golden pheasant crest*

**HEAD**  *Black head cement*

1.  Place the hook in the vise, and attach the thread.

2.  Place one end of a 6- to 10-inch length of flat tinsel under the hook shank, $\frac{1}{8}$ inch from the hook eye, and fasten it in place with a couple of firm turns of thread. Advance the thread in butting turns for about $\frac{3}{16}$ inch, and let the bobbin hang. Wind the tinsel tag in butting turns to the hanging bobbin, tie it off with a couple of firm turns of thread, and let both the tinsel and the bobbin hang.

3.  With a couple of firm, butting turns of thread, fasten one end of a 6- to 8-inch length of floss for the tip on the underside of the hook shank, on top of the tied-in end of tinsel. Next, wind the thread forward in butting turns for $\frac{1}{8}$ inch and let the bobbin hang. Wind the floss forward in butting turns to the hanging thread. Tie it off and let the bobbin hang.

4.  Select a medium feather for the tail, and cut the fuzz and short barbs at the base of the shaft to a stubble. Place the feather on top of the hook shank so the tip of the feather extends about $\frac{1}{8}$ inch beyond the point directly above the hook barb. Fasten it in place with a couple of firm, butting turns of thread, binding down the tinsel and floss, and let the bobbin hang.

5.  Select and cut off a single, full ostrich herl that's at least 3 inches long, then place the end that was attached to the shaft beneath the hook shank, about $\frac{1}{8}$ inch from the eye. Bind it in place, then continue wrapping the thread in butting turns for $\frac{3}{16}$ inch, and let the bobbin hang. Carefully wind the herl in three or four butting turns to form the butt, tie it off with a couple of firm turns of thread, and let the bobbin hang.

6.  Place one end of a 6- to 10-inch length of oval tinsel under the hook shank, $\frac{1}{8}$ inch from the hook eye, fasten it in place, and let both the bobbin and the oval tinsel hang. Attach hackle pliers to the flat tinsel or put it in a spring or clip material holder. Bind down the floss, tail butt, and ostrich herl with butting turns of thread to about $\frac{3}{16}$ inch from the eye, then let the bobbin

**silver-gray reduced feather wing**

hang. Trim the surplus tail butt, floss, and herl to ⅛ inch from the eye.

7. Wind the flat tinsel body in butting turns to the hanging bobbin. Bind it down, and cut off the surplus tinsel.

8. Wind the oval tinsel rib up the body to the hanging bobbin, allowing a space twice the width of the oval tinsel between each turn. Tie off the rib, cut off the surplus tinsel, and let the bobbin hang.

9. For the underwing, select a bunch of hair that's about as thick as a kitchen match and will extend from the hook eye to ⅛ inch short of the tail curve. Cut it off close to the hide, then pull out any fuzz or short hairs and even the tips. Place it on top of the hook shank so the tips are near the tail curve—as described above—bind it in place, and let the bobbin hang.

10. Prepare two matching feather slips that are ⅜ inch wide and long enough to extend just beyond the tip of the tail when the wing is tied in place. With their dull sides together, place the sections so they cover the underwing like a tent. Check the wing's length and position, fasten it in place with a couple of firm turns of the thread, and let the bobbin hang.

11. From the feathers used for the wing, select a section about ⅜ inch wide that has fibers at least ⅜ to ½ inch long for the throat. Apply the sections evenly to the underside of the hook shank at the head area, fasten the throat in place with a couple of firm turns of thread, and let the bobbin hang.

12. For the topping, select a feather that's at least as long as the wing. Place it on top of the wing like the ridgepole on a peaked roof. The tips of the topping should extend to just beyond the tips of the wing feathers. Bind the topping in place with tight turns of the thread in the head area, then let the bobbin hang.

13. Cut back the surplus wing, topping, and any surplus body materials to create a base for the head. Form a neat salmon fly head, and finish the fly in the usual manner.

## Orange Charm

THE METHODS OF CREATING AND TYING IN the tag, tip, tail, body, ribbing, and throat of Orange Charm, a feather-wing fly, are the same as those we used to make the Blue Charm hair-wing fly. So, at the beginning of this recipe, we will have you go to those steps instead of repeating them here.

When choosing a crest feather for the topping—or two, if the feathers are thin—note that the curve of the feather(s) should duplicate the curve of the mallard wing sections so they will lie together smoothly.

**Orange Charm**

| | |
|---|---|
| **HOOK** | *Mustad #36890, Nos. 1/0–10* |
| **THREAD** | *White 8/0 UNI-Thread* |
| **TAG/RIB** | *Silver flat Mylar tinsel, fine or medium* |
| **TIP** | *Fluorescent yellow floss* |
| **TAIL** | *Golden pheasant crest* |
| **BODY** | *Black floss* |
| **THROAT** | *Bright orange hackle feathers* |
| **UNDERWING** | *Fox or pine squirrel tail* |
| **WING** | *Brown mallard feathers* |
| **TOPPING** | *Golden pheasant crest* |
| **HEAD** | *Black head cement* |

1. Follow Steps 1–9 of the Blue Charm recipe (page 270).
2. Select a bunch of hair for the underwing that's about the diameter of a kitchen match and, and cut it off close to the hide. Even the tips and pull out any fuzz or short hairs. Place the bundle on top of the hook shank with the tips about ⅛ inch short of the tail curve and the butts over the eye. Bind it there with the hanging thread. Cut off the surplus butts and add a drop of clear head cement or nail polish before binding them down. Let the bobbin hang.
3. For the wing, prepare matching feather sections about ¼ to ⅜ inch wide and long enough to extend to about ⅛ inch beyond the tip of the tail. Place them dull sides together and align the tips. Check their length and make sure they're the same width. Make adjustments as needed.
4. Place the sections, either as a unit or one at a time, so they enclose the underwing. The section tips should be together, and the wing should sit low like a tent on the body. Tie in the wing with one turn of thread, check its

*Blue Charm Feather Wing*

5. For the topping, select a feather that has enough good color to extend from the head area to just beyond the wing tip. Cut the short fibers on the surplus portion of the shaft to a stubble.

6. Place the topping on top of the feather wing like the ridgepole of a pitched roof, check its length and position, and bind it firmly in place. Cut off the surplus shaft.

7. Form a neat salmon fly head, and finish the fly in the usual manner.

## Variations

The Blue Charm Feather Wing (reduced and simplified) is tied the same way as the Orange Charm by substituting bright blue hackle for the throat.

length and position, then secure the wing with firm turns of thread, and let the bobbin hang. Carefully trim all surplus material to ⅛ inch of the eye.

# Orange Blossom

THIS IS A SIMPLIFIED VERSION OF A COMPLI-cated and fancy Canadian pattern. It has several of the characteristics of full-dressed, feather-wing salmon flies, except for the hair wing, which is part of the original pattern.

Use silver wire for the tag on Nos. 8–10 hooks, and use two golden pheasant crest feathers for the tail if one is too thin. Although Indian crow is also listed as a tail material, we suggest you use a dyed red substitute instead. Similarly, dyed black ostrich herl, the material required for the butt, is preferred over the natural black. By carefully binding down the tied-in ends of the tag and body tinsels, floss, ostrich herl, and butts of

the tail feathers, you create a smooth base for the tinsel body.

The hackle is wound as a collar or throat, then tied back to blend with the wing, with tips extending to the hook point. The best source of hackle material is a Chinese or salt-water neck.

When choosing material for the wing, go for the finest and lightest natural brown deer hair or bucktail possible (of the two characteristics, color is the most important). Note that most bucktail hair is unsuitable in color; the white portion is too light and the colored hair is usually far too deep a brown, often shading into black, although the hair has a finer texture and is longer than most body hair. In addition, you may have difficulty finding very pale gray/tan deer body hair of sufficient length for the wings of larger flies, especially if the hide that's available came from a deer living in an evergreen forest, rather than a deciduous one where the deer usually have much lighter-colored hair. If ordering deer hair by mail you should always clearly indicate your choice of light or dark shades, although this may not guarantee that you will get exactly what you ordered. Bleached coastal blacktail deer hair may be a good substitute. It has fine texture, although its short length is not suitable for very large flies.

| | |
|---|---|
| **HOOK** | *Mustad #36890, Nos. 2–10* |
| **THREAD** | *White 8/0 UNI-Thread* |
| **TAG** | *Silver oval tinsel or wire, fine* |
| **TIP** | *Golden-yellow floss* |
| **TAIL** | *Golden pheasant crest; Indian crow* |
| **BUTT** | *Black ostrich herl* |
| **BODY** | *Silver embossed tinsel* |
| **WING** | *Palest natural brown deer hair or bucktail* |
| **HACKLE** | *Bright orange (dyed) hackle* |
| **HEAD** | *Black head cement* |

1. Place the hook in the vise, and attach the thread.
2. Place one end of a 6- to 8-inch length of oval tinsel or wire under the hook shank, about ³⁄₁₆ inch from the hook eye, and fasten it in place. Wind the tinsel tag for three butting turns toward the eye, then tie it off.
3. Fasten one end of a 6- to 8-inch length of floss under the hook shank, on top of the tied-in end of the tinsel or wire. Advance the thread in butting turns for ³⁄₁₆ inch, binding down the surplus tag material and the tied-in end of the floss, and let the bobbin hang. Wind the floss tip in butting turns, tie it off, and let the bobbin hang.
4. From a golden pheasant crest or packet of crest feathers, select a tail feather that has good color for a length equal to the hook gap. With the tip curved up, place the feather on top of the hook shank so the tip extends a hook-gap length beyond the hook bend. Fasten it there with thread, then let the bobbin hang.
5. Select an Indian crow feather (or a substitute) and place it on top of the tail so its tip extends halfway to the end of the tail. Fasten it there with thread and let the bobbin hang.
6. Select a 4- to 6-inch ostrich herl from a packet or tail feather and cut about half an inch off the tip. Place the trimmed tip under the hook shank, on top of the floss, and fasten it in place. Let the bobbin hang while you wind the herl on edge for three to four butting turns, forming the butt at the base of the tail. Tie it off, then let the bobbin hang.
7. Fasten one end of a 6- to 8-inch length of embossed tinsel under the hook shank, on top of the ostrich herl. Then

*orange blossom*

*Orange Blossom (1). Two tinsels, floss, ostrich herl in place.*

*Orange Blossom (2). Tying on the wing.*

*Orange Blossom (3). Tying on the orange hackle.*

*Orange Blossom (4). Completed fly.*

wind the thread in butting turns, over the two tinsels, floss, ostrich herl, and tail butts, to ³⁄₁₆ inch from the hook eye and let the bobbin hang.

8. Wind the embossed tinsel body in butting turns to the hanging thread. Tie it off, and let the bobbin hang while you trim the surplus tinsel, ostrich herl, and floss to ⅛ inch from the eye.

9. For the wing, cut a bundle of hair that's ³⁄₁₆ inch in diameter off the hide. Even the tips and remove all fuzz and short hairs. Place the bundle on top of the body so the butts are over the eye and the tips extend slightly beyond the hook bend and just inside the upturned tip of the tail. Fasten the wing in place with three to four firm turns of thread, and let the bobbin hang while you trim the butts to about ⅛ inch from the eye.

10. Select a webby hackle that has barbs as long as the distance from the eye to the point of the hook. Measure from the tip of the feather to where the barbs are of usable length, then trim to a stubble the barbs and fuzz on both sides of the tip to that point. Place the feather diagonally, tip forward, on the near side of the hook shank so the first usable barbs are on top of the base of the wing and directly over the hanging thread. The rest of the feather should extend to the rear of the fly. Fasten it there with two to three firm turns of thread, and let the bobbin hang while you cut off the surplus stubble end of the feather. Advance the thread five or six butting turns toward the eye, then let the bobbin hang.

11. Attach the hackle pliers at right angles to the feather shaft and, with the feather on edge, wind the collar for three to five turns and tie it off. Let the bobbin hang while you cut off the excess feather. Bind down the cut end, then take a few extra turns of thread to the left, to flatten the collar and merge it into the wing.

12. Make a neat salmon fly head, and finish the fly in the usual manner.

## Black Fairy

THE FEATHER WING OF BLACK FAIRY IS MADE with matching feather sections cut from the wide side of a matched pair of mallard Grand Nashua feathers, aka brown mallard. The wing will be more durable and easier to tie satisfactorily if you first tie in a small to medium bunch of hair as an underwing to support it. Pine squirrel tail hair is a good length for Nos. 8–10 hooks. For larger sizes, use gray squirrel tail with teal, widgeon, and other gray/black feathers, and fox squirrel tail with brown mallard or brown turkey feathers.

*Black Fairy. The topping of the golden pheasant crest should be laid on the wing like a ridgepole.*

**black fairy**

| | |
|---|---|
| **HOOK** | *Mustad #36890, Nos. 2–8* |
| **THREAD** | *White 8/0 UNI-Thread* |
| **TAG/RIB** | *Gold flat Mylar tinsel, fine* |
| **TIP** | *Fluorescent yellow floss* |
| **TAIL** | *Golden pheasant crest* |
| **BODY** | *Black fur or synthetic dubbing* |
| **THROAT** | *Black hackle fibers* |
| **UNDERWING** | |
| | *Fox squirrel tail* |
| **WING** | *Brown mallard* |
| **TOPPING** | *Golden pheasant crest* |
| **HEAD** | *Black head cement* |

1. Place the hook in the vise, and attach the thread.

2. Place one end of a 6- to 8-inch length of tinsel under the hook shank, about ⅛ inch from the hook eye, and fasten it in place. Then advance the thread in tight, butting turns for ³⁄₁₆ inch and let the bobbin hang.

3. Tie in one end of a 6- to 8-inch length of floss under the hook shank, on top of the tied-in end of tinsel, and let the bobbin hang.

4. Wind the tinsel tag in butting turns to the hanging thread. Tie it off. Advance the thread in butting turns, over the tied-off tinsel and floss, for a full ⅛ inch and let the bobbin hang.

5. Wind the floss tip in smooth, butting turns for at least ⅛ inch, fasten it with thread, and let the bobbin, floss, and tinsel hang.

6. From a packet or head/crest, select a small feather that has good golden color for a length equal to the hook gap for the tail. Place it on top of the hook shank so the feather curls up and extends a gap length beyond the floss tip. Fasten it there with firm turns of thread and let the bobbin hang.

7. Apply soft wax to the thread and dub fine wisps of fur or synthetic for the body. Wind the dubbing in butting turns to the tied-in ends of tinsel and floss, binding down the excess floss along the top of the hook shank and the short ends of floss and tinsel under the hook shank. Tie it off in the eye area with a clean section of thread, and let the bobbin hang.

8. Spiral the tinsel rib up the body, allowing a space twice the width of the tinsel between every turn, and tie it off. Let the bobbin hang while you cut off surplus ends of floss, tinsel, and dubbing.

9. Select a feather that has barbs about ¾ inch long for the throat. Remove the fuzz and short fibers at the base, then cut off a section about ¾ inch wide. Place it under the hook shank, against the body, so it extends for at least half an inch. Bind it in place, and let the bobbin hang while you cut off the surplus throat butts.

10. For the underwing, select a bunch of hair about ³⁄₁₆ inch in diameter for No. 6 hooks (adjust this proportion for other hook sizes) and cut it off close to the hide. Pull out any fuzz or short hairs and even the tips, then place the bun-

dle on top of the hook shank so the tips are over the hook bend and the butts are over or beyond the eye. Fasten the bundle in place, and let the bobbin hang while you cut off the surplus hair butts. Apply a small drop of glue or clear head cement to the trimmed butts to make a very secure wing.

11. Prepare two matching feather sections that are ⅜ to ½ inch wide and have barbs at least as long as the hook shank—preferably a bit longer. Place them dull sides together and align the tips to be sure they exactly match in the areas to be used for the wing.

12. Separate them, then set them one at a time, forming a tentlike cover over the underwing and body. Their bright sides should be showing on the out-side, with the tips directly over the hook bend and the butts over the eye area. Fasten each section firmly in place as you set them, using the soft loop technique. Then let the bobbin hang while you double-check their length and position, make any needed adjustments, and cut off the surplus butts.

13. Make a neat head, whip finish, and complete the fly in the usual manner.

**black fairy | march brown**

## March Brown

SMALLER SIZES ARE FAVORED FOR THIS FLY, especially Nos. 6–10, as they are considered to be the best sizes for salmon and sea-run trout.

Brown (natural) cottontail body fur with guard hairs left in is a good substitute for the hare's ear that's required for the body. In times past, the heads of hares—including the ears—were not used in the felt hatter trade and cost very little, whereas the longer body furs on the skins, which the hatters did use, were much more expensive. That is why old patterns call for hare's-ear dubbing. How-

*March Brown*

ever, flytiers actually used the face hair rather than hair from the ears. The same effect is achieved today by using brown (natural) wild rabbit fur—including its guard hairs—and it's easier to work with. You can still buy hare's mask (i.e., the face and ears), but now it's more expensive than cottontail body fur.

| | |
|---|---|
| **HOOK** | *Mustad #36980, Nos. 1/0–10* |
| **THREAD** | *White 8/0 UNI-Thread* |
| **TAG/RIB** | *Gold flat Mylar tinsel, fine or medium* |
| **TIP** | *None* |
| **TAIL** | *Golden pheasant crest* |
| **BODY** | *Pale tan dubbing; hare's-ear dubbing with guard hair* |
| **THROAT** | *Dark-brown speckled partridge back hackle fibers* |
| **UNDERWING** | *Pine or fox squirrel tail* |
| **WING** | *Ring-necked pheasant tail feather (from hen)* |
| **HEAD** | *Black head cement* |

1. Place the hook in the vise, attach the thread, and wrap a nonslip base for the tag.
2. Place one end of a 6- to 8-inch length of tinsel under the hook shank, about ⅛ inch from the hook eye. Fasten it in place, then bring the thread forward in butting turns to directly over the hook point, and let the bobbin hang. Wind the tinsel tag in butting turns to the hanging thread, fasten it there, and let the bobbin and tinsel hang.
3. Select a medium feather for the tail, or two if they are very thin, having a bright yellow section at least as long as the hook gap. Trim the surplus short fibers at the base of the stem to a stubble. With the tip turned up, place the tail on top of the hook shank so a hook-gap's length of feather extends beyond the hook bend. Bind it in place with firm turns of thread and let the bobbin hang.
4. Prepare and spin about an inch-long noodle of pale tan dubbing. Wind a couple of butting turns of dubbing up the hook shank, tie it off with clean thread, and let the bobbin hang. Prepare the hare's-ear dubbing, wind it in butting turns to ⅛ inch from the eye, tie it off with clean tying thread, and let the bobbin hang.
5. Spiral the tinsel rib up the body, allowing twice the width of the tinsel between each turn. Tie it off at the hanging thread, and let the bobbin hang while you cut off the surplus tinsel.
6. For the throat, select a medium to large partridge back feather that has fibers at least as long as the hook gap. Remove all short fibers from the base of the feather, then cut or strip off a ³⁄₁₆-inch-diameter bunch of usable fibers. Even the tips and place the bundle under the hook shank. Tie in and repair the throat as described in Step 7 on page 53. When satisfied with the throat, secure it with two more turns of thread,

and let the bobbin hang while you cut off the surplus butts.

7. Prepare two matching feather sections for a wing that's ¼ to ½ inch wide and long enough to extend from the head area to just beyond the tip of the tail. Place the sections dull sides together, align their tips, and set them aside.

8. For the underwing, cut a bunch of hair about the thickness of a kitchen match and long enough to extend from the head area to ⅛ inch short of the wing tip area. Measure its length against the feather sections you just prepared for the wing. Place the bundle on top of the body, tie it in, and trim the surplus butts. Place a drop of clear cement or durable nail polish to the trimmed butts to keep them permanently secured.

9. Place the feather sections, with their dull sides together and tips aligned, on top of the body and against the underwing, either as a unit or one side at a time. The feather wing should enclose the underwing and extend to just beyond the tip of the tail. Bind it there with firm turns of thread, then let the bobbin hang. Cut off the surplus wing butts.

10. Make a neat salmon fly head, and finish the fly in the usual manner.

## Dusty Miller

THIS PATTERN FOLLOWS THE ESSENTIALS of an old, standard, rather complicated but very effective, full-dress feather-wing salmon fly. After you wrap the tag, you will bring the length of tinsel forward under the tip, tail, and butt, as it will be used later for the rear half of the body. The feather you choose for the tail should not have a pronounced curve, but should have bright color. If it's thin, add another to it for better color.

The surplus ostrich herl you use for the butt will be carried forward under the body materials to the head area as you build the body. Similarly, after you wrap the rear half of the body, the flat tinsel will be bound down along with the other surplus materials, forming an underbody for the second half of the body. For the ribbing, use fine oval tinsel for No. 10 hooks, medium for No. 6 hooks, and large for No. 1/0 hooks.

The hackle you use for the throat can be from a hen, Chinese, or saltwater grade neck hackle. Chinese and saltwater necks tend to have long, webby-fibered feathers and are often available in a variety of colors. Hen hackle is usually shorter and may be softer as well. Longer fibers, which provide a "handle," are easier to use.

For the wing, you can substitute lemon wood duck flank feather with a mallard dyed wood duck feather, which is easier to obtain and less expensive. You can also substitute a matched pair of wood duck or dyed mallard feathers, each having a right or left side that's wider than the other.

**dusty miller**

| HOOK | Mustad #36980, Nos. 1/0–10 |
|---|---|
| THREAD | White 8/0 UNI-Thread |
| TAG | Silver flat Mylar tinsel, fine or medium |
| TIP | Fluorescent yellow floss |
| TAIL | Golden pheasant crest |
| BUTT | Black ostrich herl |
| RIBBING | Silver oval tinsel |
| BODY | Rear half—silver flat Mylar tinsel; front half—orange-yellow floss |
| THROAT | Orange hackle fibers |
| UNDERWING | |
| | Pine or fox squirrel tail |
| WING | lemon wood duck flank or mallard dyed wood duck |
| TOPPING | Golden pheasant crest |
| HEAD | Black head cement |

1. Place the hook in the vise, and attach the thread.

2. Place one end of a 6- to 8-inch length of flat tinsel under the hook shank, about ⅛ inch from the hook eye. Fasten it in place, bring the thread forward in butting turns for ³⁄₁₆ inch, and let the bobbin hang. Wind the tinsel tag in butting turns to the hanging thread. Tie it in place, then let the tinsel and bobbin hang.

3. Fasten one end of a 6- to 8-inch length of fluorescent yellow floss on top of the tied-in end of tinsel. Then, pulling the length of the tinsel forward, bind it down with butting turns of thread for ⅛ inch and let the bobbin hang. Wind the floss tip in butting turns to the hanging thread and tie it off.

4. For the tail, select a medium to short feather that extends from the hanging thread to just beyond the rear of the hook bend. Measure it against the hook and separate the fibers where you will tie it in. Upset the fibers from a usable portion of the feather to the butt and cut them to a stubble. Place the tail on top of the hook, double-check its length, and use the soft loop technique to fasten it in place. Then let the bobbin hang.

5. Select a full, plump ostrich herl that's at least 4 inches long for the butt. Place the end of the herl under the hook shank so the tip is about ⅛ inch from the eye. Fasten it in place with several turns of thread, then let the bobbin hang. Make two or three butting turns of herl and tie it off. At this point place the length of flat tinsel in a material clip or let it hang.

6. Fasten one end of a 6- to 8-inch length of oval tinsel under the hook shank, on top of the ostrich herl near the head of the fly. Advance the thread in butting turns to the midpoint of the body, binding down all the surplus material, and let the bobbin hang. The bobbin and oval tinsel should now be hanging and the flat tinsel should be in the material clip.

7. With the flat tinsel in hand, wind the rear half of the body in butting turns to the hanging thread, then tie it off.

8. Fasten one end of a 6- to 8-inch length

of orange-yellow floss under the hook shank, on top of the tied-in end of the oval tinsel. Advance the thread up the hook shank, binding down all surplus material to ⅛ inch from the eye, and let the bobbin hang. With the orange-yellow floss in hand, wind the front half of the body in butting turns, over the underbody to the hanging thread, then tie it off and let the bobbin hang.

9. Spiral the rib up the body to the hanging thread, allowing a space equal to twice the width of the tinsel between each turn. Tie off the rib and let the bobbin hang. Trim all surplus material in the head area.

10. For the throat, select a feather that has barbs at least as long as the hook gap.

Remove the short barbs at the base of the feather and cut or strip off a bundle of 18 to 24 fibers that are somewhat longer than the hook gap. Even the tips and place the bundle under the hook shank. Tie in and repair the throat as described in Step 7 on page 53. When satisfied with the throat, secure it to the shank with two more turns of thread and let the bobbin hang.

11. Select a bunch of hair for an underwing about the thickness of a kitchen match. The hair should extend from the head area to about ⅛ inch short of the tip of the tail, with a bit more to serve as a handle when tying it in place. Even the tips and double-check the length. Then place the bunch on top of the body so

*Dusty Miller*

the tips are in the proper location, fasten it in place, and let the bobbin hang.

12. Prepare two matching feather sections for a wing that's ¼ to ⅜ inch wide and long enough to extend from the eye to just inside the curve of the tail. Put the two sections dull sides together and align their tips. Place them, either as a unit or one at a time, so they cover the underwing and are set low on the body like a tent. Fasten them there with several turns of thread, and let the bobbin hang while you trim off the surplus butts of the wing and throat.

13. For the topping, select one full feather—or two if the feathers are thin—that has a sufficient amount of bright gold to reach from the head area to the tail when placed along the top of the wing. The curve of the feather(s) should match that of the wing as closely as possible. Cut the short fibers at the surplus butt area to a stubble and place the topping along the top of the feather wing. There should be no gap between the topping and the wing. Bind it in place with firm turns of thread, and let the bobbin hang while you trim off the surplus shaft.

14. Add a drop or two of clear cement or durable nail polish to lock all of the head materials together permanently. Form a neat salmon fly style head, whip finish, and finish the fly in the usual manner.

# Lady Caroline R/S

*Lady Caroline R/S (1). Body yarns fastened under the hook shank, on top of the tied-in ends of tinsel and floss.*

THIS IS A REDUCED AND SIMPLIFIED VERSION of the old Lady Caroline fly, which is one of the most popular and perhaps best known of the 150-year-old spey-style salmon fly patterns (see page 317 for the classic recipe).

Use fine tinsel for tags tied onto Nos. 8–10 hooks. If an eight- to twelve-fiber tail looks out of proportion on a No. 10 hook you can reduce the number of fibers to six or eight.

Applying clear head cement or durable nail polish to the trimmed butts of material in the head area will greatly strengthen the fly by gluing it into a solid unit.

| HOOK | Mustad #36890, Nos. 1/0–10 |
|---|---|
| THREAD | White 8/0 UNI-Thread |
| TAG/RIB | Gold flat Mylar tinsel, fine or medium |
| TIP | Fluorescent yellow floss |
| TAIL | Reddish-orange golden pheasant breast feather |
| BODY | Olive and tan yarns |
| THROAT | Reddish-orange golden pheasant breast feather |
| UNDERWING | Pine or fox squirrel tail |
| WING | Brown mallard |
| HEAD | Black head cement |

*Lady Caroline R/S (2). Attaching spey hackle.*

1. Place the hook in the vise, and attach the thread.
2. Place one end of a 6- to 8-inch length of tinsel under the hook shank, about ⅛ inch from the hook eye. Fasten it in place with butting turns of thread for about 3/16 inch, then let the bobbin hang. Wind three butting turns of tinsel for the tag, tie it off, and let the bobbin hang.
3. Fasten one end a 6- to 8-inch length of floss beneath the hook shank, on top of the tied-in end of tinsel. Advance the thread in butting turns, binding down the floss and surplus tinsel for about ⅛ inch, and let the bobbin hang. Wind the floss tip in butting turns for ⅛ inch, then tie it off.
4. From a medium to large feather, select

*Lady Caroline R/S (3). Spey hackle attached and ready to be wrapped.*

eight to twelve fibers for the tail. They should be at least as long as the hook gap or long enough to extend to directly over the rear of the hook barb when they are tied in. With the dull sides of the fibers inside, form a bundle and place it on top of the hook shank so the tips are directly over the rear of the barb. Bind the bundle in place.

5. Cut three 6- to 8-inch lengths of thin or medium yarn—one olive and two tan. Align them side by side—in that order —like a flat ribbon, then place one end of the "ribbon" under the hook shank, on top of the tied-in ends of tinsel and floss. Fasten them with thread, at the rear of the body area. Allow the length of tinsel to hang at this point, and wind the thread forward in butting turns, binding down the surplus floss, tail butts, and the tied-in ends of yarn to ³⁄₁₆ inch from the eye. Then let the bobbin hang.

6. Wind the body like a flat ribbon, in butting turns to where the bobbin hangs, and fasten it there with several firm turns of thread. Let the bobbin hang while you cut off the surplus yarn.

7. Spiral the tinsel rib over the body to the hanging thread, allowing twice the width of the tinsel between each turn, and fasten it with firm turns of thread. Let the bobbin hang while you cut off the surplus tinsel.

8. From the feather you used for the tail, select a bundle of fibers that's about ³⁄₁₆

to ¼ inch in diameter for the throat. The bundle should extend a hook-gap's length beyond the tie-in point. Place the bundle under the hook shank, and tie in and repair the throat as described in Step 7 on page 53. When satisfied with the throat, secure it with a couple of turns of thread and let the bobbin hang.

9. For the underwing, select a bunch of hair about the diameter of a common kitchen match (or twice that for larger than No. 10 hooks) and extending from the eye to about ¼ inch from the curve of the tail. Place it on top of the hook shank so the tips fall just short of a point directly over the barb. Bind it in place, then let the bobbin hang.

10. Prepare two matching feather sections for a wing about ³⁄₁₆ to ³⁄₈ inch wide. The sections should extend to about ⅛ inch beyond the tip of the tail. Place them dull sides together and align the tips. Double-check their length, make sure they're the same width, and adjust as needed.

11. Set the wing, either as a unit or one side at a time, so that it enfolds the underwing. Make sure the tips are together and the wing sits low like a tent on the body. Bind it there with one turn of thread, check its position, then secure the wing with firm turns of thread and let the bobbin hang. Carefully trim back all surplus material. Apply a couple of drops of clear head cement or durable nail polish, and, before it dries, wipe off

any excess glue that comes up between the turns of thread.

12. Bind down all the ends, form the head, and finish the fly in the usual manner.

## Variations

You can also use the DeFeo method to make the throat. See page 59 of the Basic Skills chapter for instructions.

lady caroline r/s

# MODERN SPEY FLIES

**M**odern spey flies have received increased attention thanks to their success in taking steelhead trout, as well as salmon. Steelhead are readily available—far more plentiful than salmon—and several recent books on taking steelhead with spey-style salmon flies have alerted fishermen to these flies and this growing fishery. You will like these flies . . . and so will the fish!

## Orange Spey

THIS MODERN SPEY PATTERN IS FROM THE Great Lakes region. For a plump front half of the body—which I prefer—use medium or large chenille; otherwise, use yarn. Note that when you apply the wing, you may need to spread the orange hackle fibers at the top of the body apart to allow the wing to go in place without binding some of them down. The hackle can be stroked apart and down to make space for the wing.

| | |
|---|---|
| **HOOK** | *Mustad #36890, Nos. 2–8* |
| **THREAD** | *White 8/0 UNI-Thread* |
| **TAIL** | *None* |
| **RIB** | *Gold oval tinsel, medium* |
| **BODY** | *Rear half—gold flat Mylar tinsel, medium width; front half—black yarn or chenille* |
| **HACKLE** | *Orange (dyed) spey hackle* |
| **THROAT** | *Orange (dyed) guinea fowl body feather* |
| **WING** | *Black hackle tips* |
| **HEAD** | *Black head cement* |

1. Place the hook in the vise, and attach the thread over the barb of the hook.

2. Place one end of a 6- to 8-inch length of oval ribbing tinsel under the hook shank, about ⅛ inch from the hook eye, and bind it in. Let the bobbin hang and put the long end of the tinsel in the material clip.

3. Fasten one end of a 6- to 8-inch length of flat tinsel under the hook shank, on top of the tied-in end of the oval tinsel. Wind the thread in butting turns to the middle of the hook shank, covering the tied-in ends of tinsel, and let the bobbin hang.

4. With the flat tinsel in hand, wind the rear half of the body in butting turns to the hanging thread. Tie it off with firm turns of thread, then let the bobbin hang.

5. Fasten one end of a 6- to 8-inch length of either yarn or chenille under the hook shank, on top of the tied-in ends of tinsel. Then let the bobbin hang.

6. Select an orange (dyed) hackle that has fibers a little longer than the hook shank. Strip the fibers off one side of the

*Orange Spey*

shaft, then place the tip under the hook shank, pointing toward the hook eye, so the first of the usable fibers begin at the hanging thread (this way, fibers of the proper length will be applied to the shank during the very first turn of hackle). Fasten the hackle in place, then continue winding the thread in butting turns to ⅛ inch from the eye, binding down tinsel butts, surplus tinsel, hackle tip, and yarn or chenille.

7.  With the yarn or chenille in hand, wind the front half of the body in tight, butting turns to the hanging thread, and tie it off.

8.  Spiral the oval tinsel rib over the entire body, allowing twice the width of the tinsel between each turn. Tie it off with the hanging thread, and let the bobbin hang while you cut off the surplus tin-sel, yarn or chenille, and hackle tips.

9.  Spiral the orange hackle tight against the front edge of the oval tinsel, over the front half of the body only, to the hanging thread. Tie it off, and let the bobbin hang while you cut off the surplus feather.

10.  For the throat, select a bunch of 16 to 24 fibers that are as long as the hook shank and cut them off the feather shaft. Even the tips and place the bundle under the hook shank. Tie in and repair the throat as described in Step 7 on page 53. When satisfied with the throat, secure it with two more turns of thread, and let the bobbin hang while you cut off the surplus butts.

11.  For the wing, select two hackle tips that are long enough to reach from the eye

to just beyond the hook bend and are about ⅜ to ½ inch wide. Place them dull sides together, even the tips, and with your fingernail, dent and bend (crimp) both shafts so the wing will raise at an angle when it's tied in. Put the ends of the shafts flat on top of the body, just behind the head area. Fasten the wing in place with firm turns of thread, let the bobbin hang, and cut off the surplus wing butts.

12. Form a neat salmon fly head, whip finish, and finish the fly in the usual manner.

# Purple Spey

FOR THE PURPLE SPEY, CHOOSE WING FEATHERS—from a Chinese or saltwater neck—that are growing side by side, and you can't go wrong. Because you will be crimping the shafts, the wing will be raised when you tie it in place. Just as with Orange Spey, you may need to spread the hackle apart at the top of the body to allow the wing to go in place without binding down some of the fibers. Again, the hackle can be stroked apart and down to make a space for the wing.

| | |
|---|---|
| **HOOK** | *Mustad #36890, Nos. 2–6* |
| **THREAD** | *White 8/0 UNI-Thread* |
| **TAIL** | *None* |
| **RIB** | *Silver oval tinsel, medium* |
| **BODY** | *Rear half—purple Poly Flash; front half—black yarn or chenille* |
| **HACKLE** | *Purple (dyed) spey hackle* |
| **THROAT** | *Dark guinea fowl body feather fibers* |
| **WING** | *Black (dyed) hackle tips* |
| **HEAD** | *Black head cement* |

1. Place the hook in the vise, attach the thread, and wrap a nonslip base for the body.

2. Place one end of a 6- to 8-inch length of oval ribbing tinsel under the hook shank, about ⅛ inch from the hook eye, and bind it in. Let the bobbin hang, and put the long end of the tinsel in the material clip.

3. Fasten one end of a 6- to 8-inch length of purple Poly Flash under the shank, on top of the tied-in end of tinsel. Then wind the thread in butting turns to the middle of the hook shank, and let the bobbin hang.

4. With the Poly Flash in hand, wind the rear half of the body in butting turns to the hanging thread, then tie it off.

5. Fasten one end of a 6- to 8-inch length of yarn or chenille under the hook shank, on top of the tied-in ends of the Poly Flash and tinsel. Then let the bobbin hang.

6. Select a purple (dyed) hackle feather that has fibers as long as the hook shank. Upset the feather and strip the

**Purple Spey**

fibers off one side of the shaft. Then place the tip under the hook shank, pointing toward the eye, so the first of the usable fibers are just to the left of the hanging thread. Tie it in place, then wind the thread in butting turns to ⅛ inch from the eye, binding down the tied-in ends of tinsel, Poly Flash, and yarn or chenille and the hackle tip. Then let the bobbin hang.

7. With the yarn or chenille in hand, wind the front half of the body in butting turns to the hanging thread. Tie it off, and let the bobbin hang while you cut off the surplus Poly Flash and yarn or chenille.

8. Spiral the tinsel rib up the entire body, allowing twice the width of the tinsel between every turn, and tie it off. Let the bobbin hang while you cut off the surplus tinsel.

9. Wind the hackle tight against the front edge of the oval tinsel, on the front half of the body only, to the hanging thread. Tie it off, then let the bobbin hang.

10. For the throat, select a bunch of 18 to 24 fibers that are long enough to extend from the eye to the hook point. Cut the bundle off the shaft, even the tips, and place the bundle under the shank. Tie in and repair the throat as described in Step 7 on page 53. When satisfied with the throat, secure it to the shank with two more turns of thread, and let the bobbin hang while you cut off the surplus butts.

11. For the wing, select two tips that are

about ⅜ to ½ inch wide and long enough to reach from the eye to just beyond the hook bend. Place them dull sides together, even the tips, and with your fingernail, dent and bend (crimp) both shafts so the wing will raise at an angle when it's tied in. Put the ends of the shafts flat on top of the body, just behind the head area. Fasten the wing in place with firm turns of thread, let the bobbin hang, and cut off the surplus wing butts.

12. Form a neat head, whip finish, and finish the fly in the usual manner.

# Green Butt Skunk Spey

THESE MODERN SPEY FLIES USE A REGULAR wet-fly or streamer wing, rather than the original, classic tent wing. Wet-fly grade necks provide cheaper wing material that is also easier to tie in and still produces successful fast-water, fish-taking flies.

When choosing wing material, select feathers that grow side by side on a neck. Although they do not have to be dry-fly quality, large feathers on dry-fly necks make useful wings, so choose Chinese or saltwater grade necks and save money. As before, you may need to spread the hackle fibers apart at the top of the body to allow the wing to go in place without binding down some of the fibers. The hackle can be stroked down and apart to make space for the wing.

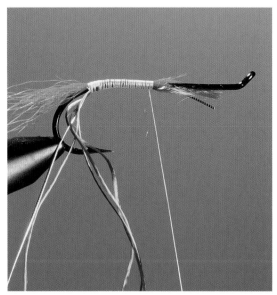

*Green Butt Skunk Spey (1). Green floss, tinsel, and red calftail tied in.*

*Green Butt Skunk Spey (2). Chenille body wound.*

***Green Butt Skunk Spey (3).*** *Tinsel spiraled over the body; hackle feather ready to be palmered.*

***Green Butt Skunk Spey (4).*** *Completed fly.*

| | |
|---|---|
| **HOOK** | *Mustad #36890, Nos. 2–6* |
| **THREAD** | *White 8/0 UNI-Thread* |
| **TAIL** | *Red (dyed) calftail (sparse)* |
| **RIB** | *Silver oval tinsel, medium* |
| **BODY** | *Rear half—fluorescent green floss; front half—black yarn or chenille* |
| **HACKLE** | *Black spey hackle* |
| **THROAT** | *Dark guinea fowl body feather* |
| **WING** | *White neck hackle tips* |
| **HEAD** | *Black head cement* |

1. Place the hook in the vise, and attach the thread over the barb or the hook.
2. Cut off a bunch of calftail hair for the tail, about 1 inch long and as thick as a kitchen match. Even the tips and place the bundle on top of the hook shank so about half an inch of the tail extends beyond the hook bend. Fasten it in place with firm turns of thread, and let the bobbin hang.
3. Place one end of a 6- to 8-inch length of tinsel under the hook shank, ⅛ inch from the hook eye, and fasten it in place. Let the bobbin hang while you put the length of tinsel in the material clip.
4. Fasten one end of a 6- to 8-inch length of floss under the shank, on top of the tied-in end of the tinsel. Then wind the thread in butting turns to the middle of the hook shank and let the bobbin hang.
5. With the floss in hand, wind the rear half of the body in butting turns to the hanging thread. Tie it off, then let the bobbin hang.
6. Fasten one end of a 6- to 8-inch length

# METHOD FOR APPLYING SPEY HACKLE FOR MODERN STEELHEAD

THIS METHOD SIMPLIFIES SPEY HACKLING, WHICH is done against the front edge of the rib, and effectively uses the best portion of the feather. The three or four tightly spaced turns of hackle at the head of the fly are also less likely to be cut by fish teeth than are the longer and more widely spaced turns used in traditional hackling procedures. This method also avoids problems of tying in the hackle at a joint between body materials or at a specific turn of the ribbing.

Please read the instructions through before starting to apply the hackle. Complete understanding of the steps and their relationship to one another is essential to success.

1. Choose a feather that has barbs at least as long as the hook shank. Upset the feather and strip the barbs on one side of the shaft, leaving a ³/₁₆-inch-wide band of undisturbed barbs at the tip of the feather. Most spey hackle (goose, pheasant rump, and so on) will have enough thin shaft for at least three turns around the hook shank. (There should be a space for at least three turns of hackle behind the head area. Push the body back to gain this space, if it is absent, and fasten the body with a couple of firm turns of thread to hold it in place.) Find the end of the thin shaft and cut the feather at least ⅛ to ³/₁₆ inch into the thicker shaft beyond it. This leaves something to tie down, and it can be clipped shorter after it is securely fastened behind the head.

2. Tie in the hackle by its base—not by the tip—either on the side or the underside of the hook shank so the thick end of the shaft is toward the eye. Bind down the shaft with tight turns of thread, and let the bobbin hang while you cut off any surplus shaft.

3. Attach the hackle pliers at right angles to the shaft, near the end of the ³/₁₆-inch-wide tip, and carefully wind that hackle in tight wraps around the hook shank toward the eye. Catch the last turn with the thread, bind it down, and cut off the surplus tip.

Make sure the barbs of the first turn point to the rear of the fly, not to the side, so the natural curve of the feather encloses the body, as with palmered hackle. By attaching the feather carefully to begin with, you can ensure that the barbs are in proper position as it is wrapped, and will thus sweep back properly. Check the position of the barbs after about a half a turn, and make adjustments if necessary.

green butt skunk spey

of either yarn or medium chenille under the hook shank, on top of the tied-in end of floss. Then let the bobbin hang.

7. Select a black hackle that has fibers as long as the hook shank. Upset the feather and strip the fibers off one side of the shaft. Place the tip under the shank, pointing toward the eye and so the first usable fibers are just to the left of the hanging thread, and tie the feather in place. Then wind the thread in butting turns to ⅛ inch from the eye, binding down the hackle tip, the surplus length of floss, and the tied-in ends of floss, tinsel, and so on. Then let the bobbin hang.

8. With the yarn or chenille in hand, wind the front half of the body in butting turns to the hanging thread. Tie it off, and let the bobbin hang while you cut off the surplus floss and yarn or chenille.

9. Spiral the tinsel rib up the entire body, allowing about twice the width of the tinsel between every turn, and tie it off. Let the bobbin hang while you cut off the surplus tinsel.

10. Wind the hackle feather tight against the front edge of the oval tinsel, over the front half of the body only, to the hanging thread. Tie it off, and let the bobbin hang while you cut off the excess hackle.

11. For the throat, select a bunch of 18 to 24 fibers that are long enough to extend from the eye to the hook point. Cut the bundle off the shaft, even the tips, and place the bundle under the shank. Tie in and repair the throat as described in Step 7 on page 53. When satisfied with the throat, secure it to the shank with two more turns of thread, and let the bobbin hang while you cut off the surplus butts.

12. For the wing, select four hackle tips that are long enough to reach from the eye to just beyond the hook bend and are about ⅜ to ½ inch wide. Pair them, dull sides together, then even the tips and crimp the shafts so the wing will be raised when it's tied in. Place the ends of the shafts flat on top of the body, just behind the head area, and tie in the wing with firm turns of thread. Let the bobbin hang while you cut off the surplus wing butts.

13. Form a neat head, whip finish, and finish the fly in the usual manner.

green butt skunk spey

# CLASSIC SPEY FLIES

These flies were developed at least 150 years ago on the River Spey in Scotland. They are somber flies with a tentlike wing of bronze mallard, a throat of teal or widgeon, and originally were hackled with long, slim, dull-colored feathers from a local breed of chickens that no longer exists. Heron hackle replaced the original spey hackle, but since herons are protected in Canada and the United States, their highly useful feathers are not available here. Hackle substitutes are blue-eared pheasant (very expensive), rump feathers from ring-necked cock pheasants, and goose shoulder feathers, or spey hackle, which are readily available in many colors at reasonable prices.

The long hackle gives both flies a great deal of action in both fast and slow water, and both have taken many salmon all over the world. They are still fished regularly in those areas where the fancy feather wings have been abandoned in favor of hair-wing salmon flies. They are an important and useful type of fly and great conversation starters among fishermen.

## Grey Heron

GREY HERON IS AN OLD PATTERN THAT'S typical of the spey style. The pattern originally called for grey heron hackle, but now we use grey spey hackle (dyed burned goose).

If you have trouble with the wings, I strongly suggest you prepare an underwing of pine squirrel tail for small flies or fox squirrel tail for Nos. 6 and up. Refer to the Silver-Gray Reduced Feather Wing (page 286) for details.

*Grey Heron (1). The hackle has been tied in under the hook and should have been pulled down and out of the way until ready for use.*

*Grey Heron (2). Hackle palmered forward.*

| | |
|---|---|
| **HOOK** | *Mustad #36890, Nos. 2–8* |
| **THREAD** | *White 8/0 UNI-Thread* |
| **TAG** | *None* |
| **TAIL** | *None* |
| **RIBBING** | *Gold flat Mylar tinsel, fine; gold oval tinsel, fine* |
| **BODY** | *Rear one-third—lemon colored yarn; front two-thirds—black yarn* |
| **HACKLE** | *Grey spey hackle* |
| **THROAT** | *Guinea fowl body feather* |
| **WING** | *Brown mallard* |
| **HEAD** | *Black head cement* |

**Grey Heron (3). Completed fly.**

1. Place the hook in the vise, and attach the thread over the barb of the hook.
2. Place one end of a 6- to 8-inch length of flat tinsel under the hook shank, about ⅛ inch from the hook eye. Fasten it in place with a couple of turns of thread and let the bobbin hang. Fasten one end of a 6- to 8-inch length of oval tinsel under the hook shank, on top of the tied-in end of flat tinsel. Then put the lengths of the tinsel, both of which will be wound later as the rib, in the material clip.
3. Fasten one end of a 6- to 8-inch length of thin lemon-colored yarn under the hook shank, on top of the tied-in ends of tinsel. Then let the bobbin hang.
4. Select a feather for the hackle and upset the fibers so you can measure them. They should be at least as long

as body of the fly, or extend from the hanging thread to the hook eye. Remove the fibers from one side of the shaft, then attach the feather under the hook shank so the tip points toward the eye and the first usable fibers are just to the left of the hanging thread. Tie it in with several turns of thread. Wind the thread forward in butting turns, binding down the tied-in ends of all the materials, until the thread covers one-third of the body length. Then let the bobbin hang.

5. With the lemon-colored yarn in hand, wind the rear one-third of the body in butting turns to the hanging bobbin, and tie it off.
6. Fasten one end of a 6- to 8-inch length of thin black yarn on top of the tied-in end of the lemon-colored yarn. Wind the thread in butting turns to ⅛ inch from the eye, and let the bobbin hang.

7. With the black yarn in hand, wind the front two-thirds of the body in butting turns over the underbody to ⅛ inch from the eye. Tie it off, then cut off the surplus yarn.

8. To create the first part of the rib, spiral the flat tinsel up the entire body, allowing about three times the width of the tinsel between each turn. Tie it off, then let the bobbin hang.

9. Spiral the oval tinsel along the front edge of the flat tinsel, tie it off ⅛ inch from the eye, and cut off the surplus tinsels.

10. Carefully wind the hackle feather tight against the forward edge of the oval tinsel to within ⅛ inch of the eye. If there is any surplus hackle when you reach this point, use it to make a couple of butting turns, then tie it off.

11. For the throat, select a bunch of 18 to 24 fibers that will extend from the eye to the hook point. Cut the bundle off the shaft, even the tips, and place the bundle under the shank. Tie in and repair the throat as described in Step 7 on page 53. When satisfied with the throat, secure it to the shank with two more turns of thread, and let the bobbin hang while you cut off the surplus butts.

12. For the wing, select a matched pair of brown mallard feathers with fibers as long as the fly body. Prepare two matching sections, ¼ inch wide. Put the sections dull sides together and align the tips. Make sure the sections are the same width. Then place them one at a time, set low like a tent so they enclose the upper half of the body. Use the soft loop technique to tie them in, then let the bobbin hang. Trim the wing butts and other materials, and apply a drop of clear cement or durable nail polish to glue them together.

13. Bind down the butts to form a neat head, whip finish, and finish the fly in the usual manner.

# Carron

THIS IS AN OLD PATTERN WITH MORE COLOR than Lady Caroline. It is one of a core of survivors that is still listed whenever spey flies are mentioned or fished.

The hackle is the first material you will tie in. If you are using burned, dyed goose feather instead of black heron, strip the barbs off one side of the shaft before using it as the hackle. You may decide to reinforce the hackle with silver wire; we recommend reviewing the instructions for this (see Variations, below) before you start the fly.

If you have only twisted floss for the rib, simply unwind it and use a single strand flat.

If the hackle fibers get in the way when you apply the wing, you can stroke the fibers down and away from the wing area before you put the wing in place. You may also find it easier to set the matched wing sections if you place the far-side section first, making sure it's in a good position, and then place the near-side section to meet it.

| | |
|---|---|
| **HOOK** | *Mustad #36890, Nos. 2–8* |
| **TAG** | *None* |
| **TAIL** | *None* |
| **BODY** | *Orange yarn* |
| **RIBBING** | *Silver flat Mylar tinsel, medium; scarlet floss* |
| **HACKLE** | *Black heron or substitute* |
| **THROAT** | *Black-and-white teal flank feathers or scaup, widgeon, and so on* |
| **WING** | *Bronze mallard strips* |
| **HEAD** | *Black head cement* |

1. Place the hook in the vise and attach the thread at almost three-quarters of a hook shank length from the eye.
2. Select a hackle that's as long as the hook shank. Tie it in by the tip so the tip points toward the eye, and let it hang. Wrap the thread in butting turns toward the rear of the hook. Stop directly over the barb and let the bobbin hang.
3. Place one end of a 6- to 8-inch length of thin yarn under the shank, ⅛ inch from the hook eye. Fasten it in with a couple of firm turns of thread, then let the bobbin hang.
4. Fasten one end of a 6- to 8-inch length of tinsel under the hook shank, on top of the tied-in end of yarn. Then fasten one end of a 6- to 8-inch length of floss in the same way, under the hook shank,

**Carron**

against the yarn and tinsel. Advance the thread, binding down the yarn and ribbing material, to ⅛ inch from the eye and let the bobbin hang. You now have the yarn, tinsel, and floss at the rear of the fly; the hackle tied in and hanging from the center area; and the bobbin hanging from the head area.

5. Wrap a thin yarn body to the head area, covering the tie-in spot of the hackle. Tie off the body where the bobbin is hanging, then cut off any surplus yarn.

6. Spiral the ribbing tinsel forward, making the fourth turn where the hackle is tied in, and continue to the head area. Tie off the rib, then cut off the surplus tinsel.

7. Spiral the floss ribbing along the front side of the tinsel, butting against the tinsel on each turn. Tie off the floss in the head area, and let the bobbin hang while you cut off the surplus floss.

8. Pick up the hackle by hand or attach hackle pliers at right angles to the shaft. Then, starting at the fourth turn of the ribbing material, palmer the feather against the rear edge of the tinsel to the head area. If there is any hackle remaining at that point, make close, butting turns to build up the shoulders of the fly. Tie off the hackle, cut off the excess shaft, and let the bobbin hang.

9. Select a flank feather that has barbs at least ¾ inch long, and cut a ½- to ¾-inch-wide section from one side of the

shaft or half that width from both sides. Place the section(s) under the hook shank, against the hackle, and fasten the throat there with firm turns of thread. Let the bobbin hang while you trim off the surplus butts.

10. Prepare two matching feather sections that are ⅜ to ½ inch wide and have barbs a bit longer than the body of the fly. Place the sections dull sides together, and align the tips to be sure they exactly match in the areas to be used for the wing.

11. Separate the sections and set them—one at a time—low over the body like a tent, with their bright sides facing out, tips directly over the hook bend, and butts over the eye area. Fasten each in place as you set them, using the soft loop technique and several extra firm turns of thread. Let the bobbin hang while you double-check the wing length and position and make any needed adjustments. Then cut off the surplus butts.

12. Make a neat head, whip finish, and complete the fly in the usual manner.

## Variations

If you desire a reinforced fly, tie in a 6-inch length of silver wire immediately after you tie in the hackle. After you wind the hackle, carefully reverse wind the wire between the fibers and over the shaft to secure the hackle and protect it from being cut by sharp salmon teeth. Fasten the wire in the head area and cut off any surplus.

# Lady Caroline

LADY CAROLINE IS AN OLD BUT STILL POPU-lar pattern that is known and fished all around the world wherever a dull-colored fly is needed. One version has a dubbed body of one part olive and two parts tan seal fur, or you can substitute synthetic dubbing or thin yarn for that endangered-species material.

Note that the body, ribbing, and hackle materials are all tied in, one after the other, in the same area of the hook shank. The three lengths of yarn required for the body will be wrapped together, flat, like a ribbon. Attach the strands to the hook in a way that will discourage them from twisting when you wind the body. The size of flat tinsel you use for part of the ribbing depends on the hook size you choose. There are usually five turns of ribbing material on the body, so plan to have yours meet this standard to be sure all the body materials show. Hackle fibers should be at least as long as the hook shank, and the feather is spiraled up the body against the front edge of the oval tinsel and is thus protected against the fish's sharp teeth. For the hackle you can substitute dyed spey hackle or, for Nos. 8–10 flies, gray ring-necked peasant rump feathers.

In rare cases, the hackle fibers may inter-

*Lady Caroline*

fere with setting the wing in the proper, low position and, if they do, they can be carefully stroked out and down from the top of the hook. Bear in mind, however, that the hackle tends to support the inside of the wing, as the use of an underwing is not recommended for the classic spey-style fly.

One final note before we begin: If eight or ten tail fibers look out of proportion on a No. 10 hook, you can reduce the number of fibers to six or eight instead.

| | |
|---|---|
| **HOOK** | *Mustad #38690, Nos. 1/0–10* |
| **THREAD** | *White 8/0 UNI-Thread* |
| **TAIL** | *Reddish golden pheasant breast feather* |
| **BODY** | *Olive green yarn; light tan yarn* |
| **RIBBING** | *Gold flat Mylar tinsel, fine or medium; silver oval tinsel, medium* |
| **HACKLE** | *Grey heron* |
| **THROAT** | *Reddish golden pheasant breast feather* |
| **WING** | *Brown mallard (Grand Nashua)* |
| **HEAD** | *Black head cement* |

1. Place the hook in the vise, attach the thread over the back of the hook, and wrap a nonslip base for the tail.

2. From a golden pheasant skin or packet, select a feather that has fibers a bit longer than the hook gap and cut off eight or ten long fibers for the tail. Even the tips and bunch them together so their bright sides show. Place them on top of the hook shank so the tips are about a hook-gap's distance beyond the bend, fasten them in place with firm turns of thread, and let the bobbin hang.

3. Place the ends of three 6- to 8-inch lengths of thin yarn—one olive green and two light tan—under the hook shank, about ⅛ inch from the hook eye. Fasten them in place—making sure they are side by side, not bunched together—then let the bobbin hang.

4. Fasten one end of a 6- to 8-inch length of flat tinsel under the hook shank, on top of the tied-in ends of yarn, and let the bobbin hang. Then fasten one end of a 6- to 8-inch length of oval tinsel on top of the flat tinsel and let the bobbin hang.

5. Select a feather for the hackle that has fibers at least as long as the hook shank, so they will extend well beyond the bend when wound in place. Tie it in by the tip and let the feather hang. Wind the thread in butting turns to about ⅛ inch from the eye, binding down the tail butts, the surplus tip of the hackle, and tied-in ends of yarn and tinsel. Then let the bobbin hang.

6. Holding the three strands of yarn like a ribbon and exerting an equal amount of tension on each, wind a thin, flat body in butting turns to the hanging thread. Tie off the body, and let the bobbin hang while you cut off the surplus yarn.

7. Spiral the flat tinsel up the body, allow-ing at least three times the width of the tinsel between each turn, then tie it off. Then spiral the oval tinsel tight against the forward edge of the flat tinsel, tie it

off, and cut off the surplus ends of the tinsels.

8. Carefully spiral the hackle feather up the shank, tight against the forward edge of the oval tinsel, to the hanging thread. If there is enough usable hackle feather left when you reach the thread, make a couple of extra butted turns. Then tie off the hackle, and let the bobbin hang while you cut off the surplus feather.

9. From the feather you used for tail material or a fresh feather, cut a bundle of 16 to 24 fibers that are at least as long as the hook gap or, better yet, almost long enough to extend from the eye to the point of the hook, if such are available. Align the tips and, with the bright sides out, place the fibers under the hook shank. Tie in and repair the throat as described in Step 7 on page 53. When satisfied with the throat, secure it to the shank with two more turns of thread, and let the bobbin hang while you cut off the surplus butts.

10. For the wing, prepare two matching feather sections that are $3/16$ to $3/8$ inch wide and have fibers long enough to extend from the eye to just beyond the hook bend. Even the tips and place the sections dull sides together. Remove any unwanted fibers or make other adjustments to ensure that the sections match.

11. Separate the sections and set them—one at a time—low over the body like a tent, with their bright sides facing out, tips just beyond the hook bend, and butts over the eye area. Fasten each in place as you set them, using the soft loop technique and several extra firm turns of thread. Let the bobbin hang while you trim the wing butts.

12. Form a neat salmon fly head, and finish the fly in the usual manner.

lady caroline

# DEE STRIP WING

Adee-strip-wing fly is a salmon fly from the River Dee in Scotland. It has turkey tail strips for wings, which are set at a 45° angle to the hook shank, it uses teal or widgeon for the throat, and it has spey-type hackle.

Do not confuse spey flies with dee flies. Both have long hackles but the wings on dee flies are tied to lay flat and extend to form a V with the hook shank in the middle instead of the tent shape of the wings of spey flies. The dee flies show more color in their complicated bodies than do the more somber spey flies.

## Glentana

DATING FROM THE EARLY EIGHTEENTH CENTURY, this is one of the oldest dee-strip-wing salmon flies, and it is still in use worldwide.

This particular pattern follows one written by Dr. T. E. Pryce-Tannatt in his book, *How to Dress Salmon Flies* (1914).

*Glentana*

The dee strip wings are tied in low and flat and form a V over the fly body. These flies once had a long, thin, black heron hackle, which has been replaced with a commercially treated goose hackle known as spey-type hackle, and a teal or widgeon throat (more about that hackle below). Do not confuse these flat-wing flies with spey flies, whose wings are always dark and placed like a tent over the body.

The hook you will use to tie this fly nearly matches the obsolete dee-style hook (Mustad #36890).

The body should be thinly dressed and slender so the fly will sink fast and to a greater depth. Originally the body was made with seal fur, but nowadays flytiers use Angora goat or other substitutes. Thin yarn is a good substitute, as little of the color shows between the turns of ribbing on small flies. When selecting tinsel for the tag and rib, use fine for Nos. 8–10 hooks and medium for Nos. 2–6 hooks.

The hackle is tied in by the tip at the front of the orange section of the body and covers the claret section. If the hackle seems too thick when you finish the fly, on the next one, strip one side of the hackle. This will produce a much sparser and quicker-sinking fly. Try tying the hackle both ways; otherwise, you will never know which style you like best. Both look good, and both will take fish.

When preparing the wing, keep the slips as long as possible so they have handles for ease of adjusting them as you tie them in place.

| | |
|---|---|
| **HOOK** | *Mustad #36890, Nos. 2–10* |
| **THREAD** | *White 8/0 UNI-Thread* |
| **TAG** | *Silver oval tinsel, fine* |
| **TIP** | *Lemon floss (flat)* |
| **TAIL** | *Golden pheasant crest; reddish golden pheasant breast feather* |
| **BODY** | *Rear one-third—light orange Angora goat dubbing or thin yarn; front two-thirds—light claret Angora goat dubbing or thin yarn* |
| **RIB** | *Silver oval tinsel, fine; silver flat Mylar tinsel, medium* |
| **HACKLE** | *Black spey hackle* |
| **THROAT** | *Widgeon, gadwall, teal, or scaup* |
| **WING** | *Cinnamon turkey tail or secondary feather* |
| **HEAD** | *Black head cement* |

1. Place the hook in the vise, and attach the thread.
2. Place one end of a 6- to 12-inch length of oval tinsel under the hook shank, $\frac{1}{8}$ inch from the eye, and bind it in place. Then wrap the thread in tight, butted turns for $\frac{3}{16}$ inch and let the bobbin hang. Wind the tinsel tag in three to five butting turns to where the thread hangs and tie it off.
3. Fasten the end of a 6- to 12-inch length of floss under the hook shank, next to the tinsel. Advance the thread in butted turns for $\frac{3}{16}$ inch, binding down the excess tinsel and forming a base for the

glentana

floss tip, then let the bobbin hang. Wrap the tip in five or six smooth, butting turns, fasten it in place, and let the bobbin hang.

4. From a full crest or package, select a short feather or tip of a feather for the tail that is either nearly straight or has only a very little curve and is long enough to extend a little beyond the hook bend when it is tied in. Place it on top of the hook, bind it in place, and let the bobbin hang.

5. Choose a medium to large breast feather for the top of the tail and cut off four to six usable fibers from the shaft. Holding them flat and bright side up, place them on top of the crest section so their tips extend to the halfway point of the tail and fasten them in place.

6. Fasten the end of a 6- to 12-inch length of flat tinsel under the hook shank, just behind the eye, and let the bobbin hang. (Go to the step below that is specific to the material you are using for the rear one-third of the body.)

7. If you are using *seal fur* or *Angora goat dubbing*, review The Common Method of Dubbing on page 68 of the Basic Skills chapter as needed. Use a soft, tacky wax because the Angora goat dubbing does not always adhere easily to the thread. Apply the wax to about 2 inches of thread immediately below the hook shank, then dub small wisps until the waxed thread is covered. Wind the loaded thread in butted turns for one-third of the body length, tie it off,

and let the bobbin hang. Then go to Step 9.

8. If you are using *thin yarn*, fasten one end of a 6- to 12-inch length of it under the hook shank, ⅛ inch from the eye, next to the last turn of floss. Advance the thread in butting turns for one-third of the shank length, binding down the tied-in ends of materials as you go. Then wind the yarn to the hanging thread, tie it off, and let the bobbin hang.

9. Select a spey hackle that has fibers as long as the hook shank. Upset the fibers on both sides of the shaft and place the feather under the shank, at the front end of the wrapped body section, so the tip points toward the eye. Fasten it there with a couple of firm turns of thread and let the bobbin hang.

10. Prepare and apply the body material you have chosen for the front two-thirds of the body, just as you did for the rear of the body. Then let the bobbin hang.

11. Spiral the flat tinsel up the body, allowing at least three times the width of the tinsel between every turn. Make two turns around the orange body section so that one of them passes the point where the hackle is tied in. Tie off the flat tinsel at the hanging thread and cut off the surplus at ⅛ inch from the eye.

12. Spiral the oval tinsel up the body, hard against the forward edge of the flat tinsel. Tie it off, then let the bobbin hang.

13. Carefully wind the hackle up the body to the eye, keeping it tight against the forward edge of the oval tinsel. The long fibers should point to the rear of

the fly, extending beyond the hook bend. If, when you reach the front of the body, any fibers remain on the thin section of the shaft, make extra turns of hackle just behind the eye to build up the shoulder. Tie off the hackle, then let the bobbin hang while you cut off the surplus shaft and tinsel.

14. Push all of the materials toward the rear of the fly, while supporting the rear end of the body with your fingers, to gain a little more space for the head and wings. A little pushing goes a long way at this stage of the fly's construction!

15. Choose a feather that has barbs at least as long as the hook gap. Remove the fibers from one side of the shaft before tying it in at the hanging thread. Wrap the feather like a collar, then tie it off, cut off the excess shaft and tip, and stroke the fibers down under the shank as a throat. Tie it there with several turns of thread, and let the bobbin hang.

16. For the wing, prepare two matching feather slips that are about one-third of a hook gap wide and long enough for the tip to reach a bit beyond the hook bend when the wing is tied in. Place one slip on the near side of the fly, on top of the body and bright side up, so the butt crosses over the head area and the tip points diagonally toward you to form a V. Using the soft loop technique, fasten the slip in place so the wing is flat on top and curves slightly down and around the near side of the fly. Tie in the far-side wing the same way, reversing the directions in which the slip is positioned and noting that the butts of both slips cross to the opposite side of the fly just behind the eye. Double-check wing length and position, adjust as needed, and cut off the excess butts.

17. Form a neat salmon head, whip finish, and complete the fly in the usual manner.

## Variations

You can also use the DeFeo method to make the throat. See page 59 of the Basic Skills chapter for instructions.

# Black Eagle

BLACK EAGLE IS AN OLD PATTERN IN WHICH black (dyed) marabou replaces eagle feathers, which are from a protected species. As always, the size tinsel you use for the tag and rib depends on the hook size you choose. We recommend fine for Nos. 8–10 hooks. For the tail, you can substitute dyed ring-necked pheasant for the Indian crow.

This recipe originally required black seal fur for the body, but nowadays flytiers use black Sealex, an artificial seal fur, or Angora goat.

glentana | black eagle

**black eagle**

| | |
|---|---|
| **HOOK** | *Mustad #36890, Nos. 2–10* |
| **THREAD** | *White 8/0 UNI-Thread* |
| **TAG** | *Silver flat Mylar tinsel, fine or medium* |
| **TAIL** | *Golden pheasant crest and red Indian crow* |
| **RIBBING** | *Silver flat and oval tinsel, fine or medium* |
| **BODY** | *Black Sealex or Angora goat* |
| **HACKLE** | *Black (dyed) spey marabou* |
| **WING** | *Dark, white-tipped turkey tail feathers* |
| **HEAD** | *Black head cement* |

***Black Eagle***

1.  Place the hook in the vise, attach the thread, and wrap a nonslip base for the tag.

2.  Place one end of a 6- to 8-inch length of flat tinsel under the hook shank, about ⅛ inch from the eye, and fasten it in place. Then advance the thread in butting turns for 3⁄16 inch and let the bobbin hang. Wind the tinsel tag in butting turns to the hanging thread, tie it off, and let the bobbin hang.

3.  For the tail, select a medium or small feather that has a section of bright color at least as long as the hook gap. (Use two feathers if one is too thin.) Cut the excess fibers to a stubble.

4.  With the tip curved up, place the feather on top of the hook shank so the usable portion starts just to the left of the hanging thread. Bind the feather in place and let the bobbin hang. Next, place the crow feather on top of the tail so its tip extends to the midpoint of the tail, tie it in, and let the bobbin hang.

5.  Fasten one end of a 6- to 8-inch length of oval tinsel on top of the tied-in end of flat tinsel, and let the bobbin hang while you place the long end of oval tinsel in the material clip. Then wind the thread forward in butting turns, binding down the tail butts and tied-in ends of tinsel, from a point about one-third the length of the body, to a point ⅛ inch from the hook eye (i.e., the length of the body) and let the bobbin hang.

6.  For the hackle, select a medium feather

that has fibers at least as long as the hook shank and strip the fibers off one side of the shaft. Upset the feather and place it under the hook shank so the first usable fibers are at the hanging thread and the surplus tip is to the right of it. Tie in the feather at about two-thirds the body length—measured from the eye of the hook, not from the bend of the hook—and let the bobbin hang. Continue winding the thread in butting turns to ⅛ inch from the eye, binding down the tip of the hackle and other materials. Then return the thread to where the flat and oval ribbing tinsel hang.

7. For the body, carefully apply a thin layer of dubbing to a well-waxed section of the hanging thread. Wind the loaded thread in butting turns to ⅛ inch from the eye, making a thin body. Fasten it in place with several turns of clean thread, then let the bobbin hang.

8. Spiral the flat tinsel rib up the body, making the third turn at the point from which the hackle is hanging, and continue on with evenly spaced turns to the hanging thread. Tie off the rib and let the bobbin hang.

9. Spiral the oval tinsel up the body, tight against the forward edge of the flat tinsel, and tie it off at the hanging bobbin. Cut off the surplus ends of tinsel.

10. Attach the hackle pliers at right angles to the hackle shaft and, starting at the third turn of the rib, spiral it up the body, tight against the forward edge of the oval tinsel. If there is usable fiber

remaining on the feather when you reach the end of the ribbing, make some butting turns for a collar, then tie off the hackle. Let the bobbin hang while you cut off the surplus hackle feather.

11. For the throat, select a bunch of 18 to 24 fibers that are almost long enough to extend from the eye to the hook point. Cut the bundle off the shaft, even the tips, and place the bundle under the shank. Tie in and repair the throat as described in Step 7 on page 53. When satisfied with the throat, secure it to the shank with two more turns of thread, and let the bobbin hang while you cut off the surplus butts.

12. For the wing, prepare two matching feather sections that are about ³⁄₁₆ to ⅜ inch wide and long enough to reach from the eye to the tip of the tail. Place the wing sections one at a time, right side up and flat—not like a tent—on top of the body. Position each at a 45° angle to the hook—so the wings themselves form a 90° angle that is bisected by the hook shank. Roll the near edge of the wings down, to the outside, about 45° from the horizontal, and fasten them firmly in place with X-wraps. (This method of applying the wings is typical of all dee-strip-wing flies.) Let the bobbin hang while you trim the butts and any surplus materials.

13. Form a neat salmon head, whip finish, and complete the fly in the usual manner.

# Jock O'Dee

THIS IS ANOTHER DEE-STRIP-WING FLY, DATing from around 1850. Use two golden pheasant crest feathers together for the tail if they are thin. Also, you can substitute a dyed red feather for the Indian crow, if you wish, and the size tinsel you use for the tag and rib depends on the hook size.

| | |
|---|---|
| **HOOK** | *Mustad #36890, Nos. 2–8* |
| **THREAD** | *White 8/0 UNI-Thread* |
| **TAG** | *Silver flat Mylar tinsel, fine or medium* |
| **TAIL** | *Golden pheasant crest; Indian crow* |
| **BODY** | *Rear two-fifths—lemon-yellow floss; front three-fifths—black floss* |
| **RIB** | *Silver flat tinsel; silver oval Mylar tinsel, fine* |
| **HACKLE** | *Gray heron or gray spey hackle* |
| **THROAT** | *Barred widgeon* |
| **WING** | *Cinnamon turkey slips* |
| **HEAD** | *Black head cement (small)* |

1. Place the hook in the vise, and attach the thread.

2. Place one end of a 6- to 8-inch length of flat tinsel under the hook shank, about ⅛ inch from the hook eye, and fasten it in place. Continue winding the thread toward the eye for about 3/16 inch, then let the bobbin hang. Wind the tin-

sel tag in butting turns to the hanging thread, tie it off, and let the bobbin and tinsel hang.

3. Select a medium golden pheasant crest feather that has bright color and will extend about ⅛ inch beyond the rearmost part of the hook bend when it's tied in. Trim to a stubble all the soft or surplus fibers at the butt of the feather. With the tip curved up, place the tail on top of the hook shank and fasten it in place. Then let the bobbin hang.

4. Choose an Indian crow feather long enough to reach about halfway to the tip of the crest feather. After measuring it for size, fasten it right side up on top of the tail and let the bobbin hang.

5. Fasten one end of a 6- to 8-inch length of lemon-yellow floss under the hook shank, ⅛ inch from the eye, and let the bobbin hang.

6. Fasten one end of a 6- to 8-inch length of oval tinsel on top of the tied-in end of floss. Advance the thread in butting turns for two-fifths of the distance from the tail to the eye, binding down the tied-in ends of the tail, tinsels, and floss, then let the bobbin hang.

7. To form the rear portion of the body, wind the lemon-yellow floss in butting turns to the hanging thread and tie it off.

8. Fasten one end of a 6- to 8-inch length of black floss on top of the tied-in ends

***Jock O'Dee (1).*** *Tail tied in; twirling the floss and tinsel.*

***Jock O'Dee (2).*** *Spey hackle tied in.*

***Jock O'Dee (3).*** *Hackle has been spiraled.*

***Jock O'Dee (4).*** *Throat and wing have been added.*

***Jock O'Dee (5).*** *Completed fly.*

of lemon-yellow floss and tinsel, and let the bobbin hang.

9. Select a feather for the hackle that has barbs as long as the distance from the tail to the eye. Upset the feather and strip the barbs from one side of the shaft. Locate where the first barbs of the feather tip are as long as the body of the fly, and trim the area up to those barbs to a stubble; leave the barbs of the required length intact.

10. Place the stubble tip under the hook shank, pointing diagonally down and toward the eye, and fasten it in place. Continue wrapping the thread in butting turns to ³⁄₁₆ inch from the eye, binding down surplus tail, lemon-yellow floss, tied-in ends of tinsel, and so on. You now have the flat and oval tinsel hanging or, better yet, in a material clip; the black floss and hackle tied in and hanging; and the bobbin hanging from the eye area.

11. To form the front portion of the body, wind the black floss in butting turns to the hanging thread. Tie it off, and let the bobbin hang while you cut off the surplus flosses about ⅛ inch from the eye.

12. Start the rib by spiraling the flat tinsel to where the thread is hanging, making the third turn where the hackle is tied in, and allowing three times the width of the tinsel between turns. Tie off the first part of the rib and cut off the surplus flat tinsel.

13. Spiral the oval tinsel tight against the forward edge of the flat tinsel, tie it off, and cut off the excess.

14. Spiral the hackle, either by hand or with the hackle pliers attached at right angles to the shaft, tight against the forward edge of the oval tinsel to the hanging thread. If there is surplus usable hackle when you reach the thread, make extra butting turns of it in the head area. Then tie it off and cut off the surplus feather.

15. Select a medium to large widgeon feather that has barbs about ¾ inch long, and cut off a section about ¾ inch wide. Even the tips and place the bundle under the hook shank. Tie in and if necessary repair the throat as described in Step 7 on page 53. When satisfied with the throat, secure it to the shank with two more turns of thread, and let the bobbin hang while you cut off the surplus butts.

16. Prepare two matching feather sections that are about ³⁄₁₆ to ⅜ inch wide and long enough to reach from the eye to the tip of the tail. Place the wing sections, one at a time and right side up, at an angle of 45° to the hook shank and 90° to each other. Fasten them firmly in place with X-wraps of thread. Let the bobbin hang while you trim off the butts and other surplus materials.

17. Form a small, neat salmon fly head, whip finish, and complete the fly in the usual manner.

# LOW-WATER SALMON FLIES

During low-water conditions salmon will frequently take a small fly but refuse larger ones. Low-water salmon flies, therefore, are based on standard patterns, but they are tied several sizes smaller. These smaller flies, however, are not tied on smaller hooks. A No. 12 hook, for instance, is too small and fragile to hold a salmon, so we tie a size 12 fly on a No. 2 or No. 4 hook that is big and heavy enough to hold and land these big fish.

The pattern and materials for low-water flies are the same as their regular-sized name-sakes, but the starting point on the hook is different. On a low-water fly begin tying ahead of the middle of the hook shank, instead of over the point or barb as you would on the larger version. The proportions are standard for each fly pattern; therefore, if you start building the body ahead of the middle of the hook shank, you'll reduce the size of the fly's other parts.

The need for low-water salmon might be limited, but when the conditions arise, they are essential.

## Low-Water Hairy Mary

THIS BASIC HAIR-WING FLY IS WIDELY USED for Atlantic salmon fishing in many sizes and many places. Follow the instructions for the Hairy Mary on page 273; however, begin tying the ahead of the middle of the hook shank, instead of over the point or barb as you would on the larger version.

*Low-Water Hairy Mary*

# Low-Water Crossfield

*Low-Water Crossfield*

FOLLOW THE INSTRUCTIONS FOR THE CROSS-field R/S on page 284; however, begin tying the ahead of the middle of the hook shank, instead of over the point or barb as you would on the larger version.

# CLASSIC FULL-FEATHER SALMON FLIES

W e have now arrived at the promised goal of the book: tying a classic full-feather salmon fly. If you have tied the flies in the order they appear on the previous pages, then you have the skills and knowledge of materials to tackle this next pattern—a fly that is suitable for presentation under glass.

## Orange Parson

ORANGE PARSON IS A CLASSIC, FULL-DRESS, feather-wing salmon fly marking the start of the apex of the fly-tying craft. When you complete this fly consider yourself a truly accomplished flytier!

This fly originated on the River Erne in Ireland, and is part of a family of "Parson" flies dating from the mid-nineteenth century that are distinguished by the use of many layers of golden pheasant crest as topping. This fly is called Golden Parson by Francis, Kelson, Hardy, and Hale, and Orange Parson by Poul Jorgenson. The pattern remains stable in its essentials, and it includes slight changes by several of these authorities on classic salmon flies.

A No. 2 hook is the easiest for first-time tiers, so we recommend you start there. For the tag, use the finest oval silver tinsel available for Nos. 8–10 flies and fine for Nos. 2–6 flies, or you can use silver wire. Oval tinsel is required for ribbing, whereas if you use wire for the tag, it will be carried forward with other body materials, forming part of the underbody, and trimmed later.

The body is divided into four equal units and extends from the base of the tail to the rear of the head area; do not count the tag or the ⅛-inch space immediately behind the hook eye as part of the body. Its size, and thus the size of each individual unit, depends on the size of the hook you use, so I can't give you one measurement to fit all sizes. Note that you will wrap a double layer of orange floss to create the rearmost quarter of the body; it is too thin otherwise. Also note that it is customary for the hackle to begin at the second turn of the tinsel ribbing on most salmon flies, so be sure that the second turn of ribbing crosses the tie-in point of the hackle.

You can substitute dyed chicken for cock-o'-the-rock, which is listed for the veiling and for the throat. For the wing, pick whole feathers from opposite sides of a cape or skin so that the curve of the shafts will match when they are tied in. It doesn't matter which side you set the wing's veiling on first, although using a mirror or turning the vise to expose the far side of the fly will allow you to set the veiling feathers properly and easily. A shaving mirror with 2X magnification is excellent for this purpose.

For the sides, you may use a barred wood

orange parson

*Orange Parson (1). Tail, body hackle, tinsel, and floss tied in.*

duck flank feather that has a center shaft, but it's expensive and hard to find. Instead, use a pair of barred wood duck flank feathers that are the same size, one from each side of a skin or patch. When looking at the bright side of the two feathers, one will have its wide side on the left of the shaft and the other will have the wide side on the right. The pair should be matched for both size and bright color.

Instead of using blue chatterer for the cheeks, you can substitute a blue (dyed) feather, from a ring-necked pheasant or kingfisher. Macaw tails, the source from which we would get the horns for this fly, are really expensive. However, 1-inch sections are usually available for about $10. There are no substitute materials that are blue on the upper side and yellow on the underside of the barb. Therefore, for reasons of price and scarcity, many flytiers omit the horns, and you may wish to also. However, the original pattern does call for them, and they do add something extra—besides cost—to the finished fly.

| | |
|---|---|
| **HOOK** | *Mustad #36890, Nos. 2–10* |
| **THREAD** | *White 8/0 UNI-Thread* |
| **TAG** | *Silver oval tinsel, finest, or silver wire* |
| **TIP** | *Lilac floss* |
| **TAIL** | *Golden pheasant crest; golden pheasant tippet* |
| **BODY** | *First (rear) quarter—orange floss; second quarter—orange SLF dubbing; third quarter—scarlet SLF dubbing; fourth (front) quarter—fiery brown SLF dubbing* |
| **RIBBING** | *Silver oval tinsel, fine* |
| **BODY HACKLE** | *Lemon (dyed) saddle hackle* |
| **THROAT** | *Cock-o'-the-rock* |
| **WING** | *Orange golden pheasant tippets with black bars* |
| **VEILING** | *Cock-o'-the-rock* |
| **SIDES** | *Barred wood duck* |
| **CHEEKS** | *Blue chatterer* |
| **TOPPING** | *Golden pheasant crest feathers* |
| **HORNS** | *Blue-and-yellow macaw tail fibers* |
| **HEAD** | *Black head cement* |

1. Place the hook in the vise, and attach the thread.

2. Place one end of a 6- to 8-inch length of wire or oval tinsel under the hook shank, about ⅛ inch from the hook eye. Fasten it in place with firm, butting turns of thread for ⅛ to ³⁄₁₆ inch,

depending on the hook size, and let the bobbin hang. Wind the wire or tinsel tag in butting turns to the hanging thread, tie it off, and let the bobbin hang.

3. Fasten one end of a 6- to 8-inch length of lilac floss under the hook shank, about ⅛ inch from the eye. Then wind the thread forward in butting turns for about ⅛ inch and let the bobbin hang. Wind the lilac floss tip in butting turns to the hanging thread, tie it off, and let the bobbin hang.

4. For the tail, select a bright, short golden pheasant crest feather from a skin, head, or packet. From the hanging thread, the feather should extend about half a hook-gap length beyond the hook bend. Upset and trim the unneeded fibers on both sides of the shaft to a stubble. With its tip curving up, place the feather—or two if one is too thin—on top of the hook shank so the first golden fibers are immediately to the left of the hanging thread. Fasten it there with several firm turns of thread and let the bobbin hang.

5. Select a medium to large golden pheasant orange neck tippet with black bars and cut off six to eight fibers that are somewhat longer than the distance from the hanging thread to the middle of the tail. Bundle the fibers bright sides out, even the tips, and place the bundle on top of the tail. The tips should extend to the middle of the tail and the butts should point toward the eye. Bind the bundle in place at the tie-

in point for the tail, using the soft loop technique and three or four butting turns of thread. Then return the thread to the tie-in point and let the bobbin hang.

6. If you used wire for the tag, tie in a 6- to 8-inch length of oval tinsel at this point, under the hook shank and on top of the lilac floss. Place the length of tinsel, whether tied in now or carried forward from the tag, in the material clip.

7. Fasten one end of a 6- to 8-inch length of orange floss on top of the tied-in end of the lilac floss. Then wind the thread in butting turns for a distance that's a little less than one-quarter of the shank length, binding down the lilac floss, wire, and the tail butt, and let the bobbin hang. Wind the orange floss in butting turns toward the hook bend, to the rear and base of the tail, and then forward again to the hanging bobbin. Tie it off and let the bobbin hang.

8. Select a lemon (dyed) saddle hackle and find the point, near the tip of the feather, where the barbs are about hook-gap length. Upset the feather from the tip to that point, then cut the upset portion to a stubble. Strip about four barbs on each side of the shaft, then put the feather under the hook shank and tie it in at the stubble area, leaving the stripped section visible. Allow the length of the feather to extend behind the tail or place it in the material clip.

9. Wax and dub about 2 inches of thread next to the hook shank with orange

*Orange Parson (2). Creating the body with floss and dubbing.*

*Orange Parson (3). Lemon body hackle wrapped. Throat hackle tied in.*

*Orange Parson (4). Body finished and throat tied in. Golden pheasant wing tied in.*

SLF. Wind the dubbing in butting turns to form the second unit of the body, then tie it off with bare thread and let the bobbin hang. Repeat the process two more times, creating the third (scarlet SLF) and fourth (fiery brown SLF) units of the body, and let the bobbin hang.

10. Spiral the tinsel rib forward so that the second turn is applied where the hackle is tied in. Continue spiraling the rib up the body, for five evenly spaced turns, to the hanging thread. Tie it off, and let the bobbin hang while you cut off the excess tinsel and surplus ends of the other body materials at ⅛ inch from the eye.

11. Raise the hackle feather at right angles above the body and double the feather. Attach the hackle pliers to the shaft and carefully spiral the feather forward—tight against the tinsel—in five even turns, constantly sweeping the fibers back into their doubled position, to the hanging thread. Then take a couple of butting turns around the body to use up the doubled feather. Tie off the hackle, and let the bobbin hang while you cut off the surplus hackle and shaft about ⅛ inch from the eye.

12. Use a bodkin to divide the butted turns of hackle directly over the shank, and stroke the fibers down to begin forming a throat. Hold it in place with an X-wrap of thread and let the bobbin hang.

13. Select a dyed-orange webby hen or saddle hackle with fibers slightly longer than the front of the lemon-yellow body

*Orange Parson (5). Completed fly. Note that the Golden pheasant crest (topping) should be pulled up and reset as a ridgepole on top of the wing. You can do this on your fly if the same problem occurs.*

hackle. Cut the fibers on a short section of the butt to a stubble, then upset the next couple of inches of the feather. Place the feather, bright side forward, on top of the body so the first long fibers are directly over the hanging thread. Allow the rest of the feather to extend to the rear. Bind the stubble end in place with a couple of turns of the thread and let the bobbin hang.

14. Make three or four butting turns of feather, either by hand or with the hackle pliers attached at right angles to the shaft, then weight the feather with the pliers. Take a look at the throat. If it seems too thin you can make another turn with the feather. Make any desired adjustments, then divide and pull down the fibers for the throat, fasten it in place with X-wraps, and let the bobbin hang.

15. Select two equal-size tippets that extend from the eye to the middle of the tail. The black bars on both should match. Place them, dull sides together and with the tips and bars matched, over the body so the tips extend to the middle of the tail. Upset the fibers on both sides of the shaft until the lowest fibers align with the hanging thread. Lift the feathers off the body and, holding them together, trim the upset fibers to a stubble and crimp the stems so the wings will be raised when they're tied in. Return the feathers to the tie-in point over the hanging thread and fasten them firmly there. Make sure you retain some space for the head as you add materials to this area! Cut off the excess wing shafts about ⅛ inch from the eye.

16. Select two webby orange hackles for the

veiling, one from each side of a wet fly-quality neck or saddle. They should extend from the eye to just inside the tip of the tail. Measure them dull sides together, then cut the excess barbs on each side of the shaft to a stubble. Place the feathers one at a time, bright side out, on the middle area of the wing so the tips point to the rear of the fly, just inside the curve of the tail, and fasten them there.

17. If you're using a center-shaft feather for the sides, use your bodkin to divide a slip 3/16 to 1/4 inch wide from each side of the feather and cut them off close to the shaft. If you're using a pair of matched feathers, cut similar strips from each of the wide sides of the feathers. The fly's sides should extend from the eye to the nearest black bar of the tippet wing; the outer black bar of the strip you've just cut should rest on top of the inner black bar of the tippet wing. Apply the sides one at a time, bright sides out, over and along the shaft of the wing tippet. Fasten them in place and let the bobbin hang.

18. For the cheeks, select a matched pair of imitation blue chatterer feathers about one-third the length of the sides. Fasten them one at a time, bright side out, over the front end of each of the sides. Let the bobbin hang.

19. Select two or three crest feathers that have bright color that will extend from the hook eye, enclose the farthest edge of the wing, and almost reach the tip of the tail. Place them one on top of the other, to form the topping, and upset any excess fibers at the butt. Cut the excess to a stubble on both sides of the shafts. Bind the feathers in place with tight, butting turns of thread, and let the bobbin hang while you cut off the surplus shafts about 1/8 inch from the eye.

20. For the horns, select two individual fibers from a blue-and-yellow tail McCaw feather, one from each side of the shaft, that extend from the hook eye to the curve of the topping enclosing the wing. Tie them in separately so they slant upward and above the wood duck sides.

21. Trim the excess materials to form a neat, short, salmon fly head, and finish the fly in the usual manner.

Congratulations! You have just completed one of the full-dress feather wing salmon flies. They are generally considered the domain of a small and select company of expert fly-tying specialists. There are more exotic and difficult salmon flies among the classic feather wings awaiting you in other books, and they should be easier to tie because of your experiences here.

I trust you will enjoy both making and fishing your flies. Here's to tight threads and tight lines!

# APPENDIX ONE
# ROADKILL AND OTHER PLEASURES OF FLY TYING

Beyond the tying of flies, I have found interest and pleasure in collecting the materials from which to make them. I look forward with great anticipation to the annual arrival of catalogues from various suppliers. New items appear in these catalogs, often following the publication of articles in books or magazines about new flies, materials, or tying techniques. Also of interest to me is the reappearance of items that had previously disappeared from supply lists, apparently because of availability problems or perceived changes in fashion among flytiers. Fashions do change, sometimes quite rapidly, because of the views expressed in some article or expert's proclamation.

The materials one can collect from roadkill or from begging sections of hide or feathers from acquaintances who are successful hunters or who keep exotic birds is another endeavor that, for some flytiers, may occupy more time than actually tying flies. Every now and then I'd get a tail from friends whose cat caught a pine squirrel. Occasionally, especially in the fall, gray squirrels are run over while crossing the road. Only rarely is the tail dirtied or damaged, although the rest of the squirrel may have been rolled out thin as pie crust. Provided the traffic is not too heavy, you can often get the carcass out of the road and, with a knife or shears, easily cut off the tail where it joins the body. The rest of the hide is usually full of dirt, blood, and guts and is thus too difficult to clean and salt down after skinning the animal. Although there is little fat or flesh on a squirrel's tailbone, it's best to skin out the tail. It needs no salt or alum to cure it. Here's how:

1. Peel back the skin from the base of the tail, cutting any of the cords and tendons that attach it to the bone. When you have exposed at least an inch of tailbone, grip it with a pair of pliers and peel/push/cut the skin, working toward the tip of the tail, to free another couple of inches of bone.
2. While grasping the mound of peeled-back skin in one hand, pull the tailbone out of the hide with the pliers. Cut any remaining cords, discard the bone, then pull the tail right side out.
3. If necessary, wash the tail in warm, soapy water, rinse it, then dry it with a paper towel. Hang it up, hair side out, and dry it like laundry.

Such tails cost between $1 and $2. All squirrel tails can be deboned in this manner, and if clean they can be kept in a box or plastic bag, moth free, for years. As a thrifty Scot, I find pleasure and profit in making flies from tails whose original owners can no longer use them, and you can be sure of the quality, which is an added advantage.

Woodchucks, muskrats, possums, and raccoons can all be skinned out, their fat scraped from the hide, and the hides washed, salted, and dried. Be sure to brush off excess salt, however, as it will pick up moisture again in damp weather. Store the hides in clean boxes or plastic with some mothballs for extra protection against moths and silverfish.

Deer, from your own bounty or that of hunting friends, provide hock hair around the scent glands on the rear legs with no loss of meat involved in procuring it. Hock hair is stiff and hollow, and it's rarely available commercially. However, while hunters use neither the hock hair nor tails from deer, other flytiers may present competition for them, so be on your toes.

To debone a deer tail, simply cut through the white hair, from the base of the tail to the tip, and peel off the skin. Then scrape off the fat, wash the skin, wipe it dry, salt it heavily, and hang it to dry like laundry. Salt draws moisture from the skin, and thus prevents rot and spoilage. Items can also be dried in the sun, on radiators, or with a handheld hair dryer, which is a speedy method and useful when you have thin-skin items like bird parts and squirrel tails.

Store all animal parts with mothballs or flakes scattered among them, as moths and silverfish feast on unprotected hair, feathers, and fur. Wings rarely require deboning or salt-ing, as they have only small amounts of meat and no fat to go rancid. But they do require protection from moths and silverfish. You can pluck feathers into bags or boxes, but you will have to re-sort them later to use them. Instead, you can skin the bird and keep the feathers intact. Whole wings and other body parts (such as the breast, from which to obtain white feathers for fan wings) can be cut off the carcass as a patch. If you need matching feathers, such as when you make fan wings, you can save much time by plucking two adjoining breast feathers from a patch or whole skin, matching them on the spot. (Adjoining feathers are as close a match as nature provides.) After you pluck adjoining feathers, tape the two shafts together. You now have a matched pair ready to use for cheeks on streamers or as fan wings, depending on their color and location on the bird. Ring-necked pheasants, both male and female, have numerous feathers you can use to make shoulders or cheeks on streamer flies. These, too, must be paired, and the above method is the simplest and most effective way to do it. Store paired feathers in a closed box, where they will stay together for years if you keep the moths out. I had some that were 6 years old that I put to good use on a recent version of a successful fly from the 1950s.

Accurate and detailed labeling of all containers is very helpful. Materials do you little good unless they are at hand when you need them, and time spent labeling and storing materials properly is never wasted!

Good standard advice is to go to your friendly local fly shop and make friends with one of the clerks. This assures personal attention and, hopefully, good service when problems arise. Unfortunately, many of us live in areas where such stores and their helpful, knowledgeable clerks are in short supply, or local prices seem beyond our means, or the shops do not carry the item or items we need at that particular moment. You may even be the only flytier within miles and must therefore turn to books rather than other flytiers for the solutions to your problems. I know! I have been there and done that!

Books, catalogues, and flyers from supply houses can all help in such situations. They may not be ideal, but can be extremely effective nevertheless. Following is an alphabetical list of mail-order (or Web) sources, all of them proven sources of tools and materials that I have used satisfactorily for several years, and all current as of this writing. Doubtless there are others that are equally good, but start with these if your needs cannot be met locally.

Cabela's
One Cabela Drive
Sidney, NE 69160
800-237-4444
www.cabelas.com
*Ask for the* Fly-Fishing Catalog *for best*

*coverage, as the shop carries much outdoor equipment.*

Collins' Hackle Farm
436 Kismer Hill
Pine City, NY 14871
607-734-1765
*This is an excellent source of good-quality hackle at very reasonable prices. Capes and saddles are sold as a unit. Personal attention is given to requests. You are buying directly from the grower, Charlie Collins, who understands his business and your needs.*

The Anglers' Den
11 Main Street
Pawling, NY 12564
845-855-5182
www.anglers-den.com
*This source has a wide range of exotic and rare materials that are especially useful for full-dress salmon flies, and has an interesting bargain column ad in* Fly Tyer *magazine.*

Feather-Craft Fly Fishing
8307 Manchester Road
P.O. Box 19904
St. Louis, MO 63144
800-659-1707
www.feather-craft.com
*This outfit carries a wide variety of tools, materials, supplies, and suggestions.*

Flyfisher's Paradise
2603 East College Avenue
State College, PA 16801
814-234-4189
www.flyfishersparadise.com
*Flyfisher's Paradise offers a wide variety of tools, materials, and supplies.*

Hook & Tackle Company
7 Kaycee Loop Road
Plattsburgh, NY 12901
800-552-8342

www.hookhack.com
*For excellent tools, materials, supplies, and service at reasonable prices, try this outfit.*

The Fly Shop
4140 Churn Creek Road
Redding, CA 96002
800-669-3474
www.theflyshop.com
*The Fly Shop offers a wide variety of tools, materials, and supplies.*

# APPENDIX THREE
# BOOKS

There are many books on fly tying, and I have chosen several that deal with important styles and types of tying to get you started.

*Art Flick's Master Fly-Tying Guide*, by Art Flick. (New York: Crown Publishers, 1972).

*Atlantic Salmon Flies and Fishing*, by Joseph D. Bates, Jr. (Mechanicsburg, PA: Stackpole Books, 1995).

*Flies for Atlantic Salmon*, by Dick Steward and Farrow Allen (Intervale, NH: Northland Press, 1991).

*Modern Atlantic Salmon Flies*, by Paul Marriner (Portland, OR: Frank Amato Publications, 1998).

*Salmon Flies: Their Character, Style and Dressing*, by Paul Jorgensen (Mechanicsburg, PA: Stackpole Books, 1999).

*Spey Flies and Dee Flies: Their History and Construction*, by John Shewey (Portland, OR: Frank Amato Publications, 2002).

*Steelhead Fly Tying Guide*, by H. Kent Helovie (Portland, OR: Frank Amato Publications, 1994).

# GLOSSARY

**BADGER** *Describes the color of a chicken feather (hackle) that has a dark center and either a white or golden edge.*

**BUCKTAIL** *A style of fly that is tied on long hooks to imitate minnows; has a hair wing (not necessarily from a buck deer) and is usually made with a red feather or hair throat and tail that represent blood.*

**BUTT/RUFF** *A band of ostrich or peacock herl that's usually tied just ahead of the tail. It may also be placed between sections of the body on salmon flies.*

**BUTTED TURNS** *Turns of thread, applied to the hook shank, that are made side by side so they touch one another, but do not overlap. Also, there are no gaps between butted turns.*

**CHEEKS** *Feathers that are tied in behind the head area of a streamer fly to represent a minnow's gill covers. Also a similar feather used on full-dress feather-wing salmon flies.*

**CHURCH WINDOW FEATHER** *A feather from a ring-necked pheasant with a color pattern in the shape of a Gothic church window. It's used as a cheek on streamer flies.*

**CLASSIC DRY FLY** *A fly that represents the adult winged phase of a mayfly's life cycle.*

**CLASSIC WET FLY** *A fly that represents the last phase of a mayfly's life cycle (i.e., a drowned insect drifting in the water). The wings are not divided and are set at about 45° instead of upright.*

**COACHMAN BROWN** *The color of a typical mahogany feather from a Rhode Island red chicken.*

**DEE-STRIP-WING FLY** *A style of salmon fly from the River Dee in Scotland that has turkey tail strips for wings, set at a 45° angle to the hook shank, and teal or widgeon for the throat and spey-type hackle.*

**DRY FLY** *A fly that is fished floating on the surface of the water.*

**DUBBING** *Thread upon which fur or synthetic fibers have been spun for the purpose of forming a fly body. Also the process used to produce this material.*

**DUN** *The phase of a mayfly's life cycle between the emerger and egg-laying adult phases. Also refers to a variety of shades of gray.*

**EMERGER** *The phase of an insect's life cycle, such as that of a mayfly, caddis, and others, in which the fully developed nymph rises to the water's surface to split its shell or shuck and dry its wings, prior to flying away.*

**FAN WING** *A wing made from two breast feathers, tied onto the fly so the feathers curve out, creating a parachute effect.*

**FOLDED-HAIR BODY** *Hollow hair bundled and folded to form a fly body such as that of a Hair Ant.*

**FURNACE** *The color and pattern name for a chicken feather that has a dark center and tan edges. Also called cochy.*

**GAP** *On a hook, the straight vertical distance between the point and the shank;*

it is often used to determine the length of a fly's hackle. Also called gape.

**GENETIC HACKLE** *Feathers that come from a chicken that was specially bred to produce the highest quality of dry-fly hackle.*

**GRIZZLY** *The color and pattern name for the barred black-and-white feather from Plymouth Rock chickens.*

**HACKLE** *A feather wound on edge to support a dry fly on the water or palmered up the body to give action to underwater flies.*

**HORNS** *Single strands, usually of macaw tail feather, tied onto the outside of salmon flies.*

**LACE** *A cable-like fiber that is made by twisting several strands of oval or round tinsel together, which is then wound as ribbing onto a salmon fly body.*

**NYMPH** *In the life cycle of a mayfly or other insect, the stage or phase after the egg has hatched. The nymph lives on or near the bottom of the water column while developing its body and wings.*

**PAINT NAILS** *Tools used to print eyes on the heads of streamers and bucktails.*

**PALMER** *The process of spiraling a hackle up the fly body.*

**PALMER HACKLE** *A hackle that is palmered, or spiraled, up the body of a fly, as in the Bomber salmon fly.*

**SADDLE HACKLE** *A long, thin feather, or one that has grown in the area next to the tail of a rooster.*

**SIDE** *Usually a jungle cock or cock-o'-the-rock feather or a strip of teal or barred wood duck feather that's tied in over the wing and is one-third to one-half the length of the wing on a feather wing salmon fly.*

**SPENT-WING SPINNER** *Describes the stage of the mayfly and caddis life cycles in which adults, shortly after mating and egg-laying, fall exhausted to the water with their wings spread.*

**SPEY HACKLE** *Exceptionally long, thin hackle originally from a special breed of chicken or heron plumage, but now from burned goose shoulder feathers (for large flies) and various pheasant rump feathers. Spey hackle is palmered over the fly body to provide distinctive action for dee-strip-wing and spey flies.*

**SPEY STYLE** *Salmon flies that are characterized by the use of long spey hackle and a tentlike wing of bronze mallard, and having a generally somber appearance. (Many modern spey flies have wings that are tied in wet-fly style instead of tent style.)*

**SPUN/CUT HAIR BODY** *A style of fly body that uses hollow hair for flotation. The hair is spun around the hook shank and then cut to the shape of a mouse, frog, or insect.*

**STILLBORN** *A nymph that dies during its struggle to shed its skin and dry its wings as it progresses toward adulthood.*

**STREAMER** *A style of fly that is tied to imitate a minnow. It has feather wings and often employs a bundle of red barbs or a feather slip for the tail and throat.*

**THROAT** *A bunch of hair, feather fibers, or a slip of feather tied under the fly body, next to the head area, on bucktails, streamers, and many salmon flies.*

**TIP/TAG** *Turns of oval or flat tinsel (tag) followed by a narrow band of floss (tip). Located immediately behind the tail on salmon flies.*

**TIPPET** *An orange golden pheasant neck feather that has black bars.*

**3X HEAVY** *Describes the wire used to make a hook whose thickness is the same as a normal hook that is three sizes larger. Also called 3X stout.*

**3X LIGHT** *Describes the wire used to make a hook whose thickness is the same as a normal hook that is three sizes smaller. For example, the wire used to make a No. 12 3X light hook is the same thickness as the wire used to make a regular No. 18 hook in that style.*

**3X LONG** *Describes a hook whose length is three sizes longer than normal. For example, a No. 12 3XL hook is as long as a regular No. 6 hook of the same style.*

**3X SHORT** *Describes a hook whose length is three sizes shorter than normal.*

**TOPPING** *A golden pheasant crest feather (or feathers) that is tied on top of a feather-wing salmon fly.*

**VEILING** *Small feathers or ends of floss that are tied between sections of a salmon fly body or wing.*

**WEED GUARD** *A length of nylon leader material that extends from the head of a fly to the hook bend. It prevents the hook from catching on weeds or debris in the water.*

**WET FLY** *A fly that is fished beneath the surface of the water.*

**WHIP FINISH** *The knot used to finish the head of a fly; it securely buries the end of the thread under several turns of thread.*

**WING BURNER** *A tool used to form dry-fly wings made from bird body plumage.*

# INDEX

# INDEX OF FLIES